Developing
Library Collections

LIBRARY SCIENCE TEXT SERIES

Developing
Library Collections

G. Edward Evans

Libraries Unlimited, Inc.-Littleton, Colorado
1979

LIBRARIES UNLIMITED, INC.
P.O. Box 263
Littleton, Colorado 80160

Library of Congress Cataloging in Publication Data

Evans, G   Edward, 1937-
    Developing library collections.

    (Library science text series)
    Includes bibliographies and index.
    1. Collection development (Libraries). I. Title.
Z687.E92   025.2   78-27303
ISBN 0-87287-145-2
ISBN 0-87287-247-5 (pbk.)

For

Tombeau and Mary Ann

with love

"No Library of One Million Volumes
can be all
BAD!"

(from a cover, *Antiquarian Bookman*)

PREFACE

Collection development is an exciting and challenging area in which to work, and selecting the right materials for your community is as intellectually demanding an activity as you will encounter. The selection of library materials is a highly personal process—something you will spend a lifetime learning—and the rewards are great. This book can serve as the starting point in that learning process. Any textbook that attempts to cover all aspects of collection development must give coverage to many topics. This text provides practical information on materials producers and distributors, community survey techniques, policies, materials selection, acquisition, weeding, and evaluation in order to minimize the variables involved in the selection process. Beyond the physical processes of collection development, though, are issues with which a selector should be concerned, as they influence how the collection will and can be developed. Thus, *Developing Library Collections* also delves into library cooperation, copyright (reflecting the newly changed statutes), and censorship as they affect the process in its entirety.

An author of a collection development textbook should acknowledge that, to a very great degree, the emphasis given each topic is based on a subjective assessment of its importance, reflecting the values and judgments of that author. Certainly, anyone with practical experience in this area knows that selection and collection development are arts, not sciences; and, as with any artistic endeavor, a person wishing to practice the art must devote years to developing the necessary skills. The basic elements of the collection development process—determining what information resources are needed; identifying the appropriate items; acquiring the items; and evaluating the collection—are rather well agreed upon. What is open to debate is how much emphasis to place upon individual steps in the process, and the interrelationship of all the elements.

A person cannot learn selection and collection development only in the classroom. A student will be able to learn the basic elements from this book; whether the student accepts the emphasis placed upon the elements is another matter. With the concepts presented in this book as a base, and using the recommended further readings, however, the student should begin to develop a solidly based, personal approach to selection and collection development.

The purpose of this book is to help students gain an overall understanding of what is involved in building *a* collection for *a* library. Within rather broad limits, one may say that all libraries share certain general characteristics, including the

7

need to assemble a collection of books and other library materials needed by its patrons. This book was written with the intent of emphasizing the similarities between types of libraries in the process of developing a collection.

Unlike any other book on collection development or book selection, *Developing Library Collections* provides an integrated approach to the process of building a library collection for a specific community of users—integrated in the sense that each element in the process is treated as flowing from one to another, and when something occurs in one element, it will have an impact on the others. Thus, as each element is discussed in detail, its relationships with the others will be examined as well, the underlying emphasis always being on the ultimate goal of the process—serving the library's community. To some degree, every chapter in this book has some application to any library. However, some aspects of collection development have more application, or at least are more widely used, in one type of library than another. For example, community analysis has been most widely used in public libraries, and as a result, chapter 4 tends to emphasize community analysis in the public library. Chapters 9 and 10, on weeding and evaluating the collection, deal with issues most pertinent to academic libraries, which is reflected in the citations. Nevertheless, every chapter provides information relevant to all types of libraries.

Many examples used in this book are drawn from personal experience in the field or the classroom. In order to avoid the use of the first person, which many persons find objectionable in textbooks, "we" has been used to mean the author and reader as librarians, not as a royal "we." Remarks directly addressed to the reader have also been employed so as to lessen formality and in the belief that this approach often achieves greater clarity.

In one sense, this is a jointly authored work. Any librarian who has written or talked about this subject has probably influenced my thinking to some degree. The bibliographies at the ends of the chapters reflect some of the works that have directly affected my point of view; they are but a fraction of the total waiting to be read. These writings will serve as an excellent starting point for your further reading, which will need to continue as long as you are involved in collection development work.

—G. Edward Evans

TABLE OF CONTENTS

PART C

COLLECTION DEVELOPMENT AND RELATED ISSUES

APPENDIX

COPYRIGHT LAW

LIST OF FIGURES

＊＊＊＊＊＊＊＊＊＊＊＊＊＊＊＊＊＊＊＊＊＊＊＊＊

PART A

COLLECTION DEVELOPMENT AND
SOURCES OF MATERIAL

＊＊＊＊＊＊＊＊＊＊＊＊＊＊＊＊＊＊＊＊＊＊＊＊＊

Chapter 1

COLLECTION DEVELOPMENT:
What Is It?

THE COLLECTION DEVELOPMENT PROCESS

Many persons tend to think of a library only as a place to go to find a book or magazine, and perhaps, a collection of both. If they are a little more familiar with libraries, they may consider approaching one for answers to various questions that they may have. But not very many persons are fully aware of the range of services that the modern library makes available to its patrons. In essence, providing the information that a patron wants, regardless of its format or location, is providing *service*, and probably every librarian in the world sees that as the reason for the existence of libraries, and indeed, of librarians.

Central to the ability of the library to meet patron demands is the collection of materials upon which its patrons and staff alike will draw. Every library's collection, though, must be consciously assembled and developed with its unique patron community in mind, or the possibilities for providing service decrease as the materials in the collection become more steadily remote from the community's needs and interests. In this spirit, "patron demand" is used in a broad sense to indicate what the patron knows is presently needed or wanted, as well as what may be needed or wanted sometime in the future. It does *not* simply mean the active user's persistent requests for the latest or the greatest, since catering to such pressures exclusively will detract from the library's ability to offer in-depth and wide-ranging service to less vocal elements of the community, which must also be served.

Collection development is a universal process in the library world whereby the library staff brings together a variety of materials to meet patron demands. This dynamic, self-perpetuating cycle consists of six definable elements: community analysis, policies, selection, acquisition, weeding, and evaluation. (Figure 1 provides an overview of the process, the individual elements of which are discussed in depth in chapters 4 through 10.) Given the sequential relationship of the elements of the collection development process, then, it is possible to begin to describe the cycle at any point. And given the concern that will be reiterated throughout this book for the library's active role in answering patron demands, the library's examination of its own community is an appropriate starting place for an overview, as community analysis is the way in which those needs can be best ascertained.

Figure 1
Collection Development Process

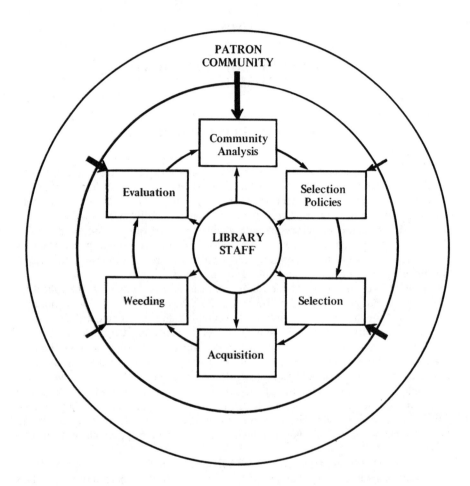

"Community" or "patron community" is used throughout this book in a generic sense to cover the group of persons that the library *has been established to serve.* It does *not* mean only the active users; it means everyone within the community's defined limits. Thus, a community might be an entire political unit (i.e., nation, region, state, province, county, city, town, etc.) or a more specialized grouping or association (i.e., university, college, school, government agency, or private organization). Also, the number of patrons that the library is to serve may range from the tens to the millions. As will be discussed in chapter 4, community analysis can be used to assemble a variety of data for library planners. For collection development personnel, it provides data on what information the patron community needs; it also establishes a valuable mechanism for patron input into the process of collection development.

One use the library can make of data collected in a community survey is in preparing a collection development policy. Clearly delineated policies on both collection development and selection (covered in chapter 5) provide librarians involved in collection development with guidelines for choosing items for inclusion in the collection. (Collection policies, it should be noted, cover a wider range of topics than selection policies. For example, *selection* policies normally only provide information useful in deciding which items to purchase, while *collection* policies will cover that topic and such related issues as gifts, weeding, and cooperation.) Most libraries have some such information available for their collection development personnel, although it is not always labeled a policy. Some libraries call it an acquisition policy; some, a selection policy; some, a collection development policy; and others, simply a "statement." Whatever the local label, the intent is the same: to define the library's goals in terms of its collection.

Using whatever written policies or statements that their libraries have prepared, then, librarians begin the actual procedures for materials selection (covered in chapters 6 and 7). For many librarians, this is the most interesting element in the collection development process. One constant factor in collection development, though, is that enough money is *never* available to buy everything that might be of value to the library. Naturally, this means that someone, usually one or more librarians, must decide which items should be purchased and which should not. Selection is thus a form of decision-making, although deciding which items would best suit the community might be no easier than deciding what to buy in any other situation involving a range of choices. The decision may be to opt for an essential, important, needed, nice, or luxurious item. Where to categorize any item in the sequence from essential to luxurious depends, of course, on the individual selector's point of view; and as someone said, "it's just a matter of perception." So it is with library materials. One significant difference, though, is that an item purchased by an individual is paid for with that person's money. When it is a question of spending the library community's money, whether derived from taxes or a company's budget, the problem is more complex, which is the great challenge in selection.

Once an item has been selected, the process continues with the library's acquiring that item. Acquisition work (as explained in chapter 8) is the only point in the collection development process involving little or no community input; it is a fairly straightforward business operation that involves the library's technical processing units. Once the decision has been made to purchase an item, the work of acquisition proceeds with the preparation of an order form, the selection of a vendor, the recording of the receipt of the item, and finally, payment. While details may vary, the basic routines remain the same around the world.

After an item has been acquired, it is processed through a series of internal library operations (beyond the scope of this book) such as cataloging and is eventually available to the patron community. But in time, nearly every item outlives its original value to the library; in most cases, these must be removed from the main collection. The activity of examining items in the library and determining their current value to *that library's collection* (and hence, to the patron community) is normally called weeding (covered in chapter 9). When a library decides that a given item is no longer of value, it will dispose of the item—sell, give, or even throw it away. If the item still has some value for the library, it will probably be transferred to a less accessible and, in most cases, less expensive storage location. A few librarians have commented that weeding is nothing more than selection in reverse.

Evaluation (examined in chapter 10) is the last element in the collection development process. To some extent, weeding is an evaluative activity, but weeding is also more of an internal library operation. Evaluating a collection may serve many different purposes, both within and outside of the library. For example, it may help to increase funding for the library; it may aid in the library's gaining some form of recognition, such as high standing in a comparative survey; or it may help to determine the quality of work being performed by the library. In order for effective evaluation to occur, the patron community's needs must be considered, which brings us back to community analysis. Thus, collection development is a dynamic, ongoing cycle that should involve both the library and its patron community.

With the exception of acquisition work, as noted, some interaction should exist in the collection development process between the library staff and the community of users (as in Figure 1). The degree of that interaction is determined by many factors: the size of the community; the original purposes of the library; and the willingness of the community to become involved. Few librarians would question the need or value of patron input, but the question is, how much should there be? The best answer would seem to be, as much as the library can afford to handle and as much as the community is willing to provide.

Bearing in mind, then, the relationship between the library's goal of service and the actual process of developing the collection to achieve that goal, it is possible to formulate several general principles about collection development. The following six statements form the philosophical foundation of this work, and have been implicit in the overview of the process just presented:

1) collection development should be geared primarily to community needs rather than to an abstract standard of quality.

2) collection development to be effective must be responsive to the *total* community's needs, not just to those of active users.

3) collection development should be carried out with knowledge of and participation in cooperative programs at the local, regional, and national levels.

4) collection development must consider all formats for inclusion in the collection.

5) collection development was, is, and always will be a subjective, biased work. The intervention of a selector's personal values into the process can never be completely avoided.

6) collection development is not something that one learns entirely in the classroom or from reading. Only through practice and making mistakes will a person become proficient in the process of developing a collection.

COLLECTION DEVELOPMENT AND THE COMMUNITY

Collection development is a complex process involving several factors both within and outside of the library. Most important among these are the library's own structure and organization, the producers and distributors of the materials available for collection, and other libraries serving similar communities. Figure 2 illustrates the complexity of the interrelationships among the library organization, the materials producers and distributors, and other libraries. (The general term "materials producers" covers both book publishers and producers of audio visual materials.)

Figure 2

Collection Development, the Library, and the Community

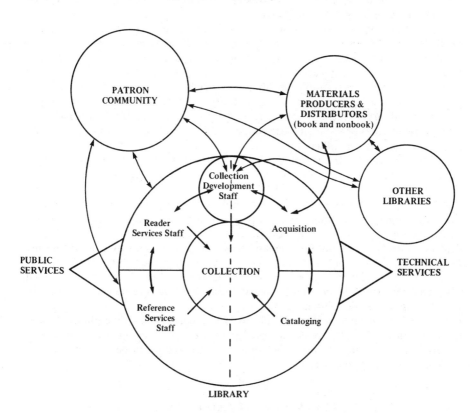

The internal activities of libraries are organized into public and technical services. Those activities in which the staff has daily contact with patrons are usually considered public services; almost all other activities are technical services. Library staff responsible for collection development supply information to the acquisition department (usually classed as a technical service), which then orders the desired items from the materials producer, or from a distributor. The producer (or distributor) then sends the material to the acquisition department. After receiving the materials and clearing the records, the acquisition department sends the items on to the cataloging department for processing; processed items are subsequently placed in the collection. Both the public service staff and the patrons using the collection provide input concerning the value of individual items, information that is then considered by collection development staff during the processes of weeding and evaluating. The information generated from these sources may eventually influence the library's written policies for collection development. (Most of these internal library interactions will be covered in chapters 4 through 10, with one exception, labeled "collection development staff" in Figure 2; this will be discussed later in the present chapter.)

Materials producers exert several significant influences. Of primary importance is that, to a very large extent, they control what is available for library purchase by their choice of whether to produce any given item. Furthermore, their methods of doing business cause the library to perform its acquisition tasks in ways that meet the producers' needs, not the other way around. A third influence is that producers go directly to the patron community to generate interest in their wares, so that the library, in responding to patron demands, is indirectly responding to the marketing activities of the materials producers.

The materials in other library collections that are accessible to the patron community may also influence an individual library's collection development, if cooperative agreements among libraries can be created. Cooperative collection development programs can enable libraries to provide more service to their communities, and they can reduce waste and unnecessary duplication of materials that can happen, for example, when a person is part of several overlapping library patron communities and influences the collection development activities of each. This person might be a business researcher who uses the company's library during the day. The person may take evening classes at an academic institution, using that library for class-related and business-related materials alike. That same individual also may rely on a local public library, because of its convenience, to supply information on both job-related and recreational concerns. Thus, one person's requests for job-related materials in both the academic and public libraries could influence three different types of libraries in the same area to collect the same material. Yet, working out effective cooperative programs can be very difficult, as we will discuss in chapter 11.

COLLECTION DEVELOPMENT AND TYPES OF LIBRARIES

Libraries may be divided into four general types: academic, public, school, and special. Broadly speaking, each of these types of library performs (or has performed for it) a number of basic functions. They have a specific population of users to serve; materials must be collected and preserved in a form suitable for patron use; and materials must be organized in a manner designed to help the patron locate what is wanted as quickly as possible. Beyond this list of basic functions, differences emerge among the various library types as a result both of the different categories of patrons served in each and of the limits set by a governing body on the services that the library may provide.

As noted earlier, collection development is, generally speaking, a process universal to all types of libraries. But as one moves from general to specific matters, differences in emphasis on the various elements of the collection development process become apparent. For example, school and public libraries tend to place more emphasis on actual selection than do academic or special libraries. On the other hand, differences in emphasis occur among libraries of the same type, so that occasionally, a small academic library might resemble a large special library in the way its collection development is handled. The approach taken in this book is to present a general view. When necessary, the varying degrees of emphasis placed on elements of the process in different library types will be pointed out.

The chapters in this book reflect, to some extent, differences in emphasis according to type of library. For several reasons, community analysis is very important in public libraries; academic, school, and special libraries have patron communities smaller in size and somewhat easier to define than public libraries. The public library also depends on librarians to build the collection, whereas in other types of libraries, patrons have a stronger voice, especially in the selection process. Thus, the public library must undertake community analysis in order to build an effectively used collection; for this reason, the chapter on community analysis has a public library slant.

It should be noted here also that the size of a library's patron community has definite bearing upon its collection development. Indeed, three "laws" of collection development can be derived when taking stock of that community:

1) as the size of the patron community increases, the degree of divergence in patron needs for materials increases proportionally.

2) as the degree of divergence in patron needs increases, the need for cooperative materials sharing programs increases.

3) a library will never be able to completely satisfy *all* of the materials needs of any single class of patron in its community.

Even special libraries, serving a limited population group, encounter problems in relation to these laws, since no two persons are identical, and it is impossible for their materials needs and interests to completely coincide. In the special library environment, the interests of patrons can be and often are similar, but even within a team of research workers exploring a single problem, individual needs will vary. The needs of a limited population group will not be as homogeneous as they might first appear.

The element of collection development that varies the least among library types is collection development policies. Simply put, as a library increases in size, its policy statements will need to become more detailed, and thus, more complex. Generally, the most comprehensive collection policy statements are found in the larger academic research libraries.

The element of the process that encompasses the greatest variety of approaches is selection. Because of this wide range, there is some danger in attempting to summarize the situation too neatly. However, with the caveat that the following statements are sweeping in scope and disregard numerous exceptions, one may make the following distinctions among types of libraries and their methods of materials selection:

1) public libraries emphasize title-by-title selection, and selection is made by one or more librarians.

2) school libraries also emphasize title-by-title selection, but it is usually made by a committee composed of librarians, teachers, and sometimes, administrators.

3) special libraries select materials in subject areas for specific research purposes, and very often, the patron is the primary selector.

4) academic libraries select materials in subject areas for educational and research purposes, but actual selection may be totally in the hands of the faculty, the librarians, or some formal group comprising representatives of each group.

The selection activities of public, academic, and large special libraries will also vary depending upon their sizes. In small public libraries, most of the librarians are involved in selection. As the library system grows, adds branches, and expands services, selection is usually delegated to department heads or branch library supervisors. A large metropolitan public library system frequently assigns selection activities to a committee composed of representatives from all of the service programs, though not from every branch library. This committee formulates a list of titles that the different service programs may select from; thus, it serves as a first level screening group.

A similar progression due to size exists in academic libraries and some special libraries, but the selectors in these cases are, more often than not, the patrons—academic or staff researchers. Even when librarians are responsible for selection in libraries serving institutions with hundreds of subject specialists, the faculty members or researchers have a significant voice in what is selected. The factor that accounts for the more limited role that librarians play in selection for academic and special libraries is the need to assess subject materials prepared for the specialist. A fairly common practice in both types of libraries is to hire librarians with graduate degrees in both librarianship and one other subject area. Even then, most materials in subject fields at the advanced levels of research are so specialized that the library must draw on all of the subject expertise available, including that of the patron community.

In small academic and special libraries, selection is in the hands of the subject specialist, unless the librarian is also an expert in the particular field. Indeed, small academic institutions usually expect the teaching faculty to build the library collection. As small budgets for materials are increased and as the collection grows proportionally, then librarians become more involved, because often broad subject fields are purchased rather than single titles in a field. This approach does not require the subject specialist. In some of the very large academic research libraries, selection does not occur in many subject areas, because the objective is to acquire everything available on a given topic. This means very little non-librarian involvement, beyond identifying the subject areas in which collecting should be undertaken.

Chapters 6 and 7, on selection, particularly emphasize public and school libraries, since selection in these library types is a major part of the librarian's activity. Selection is not unimportant in other types of libraries, but in these, it is performed also by non-librarians or on the basis of subject content that can only be accurately assessed by a specialist. Quite the opposite from selection, acquisition work is similar in all types of libraries. The organization of the work flow may vary, but the basic routines remain quite consistent. Chapter 8 provides an overview of the basic activities in acquisition work.

Once the library collection grows enough to fill all of the available shelf space, a decision may be made to reduce the size of the collection by weeding. In school and public libraries, this does not present too great a problem, as a high percentage of materials is simply used to pieces. Very often, such libraries buy multiple copies of materials; then, by keeping just one copy after demand drops, they regain some space. Also, only the very large public libraries have major archival responsibilities; thus, weeding is easier. Academic and research libraries seldom buy multiple copies, and frequently, buy titles known to be little-used. Because of space limitations, special libraries must weed on a regular basis. Very often, this results in "rules" on weeding (for instance, that all monographs five years old are to be discarded). Rules of this kind help to solve one problem—lack of staff for weeding—but they may increase the demand for interlibrary loan of items discarded as a result of this less than thoughtful approach to the problem. More research has been done on weeding in academic libraries than for all of the other types of libraries combined, which is reflected in the emphasis on academic libraries in chapter 9 on weeding.

Although the final phase of the process, collection evaluation, takes place in all library types, it is especially significant in libraries serving educational organizations. Most schools and academic institutions are evaluated by some outside agency to determine the quality of education being provided. If nothing more, the agency (governmental or private) that funds the institution will require periodic assessments, which will invariably include the library and its collection. For such libraries, the evaluation process may have far-reaching effects. Naturally, librarians in educational institutions have been very interested in improving the evaluation process, and they have written a great deal about the topic. Chapter 10, on evaluation, draws heavily upon this literature as well as on the literature of accreditation evaluations.

DEFINITIONS

The preceding pages have defined by implication four of the most important concepts discussed in this book: collection development, selection, acquisition work, and library materials. A major problem in the library profession, though, is the lack of agreed-upon definitions for the basic terms used so freely by everyone involved in collection development. Other textbooks on this subject (see the bibliography at the end of this chapter for references) do not define these terms, and most glossaries of librarianship do not list either collection development or selection in any form. That the terminology in this field has not been standardized is clearly explained in an article by Michael Bruer:

> The solution to the problem of resources is complicated by a great deal of confusion over the meaning of terms and responsibilities of resource librarians. It is not uncommon for example to find that "selection," "bibliography," "acquisitions," and "collection development" are used more or less interchangeably.[1]

Bruer's comment is important for several reasons. First, his article was the profession's own annual review of activities and publications in the field. It indicates that little agreement can be found among the professionals working and writing about the field; each has a personal, sometimes uncommunicated, definition of the various terms, making communication difficult even among colleagues. Second, Bruer's statement implies an important fact about the field: it is a highly personal and subjective activity. While there is general agreement as to the basic elements of collection development, many differences of opinion exist about which elements are more important than others, differences of opinion reflected in the few basic definitions available. And since this work is predicated on six principles whose precise meaning depends upon an understanding of the terms used therein, definitions of the four basic terms are provided here. The preceding discussion of collection development has implied much, but it seems important to state the definitions explicitly so that no misunderstandings occur.

The *Encyclopedia of Library and Information Science* (ELIS) contains a nine-page essay on "Collection Building." As close as this essay comes to an overall definition is that "building a collection may occasionally involve the selection and acquisition of these materials *ab initio*, but in most cases it is likely to mean the planned, systematic development of an already existing collection."[2] For purposes of this book, however, the following definition will be used:

> *Collection development:* The process of identifying the strengths and weaknesses of a library's materials collection in terms of patron needs and community resources, and attempting to correct existing weaknesses, if any. This requires the constant examination and evaluation of the library's resources and the constant study of both patron needs and changes in the community to be served.

Definitions of selection are even more difficult to locate than those for collection development. ELIS has not reached the letter S as of this writing; L. M. Harrod's *Librarians' Glossary* and the American Library Association's *Glossary of Library Terms* do not include the term. Other textbooks on the subject never provide an explicit definition, but rather, discuss it primarily by implication. For our purposes, the following will serve as the working definition:

> *Selection:* The process of deciding which materials to acquire for a library collection. It may involve deciding between items that provide information about the same subject; deciding whether the information

contained in an item is worth its price; or deciding whether an item could stand up to the use it would receive. In essence, it is a matter of systematically determining quality and value.

Of the four terms, acquisition work is perhaps the most standardized in its definitions. Harrod defines it as "the process of obtaining books and other documents for a library, documentation centre, or archive."[3] T. Grieder provides a longer description of the tasks of acquisition work (in this case, in a university setting):

> The duties of the acquisitions librarian are to receive requests for purchases of titles from all parts of the university community (he will almost inevitably generate a number of requests himself) and (a) to ascertain that such requests are not for titles already in the library; (b) to verify that such titles actually exist; (c) to determine if Library of Congress resources have cataloged the title, or, failing that, to determine if the title appears in other national or trade bibliographies; (d) to determine the price and availability of a given title; (e) to order requested titles that have passed through procedures a-d, above; (f) to receive and pay for ordered titles; and (g) to send all titles along with all possible bibliographical information to the Catalog department.[4]

In this book, we will use the following definition, which encompasses a slightly broader field than just the routines involved in buying materials:

> *Acquisition work:* The process of securing materials for the library's collection, whether by purchase, as gifts, or through exchange programs.

There is little reason to define library materials other than to emphasize that we will be concerned with various formats, not just books. Different authors writing about library collections have used a number of related terms—print, nonprint, visual materials, audio visuals, a-v, other media, etc.—but no single term encompassing all of them has gained universal acceptance among librarians. Library materials (or simply, materials) is a non-specific term with respect to format, while being otherwise inclusive; it will, therefore, be used throughout the text:

> *Library materials* (materials) may be books, periodicals, pamphlets, reports, manuscripts, microformats, motion pictures, video or audio tapes, sound recordings, realia, etc. In effect, almost any physical object that conveys information, thoughts, or feelings potentially could be included in a library collection.

SUMMARY

If collection development programs were to be based on the three previously-mentioned laws, existing programs would undergo several fundamental changes. First, greater stress would be placed on assessing the *current* needs of users. Not only would there be verbal acknowledgment of this "ideal," but the library's policy would incorporate statements regarding procedures for the actual assessment of patron needs on a regular basis. Second, the program would not appear to promise the patron total satisfaction of her or his library needs. Few existing programs state that the collection will take care of all patron needs. On the other hand, they seldom indicate the limits set for their specific collection.

Using the laws as a basis for formulating a program, then, the library would almost be compelled to identify the limits that it has set for collecting. Delimiters of this type would aid collection development personnel in their daily work and would keep everyone's expectations within reasonable bounds. Third, a program having recognized limits would further indicate how the library might help the patron to satisfy unmet needs through cooperative programs. Such a statement would require more than pious generalities, though. It would require indications of how the cooperative network functions, at what level, and for whom. The library would have to make practical arrangements to avail itself of such opportunities, or face the justifiable wrath of the patron community in whose interests it has been established and maintained.

NOTES

[1] M. Bruer, "Resources in 1974," *Library Resources and Technical Services* 19 (Summer 1975): 229.

[2] J. C. Shipman, "Collection Building," in *Encyclopedia of Library and Information Science*, Vol. 5 (New York: Marcel Dekker, 1971), p. 260.

[3] L. M. Harrod, *The Librarians' Glossary and Reference Book*, 4th ed. (Boulder, CO: Westview Press, 1977), p. 41.

[4] T. Grieder, *Acquisitions* (Westport, CT: Greenwood Press, 1978), p. 12.

BIBLIOGRAPHY

Broadus, R. N. *Selecting Materials for Libraries*. New York: H. W. Wilson, 1973.

Carter, M. D., W. J. Bonk, and R. M. Magrill. *Building Library Collections*. 4th ed. Metuchen, NJ: Scarecrow Press, 1974.

Conference on Library School Teaching Methods: Courses in the Selection of Adult Materials, University of Illinois, 1968. *Library School Teaching Methods: Courses in the Selection of Adult Materials*. L. E. Bone, ed. Urbana: University of Illinois, Graduate School of Library Science, 1969.

Downs, R. B. "Future Prospects of Library Acquisitions." *Library Trends* 18 (January 1970): 412-21.

Drury, F. K. W. *Book Selection*. Chicago: American Library Association, 1930.

Drury, F. K. W. *The Selection and Acquisition of Books for Libraries*. Chicago: American Library Association, 1928.

Fiske, M. *Book Selection and Censorship: A Study of School and Public Libraries in California.* Berkeley: University of California Press, 1959; reprinted 1968.

Ford, S. *The Acquisition of Library Materials.* Chicago: American Library Association, 1978.

Gaver, M. V. *Background Readings in Building Library Collections.* Metuchen, NJ: Scarecrow Press, 1969.

Grieder, T. *Acquisitions.* Westport, CT: Greenwood Press, 1978.

Haines, H. E. *Living with Books: The Art of Book Selection.* 2nd ed. New York: Columbia University Press, 1950. (Columbia University Studies in Library Service, No. 21).

Kujoth, J. S., comp. *Libraries, Readers, and Book Selection.* Metuchen, NJ: Scarecrow Press, 1969.

Melcher, D. *Melcher on Acquisition.* Chicago: American Library Association, 1971.

Shaffer, K. R. *The Book Collection: Policy Case Studies in Public and Academic Libraries.* Hamden, CT: Shoestring Press, 1961. (Case Studies in Library Administration, Ser. 3).

Spiller, D. *Book Selection: An Introduction to Principles and Practice.* 2nd rev. ed. Hamden, CT: Linnet Books, 1974.

Wulfekoetter, G. *Acquisition Work: Processes Involved in Building Library Collections.* Seattle: University of Washington Press, 1961.

Wynar, B. S. *Library Acquisitions: A Classified Bibliographic Guide to the Literature and Reference Tools.* 2nd ed. Littleton, CO: Libraries Unlimited, 1971.

Chapter 2

PRODUCERS OF LIBRARY MATERIALS

Producers of library materials can be divided into two broad categories: 1) those publishing books or printed matter (periodicals, newspapers, etc.) and 2) audio visual producers. This chapter will present a general examination of some of the important characteristics of producers in both categories. Enough depth will be attained, however, to provide a reasonable picture of what these groups do and how they go about it. We will start with publishing (the "book trade"), then go on to consider the production of audio visual materials.

WHY KNOW THE BOOK TRADE?

What is the "book trade"? The question is simple, but it is one whose answer is long and complex, reaching far beyond the activities of book publishers. The trade comprises many different persons and groups: the individuals who create the materials (writers, performers, etc.), groups that edit and manufacture the materials, and groups that distribute and sell the materials to the consumer. The businesses range in size from one person's spare room operation to a national government's publishing activities. Some of the world's largest producers of books and other materials are actually part of a national government.

Some book publishers also produce audio visual materials. For example, in the United States, such well-known publishers as McGraw-Hill and Doubleday have active, large audio visual divisions within their firms. Nevertheless, most persons would think of them as book publishers, partly because of historical factors and partly because of the emphasis they give to their publishing activities. (Conversely, some of the so-called "other media" producers occasionally publish books.) What is omitted when one discusses book publishers, though, is any consideration of newspaper and periodical publishers. These fields constitute rather special areas of publishing, both of which are important to library collection development.

In essence, the trade is a vast number of persons and organizations—some interested only in profit; some, in service; and some, in both—that create and manufacture materials in a wide range of formats that libraries collect and make available to their patrons. In response to the question "why bother with details of the trade?," several responses come to mind. When one is going to work day in and day out with an industry, even if just buying its product(s), some knowledge of that industry will make everyone's life a little easier. An understanding of the trade's characteristics—such as what determines the price of an item, how products are distributed, and what services one can expect—all improve understanding and communication between producers and buyers. Under the best of circumstances, a great deal of communication exists between the library and the trade regarding orders. If the library shows some understanding of the vendor's problems, the vendor more often than not tries to meet the needs of that library; but this only happens when the library staff takes the time and trouble to learn something about the organizations with which they are working.

All of this knowledge provides some understanding, if not sympathy, on the librarian's part for the problems of producers. Publishers who depend upon library sales know (or should know) a great deal about library problems and operations, but a number of jokes circulate among publishers about how uninformed librarians are about the book trade. The present strained relationship between libraries and publishers has occurred partly because neither group really understands or is trying to understand the other's position. (For instance, copyright, discussed in chapter 12, is an area of great controversy between the two.) Yet, we also know that when two parties can discuss problems with mutual understanding, their working relationship will usually be more pleasant. Each is more willing to make an occasional concession to the other's needs, which can often foster mutually beneficial alliances. Certainly, librarians and publishers could work more easily together if they knew one another.

Most book selection and collection development courses in library schools usually touch only lightly on publishers and their problems, teachers claiming insufficient time to give more coverage. And courses in the history of the book trade somehow seldom have time to deal with the contemporary situation—it is not yet history. Most schools do not have a place in their curriculum for a course in contemporary production, and if they did, most students would not have time for it in their study programs. But those same students are thereby lacking information that could prove invaluable to them on a basic level, since knowing what happens in publishing can affect the selection process. First, it aids in identifying the most likely sources of materials—i.e., which one among thousands of producers is most likely to have what is needed. Second, by keeping up to date with what is happening in publishing, one can anticipate changes in quality and format. Third, librarians can influence decisions about what is published, provided that the publisher knows that the librarian is knowledgeable about what is involved in developing profitable books.

Obviously, most publishers are primarily concerned with making a living, which includes getting a reasonable return on the money that they invest in producing books, periodicals, and/or newspapers. Quality and service do matter, but publishers are not in existence to provide quality material and exceptional service at a constant loss, as some librarians (and patrons) seem to believe. They are in *business*, and are not there just to meet personal information needs when those arise. Publishers must make a profit in order to stay in business, and to do this, they must produce materials that are marketable to a fairly large audience. Thus, librarians should be among the first to discard the stereotype of the publisher as a retiring, highly sophisticated literary person interested only in creative quality, just as publishers should abandon the view of the librarian as a woman with her hair in a bun, wearing horn-rimmed glasses, and with a constant "shush" on her lips.

READERS AND WRITERS

For much of the world's population, reading is still a significant leisure time activity. As the number of alternative knowledge resource formats increases, the percentage of time that people spend reading books decreases. In the United States, many people decry the drop in the percentage of active book readers. Even a superficial examination of statistical information on how Americans spend their recreational dollars reveals that it will be a long while before reading becomes America's number one indoor activity. In fact, it may be a long while before it reaches the top twenty. Indeed, given the figures, it seems amazing that books, libraries, and publishers continue to exist. Certainly these figures give the clearest indication of why both publishers and libraries place more and more emphasis on "other media." The following statistics are recent (1976), and although they are for only one state (New Jersey), they probably represent the general pattern in the United States. All of the data in this section are from the same report, *The Use of and Attitudes toward Libraries in New Jersey.*[1]

More than two-thirds of the households surveyed had one or more members possessing a public library card. That figure is impressive; however, when compared with the actual use of those cards, the first impression is changed. Only 18 percent of all of the adults visited a public library more than once a month. In fact, 54 percent said that they had not visited a public library in the past twelve months. The survey also found that the patron of a public library also utilized other types of library (school, academic, or special), while the nonpatron of the public library generally did not patronize any other type of library. This finding reinforces the point made earlier about the manner in which a single patron can influence the collection development programs of several types of library during the same time period.

Concerning audio visual materials, the nonusers expressed interest in using the library if general adult films were shown or available (56 percent) and/or if an expanded recording collection were available (42 percent). This would seem to indicate that a large number of potential patrons are not interested in books or other print formats. Finally, listening to music and watching television ranked higher (90 percent and 83 percent, respectively) than did reading (82 percent), when individuals were asked to list their two or three most enjoyable activities. Again, the difference is even greater when we consider the nonuser of libraries (the majority of adults)—music, 86 percent; television, 87 percent; and reading, 75 percent. In fact, reading and do-it-yourself projects received equal rankings from nonusers of the public library. Even though their numbers are limited, however, readers persist in their habit. And just as readers persist, so do the people ultimately responsible for books, the authors.

Making a living (earning annually more than $5,000—U.S. poverty level) by writing is very difficult. While total book sales figures continue to rise, and while the dollar amount (see Figure 3) seems impressive, the high percentage of publisher-prepared material (especially in Elhi textbook and reference book

Figure 3

U.S. Domestic Book Sales,
1976 and 1975 (Revised)

(Estimated Consumer Expenditures—
Millions of Dollars and Units)

	1976		1975		% Change		$ per Unit		
	$	Units	$	Units	$	Units	1976	1975	% Change
Trade	$862	199	$819	198	5.3	0.5	$4.33	$4.14	4.6
Adult Hardbound	495	74	462	71	7.1	4.2	6.69	6.51	2.8
Adult Paperbound	183	66	175	67	4.6	− 1.9	2.77	2.61	6.1
Juvenile Hardbound	155	36	157	41	− 0.6	−12.2	4.31	3.83	12.5
Juvenile Paperbound	29	23	25	19	13.4	23.8	1.23	1.34	− 7.5
Religious	274	75	248	70	10.5	7.1	3.65	3.54	3.1
Hardbound	156	17	148	16	5.4	6.3	9.01	9.25	− 2.6
Paperbound	118	58	100	54	18.0	6.6	2.03	1.84	10.3
Professional	550	76	491	69	12.0	10.1	7.24	7.13	1.7
Hardbound	359	23	326	23	10.1	0.0	15.61	14.17	10.2
Paperbound	191	53	162	46	17.9	15.2	3.60	3.52	2.3
Book Clubs	333	106	296	99	12.5	7.1	3.14	2.99	5.0
Hardbound	237	53	220	53	7.7	0.0	4.47	4.17	7.2
Paperbound	97	53	76	46	27.6	15.2	1.83	1.64	11.6
Mail Order Publications	358	31	287	26	24.6	18.5	11.61	11.04	5.2
Mass Market Paperback	653	434	559	446	16.8	− 2.7	1.50	1.25	20.0
University Presses	57	8	52	8	9.6	1.3	7.13	6.50	9.7
Hardbound	44	4	41	4	7.3	− 2.5	11.00	10.25	8.2
Paperbound	13	4	11	4	15.8	5.0	3.14	2.85	10.2
Elhi Text	616	231	619	243	− 0.5	− 4.9	2.67	2.55	4.7
Hardbound	308	59	335	71	− 8.1	-16.9	5.25	4.70	11.7
Paperbound*	308	172	284	172	8.5	0.0	1.79	1.65	8.5
College Text	622	83	578	85	7.6	− 1.7	7.49	6.81	10.0
Hardbound	384	33	356	34	7.9	− 2.4	11.64	10.47	11.2
Paperbound*	238	50	222	51	7.4	− 1.2	4.72	4.35	8.5
Subscription Reference	266	1	238	1	11.8	4.8	253.73	237.80	6.7
Total	**$4,591**	**1,244**	**$4,187**	**1,245**	**9.6**	**− 0.1**	**$3.69**	**$3.36**	**9.8**

Source: Table I revised by John P. Dessauer from his article "U.S. Consumer Expenditures on Books in 1976," Publishers Weekly, April 25, 1977.

Note: Dollar and unit data have been rounded to millions. Change percentages, however, are based on numbers carried to one decimal, i.e., hundreds of thousands.

*Includes workbooks, manuals, reprints, pamphlets and objective tests (but not standardized tests).

publishing) makes the prospect of making a living by the pen not so promising. Also, the number of authors sharing the field increases constantly. Accurate information about average author income is hard to come by, but it is safe to say that most authors receiving royalty payments do not expect to live just on their royalty income. A great many writers hold full-time jobs and write in their spare time. Others may work at writing full-time but only can do so because someone else provides the bulk of living expenses. Some of the best-selling authors, of course, do very, very well, but they represent a minute percentage of the total number of authors working.

Hayes B. Jacobs, a freelance writer, notes that "genuine, full-time freelance writers are as rare as genuine, full-time ghosts." In his article "Freelance at Work" in *Writer's Market '76*, he further describes the realities of being "not on a regular salary":

> Among those rare, full-time freelance writers, of whom there are only a few hundred in the United States, are a fair number who, although they appear to be getting along nicely without a regular salary, are actually undergirded by a small trust fund here, a large parcel of income-producing property there, or, quite frequently, a salaried mate. I know one with a hidden herd of Herefords, and another who rents rooms.
>
> If you're a typical freelance writer, the earnings you produce with your typewriter supplement other, steadier income. Your writing brings in $200 a year (the fledgling freelance); $20,000 a year (the high flyer); $200,000 a year (the superstars); even $2,000,000 a year (yes, it's been done, just as Halley's comet has been sighted).[2]

Despite the generally bleak prospects for achieving fiscal freedom by literary efforts, thousands of persons continue to try. A few earn nothing, most earn enough to encourage them to continue their efforts, while only a handful achieve financial independence. Enough writers gain sufficient economic and psychic rewards from their writings to continue to supply readers with new material.

WHAT IS A PUBLISHER?

What is a publisher? A simple answer is that the publisher supplies the capital and some editorial assistance in turning manuscripts into books. (Two exceptions to this are vanity and subsidy presses, discussed later in this section.) Generally, publishers in Western countries now perform six basic functions:

1)   tap sources of materials (manuscripts);

2)   raise and supply the capital to make books;

3)   aid in the development of the manuscript;

4)   contract for the manufacturing (printing and binding) of the book;

5) distribute the books—including promotion and advertising;

6) maintain records of sales, contracts, and correspondence relating to the production and sale of books.

One misconception about publishers is that they actually print books. Printing, though, is seldom a function of a major publisher, as publishers enter into a contract with an independent printer for the production of each book. A printer does *not* share in the risk of the publisher and author in the production of a book. Printers are paid for their composition of type, presswork, and binding regardless of how many or few copies of the book are sold.

In the past, a book's publisher and printer were often one and the same, as can be seen in a number of excellent histories of publishing and the book trade. However, a thumbnail sketch of a basic pattern in the development of publishing and the book trade is pertinent. The pattern seems to be worldwide and does have an impact on acquisition and selection work. In the history of publishing, there appear to be three stages of development. These stages have occurred both in Europe and America, and they also appear in developing countries as each evolves its own publishing and book trade.

During stage one, the publishing, printing, and selling of the product are combined in one firm, and often in one person or one family. The early "giants" in Europe acted as publisher, printer, and "retail" bookseller—Froben, Schoffer, Manutius, Caxton, and others. When one examines American publishing history, the same pattern appears on the eastern seaboard and moves west with the frontier; names such as Franklin, Green, and Harris fall into this period. Publishing in developing countries exhibits the same evolutionary pattern, which is in large measure a function of how the society has organized its economic, education, and human resources. In developing countries, though, limits of resources, technical skills, and market make it unfeasible, and in many cases impossible, to have specialty publishers in all fields.

From a collection development point of view, stage one development presents many interesting challenges. Large research libraries buy materials from around the world, but developing countries seldom have anything resembling a national bibliography, much less a trade bibliography (mainstays in identifying important titles). As if this were not challenge enough, most publishers operating at a stage one level do not print a large number of copies of their books. In many cases they take orders *before* they print the book. When this happens they normally print just a few more copies than the number for which they have orders. Many collection development librarians have experienced the frustration of having an order returned with the comment "unavailable, only 200 copies printed." The story of the book being out-of-print on the day it was published has a basis in fact, and it frequently occurs in areas where publishing is at the stage one level.

Stage two shows some degree of specialization, with the retail trade branching off as an independent specialization. During this stage, the one-person family operation begins to emphasize either publishing or printing. A few firms are established with a single emphasis (publishing *or* printing), the factors creating this situation again being economic, education, and human resources. Better education should and does mean that there is a greater market for books among both individual and institutional buyers. One reason the retail trade usually becomes the first separate activity is that the reading public is widely dispersed and requires outlets across the country. A single outlet in the major population center of the country is no longer adequate. Examples from this early period in American publishing are John Wiley, George Putnam, and the Lippincott Company. In 1807, Charles Wiley joined George Putnam in a bookstore operation in New York City. Over the following century and one-half, the heirs of the two men built up two of the leading publishing houses in the United States. The Lippincott Company started in 1836 as a bookstore and over the years shifted its emphasis to publishing.

When bookstores begin to develop, trade bibliography must also arise—perhaps not what most persons would call a trade journal, but some formal system through which publishers inform bookstores of what is to be or has been published. Collection development librarians expend a great deal of energy in tracking down such systems in those developing countries where the book trade has reached stage two. The usual procedure is to establish a good working relationship with one of the bigger bookstores in such an area and then to work through that shop. This may entail signing an agreement to spend a certain amount of money each year with the firm, but it will insure much better coverage, and usually better service, than working through individual publishing houses.

The third stage is the complete separation of the three basic functions, as publishers drop their printing activities. For example, John and James Harper started out as printers in 1817. Today, Harper and Row is one of the leading publishers in the United States, but it ceased printing activities years ago. (One of the last major publishers to retain a printing plant as part of its operation is Doubleday.) By the time this final stage is reached, all the trappings we see in present-day U.S. publishing are evident: specialty publishers, literary agents, trade journals, salespersonnel, jobbers and wholesalers, etc. Normally there exists something resembling a national bibliography as well as a trade bibliography, both of which are essential for collection development work.

American, Canadian, and European publishers have gone through two other changes since they reached this third level. Before 1950, most publishing houses were family owned or privately held firms. With the rapid and great expansion of the educational materials market, especially in the U.S., most publishers found it impossible to raise enough capital to expand adequately. Slowly at first, and then with increasing frequency, publishers "went public": they sold stock in the firm to the general public. Going public brought about a number of changes in the publishing field, both good and bad. On the positive side, new materials were produced and more services were offered. On the negative side there was an increased emphasis on profitability, and perhaps, a decline in over-all quality. The problems were neither as great nor as bad as the doomsday prophets predicted. Certainly, there was a new responsibility to investors to show a profit. Family- and privately-run houses, while not trying to lose money, would often be more concerned with the quality of their books and the overall reputation of the house than with the size of their profit. Under the new arrangements, though, profitability became more and more important to the now-public publishing houses.

As more and more money was poured into education in the late 1950s and early 1960s, publishing in that area became more and more profitable. This good profit made publishing an area of interest for large conglomerates looking for diversification opportunities, and large electronic and communication firms began to buy up publishing houses—RCA, IBM, Xerox, Raytheon, and General Electric, for example. One interesting combination today is Time-Life, Inc. and General Electric's General Learning Corporation. This subsidiary has controlling interest of Little Brown (trade publisher), Silver-Burdett (school textbook publisher), Peter H. Roebuck (television and educational films), New York Graphics, Alva Museum Replicas, Seven Arts Society, Book Find Club, and five publishing houses in England, Spain, Mexico, and France. There are a number of other "giants" of this type. Two excellent articles on the merger trend are Elin B. Christianson's "Mergers in the Publishing Industry, 1958-1970"[3] and a special report in *Publishers Weekly*, "The Question of Size in the Book Industry."[4]

The potential impact of these new combinations, which control a very high percentage of the total annual sales, is great. If nothing else, it will mean that market potential will take on even greater importance when publishers select manuscripts to publish. Anyone with a little imagination can build a horrible vision of the future of publishing by contemplating this danger. To date, little evidence exists that any real change has come about in the quality of books being produced, but the potential danger is there. Selection and acquisition librarians should be among the first to note any significant change, provided that they are aware both of what is happening in the publishing field and the implications of these changes.

TYPES OF PUBLISHERS

In the preceding paragraphs the terms trade, house, and specialty publishers were used. *House* is a term that goes back to the period when publishing was a family, or at least a very personal, operation. Although people still refer to "houses" and the old names still exist, it is doubtful whether the old feelings about the quality of the books being published or the rather informal method of operating still exist. *Trade publishers* are those that produce a wide range of titles having a wide sales potential, both fiction and nonfiction. Names such as Harper and Row, Knopf, Doubleday, Macmillan, Little Brown, and Random House are typical of the general trade publisher. Frequently, trade publishers have divisions similar to specialty publishers—children's, elementary-high school (Elhi), paperback, technical, reference, and so forth. *Specialty houses* restrict their output to a limited area, subject, or format. Their audience is smaller and often more critical of the product than is true of the trade publisher's audience. There are a number of categories of specialty houses: textbook (Elhi and college level), paperback, children's, microform, music, cartographic, and subject area.

Textbook publishers especially at primary and secondary school levels, are in an even higher risk area than other publishers. Most publishers in this area develop a line of textbooks for several grades, e.g., a social studies series. Preparation of such texts requires the expenditure of large amounts of time, energy, and money. Printing costs are high as school texts usually involve use of color plates and expensive presswork. This means the investment will be high before there is a chance of recovering the cost. Of course, if enough school districts adopt a text, profits can be great, while failure to secure adoption can mean a tremendous loss. Bigger textbook firms (Ginn; Scott, Foresman; etc.) have a number of different series to help ensure a profit or at least to provide a cushion against loss. Why would anyone risk this type of publishing? A look at the number of dollars school districts spend on textbooks each year provides one answer—616 million in 1976. By carefully planning a series with a great deal of educator cooperation and by focusing marketing, profits can be outstanding. Salesmen for a trade publisher have a number of choices to make—bookstores, libraries, and wholesalers. Each successful visit will mean the sale of a few copies of each title; the adoption of one textbook could mean a thousand copies sold of a single title. Because of the nature of school textbook adoption practices (a process usually occurring once a year), textbook publishers can reduce their warehousing costs, thus adding to their margin of profit.

Subject specialty houses have some of the same characteristics as textbook houses. Their market is restricted and easily identifiable; focusing on a limited number of buyers, it can achieve an excellent return. Art (Abrams), music (Schirmer), scientific (Academic), technical (American Technical Society), law (West Publishing) and medical (Saunders) books often require expensive graphic work, which increases the cost of production. While there is a higher risk in specialty publishing than trade publishers face, it is much lower than that of textbook publishers. Occasionally complaints arise, especially in the law and medical fields, that too much control is in the hands of a very few publishers, but it seems questionable whether more publishing houses in either field would change the picture significantly.

Vanity presses differ from other publishing operations in that they receive most of their operating funds from the authors whose works they publish (an example is Exposition Press). They always show a profit and never lack material to produce. They offer editing assistance, for a fee, and have printed as many copies as the author can afford. Distribution of copies is the author's problem, or again, for a fee, the vanity press will help. While providing the same functions as a publisher, a vanity press owner really takes no risks.

Private presses are not usually business operations in the sense that the owner(s) expects to make money (examples are Henry Morris, Bird, and Poull Press). In many instances, the owner(s) do not sell the products they produce— rather they give them away. Most private presses are owned by individuals who enjoy fine printing and experimenting with type fonts and design. As might be expected when the end product is given away (and often produced on hand presses), the number of copies is limited. In the past many of the developments in type and book design originated with a private press. Many of the most beautiful examples of typographic and book design are from private presses. It should be noted, though it should come as little or no surprise, that most private presses are operated as an avocation rather than a vocation.

Large research libraries often attempt to secure copies of private and vanity press items. By knowing local publishers, persons in the acquisitions department can make that work easier. Authors who use vanity presses frequently give local libraries copies of their book(s), but such gifts usually arrive with no indication that they are a gift. As will be seen in the section on processing, books without packing slips or invoices cause problems. If the staff knows the local vanity and private presses, a great deal of time can be saved by quickly identifying such possible gift items.

Academic/scholarly publishers are normally subsidized, not-for-profit organizations. More often than not, they are associated with academic institutions (University of California Press), museums (Museum of the American Indian Heye

Foundation), research institutions (Battelle Memorial Institute), or learned societies (American Philosophical Society). These presses were originally established to produce scholarly books. Generally, scholarly books have a very limited appeal, and a commercial profit-making publisher is faced with three choices when evaluating a manuscript: 1) publish it and try to sell it at a price to ensure a recovery of costs; 2) publish it, sell it at a price comparable to commercial titles, and lose money in the process; or 3) do not publish the item. Either of the first two options will cost the publisher money and for that reason, most commercial publishers will *not* publish the book. Because of economic factors and a need to disseminate scholarly information regardless of cost—even if it must be done at a loss—the subsidized (by tax exemption, if nothing else), not-for-profit press was created. As publishing costs have sky-rocketed, it has even been necessary to have entire books subsidized, almost in the same manner as in a vanity press operation.

Recently some commercial publishers have raised questions about the validity of this theory. They claim any work that does more than break even should be offered to commercial publishers. They suggest that this could be done through an auction process; if no commercial publisher bid on the title it could remain with the scholarly press. Their reasoning is that the scholarly presses (usually only university presses are the targets of these ideas) are publicly supported by tax monies and/or are tax exempt. Furthermore, they are not supposed to be making a profit. This idea was more the result of a high point in academic library purchases of scholarly works during a high funding period than it was the result of a desire on the part of commercial publishers to publish scholarly books. To some extent the scholarly presses may have caused some of these criticisms by publishing works that would and could have been published by a commercial house. Governments subsidize most of the scholarly presses either by direct payments or by tax exempt status. Yet, as costs rise, the presses are pressured by their funding agencies to at least break even on the majority of books, or to have a few "money makers" to carry the losers.

The role of the scholarly press in the economical and open dissemination of knowledge is critical. Every country needs this type of press in some form. Without such arrangements, important works with a limited appeal will seldom be published. Certainly there are times when a commercial house will be willing to publish a "loser" because it is thought to be very important, but reliance upon that type of willingness will, in the long run, mean that many important works will not be published.

Government presses are as a class the world's largest publishers. The combined annual output of government publications—international (Unesco), national (Government Printing Office), regional and local governments (Los Angeles)—dwarfs the commercial output. In the past, government publications were thought to be of poor quality, uninteresting, and generally a problem. Today some government publications rival the best offerings of commercial publishers. Most government publishing activity goes well beyond the printing of legislative hearings or actions and occasional executive materials. Often, national governments publish essential and inexpensive (frequently free) materials on nutrition, farming, building trades, travel, and a wealth of other topics.

Given this high rate of production and the quantity of sources, librarians face major bibliographic control problems. Determining what has been published at the regional and local level, if one is not physically present in the particular area, may be close to impossible, at least with any assurance as to accuracy and comprehensiveness of coverage. Only a very few of these smaller governmental units provide regular public listings of what has been published. Even if a publication is known to exist, a copy may be extremely difficult to secure because there are so few copies printed. One way around this is to get on the publisher's mailing list. Many government publishing agencies are willing to designate a library as a depository; however, this usually means that the library makes a commitment to store and make available *everything* that is sent. (Storing the material may be a major problem if a library gets on too many free, automatic mailing lists.)

Despite rising costs, government publications are still inexpensive. One good example of this is the price change for the 1970 *Yearbook of Agriculture* (Washington, GPO) which cost $3.50 when it was published; today the item goes for $6.00. In comparison, the 1970 average price for a U.S. nonfiction trade title was $11.66; in 1977, $16.32 (GPO catalogs, 1970, 1978; see page 49 for a list of sources of book trade statistics). Also, the *Yearbook*, like most other government publications, was priced only so as to allow recovery of production costs. Certainly the fee was nominal. Yet today, when prices increase up to 40 percent, this is significant—even given dramatic increases in the cost of raw materials, especially paper. But when the government's increased price is compared with what an equivalent publication would cost from a commercial publisher (assuming that it would even be considered by one), it is usually still a bargain.

Government publishing activities are also expanding in scope; just as commercial publishers are now entering the "other media" fields, so are governments. In areas where literacy rates are low, pictorial and audio formats are invaluable in the process of disseminating knowledge. For that reason governments in such areas are taking a leading role in developing and using these knowledge resource formats rather than depending solely on printed formats.

Paperback publishing can be divided into two types, quality trade paperbacks and mass market paperbacks. A trade publisher may have a quality paperback division or issue the paperbound version of a book through the same division that issued the hardcover edition. These titles are distributed in the same fashion as their hardcover books. Mass market paperback publishers are only concerned with the publication of paperback books, and distribution of the mass market paperback is very different from other book distribution. They are priced very low, and they are put on sale anywhere the publisher can get someone to handle them. The paperback books on sale in train and bus stations, airline terminals, corner stores, and kiosks are mass market paperbacks.

People talk about the "paperback revolution," but it is hard to think of it as a revolution. Certainly the softcover book has had an impact on publishers and on a few authors' incomes; and some readers seem unwilling to accept a hardcover version when the smaller, more compact size is more convenient to use. A paperback version of a hardcover edition may be released by the original publisher or by a paperback house through the purchase of paperback rights. Using a paper cover rather than a hard cover does not, however, reduce the actual unit cost of a book by more than $0.20 to $0.30, depending upon the size of the printing. The reason the price of a paperback is so very much lower is that in most cases it first appeared in hardback form. This means that many of the major costs in production have already been absorbed. The title has already sold well in hardback, perhaps made money for the publisher. Since many of the editorial costs are already recovered, it is possible to reduce the price. Furthermore, the reduced price should help sell more copies, which in turn can help push the price still lower. Naturally, original paperbacks require the same costs, except for the cover material, as a hardcover title.

Books with paper covers have been produced for a long time, at least since the nineteenth century. In some countries this is the standard format. The major difference is that most people only think of the mass market paperback as a paperback. The emphasis on very, very popular, previously published titles—issued in new and very colorful covers and sold at a low price—is apparent. Those are the elements of the paperback revolution, not the paper cover nor even the relatively compact form. Nor has the paperback created a whole new group of readers, as some over-enthusiastic writers claim. It has merely tapped an existing market for low-cost popular books.

Paperbacks are, or can be, an important element in collection development. They can supply at a relatively low cost, if they are not treated as if they were hardcover items, multiple copies of popular works. If the paperback is purchased as a multiple copy—expendable—item, libraries can make limited collection development funds go a long way toward providing breadth and depth in material more readily available for the user.

Newspaper and periodical publishers are still a different class of publishers. For the most part, book publishers depend upon persons outside their organization to prepare the material that is eventually published. Newspaper and periodical publishers are exceptions in that they retain reporters and/or writers as members of their staffs. Of course, there are exceptions to the exception. For instance, some popular and most scholarly periodicals are made up of articles written by persons not employed by the organization publishing the journal. In general one finds in the field of newspaper/periodical publishing the same range of activities as in the book field. That is, there are commercial publishers of popular materials, specialty publishers, children's publishers, scholarly/academic publishers, and of course, government publishers. They share the same characteristics as their book publishing counterparts, and sometimes are divisions of book publishing organizations.

Supplying current information is the primary objective of this type of publisher, other than securing enough income to keep operating. As to currency in book publishing, one can assume that most of the material in a majority of books was prepared at least six to twelve months prior to the publication date. The newspaper/periodical format provides the means for more rapid publishing, perhaps two to three months to less than one day. (A major exception are the scholarly and academic periodicals and newsletters that frequently are a year or two or more behind in publishing articles that have been accepted.) In order to give the community the most current information available, then, the library must acquire those newspapers and/or periodicals that suit the community's needs and interests. The problems in control and selection of these materials will be covered in chapter 6, the main point about them here being their currency as compared with books.

Two other types of publishing activities should be noted: *associations* and *reprint houses*. Professional and special interest groups/associations frequently establish their own publishing houses (American Library Association, Library Association). They may only publish a professional journal, but frequently they also issue books and even audio visual materials. The operating funds come from the association but the group hopes to recover its costs. Because associations are often tax exempt their publishing activities are very similar to those of academic presses: limited-appeal titles, relatively small press runs, relatively high price, and at least an indirect government subsidy. Many associations not operating their own press frequently contract with a commercial publisher to print their journal, conference proceedings, etc. Association publications, whether published by the organization itself or under contract, can provide the library with numerous bibliographic control headaches. Titles are announced as forthcoming but never get published. Often the publications are papers from meetings and conventions (the transactions of . . . , or proceedings of . . .); such titles frequently change title two or three times before they appear in hard covers.

Reprint houses, as the name implies, are concerned with reprinting items no longer in print. Most of the sales for reprint houses are to libraries and scholars, and many of the titles that these publishers reprint are in the public domain (no longer covered by copyright). The other major source of reprinted material is to buy the rights to an out-of-print title from another publisher. Although many of the basic costs have already been covered, reprints are expensive because of their very limited sales appeal. (In the past some reprints would be announced with a pre-publication flyer/order form; later a number of these titles would be reported as cancelled. Some suspicious persons suggested such cancellations were related to a lack of pre-publication orders.) Sometimes reprints provide as many, if not more, bibliographic headaches for libraries as association titles do. Despite many problems, reprint houses are an essential source of titles in collection development programs concerned with retrospective materials.

It is hoped that this very brief overview of some of the major types of publishing houses and what they do has whetted an appetite to learn more about the field. If so, excellent starting points would be Chandler B. Grannis's book *What Happens in Book Publishing* and Gerald Gross's *Editors on Editing* and *Publishers on Publishing*; additional references are listed at the end of this chapter.

Some of the reasons librarians need to know about the producers whose products we buy have been pointed out. Different classes of publishers are established to perform different functions. Complaining to a trade publisher about the lack of scholarly material, that their "line" is too popular, in most cases only makes the librarian appear unprofessional. Knowing which publishers are good at what helps to speed the selection process as some individual publishers are known for quality material—well written, organized, edited, and produced as a solid physical book. Also, it must be pointed out that the wide range of activities in which different groups of publishers engage makes clearer why each class of publisher has different manuscript selection procedures, marketing methods, and discount schedules.

PUBLISHING FUNCTIONS

Much of the success of a publisher depends upon the abilities of its staff of editors. Editors perform a number of critical functions:

1) secure publishable manuscripts;
2) review manuscripts;

3) work with authors to improve individual manuscripts;

4) aid in the physical design of the actual book;

5) copyedit manuscripts;

6) plan the "trade list" for each year.

If its editors do not perform well, there is little chance that a publisher will be able to stay in business. Their decisions regarding which manuscripts to publish will have a great influence on the company's total income.

Book selectors ought to learn something about the chief editors in the major publishing houses with which they deal. The reason seems clear: the editors' opinions about what is good and bad determine what will be available. It is possible to meet editors at library conventions, discuss problems, make suggestions, and thus influence what happens in the coming years. This activity is only possible when librarians know the editors and understand both their importance in a publishing house and something about the nature of the book trade in general. In addition, librarians can provide valuable marketing information to editors and publishers, provided again that they understand something of the industry beyond its products.

Securing and reviewing manuscripts is a time-consuming activity for most editors. Of a number of guesses regarding the number of manuscripts reviewed for each one accepted, the "average" seems to suggest that approximately 9/10ths of all manuscripts are rejected after the first examination. After the first complete reading still more manuscripts are rejected. Even after careful reading by several people, all of whom have favorable reactions, a manuscript may still not be published. Three common reasons for this are: 1) the title will not fit into the new list, 2) the sales potential (market) is too low, or 3) the cost of production would be too high.

Considerations concerning a company's "trade list" or list of books are very important. The "annual list" is the group of books that a publisher has accepted for publication and plans to distribute over the next six to twelve months. The "back list" comprises books published in previous years and still available. A strong back list of steady selling titles is the dream of most publishers. Editors spend a great deal of time planning the list. They do not want to have two new books on the same topic appear at the same time unless they complement one another. They want a list that will have good balance and strong sales appeal. Some consideration must also be given to past publications that are still in print (the backlist).

Publishers naturally try to consider what other publishers are doing and generally they try to avoid head-on competition with books on the same subject. One classic example of the kind of disaster that can arise from head-on competition among publishers was the flood of books that appeared after the 1967 Six Day War in the Middle East. (The "Watergate Affair" was handled differently, but, then, it lasted longer.) In the case of the Six Day War, at least five publishers issued a book on the War within a few weeks of it and of one another. The publishers all lost money on the effort, and bookstore owners had the additional cost of returning many unsold copies. Librarians and bookstore owners complained that there was too much duplication and only bought one of the five titles. No one was served by this type of competition.

An editor is confronted with a number of hard choices when a well written manuscript is presented on either a very currect subject that already has been covered or on a topic of limited appeal. In either case, adding the title to the list is not likely to improve the overall performance of the list—i.e., make a profit. On the other hand, it may be worthwhile to publish the book in the hope that the house can add another good author to its roster. Taking a broad view of the dilemma, the two preceding sentences raise two important issues for everyone concerned with the book trade, including librarians—profit and quality writers.

Librarians and readers often complain that the trade is exclusively, or at least overly concerned, with profit and has little concern for quality. What is forgotten is that publishing houses are businesses and must show a profit if operation is to continue for any length of time. Even if the presses/publishers are governments they must try to recover their costs in some manner, and those costs are rising. In time, even government publishers are forced to ask the same question—is this manuscript really worth producing, even if it will not recover the production costs? As costs sky-rocket, the answer, more and more often, will be no. What society asks of publishers is to undertake the risk of production and assume that, in some manner, their living needs will be taken care of. A capitalist system involves the right to make a profit on the use of capital. When you can make almost as much "profit" by placing capital in a no-risk savings account in a bank as by risking the loss of all of it in a publishing venture, only the compulsive gambler or altruist will try publishing. For non-capitalist systems, the decision whether to continue publishing is eventually determined by the willingness of people to continue to underwrite the expense—only society can answer that question, but generally health, safety, and the general good come ahead of books in social priorities.

This all simply means that a reasonable return is necessary in order to keep publishers operating—the benefits must outweigh the expenses. Most of the complainers fail to view the situation in a broad enough perspective. Publishers often do publish quality works at their own expense but not at the risk of having the firm fail overall.

Thus, the planning of the list is central to a publisher's success or failure. A strong list of good sellers, and perhaps one or two high sellers, can carry some money-losing items. Editors know, even if they try to select only break-even titles, that there will be losers and too many losers means going out of publishing. This means that editors must look for good and potentially high sellers to ensure a profitable list. Thus, while some persons equate quality with titles of limited appeal, to the editor this means low sales and either a high price (further cutting sales) or a loser. Whenever economically possible, an editor will go ahead and take a loss on a quality title, as publishers and editors do try to publish quality books at a reasonable price while still making a living. What the above comes down to is that an editor must *know* what will sell, and in order to know this, she or he must have reliable marketing information, both from and about the buyers. Good sales = profit; bad sales = loss.

Editors

After a manuscript is accepted and a contract agreement worked out, the author works with an editor on polishing up the manuscript—smoothing the style; rearranging, adding, or dropping sections; deciding the kind and number of illustrations (if any); setting the final title (which may even involve the sales staff, and not just the author and editor). When the editor considers a manuscript to be ready, she or he may work with the design department on questions about typeface, page layout, illustrations and jacket/cover design. The responsibility for decisions regarding costs, readability, and design will rest with the individual book's editor. Copy editors, at least in large firms, are not the same as editors. A copy editor is concerned with the final draft of the manuscript, galley and page proofs. These individuals look at the text in terms of its grammar, clarity, style, typographic and spelling errors, consistency and, to some degree, legality. Proofreading is done by copy editors and the author. All of these editorial activities take time and cost money but are very necessary to produce quality books.

Pricing

Most persons not involved in publishing assume that an author receives a royalty based upon the list price of his or her particular book. Generally, this no longer is the case. Most contracts call for royalties to be paid on net sales income and on a sliding scale, such as 10 percent of net sales income on the first 2,500 copies sold and anywhere from 12½ percent to 20 percent on sales thereafter.

The price of a book is determined in large measure by its production cost. Most publishers try to determine the price by calculating their break-even point. Experienced publishers and editors can predict fairly well how many copies of each book will be sold. They know that books on this subject usually sell X number of copies. Using this rough estimate as a guide, along with certain other factors— royalties, production, overhead, and distribution costs—a price is set. The following very simplified example (Figure 4) gives a general picture of the factors involved in price determination; it assumes that the first printing will be for five thousand copies.

Figure 4
Break-Even Example, First Printing
(List price $8.95 each)

	Alternative 1	Alternative 2
Number of copies	5,000	5,000
Number sold	4,800	4,800
Income per unit at 40%	$4.03	$4.03
Total Income	$19,344.00	$19,344.00
Less Plant Costs	2,915.00	2,915.00
Less Production (paper, ink, binding, press work)	3,750.00	3,750.00
Less Royalty (based on list price)	4,610.00 net sales—	1,932.40
	$11,275.00	$ 8,597.40
Break-Even Point (number of copies sold)	2,798	2,133
Gross Margin	$ 8,069.00	$10,746.60
Less Operating Expense (approximately 40% of gross revenue)	7,738.00	7,738.00
Net Profit	$ 331.00	$ 3,008.60

Using alternative 1 data, the publisher would show a $331 profit before taxes. Had the capital used to publish the book been placed in a passbook savings account, the company would have realized more income. Alternative 1 assumes that the royalty was calculated on the basis of the retail price. Normally, however, an author receives a royalty based upon the *net price*. If the royalty is calculated in that manner (alternative 2), the author would receive $1,932.40 rather than $4,610. This would increase the publisher's profit to $3,008.60. This is reasonable return on the investment if it occurred within one year of the publication date.

This raises the question, why take the risk for such a low return? Part of the answer is that some people like working with books and authors. More important, if the book sells more than 5,000 copies, the return will be much higher (Figure 5). Most of the editorial and overhead costs will have been recovered, the printing plates will have been paid for, and advertising costs will not increase significantly. Production costs will be for presswork, paper, ink, and binding. Overhead will be reduced by at least one-half, and the royalty will be unchanged. Thus, on the next 2,000 copies sold, the figures would be:

Figure 5

Break-Even Example, Second Printing
(List price $8.95 each)

Number of copies			2,000
Number sold			2,000
Income per copy (with 40% discount)			$4.03
		Total Income	$8,060.00
Production Costs	$1,500.00		
Royalties	1,844.00		
	$3,344.00		-3,344.00
		Gross Margin	$4,716.00
Less Operating Expense			1,612.00
		Net Profit	$3,104.00

In both figures two very important elements have been omitted—the first primarily because no one can accurately estimate its probable impact. That element is the number of copies of a book that are returned, damaged, or otherwise unsaleable; and as that number rises, of course, total income falls. Books that fail to sell may be *remaindered* (authors usually receive no royalties from remainder sales). (A remainder is a book that has been kept in stock by the publisher, but the sales of which are too low to warrant keeping it any longer. In order to sell the books to clear warehouse space, the publisher will offer them at extremely low prices, sometimes for as little as $0.10 on the dollar.) The unsaleables are a problem whose solution may cost even more money than originally thought—storage and disposal. The other factor missing is any calculation of subsidiary rights income—paperback, dramatization, translation, etc. With the vast majority of books, there will be no such additional income. For those titles that do have the potential for subsidiary rights income, the benefits for both author and publisher are great. When planning a book, an editor may hope for such additional interest in it by "outsiders," but in most cases it is not realistic to expect it. Needless to say, the main problem is to achieve the break-even point. The major concern is to reach the optimum mix between list price, size of printings, and market potential. Large printing runs are less costly per copy than small runs, but a slow seller printed in a large run can eat up any production savings in warehouse costs. A limited market may mean a high price, but a low price will not necessarily ensure reasonable sales. Total sales income for book publishing has increased steadily: 1974–$3,569,900; 1975–$3,850,700; 1976–$4,185,200; and 1977–$4,605,500. Data on annual sales amounts can be found in a variety of sources: *Publishers Weekly*, the *Bowker Annual of Library and Book Trade Information*, and Standard and Poor's *Industry Surveys*, for example.

Anyone concerned with collection development must make use of publishing statistical data in order to develop intelligent budgets and work plans. Statistical data on the number of new titles, paperbacks, reprints, etc. (see Figure 6) can be useful in planning the work load for the next year—e.g., perhaps more staff will

Figure 6

American Book Title Output, 1976 and 1977
(From Weekly Record listings of domestic & imported hardbound & paperbound books)

Categories with Dewey Decimal Numbers	1976 Weekly Record Titles Preliminary (12-month)			1976 Weekly Record Titles Final (18-month)			1977 Weekly Record Titles Preliminary (12-month)		
	New Books	New Editions	Totals	New Books	New Editions	Totals	New Books	New Editions	Totals
Agriculture (630-639; 712-719)	373	104	477	464	136	600	379	116	495
Art (700-711; 720-779)	1,101	268	1,369	1,368	313	1,681	1,198	255	1,453
*Biography	1,244	470	1,714	1,545	540	2,085	1,310	472	1,782
Business (650-659)	661	182	843	779	204	983	721	211	932
Education (370-379)	760	139	899	918	160	1,078	789	178	967
Fiction	2,067	1,391	3,458	2,336	1,500	3,836	2,001	1,250	3,251
General Works (000-099)	857	177	1,034	1,042	219	1,261	917	252	1,169
History (900-909; 930-999)	1,343	591	1,934	1,634	661	2,295	1,169	513	1,682
Home Economics (640-649)	564	126	690	660	146	806	551	85	636
Juveniles	2,039	171	2,210	2,272	206	2,478	2,326	237	2,563
Language (400-499)	307	102	409	403	120	523	336	122	458
Law (340-349)	540	158	698	668	193	861	576	182	758
Literature (800-810; 813-820; 823-899)	945	460	1,405	1,130	564	1,694	1,006	578	1,584
Medicine (610-619)	1,638	490	2,128	2,027	560	2,587	1,861	499	2,360
Music (780-789)	188	114	302	213	148	366	172	137	309
Philosophy, Psychology (100-199)	886	306	1,192	1,052	334	1,386	898	249	1,147
Poetry, Drama (811; 812; 821; 822)	1,042	265	1,307	1,254	328	1,582	826	291	1,117
Religion (200-299)	1,382	366	1,748	1,638	420	2,058	1,375	312	1,687
Science (500-599)	1,927	415	2,342	2,378	474	2,852	1,982	454	2,436
Sociology (300-339; 350-369; 380-399)	4,735	1,225	5,960	5,627	1,366	6,993	4,538	1,027	5,565
Sports Recreation (790-799)	841	193	1,034	1,009	215	1,224	766	174	940
Technology (600-609; 620-629; 660-699)	1,191	298	1,489	1,518	370	1,888	1,443	342	1,785
Travel (910-919)	352	147	499	412	169	581	273	120	393
Total	**26,983**	**8,158**	**35,141**	**32,352**	**9,346**	**41,698**	**27,413**	**8,056**	**35,469**

need to be hired if the volume of acquisition is to go up. Cost data are also essential for preparing budget requests. The average price of books and serials (see Figure 7) multiplied by the expected number of titles that need to be purchased to maintain the status of the collection, is a basic element in determining the size of the acquisition budget request submitted to funding authorities. The two most accessible sources for publishing statistics are *Publishers Weekly* (PW) and the *Bowker Annual* series. Data in both of these sources, and almost all other printed statistical data on publishing, come from the American Publishers Association (APA). Remember that the statistics represent information drawn from APA members, and *not all* publishers belong to the group. In fact, a great many small and regional publishers do not belong. One reason for their not joining is that most of the Association's activities are concentrated on the East Coast and West Coast, where the majority of publishers have their operations. Despite this limitation, though, APA statistical data is essential for collection development.

Figure 7

Average Per-Volume Prices of Hardcover Books, 1976 and 1977
(From WR listings of domestic & imported books)

Categories with Dewey Decimal Numbers	1976 WR Titles Preliminary (12-mo.)			Final (18-mo.)			1977 WR Titles Preliminary (12-mo.)		
	Total volumes	Total prices	Average prices	Total volumes	Total prices	Average prices	Total volumes	Total prices	Average prices
Agriculture (630-639; 712-719)	342	$ 4,792.97	$14.01	425	$ 6,543.15	$15.40	357	$ 5,701.30	$15.97
Art (700-711; 720-779)	1,002	19,946.03	19.91	1,235	25,053.77	20.29	1,058	21,983.97	20.78
*Biography	1,455	21,547.14	14.81	1,755	26,408.08	15.05	1,476	22,508.59	15.25
Business (650-659)	610	9,894.75	16.22	713	12,246.98	17.28	696	12,571.64	18.06
Education (370-379)	509	6,591.14	12.95	602	7,773.69	12.91	612	7,969.74	13.02
Fiction	1,887	18,619.44	9.87	2,078	20,705.26	9.96	1,654	16,656.00	10.07
General Works (000-099)	833	18,236.75	21.89	1,026	27,300.45	26.61	1,015	28,871.56	28.44
History (900-909; 930-999)	1,531	25,461.88	16.63	1,811	30,316.72	16.74	1,322	22,874.40	17.30
Home Economics (640-649)	390	3,989.65	10.23	466	5,210.39	11.18	399	4,575.81	11.47
Juveniles	2,222	13,041.36	5.87	2,464	14,819.76	6.01	2,572	17,072.39	6.64
Language (400-499)	229	3,721.97	16.25	296	4,919.49	16.62	283	4,061.57	14.35
Law (340-349)	450	8,633.64	19.19	555	11,460.49	20.65	509	12,144.08	23.86
Literature (800-810; 813-820; 823-899)	1,032	15,122.75	14.65	1,250	18,840.95	15.07	1,146	17,402.86	15.19
Medicine (610-619)	1,605	37,607.90	23.43	1,959	47,096.67	24.04	1,833	42,068.18	22.95
Music (780-789)	207	3,255.29	15.73	260	4,259.94	16.38	234	4,445.10	19.00
Philosophy, Psychology (100-199)	818	11,422.98	13.96	951	13,573.03	14.27	786	11,428.71	14.54
Poetry, Drama (811; 812; 821; 822)	764	9,480.58	12.41	939	11,884.67	12.66	795	10,676.01	13.43
Religion (200-299)	906	11,297.46	12.47	1,069	13,303.51	12.44	832	10,122.74	12.17
Science (500-599)	1,833	43,899.28	23.95	2,223	54,279.64	24.42	1,962	47,778.36	24.35
Sociology, Economics (300-339; 350-369; 380-399)	4,303	86,198.32	20.03	5,010	114,156.24	22.79	3,914	98,958.49	25.28
Sports, Recreation (790-799)	641	7,308.66	11.40	772	8,772.64	11.36	610	7,495.59	12.29
Technology (600-609); 620-629; 660-699)	1,057	21,638.30	20.47	1,327	28,117.95	21.19	1,268	29,098.87	22.95
Travel (910-919)	325	5,436.19	16.73	392	7,410.62	18.90	244	4,667.43	19.13
Total	**24,951**	**$407,144.43**	**$16.32**	**29,578**	**$514,454.09**	**$17.39**	**25,577**	**$461,133.39**	**$18.03**

Annually, two issues of **PW** report this statistical information for the previous year. One issue (in February) contains the "preliminary" figures; sometime in late summer (August or September), the revised figures are released. (The reason for the delay in final figures is that returns from bookstores and wholesalers cannot be determined quickly.) The *Bowker Annual* information is a condensation of the **PW** reports, but because it is a hardcover book, considerable delay in reporting the information is inevitable. For small libraries, which do not need to subscribe to **PW**, and for libraries in which current, reasonably accurate cost information is not required, the *Bowker Annual* is a very adequate source.

Publishers use a number of different sales outlets, selling directly to a) individuals, b) institutions, c) retailers, and d) wholesalers. Collection development personnel need to understand this variety of outlets, as they may have to employ any one of them in order to acquire a particular book. Each of these four types of outlet is further subdivided, though, which may further complicate things for the librarian. Direct sales are handled by mail order promotions, through a company's own bookstore, through its own book club system, through its own subscription sales system, and finally, by single copy personal orders. Institutional sales focus on three major groups: libraries, schools, and extension programs/services. In the retail area are independent bookstores, independent book clubs, mail-order houses, subscription companies, and mass distribution companies. Finally, there is the wholesaler/jobber.

Most publishers use all of these sales channels. Wholesalers and bookstore operators act as middlemen; a bookstore may buy from the jobber or directly from the publisher. Institutional and individual buyers may purchase books from a bookstore, a jobber, or a publisher. Each seller will have different discounts for different categories of buyers, ranging from zero to more than fifty percent. This combination of distributors ought to be complex enough, but there are at least three other outlets—mass market distributors, mail-order houses, and book clubs. Not only are there a great many choices available to the buyer, but the sources compete with one another. All of these factors combine to push up the cost of distributing a book, which in turn increases its list price. With multiple outlets, with different discounts, and with different credit conditions, the publishing industry has created a cumbersome uneconomical distribution system.

Selling practices vary from title to title as well as from publisher to publisher; however, a few generalizations can be made. Advertising will help a good book but it seldom, if ever, makes a success out of a poor book. This is not to say publicity will not help a poor book, but publicity and advertising are two different things. An interview with the author or a review of the book on a national radio or television program are examples of publicity. Generally free, such publicity will do a great deal for the sales of a book. However, the book's topic or its author was thought to be of national interest, or it would not have been selected for attention. Changes in current events can change a slow-moving book into a top seller overnight, something that no amount of advertising can do.

Advertising is done in several ways. First, trade advertising is employed, usually directed toward retail outlets rather than individual buyers. Second, an effort is made to get the book reviewed by major professional and general review media; this seldom involves advertisements but rather giving out review copies. Third, announcements are placed in professional journals, where the emphasis is on reaching individual buyers, both personal and institutional. Fourth, "cooperative" advertisements ("co-op ads") are placed in the book review sections of many newspapers. They are cooperative in the sense that both the publisher and a retail store pay for the advertisement. For instance, the following announcement is typical of such reciprocal arrangements:

> McGraw-Hill will grant promotion allowance to dealers, whole-salers, and dealers who buy from wholesalers, equal to 75% of the actual cost of advertisement in a newspaper, magazine, or on radio and television . . . but not to exceed 5% of net value of confirmed orders for wholesalers and not to exceed 15% of the net value of confirmed orders for retailers, placed between the date of agreement and the actual appearance of the advertisement of the McGraw-Hill titles so ordered.[5]

Finally, for books with a defined audience for which there is a good mailing list, the publisher may use a direct mailing campaign. Librarians may expect some patron requests to be generated by such efforts.

Some large publishers have field representatives who work with booksellers and institutional buyers. Normally they do not spend time with small libraries because it is not worth either the librarian's or the representative's time—too few titles are purchased. Bookstores, though, find the sales representative an important element in the trade, as this is their only direct personal contact with publishers. A good salesperson will also help the store owner by keeping an eye out for items with a return deadline. Librarians are used to visiting publishers' exhibits at library conventions, where they have the opportunity for regular direct personal contact with sales representatives. Bookstore owners are often unable to attend trade conventions; large chain store operations are exceptions because they must buy in great volume from many sources.

Professional and trade exhibits are also used to promote sales. In the past all publishers tried to have their own exhibits at national library, education, and other professional conferences. The cost of this type of promotion has gone up so much that many smaller publishers have had to drop out. One method that has been used to combat the cost problem at library conventions has been the "combined book exhibit," whereby books of various publishers are combined into one collection and arranged by a classification system as in the library. At both the annual convention and "Midwinter" meeting of the American Library Association, there is a large combined book exhibit. For many selection and acquisition librarians, this exhibit is a major reason for attending the conferences.

This brief overview points out some of the most basic elements in the book trade. It is intended to start a collection development novice to thinking about the trade. The next section presents a discussion of audio visual producers. Unfortunately, because of their diversity, it is not possible in a limited space to parallel the discussion of the book trade. Figure 8, page 57, provides a comparison of some elements between the two fields.

PRODUCERS OF AUDIO VISUAL MATERIALS

Any attempt to generalize about audio visual producers is bound to be inadequate; nevertheless, some attempt must be made at sketching a general picture. Media producers are a very diverse group working with a great many formats (audio recordings, film [motion and strip], video, models, etc.). The following discussion is an attempt to cover all of those audio visual formats, but it would require a full-length book to indicate all the individual variations and exceptions. The reader is reminded this is to be taken as a total overview, not as an analysis of individual mediums.

Media producers enjoy rather substantial sales every year to schools and libraries. Indeed, this market is almost the sole sales outlet for the majority of media producers. (Two major exceptions are phonograph record and tape recordings and theatrical films.) The phono record and tape industry is the major source of "other media" for most libraries. Recorded music collections are rather common in libraries and reflect the fact that the general population buys and/or listens to a lot of music. In terms of sales, however, libraries and other institutions represent only a fraction of the music industry income, just as theatrical films represent only a small percentage of the "other media" in libraries. (Theatrical films are those produced to show in cinema theaters to the general public.) There are, however, "educational" film companies or divisions of theatrical companies and art filmmakers producing material that is purchased in some quantity by libraries; since these fields are little influenced by library needs and are highly organized, they are not discussed in the following sections.

One important fact to remember about almost all media, except books and filmstrips, is that they are generally group-based and group-paced. Films, video tapes, audio tapes, and some other media require the user to follow the material as presented at a fixed pace—the pace of the machine involved. In addition, most media are geared to the average ability and knowledge in the target audience. A good number of the educational media are designed with group presentation and teacher in mind, and since libraries do have an educational function, they should have educational media available. However, it is important to keep in mind that group presentation with a teacher is usually missing. While individuals working alone can benefit from the material, they will find it of limited value because it was designed for a different use.

This, then, is the first major difference between book publishers and media producers. Media producers market a product designed primarily for simultaneous group use. Book publishers market a product designed primarily for individual use. This difference in product use has a significant influence on the distribution system employed by the two groups. Media producers place a heavy emphasis on direct institutional sales; book publishers do use this method, but outside of the textbook field it is not the primary source of sales.

One very important but generally overlooked characteristic of media production is the question of authorship. Books are usually the result of the intellectual effort of one or two persons who then try to find a publisher. Occasionally a publisher will commission a book. (Perhaps in the age of merger, this approach will become more common. At this time it is still the exception rather than the rule.) In media, the process is reversed. Normally the producer will generate the ideas and seek out the necessary persons to carry out the project if it cannot be handled by the company's staff. *This means that the producers have almost total control over what will appear.* It is also true that book publishers have the final say in what will be published. The difference is that the book publisher receives hundreds of manuscripts and ideas for books to consider each year and is thus exposed to ideas and needs that otherwise might be overlooked. In addition, even if one publisher rejects a manuscript, there is always the chance another may pick it up. In essence, the book field has a tradition of being a free market place for ideas, whereas this concept is almost nonexistent in the media field. Although this may seem to be a very subtle difference, it does have an impact on the type of material produced and, in turn, upon the library's collection.

Despite these differences, the media field is often viewed as the field of independence and freedom, an image that arises in part from the relatively low cost of entry into it. One hears many stories about the individual who started off with a few thousand dollars and some equipment and is now a major producer. One does not hear about the thousands of others who tried and failed. Mediocre equipment and a low advertising budget usually mean a mediocre product and few, if any, sales. The opportunity is there, but the chances of success are only slightly better than for any other small business venture. As noted, almost anyone may become a media producer. To become a "producer" of 35mm slides (educational, art, travel, etc.), one only needs a box camera using 35mm film and a couple of hundred dollars to pay for some advertising. Success is *not* likely, but this is all that one needs to become a "media producer" and to be listed in a directory to media sources. In general, the start-up capital (money required to begin operations) is much lower than would be necessary for a book publisher. Good quality professional media production equipment is exceedingly expensive; however, many of the so-called producers do *not* invest in quality equipment. They depend upon commercial laboratories and hope for the best.

Because of a lack of materials and the pressure to have media in schools and libraries, it has been and still is possible to sell many copies of extremely poor quality materials because only that is available. Purchases are made on the basis of need in curriculum or subject areas rather than on the basis of quality, so in this instance, the problem of quality versus need becomes acute. The need may be present, and money even available, but not truly qualified producers. Yet, a lack of quality equipment does not keep some persons from trying to produce something to take advantage of the situation. There is nothing wrong with starting off this way, if it is the only alternative available; and there is constant pressure from buyers on the producer to improve the quality. If, after a reasonable period of time for development, there is no improvement, buyers must stop purchasing material, since failure to do so will only ensure continued poor performance.

To illustrate how relatively inexpensive it is to get into the media production field, the equipment that a library might buy to have a good range of production capability is listed; for about $10,000, a library or an individual can buy equipment and supplies adequate to produce four basic formats and several mixed-media products. Eight thousand dollars would be invested in equipment; a 35mm single-lens reflex camera with extra lenses, filters and miscellaneous accessories, a super 8 movie camera with zoom lens and slow motion, two tape recording/player units with sound-synchronization, two video tape recording units (one with editing capability), one black and white video camera, two VTR/television monitors, and miscellaneous lights, tripods, and wiring. The remaining money would be used for supplies, processing, and advertising. With this beginning, the library or individual could claim to be a multimedia producer.

By the same token, any library printing booklists is a publisher, but the intent is rather different. Sales potential of a book catalog is limited, and booklists are normally given away. Also, while it is possible for an individual to become a book publisher by putting up the capital to have a manuscript printed, there will be an inventory problem. A book must be printed in fairly large quantities if a reasonable unit cost is to be achieved; large runs mean storage and warehousing problems and costs, tying up a certain amount of capital. On the other hand, media producers can, and often do, keep very small inventories. It is possible for a producer to maintain only a master copy of the material and generate duplicates on demand. A more common approach is to have a master copy, some preview copies, and only a few sale copies. Savings in this area often mean that a producer can operate out of a small house or apartment, and it is very easy to move from one location to another.

Another characteristic of media producers is that their products have a fairly high cost per unit of information conveyed. Many media items can be characterized as single concept materials. (Single concept films are a special class of educational films that deal with a very narrow concept, such as cell division, and are usually very short, 3-4 minutes long.) Books, on the other hand, have a low cost per unit of information ratio. For example, no single film video tape, audio tape, or set of 35mm slides can convey the same amount of information about American Indians as one 300-page book. This feature of media has great importance for selection, since not every medium is ideal for every purpose. Librarians must know the advantages of each and select and acquire items on this basis.

Generally, media products cost more per copy than do books. Color, 16mm sound films with a 20-minute running time have an average cost of over $300 per title—close to $20 per minute. Video tape recordings are even more expensive. Sets of 35mm slides will range from $5 to over $100. All media producers have found the most profitable item to be some combination of 35mm filmstrips and a sound track (phonograph record or audio tape is the usual system). In general, the "kit" combinations of media are high profit items. Prices on such combinations run from $20 to over $100. Also, they are the perfect medium for "building level" materials—that is, developing media collections around curriculum needs, over a period of time. Because of this cost factor, selectors normally can buy only a few items each year, thus making the selection process very important.

While book publishers use a multitude of outlets to sell their product, media producers use very few. With the exception of record and audio tape stores and a very few map shops, there are *no* retail outlets for "other media." There are no media-of-the-month clubs, no mail-order houses, and no remainder houses (except for records and some 8mm films). Even wholesalers dealing with all media are few and far between. The main source, and in some cases the only source, is the producer. Because they are the basic source, collection development personnel must spend an inordinate amount of time and energy in maintaining lists of producers' addresses. Without such records, schools and libraries would almost have to halt their acquisition of "other media." However, since many producers are small and move frequently, updating of addresses is a constant problem for the library. It also means that directories more than twelve months old must be used with great caution.

Because their material is group-oriented and has a high information unit cost, media producers have a much smaller, but more clearly identifiable, potential sales market than a book publisher. There is little chance of a media producer's having many runaway best sellers, except in the music field. Subsidiary rights, such as for theatrical films or commercial television, are almost nonexistent. Such "spin offs" from educational media do happen, but not very often; commercial television and theatrical markets exist for such items, but the basic market is educational institutions. Book clubs, which almost guarantee a profitable book, have no equivalent in the media, except for recorded music.

The one advantage to this situation is that the market for media is clearly identifiable: schools and libraries. Like the specialty publisher, the media producer is better able to focus advertising and sales activities on a small area with a very good chance of success. Trade book publishers use a broad spectrum of advertising sources, newspapers, periodicals, flyers, radio, and television. In general, the trade publisher must take a shotgun approach, while specialty publishers and media producers should have a much better idea of their market.

Books and other media are both easy to copy. The difference is the cost of the item, as normally, media items are more expensive. Most institutions having the capability to utilize media also have the capability to duplicate that material. Most producers are concerned about this problem because media buyers normally request materials for preview, and previewing can be an opportunity for copying. Awareness of this potential danger may account for the general absence of wholesalers in the media distribution system. The media for which this danger is greatest are tapes (video and audio) and 35mm slides.

The majority of media producers are small businessmen without a large capital reserve. For the small media producer cash flow is a real problem. Anything that the library can do to help the small media firm keep its costs down will help to keep the unit cost of products down as well, for example, by using cooperative previewing and keeping order and billing procedures simple.

One other important characteristic of the media field is the speed with which its technology changes. This characteristic is a central problem for everyone concerned with the field—producer and consumer. Equipment developments constantly make existing equipment almost obsolete, and occasionally a new format may, in fact, make it obsolete. One example is in video: just a few years ago many people thought that video cassettes were the wave of the future. Today it appears that a disc format is more likely to succeed, thus requiring new equipment for everyone. Because of the volatile nature of the field, many users are reluctant, with reason, to invest heavily in equipment. For the producer the problem is greater; it means deciding rather quickly whether to go with the new or stay with the old. Staying with the old too long may cut the person out of the field due to licensing, franchising considerations, or simply not keeping up to date. On the other hand, moving too soon may use up remaining capital on a change that does not last. Book publishing has some of the same problems, but only in the case of a big commitment to printing operations. Printers are more likely to be faced with the problem of changing equipment and technology than are publishers.

Figure 8 provides an overview of the basic differences between book publishers and media producers, differences that do have an impact on collection development. Again, the reader is reminded that these factors are broad generalizations and that there are many exceptions.

Figure 8

Media Producers—Book Publishers

	Media Producers	Book Publishers
Audience	Individual as part of a group	Individual
Idea authorship	Company generated	Free agent generated
Use	Group and sequential equipment paced	Self—non-sequential
Cost per concept	high	low
Selection process in library	usually group	individual
Cost to enter field	relatively low	relatively high
Inventory	low	high
Market	more clearly defined	highly variable
Potential sales volume	low	medium
Cost per copy	relatively high	relatively low
Easy of copying	easy to copy/high sales price	easy to copy/low sales price
Distribution	mostly single source	multiple source
Changes in format and equipment	very rapid with high obsolete rate	relatively slow

TYPES OF MEDIA

Up to this point the discussion has focused on some of the broad characteristics of the media field. In this section the focus is on the various types of media, with a very few notes about their potential use in the library. Chapter 7, on media selection, discusses the value and use of media in the library for the adult audience.

Any list of all available media is bound to be out-of-date by the time it is published. New technologies and new combinations of older forms seem to appear daily. Just when one thinks that the latest developments have been identified and decides to invest money in the equipment and software, a new, even more exciting and potentially valuable, format appears. With these limitations in mind, the following is offered as an extensive but not exhaustive list of media useful in the library:

1) audio tapes (single and multiple track)
2) films (8mm and 16mm, including single concept)
3) filmstrips (with and without sound)
4) flat pictures (photographs, illustrations, original art works, posters, etc.)
5) games (usually educational, but some libraries offer a variety of recreational games)
6) globes (terrestrial and celestial)
7) laser formats (including holograms)
8) maps (flat and raised relief)
9) microforms (all types)
10) mixed media packages (kits)
11) opaque projector materials (commercial and locally produced)
12) phonograph records (all speeds)
13) printed music (performance and study scores)
14) programmed learning materials (machine and printed book formats)
15) realia
16) slides (35mm and 4x4)
17) specimen collections
18) video formats (including kinescopes)
19) working models (full and scale)

Considering just this range of material, and remembering the special aspects of the media trade, one can understand why collection development in media areas presents some special problems.

Audio tapes and phonograph records are often thought of together because of the commercial music business, and commercial music (including classical) has had a place in libraries for some time. One problem has been the tendency of most libraries to handle only one speed of phonograph record—currently 33 1/3 rpm, even though the 45 rpm is also very popular with young people and many adults. The commercial music trade is reasonably well controlled in a bibliographic sense; certainly there is more control than in any other nonbook format. Audio tapes are increasing in popularity in the commercial music field and they have a special value in the language field. While language learning is always facilitated by hearing the proper sounds, the phono disc does not allow the learner to hear his own pronunciation. Dual track tapes with an instructor's voice on a non-erasable track and a learner's recording track increases learning efficiency. Another advantage is that the same tape can be used repeatedly with minimum wear.

Films are also a very popular format, at least in public and school libraries. Most libraries with film collections have emphasized the 16mm format. In recent years, with increased individual use of the super 8mm format and good quality home projector equipment, some public libraries have started 8mm collections. Theatrical films, although not frequently found in library collections, do have a place if the library is to serve fully its community's needs. Access to theatrical films is reasonably easy because production of them is a very large income business. Documentary film access is fairly good in the sense that there are a number of guides to 8mm and 16mm films. However, independent filmmakers come and go out of existence with great speed, many never get listed in guides, and others remain in guides long after they have gone out of business. Keeping up on changes in the independent filmmakers' field could become a full-time occupation for a person if serious collecting is a goal.

Filmstrips, as noted earlier, have become one of the most popular formats with producers, primarily because they have a very low production cost, and the profit margin is rather high. Many book publishers have ventured into the media field in this format. Sometimes it is the first and only format; more often, it leads into other areas. By and large, this format is still geared to the primary and secondary school market, and bibliographic control of this format is always solely focused on that market. Because of the profit factor, this format may enter the adult market in the very near future. Even the material designed for the school market has potential value in the self-education of adults, if it is made available to the user.

Flat pictures have been available in library vertical files for years, although use of these materials was usually confined to school teachers and students. With the introduction of rental collections of art reproductions and even original paintings and prints, as well as a choice of frames in some cases, the flat picture audience has expanded to include most adult patrons. Many libraries have found that these materials provide one of the most popular services they can offer. Aside from a few Unesco publications, there is little or no control in this field. Selectors and acquisition staff must learn about producers and maintain files of catalogs in order to secure these materials.

The idea of buying educational games for library collections is only beginning to develop in the United States, yet libraries in the Nordic countries have been lending recreational games for years. It is strange that when lending music seems natural for libraries, and when there is a general acceptance of lending art (at least reproductions), that lending of games is frowned upon. Could it be that most music collections are predominately classical and art collections include only "good" art? Could it be that there is some intellectual snobbery in operation? Everyone will have an opinion. One problem may be that the issue has not been discussed, and access to games is very difficult. Until more institutions enter the game-buying market, there will be little incentive to improve control. This means that a library wanting to buy games must develop its own file of sources and catalogs. (Selectors, of course, could be allowed a yearly visit to the local toy store, and what fun that could be!)

Globes and maps, although different in form and requiring very different handling, are normally secured from the same source. In the past, most libraries have had a small collection of maps and perhaps one or two globes. At the present time this picture is changing. There is an increasing variety of globes available—flat and raised relief—and in small sizes that make them true study aids. Increased leisure time has caused a great increase in interest in maps of recreational areas for boaters, campers and hikers. However, control of map production is very spotty. There are not too many commercial sources of maps, and these are easy to identify. Unfortunately, the largest producers of maps are governmental agencies, and while federal agency maps are reasonably well controlled, for state and local agencies there is no central access. Large-scale local maps are not often produced by the national government, so local sources are very important. So once again, it becomes a matter of the acquisition department developing its own lists.

Laser technology and its place in the library/information field is just being explored, and the potential of holograms is tremendous. As a storage unit of printed information the hologram far surpasses the microformats. A few technical and research libraries have small collections of holograms. Most, if not all, of these are being produced in research and development units of companies or in engineering departments of universities, but no published list of sources exists for holograms. News notes in technical and scientific journals of available holograms is the only approach to collecting at this time. Perhaps the hologram's greatest potential is in combination with other formats rather than as a separate form.

Next to recordings, microforms are probably the most common audio visual format in libraries. Because of their popularity as a compact storage medium for printed materials, bibliographic control is good. Until recently there was little or no new material appearing originally in microform, since they have been and still are used to secure copies of out-of-print books, archival material, and unique items. Microform is used as a means of storing material in a compact form, and recently it has been used to disseminate research reports to a large audience at a very low unit cost. Some firms now exist that "publish" only in a microformat: their inventory consists of the original copy, and they generate another copy when they receive an order. This format will no doubt grow in importance, if for no other reason than its storage capability and the ease with which "hard copy" can be made. The low cost per unit is another reason that this format will grow in popularity.

Any attempt to provide a complete discussion of mixed media packages would require a full-length book, as was mentioned earlier. Two very popular combinations are filmstrips with a sound track and 35mm slides with a sound track, both of which are primarily education packages. Some producers put together packages that include printed matter (workbooks or texts), records and filmstrips or slides. Slides, 16mm films, separate sound tracks, holograms, and video material have been combined, but the cost of these packages is relatively high. Many of the packages appear to have been put together with little consideration for their combined effectiveness. Thus, as with any medium, librarians must know the strengths and weaknesses of the form and only acquire those that meet their specific needs. The educational mixed media packages are reasonably well controlled and are listed in many guides. Often the package will be listed in every guide for each form in the kits, that is, a filmstrip and record kit will be listed both in filmstrip guides and record guides.

Transparencies and/or opaque projector materials are primarily school-oriented. Of all the media, this form is the most group-oriented, designed to aid in the presentation of graphic material to small- and medium-sized groups. While an individual can use the material, it has no advantage over flat pictures. A library could obtain materials related to adult education classes, especially in the science fields. Realistically, this material has very limited value to the individual user and is not likely to be found in many public or academic libraries. There are a number of guides to educational transparencies.

One rather surprising void in public and academic libraries is printed music. When both recorded music and books about music are available, why is it so difficult to secure the score? Cost is one possible explanation, but then most media cost more than books. Difficulty in handling (storage and checking in the parts) may be another aspect of the problem, but other media are also "difficult" to handle in some way. Certainly music publishers' catalogs are available, and there is a real need in the community.

Programmed learning materials, working models, specimen collections and realia are intended mainly for schools (primary and secondary). While a few items are useful for adults who are studying a subject on their own, they are bought by most public libraries only in order to supplement school library resources. A number of catalogs and guides to these items exist.

Thirty-five millimeter slides are slowly gaining in popularity for general library use. Although slide collections have existed in a few libraries for many years, they have been intended for teachers rather than for the general public. Because of the popularity of 35mm photography and availability of home projection equipment, many libraries find that a slide collection quickly becomes one of the most popular materials in the library. Perhaps the greatest problem in collecting slides is the large number of sources of highly variable quality. One must be certain to check each slide for quality, especially color purity and durability; this makes the acquisition process very time-consuming.

Video formats are probably one of the most promising forms for information dissemination. The two formats that are most likely to be used are videotape and disc. One of the newest developments in video is the disc format, which is similar to disc phonograph records, as it uses a vinyl base with the image embedded in the surface. While the disc may be the future direction for video, at the present time, two incompatible disc systems are being developed. One of the big advantages of video tape is the relative ease with which the same image can be given a new sound track. Many different languages can be used with the same image. We know of one case in the United States, where a library produced a series of video tapes on how to tune up a truck. After producing the master visual tape they produced copies with English, Spanish, and several American Indian-language sound tracks. (One can do this with 16mm sound film as well, but the cost is very high.) Because of the changing nature of the field, however, there has been little chance to develop any type of control over the output of video producers.

Just as the section on publishing only provided a broad introduction, so has this section. Unfortunately for media producers, there is no source similar to the Grannis book on publishing that would explain the field in depth. One must search for information on each format in a variety of sources—librarianship, educational, technical, and commercial. The chapters on selection criteria (chapters 6 and 7) and on acquisition (chapter 8) will explore media more fully.

PRODUCERS' PROBLEMS AND COLLECTION DEVELOPMENT

While we have looked at only some of the most basic problems of knowledge resource producers, even that discussion has taken up a fairly large number of pages. Collection development personnel need to understand some of the important issues and problems facing producers, since those factors will inevitably have impact on the library. Rising costs create problems for everyone, but publishers and media producers have some special problems. Like other producers of "luxury" items, knowledge resource producers experience pressure from two sides. On the one hand, their rising materials and labor costs put pressure on them to raise the prices of their products. On the other hand, if they do raise prices, they must realize that this may cut into sales by more than the increase might warrant. The consumer must meet basic needs first and, during periods of inflation, meeting basic needs cuts into funds available for luxury items. For the majority of individual buyers, books and media are one of the first items to be cut or reduced.

Institutional buyers will continue to need to buy materials but they face several problems. All of the producers are likely to increase their prices over a relatively short period of time. A fixed materials budget over a two or three year period in combination with increasing costs of materials means that the library will buy fewer items each year. A second problem is that most institutions are not given large increases in their budgets during inflationary periods. What increases they do receive usually only keep pace with inflation; thus, for all practical purposes, the budget remains stationary. These two factors combine to effectively cut the number of items purchased, and producers must carefully weigh them before raising prices. This in turn forces them to be more and more selective as to the items they do produce—few, if any, losers will be carried.

Resource sharing between libraries is a strongly recommended possibility. During periods of tight budgets, many libraries become actively cooperative rather than just give lip service to the concept. Sharing resources will help ensure that copies will be at least available, even if they are not conveniently so; however, such cooperation means an overall decline in the market for producers. How to handle this market decline and the concept of resource sharing have been knotty problems for producers and librarians for a long time. Librarians are concerned with how to achieve real resource sharing, while producers worry about how to react to the new system if sharing is developed. One approach for the producers is to tie the issue to the concept of copyright, which will be discussed in chapter 12; it is mentioned here to illustrate how complex the issues are.

If producers could simplify their distribution system, they could achieve significant savings. Why should the general consumer (individual or institution) be able to purchase an item directly either from the producer, a wholesaler, or retailer? The system as it now operates is cumbersome and costly. For book publishers it is a matter of having a typical marketing system (producer to wholesaler to retailer) but one that allows *any* individual customer access to any level of the system to make the purchase. Media producers, on the other hand, use a direct sales method in most cases. Both systems are costly for everyone. The book system requires complex handling procedures at each level because of different classes of customer. The media system, with single item orders to be shipped to numerous locations, runs up the cost of placing and filling an order. The impact on collection development is that as more money goes into paperwork and administrative procedures, less is available for collection development. Both producers and libraries must worry about this problem.

Perhaps the most difficult problem is the question of the right to use knowledge resources, or rather how they may be used. As noted, copyright has become a central issue among librarians, educators, and other users of knowledge resources and the producers. Yet, without copyright there is little incentive for anyone to produce a work. The problem is how far society can go in providing and enforcing such incentives and still ensure adequate access to material at a fair price. Libraries want fairly open free access and use while producers want limited free access. This issue, of course, has, or will have, an important role to play in determining how a collection can be developed.

NOTES

[1] New Jersey State Library, Department of Education, *The Uses of and Attitudes toward Libraries in New Jersey* (Trenton: New Jersey State Library), 1976.

[2] Hayes B. Jacobs, "Freelance at Work," in *Writer's Market '76*, Jane Koester and Rose Adkins, eds. (Cincinnati, OH: Writer's Digest, 1975), p. 11.

[3] Elin B. Christianson, "Mergers in the Publishing Industry, 1958-1970," *Journal of Library History* 7 (January 1972): 5-32.

[4] "The Question of Size in the Book Industry," *Publishers Weekly* 214 (July 31, 1978): 25-54.

[5] *Publishers Weekly* 207 (February 17, 1975): 21.

BIBLIOGRAPHY

Allerton Park Institute, 14th. *Trends in American Book Publishing.* Papers presented at an Institute conducted by the University of Illinois Graduate School of Library Science, Nov. 5-8, 1967. K. L. Henderson, ed. Urbana: Illini Union Bookstore, 1968.

Anderson, C. B., ed. *A Manual on Bookselling: How to Open and Run Your Own Bookstore.* 2nd ed. New York: Harmony Books, 1974.

Bailey, H. S. *The Art and Science of Book Publishing.* New York: Harper and Row, 1970.

Balkin, R. *A Writer's Guide to Book Publishing.* New York: Hawthorn Books, 1977.

Bingley, C. *Book Publishing Practice.* Oxford, England: Pergamon, 1972.

Blond, A. *The Publishing Game.* London: Cape, 1971.

The Bookman's Glossary. 5th ed. J. Peters, ed. New York: R. R. Bowker, 1975.

Bookseller: The Organ of the Book Trade. London: J. Whitaker, 1858- [Weekly].

Bowker Annual of Library and Book Trade Information, v.1- . New York: R. R. Bowker, 1923- [Annual].

Bowker Lectures on Book Publishing. New York: R. R. Bowker, 1957.

British Library of Political and Economic Science [London]. *Classified Catalogue of a Collection of Works on Publishing and Bookselling in the British Library of Political and Economic Science*. London: The Library, 1961.

"Centennial Issue: Look Ahead to What Faces the Book Industry for the Remainder of the Century, and Beyond." *Publishers Weekly* 202 pt. 2 (April 10, 1972): [entire issue].

Cheney, O. H. *Economic Survey of the Book Industry, 1930-1931*. Reprinted. New York: R. R. Bowker, 1960.

Chicorel, M. "Cost Indexes for Library Materials." *Wilson Library Bulletin* 39 (June 1965): 896-900.

Christianson, E. B. "Mergers in the Publishing Industry, 1958-1970." *Journal of Library History* 7 (Jan. 1972): 5-32.

[Comment] G. N. Hartje [letter]. *Journal of Library History* 7 (July 1972): 286.

Dempsey, D. "The Publishing Scene." *Saturday Review* (April 13, 1968): 40-41.

Dessauer, J. P. *Book Publishing: What It Is, What It Does*. New York: R. R. Bowker, 1974.

Ernst and Ernst [firm]. *Book Publishing and Manufacturing Industry in Canada: A Statistical and Economic Analysis*. Ottawa: The Firm, 1970.

Escarpit, R. *The Book Revolution*. New York: Unesco, 1966.

"Ferment in the West: Publishing, Bookselling, Fine Printing, the Great Pool of Writing Talent, Books into Films, the Los Angeles Libraries, News of Forthcoming Books from the West, Its Historical Fascination, Western Best Sellers, Plus Special Problems, Diverse Points of View and Some Outspoken Criticism of the Trade." *Publishers Weekly* 202 (Oct. 9, 1972): 34-85.

Grannis, C. B., ed. *What Happens in Book Publishing*. 2nd ed. New York: Columbia University Press, 1967.

Gross, G., ed. *Editors on Editing*. New York: Grosset, 1962.

Gross, G., ed. *Publishers on Publishing*. New York: Grosset, 1961.

Hackett, A. P. *80 Years of Best Sellers, 1895-1975*. New York: R. R. Bowker, 1977.

Handbuch der Technischen Dokumentation und Bibliographie. Bd. 2. Die Fachliteratur zum Buch-und Bibliothekswesen. 6th ed. München: Verlag Dokumentationen der Technik, 1966.

Higgins, D. "Distributing Books." *Something Else Newsletter* (April 1973): 1-4.

Jennett, S. *The Making of Books*. 5th ed. London: Faber, 1973.

Jovanovich, W. *Now Barabbas*. New York: Harper, 1964.

Jovanovich, W. *The Structure of Publishing*. New York: American Book Publishers' Council, 1957.

Kim, U. C. *Policies of Publishers: A Handbook for Order Librarians.* Metuchen, NJ: Scarecrow, 1978.

Klieman, H., and P. Meyer-Dohm. *Buchhandel: Eine Bibliographie.* Gutersloh, West Germany: Bertelsmann, 1963.

Kujoth, J. S., comp. *Book Publishing: Inside Views.* Metuchen, NJ: Scarecrow, 1971.

Lee, M. *Bookmaking: The Illustrated Guide to Design and Production.* New York: R. R. Bowker, 1965.

Lehmann-Haupt, H., et al. *The Book in America: A History of the Making and Selling of Books in the United States.* 2nd rev. and enl. ed. New York: R. R. Bowker, 1951.

Lewis, J. *The Twentieth Century Book, Its Illustration and Design.* New York: Reinhold, 1967.

Madison, C. A. *Book Publishing in America.* New York: McGraw-Hill, 1966.

Melcher, D. "Discovering the Library Market Place." *American Libraries* 3 (July-Aug. 1972): 811-14.

Melinat, C. H., ed. *Librarianship and Publishing.* Syracuse, NY: Syracuse University, School of Library Science, 1963.

Miller, W. *The Book Industry: A Report of the Public Library Inquiry.* New York: Columbia University Press, 1949.

Morris, R. "Vanity Publishing: Would You Pay $3,000 for a Book? No? Not Even If You Wrote It?" *American Libraries* 5 (Sept. 1974): 420-22.

Mumby, F. A., and I. Norrie. *Publishing and Bookselling: A History from the Earliest Times to the Present Day.* 5th rev. ed. London: Cape, 1974.

Plant, M. *The English Book Trade. An Economic History of the Making and Sale of Books.* 3rd ed. London: G. Allen, 1974.

Publishers Weekly: The American Book Trade Journal. New York: R. R. Bowker, 1872- [weekly].

Quill and Quire. The Magazine of the Canadian Book Trade. Toronto: v.1- 1935- . [monthly].

Smith, D. C. *A Guide to Book Publishing.* New York: R. R. Bowker, 1966.

Smith, R. H., ed. *The American Reading Public: What It Reads, Why It Reads; From Inside Education and Publishing, View of Present Status, Future Trends—the Daedalus Symposium, with Rebuttals and Other New Material.* New York: R. R. Bowker, 1964.

Stechert-Hafner Book News. New York: Stechert-Hafner, 1946- [9 times yearly].

Strauss, V. *The Printing Industry: An Introduction to Its Many Branches, Processes and Products.* New York: Printing Industries of America in Association with R. R. Bowker, 1967.

Taubert, S. *Biblipola: Pictures and Texts about the Book Trade.* New York: R. R. Bowker, 1966. [text in English, French, and German].

Tebbel, J. W. *A History of Book Publishing in the United States.* Vol. 1: *The Creation of an Industry, 1630-1865*; Vol. 2: *The Expansion of an Industry, 1865-1919*; Vol. 3: *Publishing Comes of Age, 1919-Present*; Vol. 4: [in preparation]. New York: R. R. Bowker, 1972- .

Underwood, R. G. *Production and Manufacturing Problems of American University Presses.* New York: Association of University Presses, 1970.

University Bookman. New York: Educational Reviewer, 1960- [Quarterly].

Unwin, S. *The Truth about Publishing.* 7th ed. New York: Macmillan, 1960.

Zeitlin, J. "Bookseller and the Librarian." *California Librarian* 23 (April 1962): 91-94.

Zeitlin, J. "Bookselling among the Sciences." *College and Research Libraries* 21 (Nov. 1960): 453-57.

[For references on audio visual producers, see the bibliography for Chapter 7.]

Chapter 3

DISTRIBUTORS OF LIBRARY MATERIALS

At the conclusion of chapter 2 three major problems for materials producers were identified: 1) economics, 2) copyright infringement, and 3) distribution. The last item will be discussed in this chapter, as a knowledge of distribution is essential for librarians since this is the system from which materials are acquired. In chapter 2, it was established that a knowledge of the system(s) outside the library makes a librarian more effective. All of the organizations described in this chapter (wholesalers, retailers, and remainder houses) are sources of material for the library collection. Often several different sources can supply the same item, so questions must be asked: Is there an important difference between sources? What can each source do or not do for librarians? For example, if one is looking for a book published last year, it is possible to acquire a copy from any of the sources. Would it matter which one? How likely is it that all three would have the book? For that matter, what exact function does each perform? These are some of the questions to be answered in the next few pages.

JOBBERS AND WHOLESALERS

Librarians generally talk about *jobbers* rather than wholesalers. There is a technical difference between a wholesaler and a jobber,* but for purposes of collection development, it does not matter. Both provide libraries with relatively small-sized orders—seldom does a library order more than fifty copies of a single title. (At this time there are very few media jobbers so most of the subsequent discussion relates to books.) Jobbers purchase quantities of books from various publishers; in turn they sell copies to bookstores and libraries. Because they buy in volume they receive a fairly high discount (reduced price) from the publishers.

---

*Jobber—"1. One who buys merchandise from manufacturers and sells it to retailers. 2. A person who works by the piece or at odd jobs" [*American Heritage Dictionary of the English Language*].

Wholesaler—A person who sells *large* quantities of goods to a retailer.

Drop shipper—A person who orders materials from manufacturers after receiving an order from a retailer (library). Unlike jobbers and wholesalers, a drop shipper does not have a stock of materials, just a telephone.

When the jobber sells a book the purchaser receives a discount off the publisher's retail price, but it is much lower than the discount that the jobber received. For instance, if the jobber received a 50 percent discount from the publisher, the discount given the library will usually be between 15 percent to 20 percent. If the library or bookstore had ordered the book directly from the publisher, the discount would have been as high or perhaps even higher.

Discounting is a complex issue in any commercial activity, but it is highly complex in the book trade. Every publisher has a discount schedule that is slightly different, if not unique, in terms of other publishers. Some items are net (no discount); these are usually textbooks, scientific technical titles, or items of very limited sales appeal. "Short" discounts are 20 percent "off" items; these are also limited appeal titles but with more sales potential than the net titles. "Trade" discounts range from 30 percent to 60 percent; these are given on popular titles. Jobbers normally receive 50-60 percent discounts, primarily because of their high-volume orders (hundreds of copies per title rather than the tens that most libraries and independent bookstore owners order).

Recently, jobbers have encountered financial problems in the form of rising costs and declining sales. A number of publishers are requiring pre-payment or have placed jobbers on a "pro forma" status, where pre-payment is required and credit extended on the basis of each one's current performance in payment of bills. Much of the credit/order fulfillment extended by publishers depends upon an almost personal relationship with a jobber. This means for libraries that the selection of a jobber must be made with care. It is *not* inappropriate to check a prospective jobber's financial status (through a rating service such as Dun and Bradstreet). Indeed, it is recommended that this be done by the library since so much depends upon its choice of jobber.

What Can They Do for You?

Why buy from an indirect source that charges a higher price for the material than the direct source would? SERVICE! Jobbers provide a very important service in that they can save a library a significant amount of time and money. Although jobbers do not give high discounts, the time saved by placing one single order for ten different titles from ten different publishers, instead of ten different orders, more than pays for the slightly higher price. Another savings can arise from unpacking only one box and writing only one check. Most jobbers also claim fast, accurate service. It is true that a few publishers, if they accept single copy orders (and most do), handle these orders more slowly than they do large orders. It is also true that jobbers do not always have a specific title when it is wanted.

"Items in stock will be shipped within twenty-four hours" is a typical claim of jobbers. Can and do they make good the claim? Generally, yes; however, the key phrase is "in stock." Frequently there are delays of three to four months in receiving a complete order because some titles are not in stock. When talking with jobbers, *do not* become impressed by numbers quoted in their advertising: "more than 2 million books in stock." What you need to know is how many *titles* and which *publishers* are represented. For various reasons, economic and/or personal, some publishers will refuse to deal with a particular jobber. Three important questions must be asked of any jobber before a library contracts for that firm's services:

1)   will you give me a list of all the publishers that you do not handle?

2)   will you give me a list of series that your firm does not handle?

3)   how does your firm handle a request for a title not in stock?

The answer to the first question is difficult to get. Sales representatives want to say they can supply any title from any publisher, with only minor exceptions. However, libraries in the same system may be given different lists, at the same time, by different sales representatives. The issue is important and must be resolved if the acquisition department is to operate effectively. Sending an order for a title from a publisher that the jobber cannot handle only delays the process. In some cases the jobber will report back that they are trying to secure the item; this usually results in a later report of failure, making the acquisition process even slower. Buying directly from the publisher is the best approach to this problem, *if* you know which publishers are involved.

Questions 2 and 3 are also important in terms of speed of service. Some jobbers will order a single title from a publisher when it is not in stock. Others say they will do this (and they do); but they actually wait until they can order multiple copies before placing the order, since by placing a large order they will receive a larger discount from the publisher. For the library the delay may be one of several months, because it will take that long for the jobber to accumulate enough individual requests for the title to make up an order of sufficient size. Jobbers who do place single copy orders for a customer usually offer a lower discount. Again, the acquisition staff must weigh the service missed against the discount. Occasionally a jobber will have a title in stock beyond the date on which the publisher listed the item as being out of print (o.p.). On occasion a jobber can supply o.p. material, and a few jobbers will even try to find o.p. items for their best customers. This is a special service which is never advertised and is given only to favored customers.

Beyond fast, accurate service, jobbers should provide personal service. A smooth working relationship with anyone, including a jobber, depends on mutual understanding and respect. When that is achieved it is much easier to solve problems when they arise, even the difficult ones. A jobber, because of its smaller base of customers, can normally give answers more quickly than can a publisher's customer service department. Even the small account customer receives careful attention (in order to hold the account), something that seldom happens with publishers.

No single jobber can stock all of the in-print items that a library will need. Most large firms, however, do carry the high-demand current and backlist items. The book trade folklore says that 20 percent of the current and backlist titles represent 80 percent of the total sales. All of the good jobbers try to stock in their warehouses the *right* 20 percent. Some are more successful than others. (Remember that this is ultimately stated in terms of sales.) Bookstores will find this concept very useful for maintaining a stock of best sellers. Libraries, on the other hand, must acquire a broader range of titles. Thus the opinion of bookstore owners about the best jobbers in your area is useful only if it is supported by the experience of librarians.

One problem with a limited stock jobber is in invoicing and billing procedures. A small jobber may ship and bill for those items in stock, then back order the rest. In this case, when the invoice is sent, the shipper expects to receive payment for the partial fulfillment of the order. However, some library systems are only allowed to pay for complete orders. Every item is either received or cancelled before a voucher (check) is issued. This procedure can be significant for small jobbers and/or libraries. Very few are able or willing to wait for payment until a particular order is complete. For small libraries with small materials budgets the problem is to find a jobber who will accept complicated procedures and delays despite a low volume. It is becoming harder and harder to find such firms.

Jobbers may handle thousands of different publishers and may maintain an inventory of over 200,000 titles. One useful service that many large jobbers offer is a periodic report on the status of all of a library's orders. Many provide a monthly report on all items not yet shipped. Each back-ordered item is listed and the reason for its unavailability is included. If the reporting system is properly organized, it can save both librarian and jobber a lot of letter writing and filing. Most large jobbers offer a flexible order and invoicing system—i.e., they try to adapt to the library's needs rather than force it to use their methods.

The services just described should be the ones offered to libraries and retail bookstores by a jobber, although most jobbers interested in selling to libraries offer a variety of other services. A typical jobber, beyond supplying books at wholesale prices, may offer libraries the following services:

1) cataloging/processing services;

2) continuation services;

3) books;

4) book rental plans;

5) other media;

6) library furniture;

7) library supplies.

As this list implies, the jobber attempts to offer a library most of the supplies and services necessary for its operation.

Many small libraries, and perhaps in the future, large libraries, may find it beneficial to buy their books already processed. A study may show this approach to be very cost effective provided that the public service staff and users find that the material supplied is adequate. Normally the technical services offered by jobbers allow the library a number of choices. "Processing kits"—i.e., catalog cards, pockets, labels, jackets, etc.—can be purchased, with the library staff then completing the processing routines. Completely processed, ready-for-the-shelf services can also be secured. Since several different classification systems are widely used in this country, a jobber will offer processing for all the major systems. Flexibility is essential in these services; yet, in order to make them cost effective (profitable) for the jobber, there must either be a high degree of uniformity or at least a high sales volume for each variation. Thus you can expect to receive a degree of personalized customer service but not custom processing.

Standing orders or continuations are a problem for most libraries. Since publishers bring out a series of titles over a period of time, selection and acquisition staff time can be consumed wastefully if each title is selected and ordered individually. Automatic shipment of each title as it is published is most desirable, but placing individual standing orders with each publisher and maintaining the records of what has and has not been received is also costly. If a jobber will place all of a customer's standing orders on its regular status report, to be included with each of the library's orders, considerable savings may be achieved for the library. Any reputable dealer will tell you just how much service to expect. Certainly, no single one will be able to handle all standing order needs, and some titles can only be secured on a direct order/membership basis. Nevertheless, jobbers can provide excellent service for a high percentage of your needs.

Most book jobbers offer only a monographic continuation service. For journals and other serials, the equivalent of the book jobber exists. A basic difference is that serial jobbers seldom offer any service except order placement. Faxon, one of the largest American serial jobbers, will place orders for almost any standard English-language and many foreign-language journals. As with monographic continuations, some journals and serials must be ordered directly. All of the questions that you would ask a book jobber should be asked of the serials jobbers. Of special concern here should be the size of the discounts or handling charges the firm employs. If one order is placed once a year for hundreds of serial titles, a large amount of library staff time will be saved. When the firm provides fast, accurate service and a good reporting system, both the library and the jobber will benefit.

There are also a few small firms functioning as jobbers for government documents. They operate in the same manner as other jobbers: their primary benefit is convenience. Small libraries, or libraries buying a limited number of government documents, will find them very useful. Libraries with large document collections will probably find it best to buy directly from the Government Printing Office rather than go through a jobber.

One problem for public libraries and others that serve current, popular reading needs is speed in supplying the current best sellers. Various programs have been devised to deal with the problem. Some years ago an American public librarian, Emerson Greenaway, came up with the idea of placing a standing order with publishers for one copy of each trade book, to be delivered on publication date. Eventually this idea developed into the "Greenaway Plan," and today one sees many variations of the basic concept. The Greenaway Plan is a contract between a library and one publisher. Some jobbers compete with the Plan by offering either date-of-publication approval copies or pre-publication lists. The basic purpose of all of these concepts is the same: to be able to select titles in advance, so as to be able to anticipate patron demand for multiple copies.

One jobber, Bro-Dart, offers a rather unusual service—the McNaughton Plan—to help solve the problem of providing an adequate number of high demand titles. Most libraries have suffered from the problem of high demand for a very popular book, but the demand may last only a few months. Do you buy many copies and discard all but one or two after the demand dies down, or do you buy just a few copies and take reservations? The McNaughton Plan offers another alternative: rent multiple copies for the duration of the high demand time. Actually, Bro-Dart describes it as a leasing program. This plan is geared to high demand items which are selected by Bro-Dart's staff; one cannot order just any book; it must be on their list. Savings occur in several areas: there are no processing costs as the books come ready for the shelf, and the leasing fee is considerably lower than the item's purchase price. Patrons will also be happier about shorter waiting times for the high interest books. All in all, public and academic libraries will find that the program is worth looking into. Academic libraries may use it to stock a variety of materials for recreational reading without taking too much money out of the book fund.

Some jobbers are now beginning to offer materials other than books and serials. Perhaps the best gauge of how far libraries in a country have gone in providing nonbook services is the number of jobbers in that country supplying both books and other media. Some jobbers offer phonorecords, film slides, etc., and a review service. They also offer a processing service for the items they sell. The opportunity to place one order for all or most formats with one jobber is something to be desired, provided that the service and quality of materials are high.

What Does a Jobber or Wholesaler Expect from a Librarian?

The preceding pages describe what can be expected from the jobber. But a librarian also has certain obligations in maintaining a good working relationship with the jobber. Simply stated, a jobber's profit is based on the difference between what is paid for the merchandise and how much it sells for. No different from any other business? Basically no. However, there is a major difference in that any buyer can buy directly from the materials producer, which is seldom true in other fields. A further difference is that all buyers can determine for themselves what the maximum price should be by checking either *Publishers Trade List Annual* or with the publisher. With every buyer knowing what the maximum price is, including any discount from the publisher, the jobber must at least match that price and provide superior service in order to hold customers.

Volume buying and selling is the only way that a jobber can hope to make a profit. Efficient plant operations and low overhead help; but no matter how efficient the operation, it may fail without a high volume. One order for 15 or 20 titles in quantities will result in a very high discount for the jobber, perhaps as high as 60 percent. Even after giving a 20-25 percent discount to the library, the jobber is left with a comfortable margin with which to work. Unfortunately, that type of order is more the exception than the rule. More often the jobber's discount is 50 percent. A smaller margin is still acceptable if all the items sell. But they do not! Yes, there is something called "returns" (where a publisher buys back unsold books). Returns normally result in credits against the current account or future purchases. Seldom does it result in a cash return for book jobbers.

Because jobbers are dependent upon volume sales, they must know their markets fairly well to project sales and to order for stock accordingly. Thus when the jobber representative stops by to talk, it is not mere public relations or, necessarily, an attempt to sell more books, but a means of determining the customer's plans for collection development. Take time to talk to the person; explain new programs and new areas to be worked on. Ask about what is available in the field, even if you think you know; you may not. Ask what the firm could do to supply the items; is it a field they carry as part of their normal inventory, or would items have to be special ordered? Such discussion takes time, but it will result in better service.

Some librarians dump their problem orders on the jobber and then order the easy items directly from the publisher in order to get the maximum discount. Nothing could be more short-sighted. Without the income from the easy high-volume items, no jobber can stay in business. Someone is needed to work on the hard order, and most jobbers will try to run down the difficult items; but give them the easy orders as well. Almost all of the problems facing the jobber involve cash flow. Since lack of cash has been the downfall of many businesses, it becomes critical for jobbers if they handle only problem orders; staff time goes up, but income does not.

Whenever possible use the order format that is best for the jobber. Do not plead legal or system requirements for a particular method of ordering unless it absolutely cannot be changed. Most jobbers, and publishers, go out of their way to accommodate the legal requirements of library ordering procedures. If libraries could come closer to a standardized order procedure, jobbers could provide better service, since they would not have to keep track of hundreds of variations. If *all* paperwork is kept to a minimum everyone will benefit. While most jobbers will accept a few returns from libraries, even if the library is at fault, returns create a lot of paperwork. If an item truly serves no purpose in a library's collection, perhaps it would save time and money to accept the mistake and discard it rather than return it, assuming mistakes are infrequent. (This refers to items sent in error, not defective ones. Any defective copy should be returned.)

Finally, pay invoices promptly. Do not hold them any longer than necessary. Since libraries seldom issue the actual payment, one cannot say that an invoice was held only three weeks. Most library systems require at least two approvals before payment will be made: first, the library's; then, the business office's. Some have three or more offices involved. Know the system, from approval to final payment. If it takes longer than six weeks, give a new jobber that information. And tell jobbers when a change occurs in your system. Most jobbers would like to be paid within 30 days since they are on a 30-day payment cycle with publishers.

Jobbers provide a valuable service to libraries. Given a good working relationship both parties benefit. Following is a summary of the basic factors at work in establishing such a relationship.

What libraries expect from jobbers:

1) large inventory of titles

2) prompt and accurate order fulfillment

3) prompt and accurate reporting on items not in stock

4) personal service at a reasonable price.

What jobbers expect of libraries:

1) time to get to know what the library needs

2) cooperation in placing orders

3) keeping paperwork to a minimum

4) prompt payment for services.

RETAIL OUTLETS

How Do New Bookstores Operate?

New bookstores—stores selling new books, not stores that just opened—are interesting places to visit, whether or not you are responsible for collection development. Many librarians started haunting bookshops long before they became librarians. If there is a bibliographic equivalent to alcoholism, many librarians have it. "Bibliomania" is defined (in the *Random House Dictionary of the English Language*, 1967, p. 145) as "excessive fondness for acquiring and possessing books." Most bibliomaniacs (librarians included) cannot stay out of bookshops and consider it a great feat of willpower and self-control if they manage to leave one without buying a book or two. Most teachers of collection development suffer from this madness and attempt to infect their students. With this end in mind, many make their students visit two bookstores, one new and one out-of-print or antiquarian.

Bookstore owners would be very happy if a high percentage of the general population suffered from bibliomania. They do not. In fact, they seem to have been inoculated with a most effective vaccine. On a percentage basis, book buyers are a minority group in most countries, although their actual numbers might be large. Because of this, bookstores generally have to exist in somewhat special environments and operate in a certain way. While most students have undoubtedly visited many bookshops innumerable times for library school ends, they are asked to visit two stores with a set of questions in mind. Basically, they are to look at a store in terms of what it might be able to do for them were they collection development personnel. They also should be able to answer this question: What are the conditions (environmental and operating) necessary for a good bookstore? In the following discussion some of the important points to consider in evaluating a bookstore as a potential source of library materials will be described.

One consideration for any bookstore owner is location. Many owners live and work in the community for a long time before they open their store. Just as the person responsible for successful collection development in a library needs to know the community, so does the bookstore owner. She or he also needs to be known and respected in the community. The dream of finding a quaint little town somewhere to retire to and then open up a small bookshop is one that many librarians harbor. Most use it as a nice daydream for the bad day in the library. Of those who go further and try to implement the idea, very few succeed. Those who do are located in communities they know and are known in as a result of frequent visits and extended stays. A successful bookshop is a busy, people-oriented organization. It is not a quiet retreat for persons who do not like working with people. Furthermore, it requires much physical work on the part of the owner, and a fairly large population base to support the required volume of sales.

The population base is a key consideration in determining where to locate a bookstore. The American Booksellers Association suggests a minimum population for a "books-only" store is 25,000 persons.[1] Thus, large cities are the most likely locations for books-only shops. The smaller the community, the less likely it is that a books-only store will survive. Cultural activities in a large city help stimulate interest in reading. In major cities it is even possible to find a variety of specialized bookstores (foreign languages and subject matter). Smaller communities adjoining a good-sized academic institution provide the primary exception to what has been said above about size.

The educational level of the population is another factor in store location. As the average level of education in a community rises, so do the chances of a bookstore's succeeding with a smaller population base. College graduates represent the largest segment of bookbuyers, outside of the course-related sales area. (The largest book market, also a captive market, is in education- and course-related sales; however, most general bookstores do not focus on this field.) Find a high concentration of college-educated persons living near a large shopping center, and you are likely to find a bookstore.

Shopping centers are considered one of the most desirable locations for a bookstore—if there is a lot of foot traffic. A store tucked in a remote corner of the busiest center is not likely to do well. If bookstore owners had to survive solely on the basis of individuals seeking a particular book, there would be even fewer stores than we now have. A store catering to the tastes of middle- and upper-income persons also increases its chances of success, because a high percentage of book sales results from impulse buying, which requires a location where the bookseller can stimulate the impulse in persons who can afford to indulge themselves in it. How many times have you gone into a bookstore looking for just one book or "something to read" and walked out with three or four paperbacks? Bookstore owners depend on such impulse buying.

The many similarities between operating a bookstore and a library success-fully are striking. Both require a solid knowledge of the community; if libraries could select sites as do bookstores, use of them would skyrocket. A new branch library in the center of Stockholm reflects an almost ideal bookstore location: on a shopping mall, in the center of the main business district, with a high volume of foot traffic, and near a concourse to a main subway station. This particular branch is the most active of all the service points in a system where high use is the norm.

Store owners attempt to stimulate buyers through a variety of sales methods. Some lures are employed in store windows and entry ways, providing clues about the basic stock before a customer enters. Only very large shops can afford ads on a weekly basis in newspapers and radio and television advertising costs are prohibitively high for most owners. For most, an occasional newspaper ad and a good storefront display are the best they can do in promoting business. Trumbull Huntington made the point that "your window, the best single advertising medium you have, tells your sales story to every passing man, woman, and child. Make sure it reflects the story that you want told, and that it does so forcefully, invitingly, and clearly."[2]

If you make it a practice to observe bookstore windows, especially those you pass frequently, you can make a fair assessment of a shop without walking in the door—an assessment of the type of material within, not necessarily of the level of service. Observing is not the same as casually looking. You can look closely, but without some guidelines you may not know what to look for or how to interpret what you see. The following broad generalizations can serve as the most basic of guidelines, providing a foundation upon which you can build as you gain experience.

An owner has two basic methods available for promoting a store through its windows: one is to focus on a particular topic or on a few best sellers; the other is a "shotgun" approach—a wide variety of titles appealing to a wide range of interests. Using a little imagination, some nonbook props, and a good supply of the book(s) being promoted, very interesting window displays can be created. The non-active reader may be stimulated to come in and buy the promoted title but will seldom pause to examine other titles in the store. Generally, the display will lead to a good sale of the promoted title or subject, but most buyers, especially those interested only in a certain topic, will not return to the store until another equally striking window on that topic is created.

"Shotgun" window displays are less likely to attract the non-active reader. One will stop a reader, if it is well done. A jumble of books in the window will not do the job, but a wealth of titles using some basic graphic techniques will. This type of window is known to attract the steady book-buying customer. Such individuals are as likely to buy four or five titles as one, and all of them may be impulse purchases—impulse in the sense that the buyers did not come into the store looking for the specific titles purchased.

Check displays in the window(s) of a bookstore that you frequently pass. If the store has consistently striking windows featuring the latest top sellers, this is very likely to reflect the orientation in the total book stock. Almost everything in such a store will have a proven track record. Backlist titles that have had steady sales (dictionaries, cookbooks, home reference items, and "classics") will comprise the majority of items in stock beyond the stacks of "in" titles and tables piled high with discount and "gift" books. While shops of this type may be willing to order single titles there will be little real advantage for the library. Almost the only reason for a library to patronize such a store is in the hope that the store will change its emphasis if the library continues to buy there. In smaller communities this may be the only type of store available. If the library were to buy $40,000 to $50,000 worth of books each year from the store, this would probably be an adequate incentive for the owner to shift emphasis. It will still be possible for the store's regular patrons to find their favorite types of books there, and perhaps it will draw in some new steady customers as a result of the change.

If a store's windows do not provide enough clues, looking in the door can provide another quick visual check. Tables of books with signs such as TOP TWENTY!, 55% to 75% OFF!, GIANT DISCOUNTS! are almost certain to announce a store of limited value to a library, especially if most of the window displays have favored the latest and best sellers. A store with a good wide range of stock cannot afford to devote much floor area to such sales methods. All stores will have sales from time to time—books that have not sold and may be past their return date, some remainders—and of course there is always the pre-inventory sale. However, the store that is always having a "sale" is never really having a sale and seldom is of value to libraries.

Another quick visual check should be for sideline items in the store. A new bookstore selling only new books needs a minimum community population of 25,000, but almost all bookstores now sell at least a few sidelines: greeting cards, stationery/office supplies, posters, art supplies, magazines and newspapers, calendars, games, and of course, "widgets." (Widgets are important impulse purchase items near the cash register: bookmarks, knick-knacks, or conversation pieces such as the one at a recent booksellers' convention—a large wooden cube with a picture of the brain on each side, labeled "Mental Block." Each block was to retail for

$2.95; but they were sold to bookstores for $0.50 each in lots of two dozen. The booth where this was on display showed a full line of widgets for bookstores, and the company making them is very successful.) Why the sideline? It is difficult to make a good living just selling books because there are few buyers and the margin of profit on books is much smaller than that on sideline items.

For purposes of comparison, let us briefly consider the possible profits on books, a complex subject given the different discount arrangements available to booksellers. Publishers offer the same general discounts (trade, long, short, net, mass market) to bookstores as they give to jobbers. Long discounts (40 percent or more) are given on most trade books, except paperbacks. In the case of very large orders (multiple copies), discounts of 50 percent are possible, and very occasionally, 60 percent. Normally the discount is 40 percent and even then there is often a required minimum number of copies (five or more) to receive this amount. A few publishers offer 35-40 percent off on an order of ten different single titles—the Single Copy Order Plan (SCOP). Librarians ordering a sizeable number of single copies from one publisher may find bookstores very willing to place such orders. However, remember that such an agreement requires the bookseller to *prepay* and to do all the paperwork. Thus if the library is slow issuing payments, only large bookstores can afford to carry its account.

Some stores will order short discount items but add on a service charge. If enough short discount items are needed from a single publisher, most stores will handle the order without a service charge. Remember, on a $20.00 book with a 25 percent discount, the bookstore will receive only $5.00 more than it pays out. By the time all the clerical and record keeping costs are taken out of the $5.00, the owner is very lucky if the transaction has not cost the store more money than was taken in.

Of the two general classes of paperbacks—quality and mass market—quality paperbacks generally sell for more than $3.00 and are only found in bookstores. (The term does not necessarily apply to the content of the book.) Mass market books are those in drugstores, grocery stores, etc., that usually sell for around $2.00. Most publishers give a long discount on quality paperbacks when they are ordered in groups of five to ten or more. A store must order 25 to 50 assorted titles of the mass market type to begin to approach a 40 percent discount. Orders for less than that amount will get discounts of 25-35 percent.

The book distribution system in the United States is very cumbersome and adds unnecessarily to the cost of books. A simplified system would benefit everyone. Perhaps the best illustration of the complexity of the system is the area of discounts, returns, billings, etc. Each year the American Booksellers Association (ABA) publishes a 500-page guide entitled *ABA Book Buyer's Handbook*. Pity the poor bookseller, confronted with all of the other problems of a bookstore, who also must work through a mass of legal forms and sales conditions for purchasing from various publishers. It does create extra work for the bookseller and publisher, and they undoubtedly pass their costs on to the final buyer.

Thus, when a sideline item offers a 70 percent to 80 percent discount, it is not surprising to find the mixed store; as much as 30 percent and 40 percent of the *total* store income is derived from nonbook sales. Indeed, such sales have become so important to the average bookstore that the ABA now issues a *Sideline Directory*. A store that devotes more than one-third of the available floor space to nonbook items probably will not be of much use to a library for developing collections, and such calculations should enter into the librarian's observations. In addition to quick visual checks, its personnel will provide further information about a store, although more and more shops are forced to use a self-service arrangement as labor costs rise. Most self-service orientations emphasize paperbacks, sidelines, and very popular trade books. Obviously such stores offer little that will be of value to the library.

A knowledgeable bookstore staff can be a great help to a library. Talk to the salespersons about books. Do they know the book trade and its current production? What authors do they know? Do they have a subject expertise? A knowledgeable sales staff can often suggest titles that might be missed. Publishers' sales representatives will often tell shop owners and staff about new books that are good but may not get publicity. They may also mention titles that are not currently high demand items but which may become so because of special promotions being planned. Just as the bookshop receives many calls for books discussed on the late night talk shows on radio and television, so does the library. Knowing in advance about these books is advantageous to both the bookstore owner and the librarian.

In general, the new bookstore can be a very valuable means of acquiring new books. Carrying out visual inspection of the local shops and discussing the library's service needs with their owners is an important link in the selection and acquisition program. Unfortunately, most libraries are not located in major metropolitan areas where there are a number of bookstores. Many are lucky if there is one bookstore in the community. Although the chances of a major portion of the library's book buying going to such small stores is slight, the possibility ought to be explored. (The reason for the low probability is that the store will probably have a very small stock [of the best sellers], many sidelines, and a very small staff, perhaps only the owner and one or two assistants.)

Out-of-Print, Antiquarian, and Rare Book Dealers

Allowing for some overlap there are two broad categories of second-hand bookstores. (It should be noted, though, that most dealers of the following types do *not* like to be called "second-hand dealers.") One type is primarily concerned with out-of-print (o.p.) books; that is, with buying and selling used books. These books often sell at a price the same as or slightly higher than it was when they were published. The other category of store here is concerned with rare, antiquarian, and/or "special" books (fore-edge painted, miniatures, private press, etc.). Prices in stores of this type range from around $10 to several thousand dollars per item. (It is possible to distinguish between antiquarian and rare book dealers, but even dealers use the terms interchangeably. A "pure" antiquarian dealer would only deal in books 100 years old or more, whereas a rare book dealer could have a book only a few months old but unusual in some way other than its age—one of 100 copies printed or signed by a famous person.) Some overlap occurs between the two categories, but a dealer generally tries to specialize in one area or the other, and often further specializes in limited subject areas—e.g., Western Americana, children's books, military history, medicine, pre-seventeenth century items, etc.

If the variety of stores dealing in new books is wide, the range for out-of-print dealers is almost infinite: from an individual working out of a house or apartment with almost no stock and functioning as a book agent, to the to-be-expected small shop, to the exclusive Beverly Hills rare bookshops visited by appointment only. The vast majority are somewhere near the lower middle of this spectrum—small shops in very low-rent areas. Because of this diversity it is difficult to make too many generalizations about this group. Sol Malkin, though, paints a very cheery picture of at least part of the out-of-print trade:

> Imagine a separate book world within the world of books where dealers set up their businesses where they please (store or office, home or barn); where the minimum markup is 100 per cent; where they can call upon 5,000 fellow dealers throughout the world and a stock of over 200 million volumes, practically from the beginning of the printed word; where books are safely packed and mailed with no extra charge for postage; where there is no competition from publishers and discount houses; where colleagues help one another in time of need to provide fellow dealers with a unique service that makes happy customers all the time—an ideal imaginary book world that never was nor ever will be? Perhaps . . . but the above is at least 99 per cent true in the antiquarian book trade.[3]

Libraries can function without using new bookstores, but they must use this second kind of distributor at some point. Replacement copies will always be needed. Often they are no longer in print and can only be found in o.p. stores. Retrospective buying is almost always confined to this category of shop, although it is possible to buy directly from private collectors.

Several directories to antiquarian or rare book dealers provide information about specialties, and anyone concerned with selection and acquisition needs to get to know these directories. Some major metropolitan areas have local directories or guides to special bookshops. In any case, a person will find it worthwhile to develop a card file on the local shops. The file can provide quick information about *real* specialties, search services, hours, etc. One can often go to a shop that advertises itself as a "Western Americana" store only to find the specialty stock very, very limited and/or overpriced; still, the shop can be studied and its true specialties and general pricing policy estimated. Maintaining this private directory can prove to be well worth the time required to keep it up to date. This is not to say that the published sources are worthless. However, owners change emphasis and their stock does turn over and is subject to local economic conditions. Annual publications are somewhat outdated even at the moment they are published. The same is true of your own file, except it can be quickly updated.

Many acquisition librarians and book dealers classify out-of-print book distribution services into three general types: 1) a complete book service, 2) a complete sales service, and 3) a complete bookshop. The first two may be operated in a manner that does not allow, or require, the customer to visit the seller's location. They can work by mail and telephone contacts and the owner may maintain only a small stock of "choice items" in a garage or basement. In type 1, a dealer actively searches for items for a customer even if they are not in stock, by placing an ad in a publication such as *AB Bookman's Weekly*. Sales service (type 2) is just what the name implies: a dealer reads the "wanted" sections of book trade publications and sends off quotes on items in his or her stock. Such services seldom place ads or conduct searches for a customer. The last (type 3) is a store operation where "in person" trade is sought; stores of this type often engage in type 1 and type 2 activities as well. Given the unpredictable nature of the o.p. trade, it is an unusual store that can afford not to exploit every possible sales outlet.

AB Bookman's Weekly (or AB, as o.p. specialists refer to it) is a weekly publication devoted solely to advertising from dealers either offering or searching for particular titles. Publications of this type are an essential ingredient in the o.p. book trade, since they serve as a finding and selling tool. Without services like this the cost of acquiring an o.p. item would be much higher, if a copy even could be located without the service.

One characteristic of o.p. and rare bookshops is that they both require a high capital investment in a book stock that may not sell. Most owners feel very lucky if there is 1½ turnover in stock during the year. Indeed, some items may never sell and most will remain on a shelf for several years before a buyer appears. Lacking the return rights of the new bookstore owner, then, a used/rare bookstore owner must be careful about purchases and have relatively inexpensive storage available.

Because of the factors of high investment and low turnover, most owners locate their business in a low rent area. Rare and antiquarian shops can sometimes exist in high rent areas, but if the shop is there, a purchaser will pay a premium price for the books. Shops in such locations seem to have more often grown with the area rather than to have resulted from an owner's deciding to move into a high rent area. Several attempts to start antiquarian shops in high rent areas have failed, despite locations that have a high volume of foot traffic, well-to-do customers with higher-than-average education, and a large university only a few blocks away.

One requisite for an out-of-print dealer is a reputation for honesty, service, and fair prices. To gain such a reputation requires a considerable period of time in this field. Unfortunately, most newcomers do not have adequate capital to carry them through this period if they locate in a high rent area. As a result most o.p. shops are located in the less desirable areas in a community. This means that a person looking for such shops must make a special trip to visit them. Out-of-the-way, low rent quarters for such a store also mean that there will be very little walk-in trade (someone just passing by). This in turn means most customers come looking for specific items and are not too likely to be diverted to something else. Sideline items are seldom found in these shops, although a few may have some used phonograph records, old photographs, or posters. Owners can only hope that they have the right items to spark some impulse book buying in the true bibliophile.

One element in the o.p. trade seems very mysterious to the outsider and even to librarians who have had years of experience with these dealers. How *do* they determine the price they ask? As Sol Malkin indicated in the earlier quotation there is at least a 100 percent markup, but how much more? How many times have you found a book in an o.p. store with no price on it, taken it to the salesperson (often the owner), and asked the price? After a quick look comes the answer, "Oh, yes. That is X amount." Sometimes the amount is lower than expected, other times much higher; but most of the time it is what was expected. Some salespersons seem to be mind readers, to know almost to the dollar how much a customer is willing to pay. Another quotation from Sol Malkin sums up the outsider's feeling about this aspect of the o.p. trade: "Many new book dealers think of the antiquarian bookseller as a second-hand junkman or as a weird character who obtains books by sorcery, prices them by cabalistic necromancy, and sells them by black magic."[4]

It may appear that magic is the most essential ingredient in successful o.p. operations. Actually it is not very mysterious after three central issues concerning this trade are understood: the source of supply, the major sales methods, and how prices are set. Once these are known, most of the mystery disappears, but for those who enjoy the o.p. trade, not the magic. With an excellent memory, a love for books, an ability and the time to learn books, enough capital to buy a basic stock of books, and finally the patience to wait for a return on the capital, anyone can become an o.p. bookseller. Sources and sales methods will be discussed before we turn to the "necromancy" referred to by Malkin, only to find none.

The question of pricing is determined to a large degree by the answers to the questions of supply and sales. The o.p. dealer has a number of sources of supply but only two can consistently produce new stock. One major source is to buy personal or business collections. Placing an ad in the telephone directory ("I buy old books") will generate a number of inquiries. Two of the most frequent reasons for a private collection's coming into the market are a family's or individual's moving and the settling of estates. Except for outstanding private collections of a well-known collector, most dealers will not enter into a bidding contest. They may come to look at a collection, but only after determining by telephone if it is very large and has some potential value. After an examination they make a flat offer with a take-it-or-leave-it attitude. A person who has no experience with the o.p. trade will usually be very surprised and disappointed at how low the offer will be. After one or two such offers a prospective seller might conclude that there is a conspiracy of o.p. dealers to cheat owners out of rare items.

Nothing could be further from the truth. Experienced o.p. dealers know how long most of the items they have bid on will occupy storage space in their shops. They also know how few of the seller's "treasures" are more than personal treasures. Grandfather's complete collection of the *National Geographic* from 1921 to 1973 may be a family heirloom but to most o.p. dealers it is so much fodder—for the $0.25 each table. Sorting out the few highly saleable items from the run-of-the-mill material takes time.

Time is the central theme in the o.p. trade. In time every edition of a book will become o.p.; in time the vast majority of the world's printed material should be returned to the pulp paper mills for recycling; in time the few valuable books will find a buyer. But when is that time? Knowing the time factor as well as they do, o.p. dealers must buy for as little as they can or they will go out of business. Knowledgeable dealers know the local and the national market; therefore, it is not surprising that several bids on the same collection are similar or almost identical. They read the same trade magazines, they see the same catalogs and to some extent, they see the same local buyers. If they are to stay in business they all most know the market.

Walk-in sales, except to libraries, are generally only a small segment of o.p. sales income. Mail order sales are the major source: buying and selling items through publications such as AB and catalogs. Most dealers prepare catalogs of selected items in stock and mail them to dealers, libraries, and book collectors. Often the catalog will list only one type of material (subject: Western Americana, European history, etc.; or form: first editions, illustrated books, etc.). Other times it will be a miscellaneous collection of titles that the dealer hopes will appeal to many different buyers.

Just as the contents of catalogs vary, so do the quality of the item descriptions and the care taken in preparing the catalog. Some catalogs are faded or smeared mimeographed or dittoed sheets that are almost impossible to read; and when you are able to read an entry it only gives the author, title, date, and price. At the other end of the spectrum are catalogs that are so well done and contain so much bibliographic information that research libraries add the catalog to their bibliography collection. A catalog of high quality is encountered less and less frequently now and the trend is likely to continue because of rising costs. In order to recover the cost it is necessary to sell the catalog to buyers who are not regular customers, which also usually means that the prices for all of the items in the catalog will be rather high ($100 to $5,000).

When you see a catalog that contains something your library needs and can purchase, RUN, do not walk, to the nearest telephone and call in your order. You will probably be too late, but the telephone is almost your only chance of getting the item. A mailed order is almost certain to arrive too late. Out-of-print folklore says that if *you* want an item so do thirty other persons. This means a certain amount of competition among buyers.

Dealer catalogs and magazines such as AB provide not only a sales mechanism but a major means of establishing prices. If an o.p. dealer in London offers an autographed copy of the first edition of Richard Adams's *Watership Down* for £10, other dealers will use this information as a guideline in setting prices for copies of the book that they have in stock. An unautographed copy of the first edition would be offered for something less than £10, assuming that both copies were in approximately the same physical condition. Other editions, including foreign first editions, would also sell for less. The foreign first editions might come close to the English first edition in price, but the *first* first usually commands the highest price.

Prices, then, are based upon a number of interrelated factors: 1) how much it costs to acquire the item, 2) the amount of current interest in collecting a particular subject or author, 3) the number of copies printed and the number of copies still in existence, 4) the physical condition of the copy, 5) any special features of the particular copy (autographed by the author and/or signed or owned by a famous person, etc.), and 6) what other dealers are asking for copies of the same edition and same condition. Without question the asking price is the major determining factor—given equal conditions in the other five areas—thus making sales catalogs and AB major pricing tools.

A few further facts about the condition of o.p. books are important for beginning librarians to know, as these bear directly on price. Most o.p. books are sold on the basis "as described" or "as is." If there is no statement about the item's condition it is assumed to be "good" or better. A common statement in catalogs is "terms—all books in original binding and in good or better condition unless otherwise stated. Items for any reason unsatisfactory may be returned within ten days." The examples of o.p. dealer catalog entries (Figures 9, 10, and 11) should be studied carefully.

The Maggs Bros. and Morrill catalogs are examples of the basic catalogs that a librarian concerned with retrospective buying would check. The sample from Heritage's catalog represents more expensive materials but still well within the limits within which a beginner might select. All three examples give information about the condition of the items offered. What does the "t.e.g." indicate about

Figure 9
Maggs Brothers [London] Catalog Sample

10 *BIBLIOGRAPHIES AND BOOKS ABOUT BOOKS*

Dickens (C.)—*continued*

61 [———] ECKEL (J. C.). THE FIRST EDITIONS OF THE WRITINGS OF CHARLES DICKENS AND THEIR VALUES. With portrait and 36 illustrations and facsimiles.
4to, *half vellum, uncut, t.e.g.* London, 1913. £8 8s
One of 250 copies on Large Paper signed by the Author and Publishers.

62 [———] JOHNSON (C. P.). HINTS TO COLLECTORS OF THE ORIGINAL EDITIONS OF THE WORKS OF CHARLES DICKENS.
8vo, *vellum (stained).* London, 1885. 10s
Some pencilling in text.

63 [———] NEALE (C. M.). AN INDEX TO PICKWICK.
8vo, *boards.* London, 1897. 10s 6d

64 [———] SHEPHERD (R. H.). THE BIBLIOGRAPHY OF DICKENS. A Bibliographical List arranged in chronological order of the Published Writings in Prose and Verse (from 1834 to 1880).
8vo, *half calf (top of spine missing).* London, (c. 1880). £1 10s

65 [DONNE (John)]. KEYNES (G.). A BIBLIOGRAPHY OF JOHN DONNE. With portrait and 27 plates. 1 of 350 copies. Second Edition.
4to, *original cloth, t.e.g.* Cambridge University Press, 1932 £5 5s

66 DRUJON (Fernand). CATALOGUE DES OUVRAGES, Ecrits, et Dessins de toute nature poursuivis, supprimés ou condamnés, depuis le 21 Oct. 1814 jusqu'au Juillet 1877. Edition entierement nouvelle, considerablement augmentée.
Royal 8vo, *original cloth (wrappers bound in).*
Paris, Rouveyre, 1879. £8 8s
Badly stained.

67 [DRYDEN]. EXHIBITION OF FIRST AND OTHER EDITIONS OF THE WORKS OF JOHN DRYDEN (1631-1700), commemorative of the 200th anniversary of his death. Exhibited at The Grolier Club.
Sm. 8vo, *original wrappers.* New York, 1900. 10s 6d

68 DU BOIS (H. P.). FOUR PRIVATE LIBRARIES OF NEW YORK. A contribution to the History of Bibliophilism in America. With 13 plates (4 coloured).
8vo, *original cloth, (spine worn), uncut.* New York, 1892. £1 5s
Embossed stamp on flyleaf.

69 DUNLOP (J.). THE HISTORY OF FICTION, being a Critical Account of the most celebrated Prose Works of Fiction.
8vo, *original cloth.* London, 1876. £1 10s

70 [EIKON BASILIKE]. ALMACK (E.). A BIBLIOGRAPHY OF THE KING'S BOOK or Eikon Basilike. With facsimiles of title-pages.
4to, *original cloth, (binding worn).* London, 1896. £4 4s

MAGGS BROS. LTD. LONDON

Reprinted courtesy of Maggs Bros. Ltd., London.

(Figure 10 is on page 84)

Figure 10

Heritage Bookshop [Los Angeles] Catalog Sample

ORIGINAL BOARDS UNCUT

31. LOCKMAN, JOHN. Travels of the Jesuits, into Various Parts of the World: Compiled from their Letters. Now first attempted in English. 6 maps and plates. London, 1743. First Edition in English. 8vo. Half vellum with cont. marbled boards, uncut. An unusually crisp set. 2 volumes. $350.00

Translation (abridged) of the first ten volumes of Lettres Edifiantes, containing particulars by Picolo on California missions, etc. Cowan, 1914, p. 143. Graff 2519. Sabin 40708. Wagner, Span. S. W., 74a. Barrett, 1499. Howes, L. 41 4.

THE FIRST LOS ANGELES COOK BOOK

32. LOS ANGELES COOKERY, Compiled by the Ladies' Aid Society. Mirror Printing and Binding House, Los Angeles, 1881. 172 pages, sm. 8vo. Original limp cloth, a very good copy. $150.00

Glozer, California in the Kitchen No. 164 (Dawson calls it the first Los Angeles cook book).

FIRST AERIAL VOYAGE IN ENGLAND

33. LUNARDI, VINCENT. An Account of the First Aerial Voyage in England, in a series of letters to his guardian, Chevalier Cherardo Compagni, written under the Impressions of the various Events that affected the Undertaking. With 2 large engraved folding plates, and a frontis portrait of the author. London, Printed for the Author, 1784, First Edition. 66 pages plus explanation of plates, 8vo. Half roan, a good, clean copy. $175.00

Vincent Lunardi was the first man in Great Britain to fly in ships lighter than air. In September 1784, Lunardi ascended from London to North Mimms in Hertfordshire, in about an hour and a half. The author's portrait by Bartolozzi is in the state before the erasure of the artist's name. With the half-title bearing Lunardi's signature.
De Vesme-Calabi, Fr. Bartolozzi, No. 865; Hodgson, History of Aeronautics in Great Britain. pp. 117-139.

THE FIRST WHITE MAN TO CROSS THE CONTINENT

34. MACKENZIE, ALEXANDER. Voyages from Montreal, On The River St. Lawrence, Through The Continent of North America, To the Frozen and Pacific Oceans; In the Years 1789 and 1793. With A Preliminary Account of the Rise, Progress, and Present State of the FUR TRADE of that Country. With the engraved frontispiece portrait of the Author by Conde after Lawrence, and the three large folding maps. London, 1801, First Edition. Small 4to. Contemporary diced calf, richly gilt

10.

Figure 10 (cont'd)

panelled back with floral tooling, floral borders on sides; a superb
copy of this great classic of the North West, complete with the
Errata Leaf. $500.00
Wagner-Camp No. 1; Sabin 43414; Smith 6382; Howes 6518; Staton and
Tremaine 658.
Mackenzie's expedition was undertaken on behalf of the North West Fur
Company which, towards the close of the 18th Century, was attempting
to break the monopoly of the Hudson's Bay Company. The account is
noted for its accuracy and for its great importance in relation to the
history of the North West Territory.

SIGNED BY EIGHT AVIATION PIONEERS

35. MILLER, FRANCIS TREVELYAN. The World in the Air, The Story
     of Flying in Pictures. First historic collection of official prints and
     photographs from government archives and private collections recording
     five thousand years of man's struggles to conquer the air. With over
     1200 illustrations. G. P. Putnam's Sons, New York, 1930. First edition.
     4to. ¾ parchment over marbled boards, a fine set. 2 volumes. $100.00
     Pioneers Edition printed on all rag paper. Limited to 500 sets signed by
     the author, publisher, and eight aviation pioneers including Glenn
     Curtiss, Louis Bleriot, Arthur Whitten Brown, etc.

THE FIRST APPEARANCE OF THE MONROE DOCTRINE

36. MESSAGE FROM THE PRESIDENT OF THE UNITED STATES, TO
     BOTH HOUSES OF CONGRESS, AT THE COMMENCEMENT OF THE
     FIRST SESSION OF THE EIGHTEENTH CONGRESS. Gales & Seaton,
     Washington, 1823 - First Edition. 15 pages. 8vo. Disbound-Minor
     staining. Basically clean, preserved in a half morocco slipcase. $400.00
     Grolier Club- 100 Influential American Books. Streeter No. 1735.

37. (MORRIS, WILLIAM). The Art and Craft of Printing. A note by
     William Morris on his aims in founding the Kelmscott Press. Together
     with a short description of the press by S. C. Cockerel and an annotated
     list of books printed thereat. 8vo. Elaborately bound in full dark
     morocco, rib bands, doublures, silk end papers, gilt extra. 1902. $150.00
     One of 210 copies printed at the Elston Press by Clarke Conwell
     (signed on half-title by Conwell). Aside from being a fine binding, all
     ornaments and decorations have been expertly hand-colored. The initial
     letter, illustrating the use of Troy and Chaucer type (designed for
     Froissart but never used), have also been colored and illuminated. All
     in all a very handsome edition of one of William Morris' most important
     lectures.

11.

(Figure 11 is on page 86)

Figure 11

Edward Morrill and Son [Boston] Catalog Sample

240. KELLOCK, HAROLD. Parson Weems of the Cherry Tree. Being a Short Account of the Eventful Life of the Reverend M. L. Weems . . . Illustrated. 8vo, original boards, cloth back (edges rubbed). New York (1928). First edition. **$7.50**

241. KEMP, FATHER. Father Kemp and His Old Folks. A History of the Old Folks' Concerts, Comprising an Autobiography of the Author . . . Portrait. 12mo (corners rubbed). Boston, 1868. **$8.50**
First edition. Inscribed by the author.

242. KENDRICKEN, PAUL HENRY. Memoirs. Illustrated. 8vo (part of binding and text water-stained). Boston, Privately Printed, 1910. **$7.50**
Presentation from the author, who came from Ireland, served in the navy and during the Civil War. His diary.

243. KENLY, JOHN R. Memoirs of a Maryland Volunteer. War with Mexico, in the Years 1846-7-8. 8vo. Philadelphia, 1873. **$15.00**
Very nice copy of the first edition.

244. KENNEDY, H. A. Early English Portrait Miniatures in the Collection of the Duke of Buccleuch. Edited by Charles Holme. Illustrated. 4to. London, 1917. **$17.50**

245.]KENTUCKY[To the People of Kentucky. Address of the Republican Executive Committee. Broadside, 16½ x 8 inches, three columns (folded; few tears, not affecting any text). N.P., n.d. (1876). **$15.00**
Urging a vote for Hayes for president.

246. KIRSTEN, A. Skizzen aus den Vereinigten Staaten von Nordamerika. 12mo, new cloth, 347pp., original wrappers bound in. Leipzig, 1854. **$10.00**
Third printing of Howes K-191.

247. KITTREDGE, GEORGE LYMAN. Witchcraft in Old and New England. 8vo. Cambridge, 1929. First edition. **$25.00**

248. KNIGHT, SARAH KEMBLE. Private Journal. Being the Record of a Journey from Boston to New York in the Year 1704. 8vo, original boards, calf back (rubbed and foxed; front cover loose). Norwich, 1901. **$10.00**
Edition limited to 210 copies. Howes K-217.

249. KOHL, JOHANN G. Popular History of the Discovery of America, from Columbus to Franklin. Translated from the German . . . 2 vols., 8vo (corners bit rubbed). London, 1862. **$12.50**
First edition in English. Howes K-245.

250. KURR, DR. J. G. The Mineral Kingdom. 24 full-page colored plates, all but one containing several illustrations of the most important mineral, rocks, and petrifactions. 4to, original cloth, leather back (lacks backstrip; hinges partly cracked). Edinburgh, 1859. First edition. **$35.00**

251. [LAKESIDE CLASSICS] CUSTER, GEORGE A. My Life on the Plains. 12mo, fine. Chicago, 1952. **$7.50**

252. [LAKESIDE] JAMES, GEN. THOMAS. Three Years Among the Indians and Mexicans. 12mo, fine. Chicago, 1953. **$7.50**

253. [LAKESIDE] FRANCHERE, GABRIEL. Voyage to the Northwest Coast of America. 12mo, fine. Chicago, 1954. **$7.50**

254. [LAKESIDE] FINEnTY, JOHN F. War-Path and Bivouac. The Big Horn and Yellowstone Expedition. fine. Chicago, 1965. **$5.00**

255. [LAKESIDE] MILFORD, LOUIS L. Memoir, or a Cursory Glance at My Different Travels . . . in the Creek Nation. 12mo, fine. Chicago, 1956. **$7.50**

256. [LAKESIDE] CONARD, HOWARD LOUIS. Uncle Dick Wootton. 12mo, fine. Chicago, 1957. **$6.00**

257. [LAKESIDE] The Siege of Detroit in 1763. The Journal of Pontiac's Conspiracy . . . 12mo, fine. Chicago, 1958. **$6.00**

258. [LAKESIDE] BOLLER, HENRY A. Among the Indians. 12mo, fine. Chicago. 1959. **$6.00**

259. [LAKESIDE] BILLINGS, JOHN D. Hardtack and Coffee. 12mo, fine. Chicago, 1960. **$5.00**

260. [LAKESIDE] COOKE, JOHN ESTEN. Outlines from the Outpost. 12mo, fine. Chicago, 1961. **$5.00**

261. [LAKESIDE] HOLLISTER, OVANDO J. Colorado Volunteers in New Mexico, 1862. 12mo, fine. Chicago, 1962. **$5.00**

[13]

item 61 in the Maggs catalog, or what is the difference between "very nice" (item 243) and "fine" (item 251) in the Morrill catalog, or between the "very good copy" (item 32) and a "good, clean copy" (item 33) from Heritage? [T.e.g. means "top edges gilt."] Some of the meanings will come only from knowing the particular dealer but some guidance can be found in books such as John Carter's *ABC for Book Collectors* (New York: Knopf, 4th ed., 1970) and/or *The Bookman's Glossary* (New York: R. R. Bowker, 1975). Carter provides illuminating and entertaining notes about dealer adjectives describing the condition of a book:

> *General.* –As new, fine, good, fair, satisfactory (a trifle condescending, this), good second-hand condition (i.e. not very good), poor (often coupled with an assurance that the book is very rare in any condition), used, reading copy (fit for nothing more and below collector's standard), working copy (may even need sticking together).
>
> *Of exterior.* –Fresh, sound (probably lacks 'bloom'), neat (implies sobriety rather than charm); rubbed, scuffed, chafed, tender (of JOINTS), shaken, loose, faded (purple cloth and green leather fade easily), tired (from the French *fatigué*), worn, defective (very widely interpreted), binding copy (i.e. needs it).
>
> *Of interior.* –Clean, crisp, unpressed, browned (like much later 17th century paper), age-stained, water-stained (usually in the deprecating form, 'a few light waterstains'), foxed (i.e. spotted or discolored in patches: often 'foxed as usual', implying that practically all copies are), soiled, thumbed (in the more lyrical catalogue notes, 'lovingly thumbed by an early scholar'), and (very rare in English or American catalogues, but commendably frank), washed.[5]

A careful review of the sample catalog pages herein will reveal many of these terms. The terms are subjective. What one dealer describes as fine another may call good. Buy on approval whenever possible, especially from a dealer that you are using for the first time.

This section, just as the one on new book stores, can only briefly outline some of the more significant points about the retail book trade. It has provided some basic information upon which you will constantly build as long as you buy and collect books for yourself or a library.

Other Media Retail Outlets

Due to the variety of their formats and purposes it is not possible to generalize about retail outlets for other media. Many of the formats are acquired directly from their producers, as noted in chapter 2, or from an educational media jobber. Others are handled as a sideline or minor element in a store actually specializing in another service.

The most common retail outlet for "other media" is the record shop. Many small communities have a record shop but do not have a bookstore. One reason is that each record has a relatively low sales price and a fairly large market exists for current popular music, especially that aimed at the young adult market. The top twenty recordings (records and tapes) of popular music may outsell the top twenty books by a 20-to-1 margin, at least in the United States.

Other than record shops, it is almost impossible to describe other media retail outlets, primarily because there are so few that it is hard to generalize. There are a few map shops in larger cities; most metropolitan areas have at least one sheet music store; and there are museums that sell slides and art reproductions. Educational models and games may be purchased from teacher supply stores. There are very few motion picture retail outlets, although there are several large mail order organizations, and a few rental stores in larger cities. Video recordings and microforms are generally purchased from their producers. In the chapter on selecting other media (chapter 7) sources will be discussed in more detail.

The distribution system for books and other library materials is varied and complex. You must know something about the system before you begin developing a library collection. This chapter has provided the *highlights* of what you need to know. It is just the beginning of a long, enjoyable learning process. Jobbers, bookdealers and media vendors are more than willing to tell you about how their work is affected by library activities when they know that you have taken time to learn something about their operations.

NOTES

[1] Ron Barney, "Opening a Bookstore," in *A Manual on Bookselling*, ed. for the American Booksellers Association by C. B. Anderson, G. R. Smith, and S. Cobb, 2nd ed. (New York: Crown Publ., 1974), p. 3.

[2] Trumball Huntington, "Store Windows and In-Store Displays," in *A Manual on Bookselling*, p. 257.

[3] Sol M. Malkin, "Rare and Out-of-Print Books," in *A Manual* . . . , p. 208.

[4] Ibid.

[5] John Carter, *ABC for Book Collectors*, 4th ed. (New York: Knopf, 1970), pp. 67-68.

BIBLIOGRAPHY

Jobbers and Wholesalers

American Library Association, Book Dealer-Library Relations Committee. *Guidelines for Handling Library Orders for In-Print Monographic Publications*. Chicago: ALA, 1973.

American Library Association. *Guidelines for Handling Library Orders for Serials and Periodicals*. Chicago: ALA, 1974.

Andersen, D. C. "Book Discounts and Cost-Plus Pricing." *Library Resources and Technical Services* 18 (Summer 1974): 248-52.

Bennett, F. "Prompt Payment of Book Dealers Invoices: An Approach to Standards." *College and Research Libraries* 14 (Oct. 1953): 387-92, 395.

Bromberg, E. "How the Birds (Pigeons) and Bees and Butterflies DO IT." *Special Libraries* 61 (April 1970): 168-70.

Bry, E. "International Distributors Convene in San Francisco." *Publishers Weekly* 206 (Sept. 30, 1974): 44-45.

"Buying and Selling Books and Manuscripts: Some Canons of Good Practice." *ALA Bulletin* 51 (Nov. 1947): 777-79.

Coppola, D. "Library-Book Trade Relations in the Field of Current Books." *College and Research Libraries* 17 (April 1956): 330-33.

Coppola, D. "The International Bookseller Looks at Acquisitions." *Library Resources and Technical Services* 11 (Spring 1967): 203-206.

Davidson, J. S. "Direct from the Publisher." *Publishers Weekly* 193 (July 1, 1960): 40-41.

"The 'Get-'Em-All' Theory of Book Buying." *Library Journal* 85 (Oct. 1, 1960): 3387-93.

Holt, P. "The Off-Beat World of Book People." *Publishers Weekly* 206 (Dec. 9, 1974): 33-34.

Jacobs, E. "Automatic Purchase of University Press Books." *Library Journal* 83 (March 1, 1958): 707-708.

Jordan, R. T. "Eliminate the Middlemen in Book Ordering." *School Library Journal* 86 (Jan. 15, 1969): 15-17.

Kim, U. C. "Purchasing Books from Publishers and Wholesalers." *Library Resources and Technical Services* 19 (Spring 1975): 138-47.

MacManus, G. S. "What Librarians Should Know about Book Buying." *Library Journal* 85 (Oct. 1, 1960): 3394-97; (Nov. 15, 1960): 4074; (Dec. 15, 1960): 4402.

Magruder, M. "The Big New Sound from Nashville." *Publishers Weekly* 203 (April 30, 1973): 42-43.

Melcher, D. "Discount Diversity." *Library Journal* 86 (Feb. 1, 1961): 960-62.

Obeirne-Ranelegh, E. "A Librarian Makes a Case for Ordering Direct." *Publishers Weekly* 205 (Jan. 14, 1974): 84.

"Open House Ritual at Raymar." *Publishers Weekly* 206 (Dec. 9, 1974): 36-37.

Paige, N. "Is It Habit or Law? Cutting the Red Tape of Library Book Buying." *School Library Journal* 89 (Feb. 15, 1964): 9-12.

Peckham, S. "A New Book Jobber for the Mountain States." *Publishers Weekly* 206 (Dec. 9, 1974): 34-35.

Pickett, A. S. "Advice to Book Dealers." *Library Journal* 85 (Dec. 15, 1960): 4402-4404.

Potter, F. H. "Book Wholesaling and Supply in California." *Publishers Weekly* 198 (Nov. 22, 1965): 57-59.

"Publishers Accused of Price Fixing." *Library Journal* 91 (May 1, 1966): 2292-94.

Ready, W. B. "Acquisition by Standing Order." *Library Resources and Technical Services* 1 (Spring 1956): 85-88.

Smith, R. H. "Ordering Books for the Christmas Rush." *Publishers Weekly* 206 (Aug. 19, 1974): 50-52.

"Suits News Company—Paperback Success Is an Educational Experience." *Publishers Weekly* 208 (Sept. 8, 1975): 44-48.

Veenstra, J. J. "The Stormy Marriage." *Library Journal* 88 (July 1963): 2634-36.

Veenstra, J. J. "When Do You Use a Jobber?" *College and Research Libraries* 23 (Nov. 1962): 522-24.

"What Wholesalers Think of Library Customers." *Library Journal* 84 (Feb. 1, 1959): 369-70.

New Book Stores

AB Bookman's Yearbook, 1959: Buying and Selling Books. Newark, NJ: ABA, 1959.

AB Bookman's Yearbook, 1960: ABC of Bookselling. Newark, NJ: ABA, 1960.

Anderson, C. B. *A Manual on Bookselling.* 2nd ed. New York: Harmony Books, 1974.

Anderson, C. B. *Bookselling in America and the World.* New York: Quadrangle, 1975.

Baker, R. E. *Books for All: A Study of International Book Trade.* Paris: Unesco, 1956.

Battle, G. "Let's Tackle the Publisher Practices That Frustrate the Bookseller." *Publishers Weekly* 207 (June 30, 1975): 46-49.

Brent, S. *The Seven Stairs.* New York: O'Hara, 1973.

Dessauer, J. P. "How to Make a Profit in Bookselling." *Publishers Weekly* 203 (April 2, 1973): 39-41; (April 19, 1973): 54-56; (April 16, 1973): 39-42.

Dickson, L. "Oxford (Blackwell's) as a Microcosm." *Bookseller* (Sept. 19, 1964): 1440-46.

Effron, J. "Fear and Loathing on the Discount Trail." *Publishers Weekly* 205 (June 17, 1974): 52-53.

Freilicher, L. "An Interview with Richard Noyes." *Publishers Weekly* 206 (Nov. 18, 1974): 43-44.

Harmon, G. "Eliot Leonard: 38 Years in Bookselling." *Publishers Weekly* 205 (June 3, 1974): 92-93.

Holt, P. "Community Consciousness Is Good Business for Berkeley's Unlimited Co-op." *Publishers Weekly* 208 (Sept. 1, 1975): 58-60.

Kimball, R. "Urban Explorer: Bookstores with Something for Just a Few." *Library Assistant* 20 (March 1975): 39-40, 42, 44.

Kimbrough, E. *Through Charley's Door.* New York: Harper, 1952.

Littleton, I. T. "The Bull's Head Bookshop—A Unique Library Bookstore." *College and Research Libraries* 43 (Dec. 1972): 232-33.

Maryles, D. "Crime Buffs Now Have Their Own Bookshop: 'Murder Ink.'" *Publishers Weekly* 202 (Dec. 4, 1972): 32-33.

Mitchell, S. "Texan Builds Dallas Bookstore into Million-Dollar Business." *Publishers Weekly* 207 (Jan. 13, 1975): 46-47.

"Most Children's Bookstore Owners Find It a Struggle—But a Highly Rewarding One." *Publishers Weekly* 207 (Feb. 24, 1975): 104-106.

Navasky, V. S. "In Cold Print: Thriving in Chairs." *New York Times Book Review* (April 20, 1975): 3, 34.

Noyes, J. "American View: Selling Children's Books in London, Penzance and Paris." *Publishers Weekly* 194 (Dec. 16, 1968): 14-17.

Pogrebin, L. C. "A Heroine of Gotham." *New York Times Book Review* (Dec. 31, 1972): 6.

Powell, L. C. *Vroman's of Pasadena.* Los Angeles: Ritchie, 1953.

Rogers, W. G. *Wise Men Fish Here: The Story of Frances Steloff and the Gotham Book Mart.* New York: Harcourt, 1965.

Rosenberg, B. "The College Bookstore in the U.S." *Journal of Documentation* 21 (Sept. 1965): 190-98.

"Rubbing Shoulders with the Right People at New York's Madison Ave. Bookshop." *Publishers Weekly* 205 (Feb. 18, 1974): 63-64.

Russ, L. *The Girl on the Floor Will Help You.* New York: Doubleday, 1969.

Smith, R. H. "Books and Men at Yale." *Publishers Weekly* 203 (June 10, 1973): 50-55.

"Views on Bookselling: Salt Lake City's Sam Weller Champions the Cause of Regional Bookselling." *Publishers Weekly* 205 (March 4, 1974): 54-55.

Antiquarian and Out-of-Print Bookstores

AB Bookman's Yearbook. Newark, NJ: AB Bookman's Pub. [Annual].

Adams, S. *The O.P. Market: A Subject Directory of the Out-of-Print Book Trade.* New York: R. R. Bowker, 1943.

American Book-Prices Current. New York: American Book Prices Current, 1895- [Annual].

Antiquarian Booksellers Association of America. *Book Dealers in North America.* New York: ABAA, 1970.

Antiquarian Booksellers Association of America. *A Directory of Secondhand and Antiquarian Booksellers in the British Isles.* New York: ABAA, 1972.

Benjamin, M. A. "Catalogs and Cataloging." *The Collector* No. 5-8 (1966). [All issues].

Bookman's Glossary. 5th ed. New York: R. R. Bowker, 1975.

Bookman's Price Index. Detroit: Gale, 1969- .

Book-Prices Current. London: Sargeants Press, 1888- [Annual].

Bradley, V. A. *The Book Collector's Handbook of Values.* New York: Putnam, 1972.

Carter, J. *ABC for Book Collectors.* 4th ed. New York: Knopf, 1971.

"Current Trends in Antiquarian Books." *Library Trends* 9 (April 1961): [entire issue].

Dorn, R. W. "Otto Harrassowitz, Buchhandlung-Verlag-Antiquoriet: The First Century." *Harvard Library Bulletin* 21 (Oct. 1973): 365-67.

Edelstein, J. M. *A Garland for Jake Zeitlin on the Occasion of His 65th Birthday and the Anniversary of His 40th Year in the Book Trade.* Los Angeles: Dahlstrom, 1967.

Hanff, H. *84 Charing Cross Road.* New York: Grossman, 1970.

Heard, J. N., and J. H. Hoover. *Bookman's Guide to Americana.* 7th ed. Metuchen, NJ: Scarecrow, 1977.

Johnson, M. D. V. *American First Editions.* 4th ed. New York: R. R. Bowker, 1942.

Magee, D. *Infinite Riches: The Adventures of a Rare Book Dealer.* New York: Eriksson, 1973.

Malkin, S. M. "Catalogs Are the First Reading for Any Bookman." *AB Bookman's Weekly* 53 (Jan. 20, 1964): 114-21.

Malkin, S. M. "Some ABCs of the Antiquarian Book Trade." *AB Bookman's Weekly* 55 (Jan. 31, 1972): 351-53.

Perez, E. R. "Acquisitions of Out-of-Print Material." *Library Resources and Technical Services* 17 (Winter 1973): 42-59.

Peters, J. *Book Collecting: A Modern Guide.* New York: R. R. Bowker, 1977.

Ricci, S. *Book Collector's Guide.* Philadelphia: Rosenbach, 1921.

Rostenberg, L., and M. B. Stern. *Old and Rare: Thirty Years in the Book Business.* New York: Schram, 1974.

Schiller, J. G. "Memoirs of an Antiquarian Bookseller." *Horn Book* 49 (Oct. 1973): 442-43.

Tarshish, M. B. "Goodspeed's: The Yankee Bookseller from Boston." *Publishers Weekly* 197 (June 30, 1969): 54-56.

Tyler, R. "The Book Detectives." *Bookviews* 1 (Feb. 1978): 12-17.

Zeitlin, J. "The Bookseller and the Librarian." *California Librarian* 35 (April 1964): 91-94.

Zeitlin, J. "Bookselling among the Sciences." *College and Research Libraries* 21 (Nov. 1960): 453-57.

Zeitlin, J. *Some Rambling Recollections of a Rambling Bookseller.* Los Angeles: Dahlstrom, 1970.

PART B

COLLECTION DEVELOPMENT PROCESS

Chapter 4

COMMUNITY ANALYSIS AND SURVEYS

Community analysis is defined as an attempt to enumerate the needs of a population living in a community. It may take the form of a community survey, study, or needs assessment. No matter what term is used, it is an essential element in any sound library service program for the community. Librarians cannot accurately assess the information needs of their communities by intuitive knowledge gained through observations at the circulation or reference desk. They must systematically analyze the community, using every available tool. Variables that may have an impact on community library service must be identified, the first step in the process. Data related to these variables are then gathered from various published sources. Additional relevant data that are not available must be generated by the library through such techniques as interviews and questionnaires.

WHY KNOW THE COMMUNITY?

The data are analyzed and interpreted in terms of the library's service goals for its community. New objectives may be established if it is determined that the library's present objectives are not in alignment with the needs of the community. The collection development policy can then be adjusted to reflect the new-found needs of the community. New programs will then be established to reach those segments of the community identified as the non-users. And of course, book selectors will use the data to plan their work. The last step of the process is to implement a policy of continuous study so that the library's objectives, programs, and collection can be adjusted on an on-going basis to meet the changing needs and interests of the people in the community.

One may ask, how does a library attempt such a monumental task? At this point in time, it would be extremely difficult to do, for nowhere in the library literature is there a manual or handbook that describes, step-by-step, how to carry out a community survey. ALA's Public Library Association (PLA) has recognized this shortcoming and is taking steps to remedy the situation by restructuring their 1966 *Standards.*[1] In establishing new standards for public library service, the PLA is using the concept of total community needs, as opposed to national or regional needs, as the basis for developing the new standards. Standards will emerge in each community through a five-step process: needs assessment; evaluation of existing library/information services; priority establishment; program development; and evaluation. The PLA's Goals, Guidelines and Standards Committee will develop a manual for each of the aspects used for determining the new standards, but the new standards will not be completed until 1981 or 1982. When completed, it is hoped that the proposed manual of needs assessment will go beyond the generalizations put forward over the years in the literature of the library community survey.

In the meantime, librarians must work independently to determine how to accurately assess community information needs. Consequently, in this chapter we will examine a method of community analysis for libraries using community participation. A great library resource, the people of the community, has been generally overlooked, yet citizen participation in community analysis serves a four-fold function: 1) publicity, 2) direct expression of needs, 3) voluntary help, and 4) involvement of citizens in library affairs. Publicity can make people in the community aware of the library, and it can inform them that the library is interested in their needs. Direct expression allows citizens the opportunity to voice their needs and interests to the body conducting the community survey. Voluntary help provides a pool of labor to help conduct the survey and, at the same time, promotes interest by involving citizens in library affairs (the concept will be fully described later in this chapter).

EXAMPLES OF COMMUNITY STUDIES

At just about the same time that McColvin was writing about the need to respond to community demands (in *The Theory of Book Selection for Public Libraries*), Joseph Wheeler published *The Library and the Community: Increased Book Service through Library Publicity Based upon Community Studies* (Chicago: ALA, 1924). He was among the first to identify community leader groups that could influence and help library service by aiding in an assessment of community needs. Probably the most frequently cited American monograph on library community studies is Everett McDiarmid's *The Library Survey: Problems and Methods* (Chicago: ALA, 1940). This is the closest that librarians can come to finding a step-by-step how-to-do-it library community analysis manual. Despite the book's length, its material on community analysis is limited and is presented in rather general terms. McDiarmid suggests some methods for measuring reading interest and the desire for reading materials, drawing distinctions between different purposes of surveys and types of libraries. He makes a strong case for studying the total community, not just the library's users.

The best manual presently available is Roland Warren's *Studying Your Community* (New York: Russell Sage Foundation, 1955). This work, despite its general social science orientation, is a good practical guide to general methods to employ. It must be supplemented with more current library-related studies and techniques. Nevertheless, you should add this to a reading list if you are serious about becoming a book selector.

One classic user study, Bernard Berelson and Lester Asheim's *The Library's Public* (New York: Columbia University Press, 1949), analyzed library user studies published between 1930-1949 and Berelson's own findings. By generalization and synthesis, he was able to develop an overall picture of public library users in the United States at that time. Some of his more important conclusions are that public libraries are: only used by 10 percent of the adult population, that they are essentially middle-class institutions, and that education is the most significant factor correlated with use. These results are probably still reasonably operative, although some later studies have cast some doubt on the degree to which Berelson's factors were independent variables.

Philip Hauser's "Community Developments and Their Effect on Library Planning" in *Library Journal*[2] gives a brief history of population changes in the United States, including total population growth, concentration of population in metropolitan areas, the shift away from the inner city, age structure, ethnicity and race, and family characteristics. He concludes that the "library and its branches will be faced with the need to adjust to the changing physical structure of the metropolitan area and changes in population composition and population type."[3] In other words, library use will depend upon the makeup of the community's population and where this population is located. These factors have implications far beyond collection development—new services, staffing, and even new physical facilities.

In "Patterns of Adult Library Use: A Regression and Path Analysis,"[4] Carol Kronus uses multi-variate analysis on a large sample of survey data gathered from adult library users in Illinois. The analysis reveals three principle factors as predictors of the rate of library use. Education (both in the number of years and plans for further education) is the most powerful, followed by family lifecycle factors (marital status and family size), and urban residence (as opposed to rural). Factors of age, sex, and race, which are commonly described as having a high influence on library use, had no independent effect on how often people used library resources. Kronus concluded that "the question of the causes behind library use is, therefore, wide open for study."[5] If we do not really know the causes of library use how can we build collections that people will use?

Urban Analysis for Branch Library System Planning[6] by Robert E. Coughlin and others, is the report of a study of the Philadelphia Free Library system aimed at discovering whether there are statistical relationships between the quality of the library itself and a branch's location relative to a population of varying social characteristics. One of the conclusions reached is that the socioeconomic level of a community's residents is the most important factor determining the amount of library use. Although not directed toward collection development problems this study provides insight into good community analysis techniques.

Charles Evans, in *Middle Class Attitudes and the Public Library Use*,[7] states that studies have shown several variables that distinguish users from non-users. They include age, education, sex, occupation, economic status, marital status, race, residence, and influence within the community. Why then, he asks, are there users and non-users who have the same social and economic characteristics? His answer is that use ultimately may depend upon their attitude toward the library, and that it may be possible to stimulate use by improving public attitudes toward the library. Clearly, one focus of any public relations program would be the collection.

Aleta S. Benjamin conducted a survey of registered voters in Ventura County, California,[8] in which she found that knowledge about the library is highly correlated to library use. Also, both occupation and distance from the library were related to knowledge about it. But there was no relationship of library knowledge to age, sex, marital status, duration of residence, income, or level of education. Finally, Arthur A. Kunz, in "The Use of Data Gathering Instruments in Library Planning,"[9] lists certain variables that he assumes have an effect on library use: age information used in conjunction with total population; educational level or number of people in institutions of higher learning; income by itself or used in conjunction with education and place of employment; and racial or ethnical background. In addition, he briefly outlines how librarians can gather this data for use in a community study.

This is an extremely diverse group of opinions and variables, many of which directly contradict one another. There is obviously a need for further research in this area. Lowell Martin insists that the problem lies in areas that usually are considered outside the scope of the librarian's role.[10] American librarianship has been hesitant to explore geographical and sociopsychological areas that would reveal variables explaining why libraries are used and whether that use benefits the individual and the community. Until this area is thoroughly researched and a set of variables is established that can accurately indicate use and the benefits from it, the outcome of social factor studies will be marginal. At this point it may be necessary for libraries involved in community studies to choose variables that are thought to influence library use in their own communities, since general research up to the present has been inconclusive.

Hundreds of libraries (perhaps even thousands) have managed to survive without a survey. However, have such libraries just *survived*? How much longer will they survive? Why is it so difficult to get library bond issues passed? Why is it that more and more commercial firms are coming into existence that charge fees for and make a profit by providing information and services that libraries have been offering for free? The answers to these questions are complex but two elements are relevant to this book in general and to this chapter in particular. First of all, libraries do *not* serve the *total* community and the staff does not know what the community needs. Second, commercial organizations emphasize their finding the best information—a selection process of a high order—while libraries tend to be satisfied with having something rather than the best: "Find out what the user needs and then supply it" is their motto. At first they must search out the information in various sources in libraries, although in time such firms acquire most of the basic sources in order to have them immediately available. Despite this, they keep going back to the user (buyer) for feedback; they also keep checking to determine if new needs exist or old needs have changed. What they are doing is providing a special library service, in this case, to a group of businesses or the general public. Special libraries have always made it a point to stay current with patron needs; if they do not they cease to exist. Only academic and public libraries have been able to more or less ignore user needs and still survive.

ELEMENTS OF THE SURVEY

As soon as you decide that a full-scale community study is needed, you must answer a number of essential questions: 1) who is to collect the information? 2) what information do you want? 3) what methods will be employed to collect the data? 4) where can the data be found? 5) how will the data be interpreted?

Who Will Do the Study?

A number of factors will enter into the decision as to who will carry the primary responsibility for supervising and running the study: the financial support (library budget or supplemental funds), the number and qualifications of personnel available (staff members or outside consultants), and the depth and breadth of the study.

Any survey of major proportions must have the financial backing to hire a qualified and experienced consultant. Often the only way in which a major study can be handled is by a committee comprising both paid and volunteer workers. Committees do pose many problems, but lack of sufficient funding for other approaches may force use of them. The head librarian and the rest of the library staff must be strongly involved if the project is to succeed. The use of a library staff team, while a financial saving, needs to be carefully considered. An inexperienced team can waste inordinate amounts of time and energy. Furthermore, to be effective, team members should be allowed to do the survey during their regular working hours, which can cause staffing problems. A staff team may also draw conclusions based upon individual members' personal biases concerning a particular area or aspect of the community rather than from the actual research efforts of the project.

A compromise solution is to hire an outside consultant to formulate a plan of attack that is then implemented by the library staff. One problem in using this approach is that the consultant must divide the tasks into units small enough to be handled by personnel who are not fully trained in survey methods. The staffing problem, which is a significant one, must be weighed against the consequences of failing to conduct any survey at all. One way to overcome the problem of a lack of staff time and experience in community survey work is to make the project a regular aspect of collection development activities. Many of the larger academic libraries have started moving in this direction already with subject specialists. To some degree this movement is accidental, as the literature on the reasons for and functions of the subject specialist gives little indication that formalized survey work is ever a primary concern. Contact with faculty, working in conjunction with faculty and specialized users, developing subject areas in the light of institutional and patron needs—all are commonly cited activities. In essence, the foundation is present in such libraries for subject specialists to conduct on-going community surveys. A meeting once a year with each faculty member whose subject interest touches on the area of responsibility will maintain close contact with community needs.

If the job description for selection personnel includes community survey work, the problem is solved. That is, a person hired for the position should have a background in survey work. By including the survey as one of several tasks making up the full-time position, the library builds in adequate time and staffing in order to develop and maintain an on-going community survey program. Of course there is the problem of convincing funding authorities. Adding survey work to job descriptions would, in effect, increase the staff size by one (or more) full-time position(s). Apparently community survey work has not been thought to be that important because very few libraries employ this technique.

Using the library staff as the surveying group offers several advantages. First, although a less thorough study may result, there is a more practical basis for the formulation of a collection or a selection policy because the data will be collected with a thorough understanding of how it is to be used. A library team should have already gained useful information through day-to-day work; for example, they will have taken requests for and/or attempted to locate information that the library did not have; or have been involved in programs that involved users of all ages, backgrounds, and professions, and thus provide(d) data for the study.

Another useful outcome of using a library staff team comes from the personal commitment that can be gained through the process of the team's members learning about their community. Also there is a greater willingness of those involved in such a project to accept the results and to use those results on a day-to-day basis. Less time is required to inform the rest of the staff about the results because normal social interaction cuts across many barriers; more time often is needed when the study is handled by an outside consultant, as resistance may be higher and communication of results more difficult. Once the decision as to "who" will run the project has been made, though, the other issues must be handled. A clear statement of the study's objectives and a detailed listing of the steps to be taken and the questions to be asked must be developed.

What Will Be Studied?

Each type of library will have a slightly different definition of the word community. In the context of the public library, it will mean the political jurisdiction that such a library serves; for the academic library it will be the institution it is to serve; and for the special library it will be the company, business, institution, or foundation that established it. With these basic distinctions in mind it is possible to identify eleven broad categories of what data to collect for all types of libraries.

1) *Historical* data is useful in several ways. Understanding a community's historical development may lead to a better, and sometimes quicker, understanding of where that community stands today. Historical background information may also provide clues as to which areas of the collection might be weeded or areas in which it is no longer necessary to acquire material.

2) *Geographic* information may involve such questions as: in which physical direction is the community growing? are there physical barriers to growth? what is the distribution of population over the geographic area? This type of information helps in the determination of service points, which in turn influences the number of duplicates that the library needs to acquire. (Duplicate copies cut into the number of *titles* the library can buy.) Geographic and transportation data, considered next, are intertwined and should be considered together.

3) *Transportation* availability combined with geographic factors are important in deciding on how many service points are needed and their locations. Merely noting the existence of a bus service does not provide enough information for a meaningful survey. How often is there service? What does it cost? What are the hours of service? What is the

level of use? Answers to these questions become vital to answering questions regarding service points and service hours. As noted above, service points and hours have impact on plans for developing the collection. Often large academic and industrial organizations provide their own internal transportation systems, especially in urban areas. The existence of its own good internal transportation system may help a library to build a more varied collection. A courier system may help alleviate the need for as many (or as large) branch operations. Reduction in the number of branches, while still maintaining the same level of service, can reduce the need for duplicate materials.

4) *Legal* research will not be too difficult nor will the amount of data be large. Nevertheless, it may determine how the collection is to be developed. In some academic institutions the teaching faculty has the legal right to expend all book funds. Although there is no longer any institution where this legal authority is exercised to its fullest, cases of limited implementation do exist. Also the right may exist but most persons—including the librarians—will have forgotten about it until a problem arises. Preparing for a possible problem is usually less difficult than dealing with an existing one, or a surprise. Clear-cut policies about the delegation of selection authority and responsibility may help to avoid a problem.

Knowledge of how a community's legal system functions can also be important. Where does authority lie? To which bodies is the library accountable, especially for collection development? Are there any legal restrictions on what the library may buy with monies allocated for collection development? Some jurisdictions, up until a few years ago, had regulations making it illegal to buy anything except books, periodicals, and newspapers; thus, other media could not be purchased. How does one go about changing the regulations? Knowledge of the library's legal position will help answer the questions.

5) *Political* information is related to legal data on both the formal and informal levels. Formally, such questions arise as: to what extent is the library a political issue? if political parties exist, are there differences in their attitudes toward library and information services? what is the distribution of party affiliations in the community? are some areas more politically conservative or liberal than others? should library service point collections reflect these philosophical differences? Informally, questions concern: how do the politics of the community work? who are the individuals who influence fiscal decisions? in an academic or special library environment, what are the politics of the allocation of collection development funds? Answers to most of these questions will not have a direct bearing on which actual titles go into the collection. They will, however, influence the way in which funds are secured and allocated.

6) *Demographic* data is fundamental in formulating a knowledgeable collection development program. Basic changes in the composition of the population are inevitable, but only by monitoring the community

can such changes be anticipated. Waiting until change has occurred creates an image of a slow-to-change "Establishment" institution at best. Libraries have enough problems with their image without adding to them unnecessarily. For example, academic institutions and libraries operated for years on the premise that their student bodies would continue to grow in size. Census data in the 1960s indicated a sharp drop in the birth rate. This fact, combined with widespread discontent with the higher education system, should have been clear indication that the growth would not continue. However, only after several years of declining or stable enrollment did academic institutions react to the "news," which was available for more than 18 years. Public libraries had a somewhat similar problem with shifts of population out of the inner cities. Occasionally such shifts can change the city's tax base, which in turn affects the library. Other changes in the population (age, education, nationality, health, etc.) should be considered in developing a collection.

7) *Economic* data are useful from the standpoints of planning and of the overall collection. Knowledge of the existing economic base of the community and possible changes in it can be used to plan overall collection development activities. Anticipating increases or decreases in funding can lead to a more even collection, especially for serial publications. Viewing the collection as a whole, an economy based upon semiskilled or unskilled workers will call for one type of collection; a skill-based economy, another; while the group termed "knowledge worker" would require still another. Communities with a seasonal economy or a predominantly worker population will be faced with several problems. If the seasonal population is to be given service, what type of service, what formats would be best? When you know the answers to these and similar questions you can begin to build a useful collection.

8) *Communication systems* available to the community can be of some importance to the library's mission. Closed circuit and cable television may become very valuable resources. Already important in the primary and secondary schools, television is becoming a factor in higher education and in the education of the whole community. Public access to cable television—one channel exclusively reserved for community use—has already had some impact on libraries. One community has reference service by cable television and telephone;[11] several have story hours on cable.[12] Use of cable television will open up new areas of service, patron access, and collection development needs.

9) *Social* and *educational* organizations reflect the values of the persons making up society. While social patterns are slower to change than individual attitudes, such patterns must be considered in planning an integrated collection building program. Social clubs, unions, service organizations all have an impact and reflect community interests. The most influential group of organizations at their level of use is the existing educational programs. An academic institution is not just a 2-year, 4-year, and post-graduate program anymore. Evening adult

education classes, day and night degree programs, off-campus classes, and even some "remedial" high school level course work make for a complex instructional program, each facet having rather different information needs. Public libraries need to be concerned not only with public and private primary and secondary schools, but also with adult vocational programs and higher education. Special libraries in business are usually set up to serve specialized research and development needs; however, in-house training programs may also require public or academic library support.

10) *Cultural and recreational organizations* also reflect community interests. As with social organizations these formal groups give useful clues to highly specialized interest areas *with* enough community interest to sustain a formal group. Such groups, when given library service, often become some of the library's most solid and influential supporters. (This category does not really apply to the special library because its collection and service areas are clearly defined by the organization it serves.)

11) *Other community information sources* are, in some respects, the most important elements in the collection development program. If a number of community sources are identified, and if a working cooperative agreement is reached, everyone will benefit. All too often the public, school, and academic libraries in the same political jurisdiction will operate as if they existed in total isolation. When all of the libraries are publicly supported, considerable resources and service are wasted if there are no cooperative programs. The first step in achieving a cooperative arrangement is to know what resources exist and what is available. In addition to knowing what library resources exist in the community, the librarian should know about other information resources such as bookstores, record shops, newspapers, radio and television stations, and motion picture theaters. Some writers on selection, among them David Spiller,[13] have suggested fewer recreational materials in the library if other recreational outlets are available to the community. What things does the local community respond to? Again this applies primarily to public and academic libraries, and the latter often must work out a meaningful agreement with the media center (learning resources center) as to formats to be acquired.

How and Where Are Data Collected?

Knowing what you need to know is only one-third of the battle; knowing how to get the information is the second two-thirds. The fields of social welfare and sociology have developed a number of methods for systematically studying the community. Community studies may be divided into four primary types: 1) Key Informant, 2) Community Forum, 3) Social Indicators, and 4) Field Survey. All of these methods can be employed in various combinations—they are not mutually exclusive. Furthermore, they may be conducted by an outside consultant, by the library staff, or by the citizen/library committee.

Key Informant. Key informants are citizens who are in a position to be aware of the needs of the people of the community. Included are public officials, officers of community organizations, business leaders, the clergy, and certain unofficial leaders in the community who are nonetheless influential and are viewed as knowledgeable about community affairs. These individuals are contacted and interviewed to ascertain their opinions and ideas concerning the community's information needs. In order to be effective, a tested interview schedule needs to be drawn up. A tested interview schedule is one that has been pre-used (tested) to determine the types of answers that questions would generate. Individuals will always differ as to what a question "really means." Pretesting questions allows a team to reduce the range of interpretation by rewording ambiguous or confusing questions. There should not be too many interviewers, and unless they have had extensive experience in interviewing, they *must* have strong training before they begin.

There are some disadvantages to the key informant approach. The informants are not actually representative of the community in terms of statistical probability, since they are not randomly selected. They may not be aware of all segments of the population that are in need of library services, nor of their needs. Their opinions have a personal bias; they may perceive the community's information needs much differently than do the individuals who make up the community. In essence, this kind of interview supplies a great deal of subjective information about the community, which is necessary input to a total study.

Despite these disadvantages, the key informant approach is relatively easy to prepare and implement, it requires the least amount of time to collect the data, and it is very helpful in making key community people aware of the problem of providing the information needed by a diverse community. You should, however, supplement this data with other statistical data and, when possible, with a more representative cross-section of community opinion.

Community Forum. The community forum can be compared to an old-fashioned town meeting. This approach is not selective, as all members of the community are invited to participate in a number of public meetings, and to express their opinions about what can or should be done to improve library services. The key to success for this approach lies in extensive publicity. Several ways can be used to encourage people to attend. Letters can be mailed to individuals and selected organizations to publicize the meeting and its purpose. Utilization of the mass media, including newspapers, radio and television, is also a standard means for advertising public meetings. In a large community, a number of meetings may have to be planned in order to keep the groups small enough so that people will feel comfortable in expressing their opinions, since many individuals have difficulty speaking up in a large crowd. In order to make these meetings useful some structure must be provided by the survey team. Certain questions must be raised at all of the meetings. It is usually desirable to have the entire survey team present at all meetings or to tape the meetings. There also needs to be a certain period of time set aside for comments from the group which are not related to the survey team's questions.

The advantages of the community forum are that they are easy to arrange and inexpensive to conduct. Forums also help to identify those individuals who are interested in improving the quality of library service in their community. These people may later be persuaded to help implement the programs that are necessary to correct any deficiencies in library service. One glaring disadvantage of the community forum is that people who are non-users of the library will not, in all probability, attend the meetings. If they feel they have no need for the library, why should they be interested in spending their time to improve services they never use? Another major disadvantage is that the data obtained are mostly impressionistic and subjective. This type of data is extremely difficult to categorize, and it is not readily amenable to systematic analysis. Although these disadvantages are serious, the community forum still stands as a major grassroots democratic process in soliciting opinions, ideas, and criticism from the general population.

Social Indicators. Over the last few years a method has been developed in the social sciences for determining the needs of certain segments of a community. "Social indicators" is the recently adopted term that describes this method. "The notion of the city as a constellation of 'natural areas' has . . . proven useful as a method of describing social subdivisions within communities."[14] A "natural area" is a unit within the community that can be set apart from other units or areas by certain characteristics. Those characteristics, or social indicators, may be: 1) geographical features such as rivers or transportation patterns; 2) sociodemographic characteristics, such as age, sex, income, education, and ethnicity; 3) population factors, including distribution, density, mobility, and migration; 4) the spatial arrangements of institutions; and 5) health and social well-being characteristics, such as condition of housing or suicide rates.[15]

The social indicators approach to needs assessment can infer certain needs of a community by studying the relevant indicators. By using descriptive statistics found in public records and reports, the library involved in community analysis can deduce certain of the information needs of the community's population. In selecting factors that have been determined to be highly correlated with those people in need of information, surveyors are able to extrapolate the information needs of the whole community. What these social indicators (in library parlance, "factors," "variables," or "characteristics") may be is a point of much disagreement among researchers in the field of library science. The following are some examples of social indicators found in the literature that illustrate the great diversity of opinion:

1.	age	5.	health
2.	sex	6.	employment
3.	education	7.	marital status
4.	income	8.	domicile location

Once the indicators have been selected, the needed data can then be collected from several existing sources. The most detailed and accurate source is the U.S. Census. Census tracts (the breakdown into neighborhoods or communities of a few thousand people) are excellent sources available from the Bureau of the Census. The major drawback with census data is that it is taken only once every ten years. (A population estimation is done annually, but statistics are not compiled for areas smaller than counties.) In rapidly changing communities, this can be a problem, as the statistics may be misleading once several years have elapsed since the last census. But other sources are available for up to date local data. Regional, county, or city planning agencies gather statistics and make projections that can be useful.

In addition, school boards, chambers of commerce, and police departments compile statistics.

For the actual investigation, a unit of analysis such as census tracts or block groupings must be selected. Census tracts appear to be the most widely used unit of analysis for community studies, and the data from the tracts are readily available. If a large area is being covered, the sheer number of workable units will not become unwieldy.

The Field Survey. The field survey approach to community analysis is based on the collection of data from a sample or entire population of people living within a given area. The most common means of collecting data is through interview schedules or questionnaires. The methods most frequently used are the telephone interview, the person-to-person interview, and the mailed questionnaire, each of which employs a series of questions. In the community survey for public libraries, questions may be designed to elicit from an individual or household information regarding their frequency of use of the library, reading habits, economic and/or educational background, or any other information that the library feels will provide insight into use, and especially non-use, of the library. An example of a questionnaire is shown in Figure 12.

Care must be taken when designing questions so that the individual's rights to privacy are not violated. If the person or group designing the questionnaire is not certain of the legality of the questions, reliable legal counsel should be consulted. Questions that are asked of the community should have a direct relationship to the objectives of the survey. Those questions that are designed to elicit peripheral information tend to fatten the questionnaire, raise the cost of the survey, and overburden the respondent. This, in turn, may decrease the response rate and reduce the validity of the findings.

A choice should be made between a structured or unstructured format for the questionnaire/schedule. Open-ended questions (unstructured format) take more time to answer than the fixed-alternative type of questions (structured format), which in turn affects the response rate. Open-ended questions are also much more difficult to code and analyze and are limited to only a few methods of statistical analysis. When using volunteers to conduct interviews or to code and analyze the data, the structured format is much easier to administer and, because of the homogeneity of the responses obtained, is more readily coded and analyzed. Use of volunteers also requires that careful instructions be prepared to assure accurate results. Instructions for the use of the questionnaire form that appears in Figure 12, can be found on pages 112-13.

The next step in the field survey is to select a sample. "The selection of the sample depends largely upon the information needed: the unit for analysis, i.e., individuals, households, etc.; the type of data gathering techniques used; and the size it must be to adequately represent the population from which it is drawn."[16] Also, cost must be taken into account when selecting a sample. A large sample may call for complex selection methods and may take several work-hours to conduct the survey. Of course, the use of volunteers can keep the cost down, but the survey method, including sampling, is not a simple procedure. This is an area in which the services of a paid consultant may be required.

A popular method of obtaining information from respondents is through the personal interview. This permits face-to-face contact, stimulates a free exchange of

Figure 12

Community Survey Sample

GK

Griffenhagen-Kroeger, Inc.

PUBLIC MANAGEMENT CONSULTANTS / LOS ANGELES, 1543 West Olympic Blvd., Calif. 90015 (213) 381-7058

January 15, 1975

Dear Pasadena Area Resident:

You can assist in the continued success of the Pasadena libraries by filling out this form and returning it in the enclosed self-addressed stamped envelope before February 2, 1975. This will take only a short time. All answers are confidential. DO NOT SIGN.

Thank you for your assistance.

Very sincerely,

Edward W. Kelley

Edward W. Kelley, Vice President

INSTRUCTIONS

Please answer and return this form, even if you have never used one of the Pasadena public libraries. There are spaces for as many as five different people in one home to answer. Each person should put his answers in the same lettered column each time. Each person should answer by putting an "X" in the proper box in his column. An example is shown below:

EXAMPLE

How many books did you borrow from a Pasadena library in the month of December 1974?

	First Person A	Second Person B	Third Person C	Fourth Person D	Fifth Person E
None			X		
1-3 books	X	X			
4-10 books				X	
more than 10 books					

In this example:

The person answering in column A borrowed 1 to 3 books last December.
The person answering in column B also borrowed 1 to 3 books last December.
The person answering in column C did not borrow any books last December.
The person answering in column D borrowed 4 to 10 books last December.
There are only four people in this home, so no one answers in the fifth column.

QUESTIONS

1. Where do you live?

	A	B	C	D	E
Pasadena					
Altadena					
South Pasadena					
San Marino					
other_____					

2. If you live in Pasadena, use the map on the back side of this questionnaire and tell us in what lettered part of the City you live.

	A	B	C	D	E
Section A					
Section B					
Section C					
Section D					
Section E					
Section F					
Section G					
Section H					
Section I					

Reprinted courtesy of Griffenhagen-Kroeger, Inc.

(Figure 12 continues on page 110)

Figure 12 (cont'd)

Page 2

			First Person A	Second Person B	Third Person C	Fourth Person D	Fifth Person E

3. Age

	A	B	C	D	E
Under 6 years					
6-12 years					
13-17 years					
18-25 years					
26-45 years					
46-62 years					
Over 62 years					

4. Highest Grade Completed

	A	B	C	D	E
8th grade					
12th grade					
College, 4 years					
College, 4 years +					

5. Occupational Status

	A	B	C	D	E
Employed					
Housewife					
Retired					
Student(full-time)					
Looking for work					

6. Have you used one of the Pasadena Public Libraries during the last 12 months?

	A	B	C	D	E
Yes					
No					

If "NO" please tell us why in your own words or choose one or more of the following reasons.

	A	B	C	D	E
Does not have the records I want.					
Does not have the books I want.					
Library is not open when needed.					
Parking is difficult.					
I use another library.					

IF YOU ANSWERED "NO" PLEASE OMIT THE REST OF THIS FORM.
IF YOU ANSWERED "YES" PLEASE GO ON TO THE NEXT QUESTIONS.

7. How often do you use one of the Pasadena Public Libraries?

	A	B	C	D	E
Less than once a month					
Once a month					
Once a week or more					

8. How do you use the Pasadena Public Library?

	A	B	C	D	E
Phoning for information.					
Going to the library.					
Both.					

9. Do you usually use the

	A	B	C	D	E
Central Library(on Walnut)					
Allendale Branch					
Hastings Branch					
Hill Avenue Branch					
Lamanda Park Branch					
La Pintoresca Branch					
Linda Vista Branch					
San Rafael Branch					
Santa Catalina Branch					

How many blocks is this library from your home?

Figure 12 (cont'd)

Page 3

		First Person A	Second Person B	Third Person C	Fourth Person D	Fifth Person E

10. What other branch libraries do you use?

Central Library(on Walnut)
Allendale Branch
Hastings Branch
Hill Avenue Branch
Lamanda Park Branch
La Pintoresca Branch
Linda Vista Branch
San Rafael Branch
Santa Catalina Branch

11. What other libraries do you use? Please list:

12. How do you usually get to the library which you use most often?

	A	B	C	D	E
Walk					
Bus					
Drive					
Bicycle					
Ride with someone else					

13. How long do you usually stay?

	A	B	C	D	E
1/2 hour or less					
1 to 2 hours					
3 hours or more					

14. When do you usually use the library?

	A	B	C	D	E
Mornings					
Afternoons					
Evenings					
Saturdays					
Lunch Hour					

15. Why do you use the library?

	A	B	C	D	E
Pleasure					
Attend Programs					
General Information					
Technical Research					
Business & Financial Info.					
As a study hall					
Job Preparation					

16. What services of the CENTRAL library do you use?

	A	B	C	D	E
Childrens					
Reference					
Business/Industry					
Fine Arts					
Borrow Material					
Non-Fiction Books					
Fiction Books					
Films					
Records					
Readers' Advisory Service					
Newspapers/Magazines					

17. What services of the BRANCH library do you use?

	A	B	C	D	E
Childrens					
Reference					
Business/Industry					
Fine Arts					
Borrow Material					
Non-Fiction Books					
Fiction Books					
Films					
Records					
Readers' Advisory Service					

(Instructions for use of questionnaire form are on page 112)

Instructions for Use of Questionnaire Form

A.   Read questionnaire form thoroughly once or twice to be sure you yourself are familiar with the format.

B.   Approach.

1.   Stand or sit where you can easily approach individuals coming in but so that you do not obstruct traffic or work flow.

2.   Smile and courteously hand out a copy of this questionnaire to each individual coming into library with explanation (see below).

3.   DO NOT FORCE the questionnaire on to anyone, but try to distribute to a "mix" of people, i.e., some adults (male & female); some teen agers (male & female); some children.

C.   Explanation.

1.   Be prepared to explain to those receiving the questionnaire.

"Would you take a few minutes while you are in the library today and complete this questionnaire?

It will take only a short time. All answers are confidential.

Do not sign your name.

Please fill out *even* if you do not regularly use the library.

We appreciate your cooperation, you can truly assist in the continued success of the Pasadena Library by filling this out.

Thank you."

Give only one questionnaire to each individual; advise individuals where they can sit; hand out pencils. Also say—"Please return the completed form to this box." (Show the box.)

2.   Some patrons may take the questionnaire and dash off without listening to the instructions. Do not pursue them, all questions are self-explanatory.

Instructions for Use of Questionnaire Form (cont'd)

3.   DO NOT answer any questions except those related to the mechanics or procedures re filling out and depositing the form.

Since each patron will be filling out an individual form, he or she will answer only Column A. Patrons should not fill it out for other family members who use the library but are not present at the time you hand out the questionnaire.

Questions about other library services should be referred to a library employee.

Questions about how the forms will be used should be answered simply by saying—"The City of Pasadena is interested in reviewing its library services; your responses will assist in the continued success of the Pasadena libraries."

SPECIAL NOTE: We want to be sure everyone answers question 2 (bottom of front page). Be sure to read this yourself and check the procedure so that if someone does not understand it and asks for advice you can explain it.

---

ideas, and has a high response rate. The telephone interview can also be used, but there is a limit to the amount of time that the interviewer can hold the interest of the respondent. Twenty minutes appears to be the maximum length for an efficient telephone interview. If the interview schedule is highly structured and the interviewer well trained, this can be an adequate amount of time to gather the necessary data.

Mail surveys also have certain inherent advantages and disadvantages in approach. They require lower staffing and less training than those surveys that depend on in-person interviews. These two advantages can greatly reduce the cost in time and money in conducting a survey. However, there are two significant disadvantages to the mailed survey.

One disadvantage is that generally there is low response rate. Organizations conducting mail surveys have reported a response rate as low as 35 percent, and such rates can seriously affect the validity and reliability of the collected data. Even with repeated mailings the response is low, and the cost of keeping track of who has or has not responded is high. Secondly, some persons in the community are unable to respond to anything but the simplest of questions. This may be especially true in communities where English may be the second language or may not be used at all. Of course, the problem of language can be overcome by printing the questionnaire in English and in one or two other languages that may be used in the community; but there is still a problem of the literacy level, no matter what language is used. Because of these disadvantages, then, libraries using the mail survey must carefully design the questionnaire, using the simplest and most succinct language possible, while still meeting their established objectives for gathering the needed information. They should also attempt to determine what the response rate will be before expending the time and money for a survey that could be of questionable value.

The survey approach, like the other needs assessment approaches, has certain advantages and disadvantages. The primary disadvantage is its cost. Designing large-sample methods, extensive interviewing, and advanced statistical analysis, for example, tend to raise the cost of this approach as compared with other approaches. Another disadvantage is that many individuals refuse to supply information about themselves or other family members. In many communities, the refusal or non-return rate may be so high as to make the data of questionable value.

However, one important advantage to the survey approach is that a survey, if carefully designed and administered, will produce the most accurate and reliable data for use in determining the information needs of the individuals who constitute the community. The other community needs assessment approaches are useful, but they have basic drawbacks: the key informants approach is not necessarily representative of the community; the community forum will probably not draw non-users; and variables indicating library use and what benefits are derived from that use have not been established yet for the social indicators approach. But when the field survey approach is combined with one or more of the other methods, it greatly enhances the findings. Results from the different methods can be compared and contrasted; especially valuable is the comparison of data from a user study with the data gathered by a field survey approach.

How Are Data to Be Interpreted?

Once collected, information must be prepared for analysis. The method chosen will depend upon the approaches used to collect the data and the capabilities of the agency or group performing the analysis. Tally sheets should be established so that each aspect or question of the study is listed along with its variables or responses. Each element is then manually tallied and the totals are calculated. Elementary statistical analysis, such as averages and standard deviations, can be performed at this time.

One simple and inexpensive method of analysis is to prepare maps indicating the units of analysis (e.g., census tracts) and the variables or responses analyzed. This method can be improved upon by using overlays, which can illustrate distribution of and relationships between the selected variables. This produces the best results when there are a small number of variables; analysis involving a large number of variables should be carried out by use of a more sophisticated technique. If a computer is available, the data can be punched onto cards or placed on magnetic tape, permitting advanced statistical analysis to be performed.

In order to present the findings of the study, a suitable format needs to be selected. The format will depend upon the community being studied, the type of survey, and the audience being addressed. Advanced statistical analysis may be a suitable format for those audiences that can understand the assumption and implications of such tests. But assuming that community analysis is to improve library services in the community, the findings always should be presented in such a way that individuals in the community, in public office, and in the library can easily understand their implications. This is best accomplished by descriptive summaries, charts, diagrams, and other visual aids.

Of course, the group who is primarily responsible for the analysis and presentation of the data is the project team. But just as they solicited the help of individuals and groups within the community to conduct the study, they should also ask these individuals to help with the analysis and presentation of the findings. The team should first present their findings in a preliminary report, which should be distributed to all those groups involved for their comments and suggestions.

The examination of the data by several citizens and groups allows for the identification of areas requiring action. This can be done by providing the opportunity for group discussions of the preliminary results; for instance, meetings such as those discussed in the section on the community forum approach can be utilized to obtain citizen feedback. If the preliminary conclusions are weak or unsubstantiated, group discussion will reveal that. These discussions will also reveal to the community the areas where action must be taken to improve library services. This type of public discussion will create a strong commitment for all those involved in the study to see that action is taken to improve services. Another advantage of involving several groups in the analysis is the disclosure of certain unmet needs and interests of the community that are not the responsibility of the library. Public disclosure of such community problems will bring them to the forefront, and possibly force some agency or group to assume responsibility for their correction. In this matter, not only will the study help to improve community access to information, but it can also benefit all aspects of community life.

Once the project staff has gathered all of the comments, suggestions, and citizen feedback, they should analyze their conclusions once more in preparation for the final report. The final report should include: the objectives of the study; methodology used to collect the data; a list of the identified problem areas; and a list of recommendations with priorities indicated for their implementation. The recommendations should include ones that are easily and economically implemented as well as solutions that call for extensive programming changes, but *all* recommendations should be realistic and feasible. "Blue sky" reports, where recommendations are uneconomical or unfeasible, are usually considered as pipe dreams by those who are responsible for the allocation of funding. The present and future resources of the library must be considered when making recommendations that will improve its services.

Each unit of the library should then take the report and examine it for implications for their work unit. Only after all units have completed their work can the selection staff start to assess the impact of the report. Only after all of the new needs and desired changes in programs and service are determined can a realistic collection development program be formulated.

The study finally may reveal segments in the community that are not being served by the library. The findings should indicate what areas of library service have contributed to this failure. Hours of service, location or lack of service points, attitude of staff, citizens' lack of knowledge about library programs, etc., are problems that could be identified and then corrected through recommended programs. For example, an extensive publicity campaign can be implemented using newspapers, radio, posters, and bulletins to inform the community of new and existing programs.

Since the information needs and interests of the community have been researched and identified, the collection development policy can be adjusted accordingly. For example, more older people may have moved into the community, requiring large print books and materials dealing with the problems of living on a limited income. But the most important element is: *do the present objectives of the library coincide with its new knowledge of the community?* Are the objectives in line with the current needs of the community, or do they reflect a past need, or do they only fulfill a self-serving purpose? The findings of the study should make this apparent, and if the objectives of the library do not reflect the needs and interests of its community, recommendations should be made for specific changes to assure that they do.

Following the completion of the study and the implementation of the recommendations, a program of continuous community analysis should be initiated. Statistical information can be easily kept current and additional information can be gathered by a smaller sample than that of the original survey. The amount of time and manpower needed for continuing analysis will be a fraction of that devoted to the original study. Once the initial study has been completed, the library's objectives, programs, and collection can be continuously adjusted to meet the changing information needs and interests of the people in the community, as reflected in the ongoing analysis.

CITIZEN PARTICIPATION

The idea of citizen participation in community analysis is drawn both from the literature of library science and from that aspect of social welfare called community organization. "Community organization refers to various methods . . . whereby a professional . . . helps a community . . . composed of individuals, groups or organizations to engage in planned collective action in order to deal with social problems within a democratic system of values."[17] Practitioners in community organization see "the participation of service users in institutional decision-making (as) one means of promoting consumer needs and protecting consumer interests."[18] In other words, in community organization the people of a community are seen as having a definite role in determining the type and quality of services that their institutions can provide to fulfill their needs.

Participation of citizens in the operation of public institutions is part of the democratic heritage: citizens must share in the decision-making process of the institutions that exist to serve them. To do otherwise is to undermine the very foundations upon which a free society is built. However, a select few have always tended to dictate to others what they think is best for the general welfare. During the past few years events have made most citizens aware that if public officials are allowed to make all decisions concerning public welfare, the people may suffer. Consequently, if legislation has not mandated citizen participation, then the people themselves have demanded it. Libraries are not exempt from this phenomenon. They are beginning to see the writing on the wall regarding community participation in policy-making. Lowell Martin expressed it this way:

Policy-making for libraries has been mainly in the hands of the professionals; the administrator and staff determine aims and programs for the most part, with trustees furnishing the stamp of approval. This may not be the structure of the future. Our institutions are being questioned, as is the role of professionals within them. If and as libraries become more essential, people will seek a more direct and active voice in what they do.[19]

Ensuring citizen participation in library affairs, especially in community analysis, is not an easy task, and several problems will be encountered when initiating a program of community participation. For example, it is difficult to find citizens who are both representative of the community and willing to participate. Recruitment and training of volunteers is also a difficult and time-consuming task. However, the greatest problem lies with librarians themselves. Most library administrators are trained professionals who feel that they have the expertise to run the library without the help of citizens in the community. They contend that citizen participation will be extremely time-consuming and actually may hinder the library's overall operation. They also contend that the general population does not have enough knowledge about libraries and librarianship to participate in decision-making functions concerning them.

These objections have some validity, but they can be overcome if the library administration believes that community service is the library's primary function, and that this service can be immensely improved by community analysis with the help of participating citizens. Of course, citizen participation *is* going to be a time-consuming affair, but there are few new programs in a library that will not require large amounts of time to initiate. In response to the criticism of the public's lack of knowledge in library affairs, this book is written in the belief that people in the community cannot learn about their library and its operation unless they are invited to participate. Participation becomes an educational experience for those citizens who volunteer or are asked to volunteer their services.

The traditional means of citizen participation—such as library boards, friends of the library groups, and volunteers—often overlook the disadvantaged and the non-users. These traditional methods do not encourage participation from all segments of the community, especially the group served. However, by relying mainly on citizens from all segments of the community (as opposed to one or a few experts) to conduct the community study, the library is soliciting a diverse number of opinions and ideas, some of which may never have been considered or explored by the experts. Also, who could be more knowledgeable about a community than its own residents?

Libraries have a democratic responsibility to utilize citizen participation to provide improved library services. By combining citizen participation and community analysis, the library is reaching out to the community and fulfilling its democratic obligations, while at the same time, it is determining what information the community both needs and desires. Community analysis is an essential element in providing sound library service to fulfill the information needs of the community. However, by utilizing citizen participation to conduct community analysis, the library can also fulfill the four-fold purpose of gaining publicity, voluntary help, direct expression of needs, and involvement of the people in library affairs. This democratic process will benefit both the library and the community.

NOTES

[1] Public Library Association, Standards Committee, *Minimum Standards for Public Library Systems, 1966* (Chicago: ALA, 1967).

[2] Philip M. Hauser, "Community Developments and Their Effect on Library Planning," *Library Quarterly* 27 (October 1957): 255-66.

[3] Ibid., p. 264.

[4] Carol L. Kronus, "Patterns of Adult Library Use: A Regression and Path Analysis," *Adult Education* 23 (Winter 1973): 115-31.

[5] Ibid., p. 130.

[6] Robert E. Coughlin, F. Taieb, and B. H. Stevens, *Urban Analysis for Branch Library System Planning* (Westport, CT: Greenwood, 1972).

[7] Charles Evans, *Middle Class Attitudes and Public Library Use* (Littleton, CO: Libraries Unlimited, 1970).

[8] Aleta S. Benjamin, *The Relationship between Selected Personal Factors and Knowledge of the Public Library of Selected Adults in Ventura County, California* (Washington: U.S. Department of Health, Education and Welfare, National Institute of Education, 1974).

[9] Arthur A. Kunz, "The Use of Data in Gathering Instruments in Library Planning," *Library Trends* 24 (Jan. 1976): 459-72.

[10] Lowell Martin, "User Studies and Library Planning," *Library Trends* 24 (Jan. 1976): 486.

[11] K. E. Dowlin, "Four Tools for Information Services in Libraries," *Wyoming Library Roundup* 29 (Dec. 1974): 7-10.

[12] L. E. Harrelson, "Cable Television and Libraries," *RQ* 14 (Summer 1975): 321-33.

[13] David Spiller, *Book Selection: An Introduction to Principles and Practice*, 2nd ed. (Hamden, CT: Shoe String Press, 1971).

[14] G. J. Warheit, R. A. Bell, and J. Schwab. *Planning for Change: Needs Assessment Approaches* (Rockville, MD: Alcohol, Drug Abuse and Mental Health Administration, n.d.), p. 48.

[15] Ibid.

[16] Ibid.

[17] R. M. Kramer and H. Specht, *Readings in Community Organization Practice*, 2nd ed. (Englewood Cliffs, NJ: Prentice-Hall, 1975), p. 6.

[18] G. Brager and H. Specht, *Community Organizing* (New York: Columbia University Press, 1969), p. 34.

[19] Martin, p. 495.

BIBLIOGRAPHY

American Library Association. Library Community Project. *Studying the Community: A Basis for Planning Library Adult Education Services.* Chicago: ALA, 1960.

American Library Association. Public Library Association, Goals, Guidelines and Standards Committee. "Goals and Guidelines for Community Library Service." *PLA Newsletter* 14 (June 1975): 9-13.

Babbie, E. R. *Survey Research Methods.* Belmont, CA: Wadsworth Pub. Co., 1973.

Benjamin, A. S. *The Relationship between Selected Personal Factors and Knowledge of the Public Library of Selected Adults in Ventura County, California.* (ED 090943). Washington: U.S. Department of Health, Education and Welfare, National Institute of Education, 1974.

Berelson, B., and L. Asheim. *A Report of the Public Library Inquiry: The Library's Public.* New York: Columbia University Press, 1949.

Bloss, M. "Standards for Public Library Service—Quo Vadis?" *Library Journal* 101 (June 1, 1976): 1259-62.

Brager, G., and H. Specht. *Community Organizing.* New York: Columbia University Press, 1969.

Brieland, D. "Community Advisory Boards and Maximum Feasible Participation." *American Journal of Public Health* 61 (Feb. 1971): 292-96.

Burke, E. M. "Citizen Participation Strategies." *Journal of the American Institute of Planners* 34 (Sept. 1968): 287-94.

Carnovsky, L., and L. Martin, eds. *The Library in the Community: Papers Presented before the Library Institute at the University of Chicago, August 23-28, 1943.* Chicago: University of Chicago Press, 1944.

Clift, V. A. "Community Control of Libraries: A Philosophical Position." *American Libraries* 1 (June 1970): 610-11.

Coughlin, R. E., F. Taieb, and B. H. Stevens. *Urban Analysis for Branch Library System Planning.* Contributions in Librarianship and Information Science, No. 1. Westport, CT: Greenwood Pub. Co., 1972.

Cox, F. M., J. L. Erlich, J. Rothman, and J. E. Tropman, eds. *Strategies of Community Organization: A Book of Readings.* 2nd ed. Itasca, IL: F. E. Peacock, 1974.

Drott, M. "Random Sampling: A Tool for Library Research." *College and Research Libraries* 30 (March 1969): 119-25.

Dunbar, E. M. "Library Resources. An Overview." *Library Trends* 10 (Oct. 1961): 243-48.

Evans, C. *Middle Class Attitudes and Public Library Use.* Littleton, CO: Libraries Unlimited, 1970.

Evans, G. E. *Management Techniques for Librarians.* New York: Academic Press, 1976.

Faibisoff, S. G., and D. P. Ely. *Information and Information Needs.* Washington: U.S. Office of Education, Division of Library Programs, 1974.

Fuller, M. L. "Looking at Your Community." *Illinois Libraries* 57 (Feb. 1975): 76-82.

Gotsick, P. *Community Survey Guide for Assessment of Community Information and Service Needs.* Public Library Training Institutes Library Service Guide, No. 2. Morehead, KY: Appalachian Adult Education Center, Morehead State University, n.d.

Hauser, P. M. "Community Developments and Their Effect on Library Planning." *Library Quarterly* 27 (Oct. 1957): 255-66.

Hiatt, P. "Standards for the Future: A New Approach." *PLA Newsletter* 15 (Fall 1976): 7-8.

Kramer, R. M., and H. Specht. *Readings in Community Organization Practice.* 2nd ed. Englewood Cliffs, NJ: Prentice-Hall, 1975.

Kronus, C. L. "Patterns of Adult Library Use: A Regression and Path Analysis." *Adult Education* 23 (Winter 1973): 115-31.

Kunz, A. A. "The Use of Data Gathering Instruments in Library Planning." *Library Trends* 24 (Jan. 1976): 459-72.

League of Women Voters Education Fund, State and Local Government Department. *So You Want to Do Something about Your Library.* Washington: The League, 1976.

McClarren, R. R. *Community Analysis.* Arlington, VA: U.S. Educational Resources Information Clearinghouse, 1967.

McDiarmid, E. W. *The Library Survey: Problems and Methods.* Chicago: American Library Association, 1940.

Martin, L. A. "User Studies and Library Planning," *Library Trends* 24 (Jan. 1976): 483-96.

Mogulof, M. G. "Local Experiences in Citizen Participation in the United States." *British Journal of Social Work* 2 (Autumn 1972): 387-99.

Monroe, M. E. "Community Development as a Mode of Community Analysis." *Library Trends* 24 (Jan. 1976): 497-514.

Newhouse, J. P., and A. J. Alexander. *An Economic Analysis of Public Library Services.* Santa Monica, CA: Rand, 1972.

Robbins, J. *Citizen Participation and Public Library Policy.* Metuchen, NJ: Scarecrow Press, 1975.

Warheit, G. J., R. A. Bell, and J. J. Schwab. *Planning for Change: Needs Assessment Approaches.* Rockville, MD: U.S. Alcohol, Drug Abuse and Mental Health Administration, n.d.

Warncke, R. "Analyzing Your Community: Basis for Building Library Service." *Illinois Libraries* 57 (Feb. 1975): 64-76.

Warren, R. L. *Studying Your Community.* New York: Russell Sage Foundation, 1955.

Webb, K., and H. P. Hatry. *Obtaining Citizen Feedback: An Application of Citizen Surveys to Local Governments.* Washington: Urban Institute, 1973.

Weinberg, E. *Community Survey with Local Talent: A Handbook.* Report No. 123. Chicago: National Opinion Research Center, 1971.

Wheeler, J. L. *The Library and the Community: Increased Book Service through Library Publicity Based on Community Studies.* Chicago: American Library Association, 1924.

Chapter 5

COLLECTION DEVELOPMENT POLICIES

Collection development policies, selection policies, acquisition policies—are they all one and the same? Given the definitions in chapter 1, you know this is not so. However, many librarians use the terms interchangeably. You will even find some of the same information in policies variously identified as a collection development, a selection, or an acquisition policy, assuming that the library has a written policy. One library school professor who teaches collection development tells her classes, "On the first day you go to work in collection development ask to see the written policy so you can study it. When they tell you they don't have one, faint. By the way, you need to practice fainting and falling so you don't hurt yourselves—not many libraries have written collection development policies." In a way her story tells it all. To work effectively in collection development a selector must have some guidelines. Without them, fainting may be as productive and worthwhile as anything else you could do.

WHAT ARE COLLECTION DEVELOPMENT POLICIES?

Although selection and acquisition policy statements may contain most of the information to be found in a good collection development policy, they also tend not to include some important items. Remember, the definition of collection development is the process of assessing the strengths and weaknesses in a collection, and then creating a plan to correct the weaknesses and maintain the strengths. The collection development policy is the *written statement* of that plan, providing details for the guidance of the library staff. Thus a policy statement is a document representing *a plan of action and information* that is used to guide the staff's thinking and decision-making; specifically, the policy is consulted when deciding in what subject areas to consider buying and how much emphasis each area should receive.

Why is it that libraries frequently do not have or do not update their collection development policy? One of the major reasons is that a good policy statement must be based on a great deal of data. You must know 1) the strengths and weaknesses of your collection; 2) the community you are serving and where that community is going; 3) other resources available locally (to your patrons) and those accessible through interlibrary loan. Only when you have all of this knowledge in hand are you ready to start developing a policy.

Another reason policies are lacking is that they require a great deal of thought. As you would expect, a policy needs to change to reflect a changing community and, therefore, your thinking and data collecting are never finished. Some librarians say it is not worth the trouble: as soon as the plan is on paper, the situation has changed so much that the plan is out of date—so why bother?

Why bother? A policy statement can provide a framework within which individuals can exercise their own judgment. Unless the library has a dictatorial style of management, its collection development work will involve a number of persons at any one time and a great many throughout the history of the library. Whenever a number of persons set policy, many slightly different views of the library's purpose will emerge. Without written statements the divergence of opinion can be confusing. With a policy statement, though, everyone has a central reference point. Differences in opinion can be discussed with some hope that a basic understanding, if not agreement, will be possible, using the policy statement as the base. Also, as individuals join and leave the staff, a great danger looms of very important gaps occurring in the library's collection. Each individual's interests and views are unique to some degree, and if there are no guidelines, there is little hope of building the type of collection the library needs to serve its community.

In an academic situation with faculty in charge of selection, numerous points of view come into play. For example, four different anthropology professors might be selectors over four successive years. Lacking a policy statement, each professor would be free to, and sometimes would, buy heavily in a particular area of interest. The result might be one year of almost exclusive purchases of North American ethnology, one of Bantu studies, one of physical anthropology, and one of Oceanic material. In one way the entire field is thereby covered—given enough changes in selectors. The problem is, of course, that many fields are completely ignored and are likely to remain so for many years. A professor may not stay long enough to fully develop an area, so the library cannot claim strength in *any* area. If the professors have full authorization for the selection process, the library can do little to keep a bad situation under control.

Admittedly, a written policy statement will *not* completely solve this problem. A selector (in this case, a faculty member) occasionally has the authority to make final decisions. However, if the library has a document outlining in which fields coverage is required, the policy can serve as a reminder that areas other than the selector's favorites need materials as well. Although the example is from an academic environment, the same type of problem can arise in a public school or special library.

A policy statement thus can do the following:

1) help achieve a unified view of what areas of the collection should be developed;

2) help develop coordination between different individuals responsible for the collection, both currently and through time;

3) help achieve a consistency in the collection;

4)   help reduce the number of ad hoc decisions that have to be made regarding the collection;

5)   help avoid confusion in the minds of selectors and patrons as to what the collection is and is not.

The final point is important. A policy statement can be an effective means of communication to the patron. While a complete policy statement runs to many pages of text, something that few patrons would want to read, a summary of its major points can be a valuable information tool. This especially is true if the patrons have had some say as to what went into the policy.

GENERAL ISSUES IN LIBRARY POLICIES

Some years ago the Association of Research Libraries funded a study of academic library policies.[1] While the study focused on the academic environment some important facts came out of the work that apply to all libraries. In one of the appendices of the study, the researchers outlined the overall policy issues for academic libraries, which with only a very slight rewording here and there can be applied to all libraries. The slightly reworded outline is included here because 1) it clearly illustrates the importance of the collection to library services; 2) it illustrates the interrelationships between all aspects of service and policy matters; and 3) it demonstrates the need to have a carefully and fully developed statement about collection development.

Basic Policy Issues

I.   Educational
    1.   Library support for formal community instructional programs
          —materials
          —facilities
          —staff
          —services
    2.   Library support for informal self instruction
          —materials
          —facilities
          —staff
          —services
    3.   Magnitude and proportion of resources to be allocated to these programs
    4.   Priority of these services

Basic Policy Issues (cont'd)

II. Information
1. Library support for formal community "research" programs, both individual and organizations
   —materials
   —facilities
   —staff
   —services
2. Magnitude and proportion of resources to be allocated
3. Priority of these programs

III. Recreational
1. Library support of formal recreational programs in community [same subdivisions as II.1]
2. Library support of individual recreational needs [same subdivisions as II.1]
3. Magnitude and proportion of resources to be allocated
4. Priority of these programs

IV. Collections
1. Scope, depth and organization of general collection
2. Types of materials to be provided and maintained
3. Responsibility for selection decisions
4. Involvement of user in development of collections
5. Communication of collection policies to users
6. Preservation, weeding, replacement, and duplication issues
7. Size and proportion of resources allocated to this area
8. Priority of library activities in this area

V. Access to Services and Materials
1. Clientele to be served and priorities
2. Charges for services
3. Provision and organization of physical facilities
4. User orientation, interpretation and instruction
5. Branch and mobile services
6. Public service obligation (non-community services)
7. Service attitudes and posture
8. Scope and extent of services

VI. Staff Resources
1. Staff requirements—professional, paraprofessional, clerical
2. Provision of special skills
3. Status and role of staff categories
4. Staff development

(Outline continues on page 126)

Basic Policy Issues (cont'd)

VII. Management
　　1.　Administrative relationships with governing body
　　2.　Library governance
　　3.　Stewardship and utilization of limited resources
　　4.　Cooperative relationships with other libraries.

This is a comprehensive listing of basic issues. Not all of the seven sections have equal impact on collection development, but each major section has some. Item 4 of staff resources (staff development) could be important in terms of emphasis—if any—on acquiring professional and paraprofessional books, journals, and other materials. As the section on collections makes no mention of cooperative activities, then that item (4, under management) certainly would have an impact on how the collection is to be developed.

ELEMENTS OF A COLLECTION DEVELOPMENT POLICY

Everything to this point has been general, but what are the precise elements that ought to go into a good collection development statement? The following list illustrates why policy formulation is so time consuming, but also so critical to success. (Once the basic work has been done and the policy has been written, keeping the policy up to date is not a monumental problem; updating does take time but if it is done annually, it is next to painless.) The list of elements, then, can be divided into three parts: overview, details, and miscellaneous.

Element One—Overview

The first element should be a very clear statement of overall institutional objectives in reference to the library. Statements such as "geared to serve the needs of the patrons of the community" have little value or concrete meaning. In order to ensure that the statement is of help to the selectors and has meaning, all of the following factors should be present in the first section:

1)　A brief general description of the community to be served (town, country, school, business, etc.). What is the general make up of the community and where is it going? If you have done a thorough job of community analysis (chapter 4), this part of the policy and many of the following sections will be very easy to prepare.

2)　Specific identification of the clientele to be served. Anyone who walks in the door? Probably not, or at least they probably will not be served at the same level as the primary clientele. Who are the primary clientele? Is it all citizens of the local area, all staff and students of the educational institution, all employees of the business? Will you serve others? If so to what degree? Will the service to others be free or will there be a fee? Are there to be other differences in service primarily for adults, children, faculty, students, etc? Must the patron come to the library? Will there be service for the handicapped, the institutionalized, users with less-than-average reading ability or other communication problems? There are no universal answers for these questions and many others that might be listed regarding the clientele to be served. There is only a right answer *for your library at this time*, and this right answer will change through time.

3)   A general statement regarding the parameters of the collection. What subject fields will be represented? Are there any limitations set on the type of formats that the library will acquire? Just printed materials such as books, periodicals, and newspapers? What are the limits in audio visual areas? This section should provide an overview of the details that will be given in the second major element of the policy.

4)   A detailed description of what types of programs or patron needs are to be met by the collection. In a public library, to what degree is the total collection to be oriented toward educational purposes, that is, support of formal educational programs and self education? Will recreational needs be met and to what degree? Is the collection to be a circulating (loan) collection, or is it for reference purposes only? Academic libraries need also to be concerned with how much emphasis will be placed on research material. In the special library all of these questions may have to be considered.

5)   A section on the general limitations and priorities that will determine how the collection will be developed. To what degree will the library collect retrospective materials? One very important issue to cover in this section of the policy is whether the library will buy duplicate copies of an item; if so, what factors will be used to determine the number of copies and how long will the duplicates be retained? The question of duplicates is complicated and difficult. One excellent book that can be of great value in deciding the duplicate question is Michael Buckland's *Book Availability and the Library User* (Pergamon Press, 1975). This is one of the *essential* books to read if you want to become a member of a collection development staff.

6)   A detailed discussion of the library's role in cooperative collection development programs. To be effective this section must leave no doubt in a reader's mind as to whether the *basic* philosophy is one of self-sufficiency or cooperation. If the reader is in doubt, it means either that the writer(s) did not want to make a decision on this very critical issue or that they wanted to avoid a public stand. Furthermore, if the library is involved in cooperative programs, this section should detail those programs in which participation is to be active and identify those areas for which the library has a major responsibility. For subject areas not of major concern, the reader should be told where to find information on who does have major responsibility for their collection.

Element Two—Details of Subject Areas
and Formats Collecting

It is first necessary to break down the collection into its constituent subject areas, identify each type of material to be collected for that subject and the class of patron for which this area is primarily intended. This may sound like a lot of work—it is. You must spend hours talking to patrons about the problem and then spend many more hours thinking about the information. After that you have to assign priorities to each area (perhaps even by format within each area), all of this with an eye toward achieving the proper balance of all subjects, given your particular community of users and their needs. The following is a reasonably comprehensive listing of patrons and formats to consider. There is no point in trying to list subjects.

Patrons

1) adults
2) young adult
3) school-age children
4) pre-school children
5) physically handicapped (blind, partially sighted, wheelchair patients, etc.)
6) shut-ins and institutionalized persons (hospitals, homes, prisons, etc.)
7) teaching faculty
8) researchers
9) staff
10) undergraduate students
11) post-graduate students
12) alumni

Formats

1) books (hard or paper bound, monographs, textbooks, etc.)
2) newspapers
3) periodicals
4) microforms
5) slides
6) film and filmstrips
7) pictures
8) audio recordings (tapes and records)
9) video recordings (tapes and discs)
10) printed music
11) pamphlets
12) manuscripts and archival material
13) maps
14) government documents
15) laser formats
16) realia
17) games
18) specimens

Although these lists are fairly long, they are not comprehensive; formats are likely to change constantly. The lists do provide, though, a rather clear picture of the magnitude of the project, especially when you further subdivide each for subject considerations. Before you decide that this would indeed be too time-consuming, remember that not all of the categories, formats, or subjects will be considered for any one library.

The setting of priorities, or levels of collecting intensity, can be handled in a number of ways. Two of the more typical methods that use labels for identifying priorities are described below. One uses a five-level ranking system and the other four. Either one could be used in any type of library. The four-level system is more widely used and will, therefore, be described more completely:

1) general coverage: Acquire only light popular works. Acquire books for average adult reader. Do not buy reference books in this field. Weed the collection annually, discarding books more than three years old unless there is a significant reason to retain (high use, widely cited, field is becoming a new area of collection interest for the library). The collection remains a constant size.

2) instructional or working collection: Acquire current materials with an eye to all points of view. Do not buy retrospective materials. In addition to books, consider periodicals and newspapers (only current volumes and those that are indexed). Microforms and other formats should only be acquired if the information is *not* available in books or serials. Develop a working reference collection, again based on current (in print) items. There should be a selective annual weeding program; however, it is expected that collections in this level will exhibit small (1-2 percent) increases in size each year.

3) comprehensive/research collection: Acquire *all* current printed materials both for the circulating and reference collections. Buy as much retrospective material as possible in the area of printed materials for both the circulating and reference collections. Give very serious consideration to all other current formats, including rare books, manuscripts, and archival materials. There should be little or no weeding for discard, but it may be necessary to review the collection every two or three years to identify items that might be housed in a low-use, compact storage unit.

4) exhaustive collections: Acquire everything possible including physical objects that might be considered museum pieces. Maximum efforts should be made to acquire all possible retrospective materials, especially archival material and manuscripts. There will be no weeding of these collections. Special funds should be sought when a particularly important item becomes available. Information about all potential major additions should be given to the head of the department concerned and to the director of the library.

Given this type of detail, a selector can focus attention quickly on the items appropriate for the collection. These statements are only guidelines, with ample room for individual interpretation, but they do narrow the scope of a person's work. Combine this section with the patron list and subject listing, and you have a solid framework on which to build.

Most subject areas will fall either into the working or comprehensive levels. In most libraries there will be only one or two topics in the exhaustive class; they will be highly restricted in most instances to one person (e.g., Goethe) or topic (e.g., pre-Columbian writing systems). General coverage is usually represented by only a few subject areas.

Finally in this first section, you should identify the strengths in the existing collection, what the actual level of collecting is, and what the desired level ought to be. To some extent, the assignment of levels does some of this; however, you may find significant differences between what is desired and what was and is being done. This last step helps to ensure some consistency in the library's program and policy.

Section two of this element will probably be short but it is very important: it identifies where responsibility for collection development lies. Ultimate responsibility, of course, lies with the head of the library, just as does the final responsibility for all library activities; but no one expects the head librarian actually to do all the tasks for which she or he is responsible. Since the collections are the central focus of the library's programs, the question of who will actually develop them is a vital one. This *must* be decided upon after careful examination of the needs of the library. This section of the policy, then, should be a clear statement of who will be responsible for selection, what guidelines that person must use, and how the selector's performance is to be evaluated.

In each type of library, and even among libraries of the same type, this responsibility will vary. There are, however, only a few basic groups from which to select the responsible person(s). Then one can develop small local variations.

Who Shall Select?

1) patrons/users

2) librarians from public service areas, with no special background or training beyond basic library education

3) librarians from technical service areas—no special background or training beyond basic library education

4) subject or service specialists, with special advanced training in subject or service area

5) department heads

6) head librarian

How Shall They Select?

1) independent, with or without a systematic alerting program from the library

2) committees

3) centrally prepared list from which selections are made

A few generalizations may be made about differences between types of libraries. Many exceptions to these generalizations exist, but a pattern is apparent in most areas. Teaching institution libraries tend to have a higher patron involvement and greater use of subject specialists than is found in public libraries. Special or technical libraries are often staffed with librarians who have advanced training in the field in which the library specializes, and they are responsible for selection, with the advice of patrons being constantly sought. Public libraries normally use librarians from public service areas (often the department heads) as selectors, working through selection committees or from lists prepared by a central agency.

When non-librarians have an active voice in selection matters, it is usually only in terms of the working or loan collection. Reference collection matters are normally the sole responsibility of the library staff. Sometimes there are variations, but patrons are generally more concerned with current items, books, and monographs, whereas librarians will tend to regard retrospective buying, serial items, and "other media" favorably. When such variations occur the responsibility for the more "unusual" items (retrospective, serials, "other media," etc.) is almost always given to a librarian with special training and/or knowledge of the form. Allocation of that responsibility in any given library will depend in large measure upon the type of library and the local conditions. Just remember, whatever is decided, put it in writing so there will be no question about where the responsibility/accountability lies.

Third, this section should provide some general guidelines about what, or what not, to select. Normally, such written guidelines are more important to have in public and school library situations, because there are usually a wider range of interests involved and a great deal of concern about the impact of the collection upon the children using it. Some examples of guideline criteria statements are:

1) select and replace items found in standard lists and catalogs;

2) select only those items that have been favorably reviewed in at least two review sources;

3) do not select anything that has received a negative review;

4) try to provide both, or all, points of view on a controversial subject;

5) do not select textbooks;

6) do not select items of a sensational, violent, or inflammatory nature;

7) select only items of lasting literary or social value.

The list could go on and on; however, most of the statements are really only variations of the selection criteria discussed in chapters 6 and 7 and do not need to be repeated here. Whatever criteria are used they should be clearly delineated in this section of the statement.

Element Three—Miscellaneous Issues

The term miscellaneous may make this section appear to be of lesser importance: this is *not* the case. Each of the subtopics in this section is important, but none of them needs to be very long; nor are they interrelated in the same manner as are the first two elements. Five topics need to be covered in this element: gifts; weeding and discards; replacements; complaints and censorship; and evaluation.

Gifts

Gifts should not be added to the collection on any other basis than that used for items you buy. All too often libraries tend to add any free items. As indicated in the chapter on cooperation, no donated item is free. It still must be processed in the same manner as a purchased item. To expend the energy to add something to the collection just because it is free, when it is not essential to the library's purpose, is a very poor practice. Apply the same standards to gifts as you do to purchased items, and weeding problems will be greatly diminished.

You need to have your policy on handling gifts in writing. That is, state whether you will accept only items that you plan to add to the collection or will you accept anything with the proviso you can dispose of unwanted items in any manner the library sees fit? It is very important to have something in writing about gifts with "strings." Will you take private collections and house them separately with special labels identifying their donors? Will you create special areas (rooms) for a collection if the donor provides the funds? Will you accept funds earmarked for certain classes of materials or subjects? Will you try to sell or trade duplicate or unwanted materials and acquire new materials? If you are going to try to expand the collection through gifts and endowment monies, who will be responsible for this activity? Will it be coordinated? These are some of the major questions that should be addressed in a section on gifts.

Gifts and endowment monies are excellent means of developing a collection *when and if* the library has complete freedom for their use and is not restricted by the donor. A very important public relations question must be answered here: is it better to accept all gifts, regardless of the conditions attached to them, or should the library avoid conditional gifts? If there is a clearly reasoned statement as to why gifts with conditions are not accepted, there should be no public relations problem.

Weeding and Discards

As in the section on levels of collecting (pages 126-27), weeding and discarding materials must be specifically discussed. Again the level and type of weeding program will vary from library to library, but all libraries will have to face this issue eventually. Chapter 9 provides a fairly detailed discussion of this issue. Once such issues as the criteria, scope, frequency, and purpose of weeding have been decided upon, these decisions should be incorporated into the policy statement.

Replacements and Duplicates

When do you buy replacement items? Are there any guidelines about when to buy and how many duplicate copies one should buy? Neither of these questions is very complicated, but if there are no guidelines the staff can waste time making a new decision each time these problems come up. Should you bother to look for a replacement for every old worn-out title in the collection? Probably not, especially if the item has not been used for many years. Ad hoc decisions each time this question arises will consume time and very likely result in inconsistent decisions. Statements such as "replace worn-out copies of titles still in print and used within the last five years" or "do not attempt to locate replacement copies of out-of-print, worn-out or damaged copies unless there are special reasons to do so" can save a great deal of time. Guideline statements are just that, and exceptions can always be made. (These should be noted for possible use in future policy revision.)

The number of duplicates to acquire, if any, requires careful consideration. All libraries, except special libraries, are confronted with this problem to some degree. At the present time, except in school libraries, the question seldom arises for anything but books. However, public and academic libraries face this every day in terms of best seller and popular titles and textbook-like titles. To some extent the popular title problem can be alleviated by employing a rental program such as the McNaughton programs (discussed in chapter 3). Such plans help reduce the cost of and long-term storage problems with books in high demand for a short period of time; however, they do not resolve the question of how many extra copies to acquire. There are no easy solutions to the problem of extra textbooks unless you have a low-cost rental system. Some possible guideline statements would be: "buy one copy for every ten potential readers during a six month period," "buy one copy for the general collection and acquire one copy for every five readers during X months for the high use or rental collection." Of course, the length of time, number of readers, etc., will be determined by local conditions.

Complaints and Censorship

Another short section of the collection development policy statement that can save time and trouble is one spelling out the steps to be taken in handling complaints about the collection. Eventually every library will have a few complaints about what is or is not in the collection. Naturally it is easier to handle questions about what is not there, especially with a good collection development policy statement. (You can always try to buy a missing item.) Your major problem will be complaints about what is in the collection or questions as to why the policy says what it does.

An irate patron on the other side of your desk, more than slightly livid because this "terrible" item has been purchased, can cause you more than passing discomfort. How do you reduce the person's anger? One solution is a cop-out—pass the buck to a supervisor. Such buck-passing does nothing to calm an upset patron; if anything it tends to increase their level of frustration. In the absence of guidelines, however, it is dangerous to try to solve the problem alone. Normally the patron wants the offending item taken out of the collection—which is in effect patron censorship.

You should *not* promise to remove the item. You can and should agree to review it if the library has an established review procedure. It is then necessary to identify who, how, and when the review will be handled. One method of doing this is to have a form for the patron to fill out concerning the offending item. While this tends to be "bureaucratic" in approach, it does help everyone to identify the problem. Usually it consists of two parts, one explaining the library's review procedure, the other asking the patron to *specifically* identify the offending sections or qualities of the item in question. At times this approach only increases anger; but since you are offering to do something, more often than not the patron becomes less angry. Naturally, if the patron demands to speak with a supervisor, do your best to arrange this promptly.

There are other alternatives, but whatever your library is going to do about complaints should be decided upon *before* the first complaint. Ad hoc decisions in this area can cause a library a great deal of trouble in its community. Consistency is not always a good thing, but in this area its merits far outweigh its drawbacks. The basic issues concerning censorship are discussed in chapter 13. As with weeding, whatever decisions are reached after due consideration of the basic issues involved should be incorporated into the written collection development policy.

Evaluation

The statement's final section will specify how the collection will be evaluated and for what purposes. Chapter 10 describes all of the basic methods for evaluating a collection along with the advantages and disadvantages of each. What you need to do in the section of the policy concerned with evaluation is to indicate whether you will evaluate only for internal purposes (i.e., identifying collection strengths and weaknesses) or for comparative purposes—or perhaps as a review of how well the selectors have been doing their job. Each of these is slightly different and requires different techniques or emphasis. Again, making decisions ahead of time, putting them in writing, and getting them approved can save time and trouble for staff, patrons, funding agencies, and governing boards.

GETTING THE POLICY APPROVED

You can now understand why the process of preparing a comprehensive collection development policy statement of this type is thought to be very time consuming. If the staff—and it should be the library staff—has spent all the time necessary to prepare such a comprehensive policy, it is important that it be approved by the library's governing board. With such approval everyone has a set of commonly agreed-upon ground rules for building the collection required to serve the local community.

These are the basic steps in an ideal policy development process:

1) the head librarian should appoint a staff committee to draft a basic policy statement, which will first be submitted back to the head librarian;

2) the head librarian then both reviews and comments on the draft personally and has it distributed to the entire library staff for comments and suggestions;

3)   the original drafting committee then incorporates the comments and suggestions into a revised, final statement. Perhaps a general meeting will be needed to discuss the interim draft before the final version is prepared;

4)   the final draft statement is then given to the governing board to review, possibly revise, and eventually approve;

5)   another valuable step can be taken between board review and final approval. That step is to have an open meeting for patrons to hear about and comment upon the proposed policy. Members of the drafting committee, the head librarian, and representatives of the governing board should be present to explain, describe, and if necessary, defend and modify the statement;

6)   the final step is to prepare multiple copies of the final statement for the library staff and those patrons desiring a copy. A good public relations device is to prepare a brief condensed version for distribution to each new user of the library.

These steps can ensure community, staff, and administrative consensus before a problem arises. It is much easier to agree theoretically on evaluation procedures, review procedures, levels and areas of collecting, etc., in advance than it is to try to handle them in the heat of specific spontaneous disagreement. It also means that later disagreements can be more easily resolved as there is a body of previously established and agreed-upon ground rules.

SUMMARY

Is all the work that must go into a policy statement really worth it? It is! Collection development is a complex process, highly subjective, and filled with problems and traps for even the most wary individual. A solid, comprehensive written policy, developed with the advice and involvement of all parties concerned, helps to make the process much less ad hoc and, therefore, less problem-filled. A few examples of policy statements are included in the appendix to help illustrate how the theory of preparing a policy statement is applied in real libraries. None of the examples are ideal—rather they represent what you may encounter on the job. The bibliography includes several collections of policy statements to consult for even more background.

NOTES

[1] D. Webster, *Library Policies: Analysis, Formulation and Use in Academic Institutions.* Office of University Library Management Studies, Occasional Papers, No. 2. (Washington: Association of Research Libraries, 1972).

BIBLIOGRAPHY

American Library Association. Resources and Technical Services Division. Collection Committee. "Guidelines for the Formulation of Collection Development Policies." *Library Resources and Technical Services* 21 (Winter 1977): 40-42.

Association of Research Libraries. *Library Policies.* Chicago: ARL, 1972.

Boyer, C. J., and N. L. Eaton. *Book Selection Policies in American Libraries.* Austin, TX: Armadillo Press, 1971.

Corrigan, D. D. "Public Library Policies for People." *Illinois Libraries* 48 (Feb. 1969): 103-105.

Deller, A. M. "Your Book/Media Selection Policy: A Public Relations Opportunity." *Michigan Libraries* 39 (Summer 1973): 5.

Futas, E. *Library Acquisition Policies and Procedures.* Phoenix, AZ: Oryx Press, 1977.

Gregory, R. W. "Principles Behind a Book Selection Policy Statement." *ILA Record* 10 (Oct. 1956): 23-26.

Lake, A. C. "Pursuing a Policy." *Library Journal* 85 (June 1, 1960): 2491-94.

Nash, W. V. "Policy-Making in Libraries." *Illinois Libraries* 44 (May 1962): 348-58.

Wasserman, P. "Policy Formulation in Libraries." *Illinois Libraries* 43 (Dec. 1961): 772-79.

Chapter 6

SELECTION OF BOOKS

The central issue in the selection process is whether you should select for quality or select primarily for use. Is it an either/or situation? If not, what is the best blend, or how can you blend the two concepts? At one extreme, some librarians say that a library is the primary means of raising the literary awareness of the community and therefore should contain only the "best" literature. At the opposite end of the spectrum, other librarians claim that a library is a public institution supported by tax monies and therefore the public should be able to find whatever materials they need and want.

QUALITY VERSUS DEMAND

Community demand as the basis for library collection development was outlined most thoroughly in Lionel McColvin's 1925 monograph, *The Theory of Book Selection for Public Libraries.* His premises, and those of most librarians who support this concept, are that:

1) public libraries are established in response to, and in anticipation of, demand;

2) the process of book selection involves both supply and demand: the library's function is to discover and assess community demand, then to satisfy those demands.

To some extent, McColvin's premises can be applied to any type of library, not just to public libraries.

Advocates of quality selection find excellent support in Helen Haines's work, *Living with Books* (2nd ed., 1950). Haines was concerned with all types of libraries although many people tend to think of her book as oriented to the public library. Her basic premises were that a librarian selects books that will develop and enrich the lives of the persons being served by the library. Obviously this requires an extensive literary background, including a comprehensive knowledge of the "foundation" or "classic" works. Demand is to be met by selecting the highest quality books. She assumed that people exhibit demands (needs) both for ephemeral materials (which can be supplied in other ways) and for materials from "deeper life channels."

No one takes an extreme position on this fundamental issue, so an either/or situation does not really exist. Many individuals, however, are closer to one end of the continuum or the other than they are to the middle. Where you will fall on that continuum will depend upon your feelings about library service and the community your library is serving. Thus, at the very outset of the discussion of selection, we are confronted with one essential fact about the process: It is a highly personal, highly subjective activity.

A brief historical review of some of the major monographs on book selection and collection development will provide a good overview of the basic issues, selection criteria, and how these factors have changed through time. Starting with Lionel McColvin (1925) and ending with David Spiller (1974), we will examine fifty years of writing on book selection. Although monographs (at least in librarianship) seldom represent the first appearance of a concept, textbooks generally attempt to summarize developments and reflect thinking on the subject as of the time they are published. We look at the works of: Lionel McColvin; Arthur Bostwick; Francis Drury; Harold Bonny; S. R. Ranganathan; Helen Haines; Mary Carter, Wallace Bonk, and Rosemary Magrill; Robert Broadus; and David Spiller. While not comprehensive in coverage, this list does cover the major works and is international in scope. (Full citations for each will be found in the bibliography to this chapter in the "General Works" section.)

LIONEL R. McCOLVIN
The Theory of Book Selection for Public Libraries (1925)

As already noted, McColvin was one of the first persons to write a major text on collection development and to advocate the principal that libraries respond to the demands of their communities. As noted, McColvin made two assumptions about collection development. First, public libraries (unlike private, national, or general research libraries) are established in response to and in anticipation of demand; their "service" is derived from demand. He further assumed that the process of book selection involves both supply and demand. Therefore, the library's function is a double one—to discover and assess demands and then to try to satisfy them.

His basic principle was that book representation must be comprehensive of and in proportion to demand, *not* to subject content. In using the term "comprehensive," he was concerned that the demands be judged not only on their own merits but also in relation to the entire body of demands. Thus representation becomes a matter of proportions, not of actual volume counts. A large demand may be met by a relatively small number of books on the subject, a situation illustrated by the fact that a very small proportion of the total collection (25-30 percent) usually satisfies anywhere from 60 to 70 percent of the total demand. The proportion is also influenced by such factors as library budget, space, availability of titles, etc. Intentional duplication is also very important in the representation picture— multiple copies of a title, as opposed to unintentional duplication. In McColvin's terms there is a surprising amount of "unintentional duplication"—a number of titles on a subject that all provide basically the same information with only slight variation. The question is—would it be better to have only one or two titles in multiple copies rather than numerous similar titles? At this point, some of the basic criteria for selecting materials come into play, and according to McColvin, there are seven basic criteria for selection:

1) the information should be as accurate as possible;

2) the book should be complete and properly balanced, with due regard being given to its subject and intended scope;

3) the author should have distinguished between fact and opinion;

4) the currency of the information is frequently the determining factor;

5) the writing style and treatment of the subject should be appropriate to the type of demand to be met;

6) the title reflecting the cultural values of its country of origin is to be preferred; that is, when the subject matter is treated differently in various countries the treatment from the country of origin is to be preferred;

7) the physical characteristics of the book are generally of minor importance unless there are two books similar in terms of content; when this occurs, such factors as type face, illustrations, binding, paper, indexes, bibliographies, etc., may help make the final decision.

In essence, McColvin suggested that the size of the collection in a particular subject ought to be proportional to the demand for that subject regardless of a librarian's subjective assessment of the importance of that topic. He recognized that patrons tend to be inconsistent, responsive to fads, and highly changeable in their demands. He also recognized that librarians and the general public assign relative values to various subject areas. In order to determine the size of the collection for given subjects, two values were to be used. One was the relative importance of the subject—some numerical value. A second number was to be assigned on the basis of the number of requests received for books on that subject. These two numbers would be multiplied to obtain a "representative number." (Another possible manner of numerically determining the relative value of a subject would be to rank a subject from one to ten according to the column inches devoted to that subject in general encyclopedias for the particular country in which the library is located. A very articulate critic of this approach is Rinaldo Lunati [see *La scelta del libro per la formazione e lo sviluppo delle biblioteche.* Firenze: Leo S. Olschki Editore, 1972].)

A number of flaws exist in McColvin's concept, but it was an attempt to meet demand and, to some degree, to take quality into account. In essence McColvin's approach (and that of others who follow the demand concept) places a very heavy emphasis on community analysis in order to determine changing demands. Some persons have suggested that this approach creates a situation in which the librarian is converted into a sociologist and is thus taken away from "real" library work. True, community analysis does take time and draws heavily on sociology. It is difficult to understand, however, how you can develop an actively used library collection if you do not know the community (see chapter 4).

The suggestion that librarians leave this work to sociologists and only use sociological data as the library needs it seems faulty. Librarians planning a new library building should not expect a functional building if the project is left solely in the hands of an architect. Day-to-day library involvement in the design process, as well as with supervision of the construction work, is the only way to *help* ensure a satisfactory physical facility. The same is true of a community analysis project. Without direct on-going involvement by librarians, data may be of limited value. Furthermore, while a building project lasts for only a short period of time, community analysis is an on-going project. Unless the library has enough funding to hire a resident sociologist, librarians need to learn how to make this activity an on-going activity that they can handle.

The socioeconomic emphasis in American and British public librarianship was very strong during the 1920s, 1930s, and late 1940s. Considerable emphasis was placed on community studies and developing programs and services, particularly book collections, to meet local community needs. During the 1950s and 1960s this emphasis faded somewhat: the economic picture was bright and there was an increasing flow of funds to libraries. For many American academic libraries and a few large public library systems there seemed to be no concern with selecting, just with collecting—everything in sight. We have now come full circle. Selection is again the keyword.

ARTHUR BOSTWICK
The American Public Library (1929)

A number of subsequent writers followed McColvin's lead and focused attention to the demand concept. Arthur Bostwick discussed the problem from the point of view of American public libraries. He phrased the dilemma as: let the public have what they want and run the risk of having the collections fall to an "unacceptably low level," or collect only the best and risk having a library without readers.

Most of the emphasis in McColvin's seven criteria was on nonfiction. Bostwick explored the issue of fiction as well and made a strong case for the inclusion of it in the public library since recreation is a general need and there is a high demand for recreational reading. Perhaps the emphasis on fiction—usually more difficult to judge than nonfiction, especially when there are questions about style and treatment—caused him to take one of the more questionable stands on who should be responsible for selection. He indicates that the board of trustees should have the responsibility unless the librarian knows his job. Unfortunately, Bostwick does not indicate who will determine the extent of the librarian's subject knowledge. Library literature is filled with cases of disagreements between library boards and librarians about who knows what. (It must be remembered, though, that his book covered all aspects of American public library operation, and the chapter on book selection was only sixteen pages in length.)

Bostwick also lists characteristics that he would require of selection librarians. Although his list is not as formidable as some later listings (especially those of Drury and Haines), it is still rather impressive. Most of the characteristics—forceful, self-confident, sociable, and influential—seem to be required for any librarian, not just a book selector in a public library. He does indicate that book selectors must be dependent in part upon the judgments of other persons because the scope of knowledge and output of material is too high for any one person to handle. Certainly this was true in 1929 and is even more important today when a library subject expert in a field such as chemistry or history cannot be equally knowledgeable in all of the subfields.

As so many others have done, Bostwick suggests a middle ground for book selection: "average taste of users." In many respects this solution is no better in terms of workload than the demand approach—both require extensive sociocultural investigations to determine the community's level of needs or "average taste." Furthermore, the average taste of users would preclude consideration of the non-user population as a new service need. In fact, the focus of attention still would be on the users and their tastes rather than on the entire community. A community-wide focus would at least *identify* non-user groups and perhaps even provide a mechanism for assessing their interests and needs. That information in turn might suggest new programs or collection development areas for the library.

FRANCIS DRURY
Book Selection (1930)

Francis Drury's textbook, *Book Selection*, appeared a year after Bostwick's book was published. Drury took the position that the value of a book is the basic reason to include it in a collection. He further indicated that selection should operate on the basis of three factors—the books or titles as individual entities, the patrons using the collection, and the library's resources. A one-phrase summary of his philosophy would be: the best quality reading material for the greatest number of patrons at the lowest possible price. Certainly this is a highly desirable goal for any library.

Drury's concept of "best" is qualified in several ways. That is, it could be the best in the field in which the book will be used; that the use will be "good use"; and that it meet certain demands. The best of any type of reading, according to Drury, is characterized by four qualities: truth, clarity, good taste, and literary merit. Of the four, truth is perhaps the easiest to determine, but even this factor is often a question of perspective—"the truth as I see it" is not an uncommon statement. As for the remaining three factors, clarity can often be a function of educational level, while individual preference and experience almost completely dominate judgments as to levels of taste or literary merit. If this were not so, judicial systems would not have so much trouble deciding such issues as pornography or libel.

Drury set up a number of guidelines for selectors, and the following were suggested in order to choose the best books:

1)   establish suitable standards for judging all books;

2)   apply criteria intelligently and evaluate the book's contents for inherent worth;

3)   strive to get the best on any subject, but do not hesitate to add a mediocre title that will be read rather than a superior title that will be unread;

4)   duplicate the best rather than acquire the many;

5)   stock the classics and "standards" in attractive editions;

6)   select for positive use—not just good books but ones that serve usefully;

7)   develop the local history collection—these items will be sought in the library if anywhere;

8)   be broad-minded and unprejudicial in selection; represent all sides fairly—although propagandistic and sectarian titles should only be added as far as use demands it;

9)   do select fiction—it has both educational and recreational value;

10)   buy editions in bindings suitable for library use—circulation and borrowing;

11)   know publishers, costs, and values;

12)   know authors and their works—if possible, develop a ranking system.

These factors are an interesting mixture of achievable and non-achievable goals. "Suitable standards" and "apply intelligently" sound good, but what do the phrases really mean? Each person who reads those words will give them slightly different meanings, and if such is the case, how can there be any consistency from library to library, or within a library if more than one person does the selecting?

The second aspect of Drury's basic philosophy—greatest number—resulted in another list of guidelines:

1)   study the library's constituency with an open mind to determine and assess their needs and demands;

2)   develop a selection program that will satisfy community needs and demands and that will develop the community's intellectual level—thereby increasing the sum of its systematic knowledge;

3)   apply the Golden Rule in selecting books for readers;

4)   provide for both actual and potential users: satisfy the former's general and specific demands as far as possible; anticipate somewhat demands that might or should come from the latter;

5)   discard or do not add titles for which there is no actual or anticipated demand—except for classics and standards;

6)   use restraint in responding to demands of aggressive patrons and recognize the inarticulate patron's demands;

7)   buy many works for specialists and community leaders' needs insofar as this does not draw off too much of the book funds available to obtain material for the primary constituency;

8)   do not attempt to complete sets, series, or subject areas unless there is actual demand for completeness.

These guidelines are general in scope and are to some degree subjective. However, a group of persons responsible for collection development could use them as a basis for establishing their own agreed-upon meanings.

The cost aspect is rather self-explanatory except for one statement: Drury suggests that you not buy any book without first asking whether its purchase is depriving the library of a better book in as great or greater demand. This is a useful question to ask, but again, it places great emphasis on quality and does not take into account subject matter. For example, the choice is between a mediocre title on a new field of anthropology with only a limited demand and a good title on gardening, which is in high demand. You have nothing in the new field of anthropology; you have a number of titles on gardening but not the new one. There is only enough money to buy one of the two books—which would you select? Using Drury's guidelines; using your own judgment—why?

All of Drury's guidelines are geared to creating a value system for selecting books. A selector is to operate in a milieu in which this value system has been converted into a permanent and general scale of literary values, a scale used to judge the merits of any particular title. Furthermore, the librarian should be able to review, critique, and decide what type of library should buy a particular title. In many ways the journal *Booklist* (an ALA publication) reflects this concept. It is prepared and published by librarians for librarians and only lists books recommended for purchase by public libraries.

Drury recognized that no one person could possibly know enough about all subjects to be able to effectively evaluate all books—assuming that there was time to read all the books. American public libraries have taken this concept to heart and a great many hours of professional time are spent in reading new books (normally on the librarian's own time—nights and weekends) and discussing them in book selection meetings. Personal experience with such meetings indicates that perhaps somewhere in the dim dark past, a permanent general scale of literary values may have been established upon which to weigh each book; but somewhere in the more recent chaotic past the scale was misplaced. (This observation is based upon listening for what seemed to be eternities to two normally friendly individuals argue vigorously, if not shout at one another, about the merits of a particular book.)

Generally speaking the basic precept of all collection development—the right book for the right reader at the right time—becomes modified using the quality approach. It becomes the best book for all readers all the time. If assessing community needs is a time-consuming activity—and it is—think how much more complex the quality factor is to assess. Despite the difficulties, there are important reasons for only buying the best. An important one is not to waste limited collection development funds. Tax money is always difficult to secure and wasteful practices never make sense. The question you have to answer is what is "best." Does this mean physical characteristics or content? Not too many years ago public librarians tended to view paperback books as being of poor quality. Some claimed that the type of material published in paperback was too low in quality for inclusion in a library collection. Others said that it was just a question of how long the book would last—only a few circulations and it would fall apart.

Poor content rather than poor physical characteristics is the usual concern. The main consideration is to maintain the very highest literary quality. A collection of the great books and great authors has been the goal of some libraries, which means that raising the community's literary taste has been given the highest priority in collection development. When using the "buy only the best books" principle, however, certain fundamental questions must be considered. One is, are there lists of the best books or can one be developed? Do such lists exist? Yes, there are dozens of "Basic Books for . . . ," "Best Books of . . . ," "All Time Classics," etc. Some, such as *Standard Catalog for Public Libraries*, carry with them a certain official aura. Some librarians feel that their collection must contain all of the books that they consider basic before any other items are acquired. If a library did not have most, if not all, of the items on the list, then that library would be considered a failure, given that standard.

Other questions concern the character of a "best book" list. Was it developed by one or more persons to serve a specified objective? If so you need to know the identities of the individuals who made the selection, the objectives of the selection process, and what criteria were employed. You also must decide whether the published list of objectives is sufficiently close to your library's objectives to warrant using the list. (A representative sample of best books lists and other selection aids is given at the end of this chapter.) Just the fact that so many lists exist indicates some of the problems involved in listing the best books. Each person has an individual, unique value system that will result in differences of opinion about which book(s) should be labeled best. Philosophers have debated value concepts for several thousand years, with no resolution in sight. Why should librarians expect to accomplish the task in less than two hundred?

Authors writing about this concept—buying the best—recognize that in order to select the best a librarian must have an extensive literary background. The length of time a student spends in library school almost presupposes that most librarians come to library school with a literature and subject background if they are to be successful in collection development. Library schools can only help sharpen critical skills and teach a few basics about preparing annotations. (Perhaps the best discussion of how to prepare a library annotation is in Helen Haines's book, *Living with Books*, a standard textbook in many American library schools for many years; it is examined below.)

Lasting worth or value is easy to determine for books one-hundred or perhaps even fifty years old. Current books are a different problem. In essence there is a significant difference between current and retrospective selection, if only in terms of the number of items to be considered. Retrospective selection is aided by time itself. Many titles no longer exist or exist in only limited quantities—primarily in libraries. An interesting study would be to examine the proportion of 1870 imprints still available as compared with the proportions of those published in 1925, 1950, and 1970 and still available. As the volume of books published increases each year and if the number of librarians does not increase proportionately, the amount of time available for review per book decreases. No one is able to examine every new book published in English each year, let alone read them all. Less and less time for more and more books means that you, the librarian, *must* depend upon others for judgments about the worth of a particular item.

It is important to note the concept of acquiring "quality" material is normally only applied to selecting books. Media is a completely different matter as we will see in chapter 7. However, periodicals, serials, and other printed matter are also generally excluded from the quality evaluation process—excluded in the sense that often you must accept a particular item or nothing at all. Another factor, especially with periodicals, is that the evaluation should be on-going. Periodicals or serials constantly change in nature: new editors, new contributors, and changing areas of interest all create an environment where frequent review is necessary. A title once though to be *the* best (or worst) may change completely between two issues.

One interesting feature of Drury's work is that he recognized that, despite the best efforts, a considerable number of current selections would *not* have lasting value. Removal of obsolete items must be considered part of the normal work of persons responsible for collection development, but unfortunately, this aspect of collection development has not received the attention it should in most library schools and libraries. In spite of the recognition of the need to weed, the process is usually ignored until the need has reached crisis proportions (see chapter 9).

Perhaps the section of Drury's text that most reveals the difficulties in developing meaningful selection guidelines using the quality approach is his extended discussion of the personality and skills required of a person who is to become a selector. If Bostwick's list is impressive, Drury's is overwhelming. He identifies over 24 "essential" characteristics, ranging from judgment, intelligence, and imagination to accuracy, speed, and industriousness to health. Many of the characteristics are desirable in any employee in any situation; some seem essential requirements for acquisitions personnel but marginal for selectors. Finding the persons with all of Drury's preferred characteristics would be a time-consuming job, as the ideal individual would be a paragon of virtue and skills. Developing a means of assessing the abilities of each person is almost more difficult than actually carrying out the selection process. Everyone possesses the characteristics identified by Drury; the problem lies in determining the amount and quality.

By the time you finish reading Drury you may well conclude: this is all very interesting but how can I apply it to the "real world" of collection development? This is difficult to answer, since basically, only time and experience will show you the way. A more practical approach is found in Harold Bonny's work.

HAROLD V. BONNY
A Manual of Practical Book Selection for Public Libraries
(1939)

Bonny does not claim to add anything new to the theory of collection development, but he does provide excellent practical advice on how to go about building a library collection. Generally, the practical advice revolves around knowing the community's tastes and needs. Bonny sees input to the selection process coming from three sources: the selection librarian(s), the patrons, and a committee of specialists. Patrons are encouraged to suggest titles for the collection and to volunteer to serve on the selection committee. Another practical suggestion is to form a selection committee composed of persons with a variety of subject backgrounds. This committee could suggest appropriate additions to the collection (note that the committee in most cases would *not* be made up of librarians). Another use of the committee, as conceived by Bonny, would be as a means of assessing the value of titles suggested by patrons. Such a committee accomplishes several things: it allows community participation in collection development; it helps to ensure a workable level of community input—not too much or too little; and it helps to reduce the need for "super" librarians who know everything about all subjects. As far as Bonny is concerned, this committee is only advisory, as the final responsibility for selection remains in the hands of librarians. Although the book was written in terms of a public library environment, Bonny's basic concepts apply as well to any type of library. Educational institutions usually have an advisory committee for the library. If the rules governing the committee's powers (whether advisory or decision-making) are properly drawn up, such a committee can be very helpful in collection development. Special libraries often establish a committee of this type because the library staff is too small to handle the total workload.

After World War II several more collection development textbooks were published. None of them provides any new insights into the problem of quality and demand. Each does provide a slightly different perspective, with more ideas and opinions to be sorted. Nevertheless, the final message is that collection development is an art, not a science.

HELEN HAINES
Living with Books (2nd ed., 1950)

Living with Books has almost attained classic status in this field. Haines's general approach to the problem of collection development is a combination of the ideal and utilitarian. She acknowledges that in some of her principles there are inconsistencies. However, she feels that the matter, when viewed as a whole, is a dynamic situation in which adjustments must be constantly made in order to achieve some degree of equilibrium. Her basic assumption is that people need and demand not only ephemeral materials such as literature, but also materials for "deeper life channels," which require education and lasting, high quality materials.

Haines provides two major principles and a number of related ones. The basic principles are:

1) Select books that tend toward the development and enrichment of life. (In order to accomplish this type of selection, one must know the foundation books—usually the older titles and the "valuable" ones in the current output. The purpose of collection development thus seems to be to enlighten, to lessen patterns of mass thinking that may be prevalent but are not conducive to tolerant living, or to help patrons comprehend vital current issues. This seems, though, to place an inappropriate burden on the selector, since that person must make judgments as to what the community should or should not read.)

2) Make the basis for selection positive, not negative. Every book should be of service, not simply harmless.

Her list of related principles is rather extensive and may leave a person wondering when or how *all* of that can be done:

1) know your community's general and special character and interests;

2) be familiar with subjects of current interest—general, national, local;

3) represent in the collection all subjects applicable to these conditions;

4) make the collection of local history materials useful and extensive;

5) provide for organized groups whose activities and interests can be related to books;

6) provide for both *actual* and *potential* readers: satisfy *existent* demands and *anticipate* those suggested by events, conditions, and increasing use;

7) avoid selection of non-demand books; remove those past a useful life;

8) select some books of permanent value regardless of their potential use; great literary works must remain the foundation of the library's structure;

9) practice impartiality in selection: no favored hobbies or opinions; in controversial or sectarian subjects, accept gifts if purchase is undesirable;

10) provide as far as possible for the needs of specialist users: those requiring books as tools have a special service claim on the library, so long as the books aren't too esoteric in nature;

11) strive not for a "complete" collection, but for the "best": the best books on a subject, best books of an author, most useful volumes of a series. Ignore the practice of getting full sets without a need for all of the parts of each one;

12) prefer an inferior book that will be read over a superior one that will not. With wide and discriminating knowledge, it is usually possible to choose a book with both value and interest on its own level;

13) keep abreast of current thought and opinion; represent adequately significant and influential scientific, intellectual, and social forces;

14) maintain, so far as possible, promptness and regularity in supplying new books—especially in the case of books both good and popular.

In many ways, this list reflects Drury's work, as it should, since Haines's work was in essence an updating of the earlier title. If anything, however, her list makes an even stronger case for the "quality" collection. Most of the demand principles are modified; some are qualitative statements. As does anyone writing on this subject, Haines recognized the impossibility of one person's handling all the titles in just one major field of interest for a library. She also was one of the first to describe a comprehensive method for handling this problem, her solution being to make extensive use of the bibliographic/selection aids supplemented with local input. She lists six types of selection aids, and while one may not agree with her ranking of importance, the types seem to be comprehensive in coverage. The aids are listed in her rank order:

1) those issued by library organizations (IFLA, LA, ALA, etc.);

2) those issued by individual libraries (British Museum, Library of Congress, Bibliothèque Nationale, etc.);

3) those issued by societies and educational institutions (Unesco, Modern Language Association, etc.);

4) those issued by publishing organizations (*Publishers Weekly, Bookseller*, etc.);

5) those issued by individual publishers (catalogs, announcements, flyers, etc.);

6) those issued by other groups as part of their service (book reviews in periodicals and newspapers).

Without an extensive knowledge of these aids and without using them constantly, it would almost be impossible to function as an effective book selector. You must spend a considerable amount of time simply in getting to know the tools and their assets and limitations. Just as experience is the only way to get to know authors and publishers, the same is true for selection aids.

Haines goes further than earlier writers in recommending a specific system for selection work. Although it is general in nature and could be applied, within limits, in any country in any type of library, she presumes that an extensive and effective bibliographic network exists in the country. She suggests the following procedure:

1) examine the bibliographic aids on a regular and systematic basis— publishers' flyers and catalogs, lists of new books published or received, and book review sources;

2) prepare cards for titles that seem to be of potential value; be certain to indicate the source of the information;

3) solicit and accept recommendations from patrons;

4) incorporate into one "possible order" file both suggestions from patrons and those from bibliographic tools;

5) search for published reviews of titles in the file;

6) sort the file into two groups—one to order immediately and a "hold" group (usually those for which no reviews could be found);

7) transfer cards for titles ordered to an "on-order" file; this will save time and effort by avoiding unintentional duplication.

This is a workable system but it does place great emphasis on reviews and reviewers, whose judgments about a title are made without particular reference to the local situation. Naturally there is a need for local professional judgments to be involved in the final decision. A particular problem for academic, research and special libraries is that the titles they acquire are in many instances highly technical and reviews, if they appear at all, are very, very slow—anywhere from one to two years after publication. In most cases the library cannot wait that long to buy the title. Thus there is a need for a local review process.

Published reviews, although of great potential use, must be used with care and understanding, as all of the several types of them will be encountered by librarians engaged in selection. Haines identifies four types:

1) "reviews" that are solely intended to promote the sales of a title. Although often presented so as to appear to be reviews, these are more rightfully termed announcements and are usually prepared by the publisher at the time of publication;

2) reviews published in library periodicals. Even being written with library needs in mind, however, these publications cannot review every title published. Such reviews usually appear shortly after a title's publication;

3) reviews published in mass market newspapers and periodicals. If the book review editor is knowledgeable, these are useful in identifying potential high demand items. This type of review appears within two to six months after publication of a title;

4) reviews published in specialized subject publications. Usually written by specialists in the field the book is about, these are scholarly assessments of nonfiction titles of scholarly interest—no fiction. These will not appear until nine months to eighteen months after a book's publication.

No matter what type of review medium you are using, you must get to know the abilities and biases of the editors and the reviewers. Thus it is more beneficial to use reviews that are signed, and over a period of time you can get to know reviewers. But human nature being what it is, we tend to respect and accept the opinions of persons who share our personal biases. Nevertheless, use of reviews does provide a backup, outside opinion that supports a decision concerning a particular title.

One useful aspect of the review process, if the title is widely reviewed, is that you will frequently observe a wide range of opinion about its value. Some persons may find this difference of opinion a problem; they want to buy titles getting only good reviews. Mixed reviews require more local judgment but the differences in viewpoint may provide just the insight needed to make an informed local decision. It is possible that what was viewed in a negative light by a reviewer could be just the factor that a library may be looking for, and thus supports the decision to buy the title.

A major problem is that no single review medium in a country with an active book trade is able to review more than a fraction of the annual output. Consequently, some titles never get a published review, while others seem to be reviewed more widely than their subject matter seems to warrant. Because only a small percentage of titles can be reviewed in a year, the role of the book review editor becomes critical. An editor may receive hundreds of titles and be able to review only half of the number received. Thus, this person's judgment of what will and will not be reviewed is significant. You may never know which titles were rejected for review, but given time and experience, you will soon learn those sources that review the highest percentage of titles that you need to consider. Generally, you will have to use a number of sources in order to achieve any degree of comprehensive coverage.

What is a good review? Haines supplies not only a good discussion about what to look for but also tells how to prepare a good review:

1) there should be a brief, accurate description of the book's subject(s) and its contents. This should be factual in presentation and should include information regarding the stated purpose of the book;

2) there should be, when appropriate, a comparison to similar works by the same or different authors. This should be factual; however, it is also

an appropriate place for a reviewer to take a personal stand on the quality and utility of the title under review;

3) there should be a straightforward style in the review. This is not the place for the reviewer to demonstrate literary style and wit at the expense of conveying useful information about the title under review;

4) there should be a limited range of topics reviewed by a single reviewer. A reviewer who attempts reviews on almost any subject must be suspect. As a librarian you need opinions based on in-depth subject knowledge;

5) there may or may not be a clearcut statement—"recommended" or "do not bother to read this one." Regardless of whether such statements are made, the review should be free of bias. Suspect the reviewer who never has anything good or bad to say about any book.

No one would ever say *always* or *never* depend upon published reviews. They are a useful *aid* in the selection process, and as you gain experience, you will learn how to make the most effective use of them.

In summary, Haines's book provides a detailed statement about the why, wherefores, and hows of selecting quality books. No matter what stand is taken on the issue of the library's setting and maintaining literary standards for the community being served, her book is essential reading for anyone wishing to become a book selector.

S. R. RANGANATHAN
Library Book Selection (1952)

One of the post-War writers who did all he could to create a more scientific approach to collection development was S. R. Ranganathan. (Without question Ranganathan was one of the leading thinkers about librarianship. He demonstrated that the central issues and problems of librarianship are international in scope. All librarians ought to read one of Ranganathan's works on cataloging/classification, administration, or collection development.)

In various places in *Library Book Selection*, he enunciates five laws of librarianship, laws that underlie all of his concepts of librarianship and his view of how a library collection should be built. The five laws are:

1) books are for use;

2) every reader his book;

3) every book its reader;

4) save the time of the reader;

5) a library is a growing organism.

The list would seem to be very pragmatic. Clearly his first concern was in developing a library that would be a valuable asset to the community being served. Utility was the first consideration; after that, one should be concerned with quality.

Ranganathan suggests two important means of having some quality control, even when there is only a limited knowledge of the content of a specific title. If you know something about previous works by the same author, you will have a clue as to the general quality of the new work. (Of course, this assumes the author is writing in the same general field.) By using current reviews, when available, and a knowledge of past efforts by the same author, you can almost make your decision about the purchase of the item without examining the title. The danger in this approach is in being certain of having a sufficiently narrow definition of the phrase "in the same general field." A recent example of the type of difficulty that can happen concerns the American novelist, Allen Drury. As a writer of contemporary political novels, Drury is well known and respected; over the past several years though, he also has published two novels with an ancient Egyptian setting. Unfortunately, these latter novels do not come up to the same level of his earlier works. He is still a novelist, but the change in content from contemporary to historical plots has caused a change in style and quality. With an author such as Drury, you might well continue to buy his historical novels but perhaps in smaller quantities, at least in public library situations.

The second important suggestion of Ranganathan is to study publishing houses. (He does not actually discuss media producers, but his basic ideas apply to them just as much as to book publishers.) Many times just knowing the publisher or producer will provide enough information to make the selection decision. Some firms have such an extensive reputation for producing only "quality" material that 99 percent of the time you are completely safe in selecting one of their products sight unseen and even unreviewed. Unfortunately, a few firms have just the opposite reputation and you should never buy anything from them without extensive individual review of each item. As with any changing situation, one can never produce the definitive list of good and bad companies. Experience and input from colleagues in other libraries will provide the necessary on-going assessment, but the assessment must be continuous.

In addition to the company's overall reputation, one should consider the reputation of any series produced. Frequently a firm establishes one or more series; each series focuses on a limited area of concern—subject, format, purpose, etc. For example, this book is in Libraries Unlimited's Library Science Text Series. Some series are "house series," that is, handled by a firm's resident staff. Other series have editors who are not full-time members of the firm's staff; this is particularly true in the area of educational materials. Knowledge about series editors will affect the volume of selection work in accordance with the degree of confidence that you have in the series editor's judgment.

Ranganathan's book is a complex mixture of practical advice and philosophy. The five laws are straightforward, but their means of application is left to the reader. To some extent if any one law is rigorously followed, the others will be violated on occasion. Despite this unusual mix, however, his book is well worth reading.

CARTER, BONK, AND MAGRILL
Building Library Collections (4th ed., 1974)

Building Library Collections by Mary D. Carter, Wallace J. Bonk, and Rose Mary Magrill is certainly one of the standard American textbooks on the subject. Perhaps one reason for this success is that the authors are never prescriptive; instead, they present general principles and do not attempt to create a self-consistent body of principles. They observe that each librarian's conception of the library's purpose determines that person's attitude toward and application of the various principles. To some extent, the size and resources of a particular library will further affect the execution of individual assessments. Above all, there is no magic formula for effective selection beyond the use of informed professional judgments. They place more emphasis upon developing a plan of action and viewing the problem as building a *collection*, than on selecting individual titles.

Their list of principles reiterates what has been listed previously; in fact, they simply list a number (154) of principles that various writers have proposed and indicate which author(s) suggested which ideas. Essentially it is a book selector's smörgåsbord of principles from which an individual must then create a personal list. They seem to place greater emphasis on demand than on quality, although they do make it clear that they feel "basic items" and a "well rounded collection" are important.

Carter, Bonk, and Magrill emphasize the impact of the different types of library on the selection process more than any of the other authors discussed. Their ideas on this subject are worth repeating here:

1) large public libraries with both a heterogeneous community to serve and a reasonable book budget theoretically can apply most of the principles with very little modification within the total library system;

2) medium-sized public libraries are also in a similar position except the level of funding usually forces greater care in selection—mistakes are more costly;

3) small public libraries are the ones most limited, and generally they can only hope to meet the most significant community demands from their collections. They lack both the professional staff and money to do more than this;

4) college libraries serve a more homogeneous population or rather, the service goals are more homogeneous. In most cases, demand is the operative principle: materials needed in support of the instructional program are acquired and the quality of the material is not usually questioned if the request originated from a faculty member or department;

5) university libraries serve a more diverse population than do college libraries but their populations generally are more homogeneous than those of public libraries. Again, the first priority goes to meeting academic and research demands of the faculty and students; after those needs are met the collection is "rounded out" as funds permit;

6)   community college libraries are often closer to public libraries than to academic libraries in terms of the diversity of needs that must be met, a result of the wide variety of vocational programs that most community colleges offer. Demand and quality are almost equal factors in this case—limited funds and broad coverage usually mean that the library and faculty must work closely to select the "best" items for their institution;

7)   special libraries are very homogeneous and "develop" their collections almost solely by demand;

8)   school libraries are unique in that school librarians seldom have sole responsibility for developing the collection. The school system makes the decisions as to what to include; certainly the librarians have input, but their voice is not as strong as in other types of libraries.

DAVID SPILLER
Book Selection: An Introduction to Principles and Practices
(2nd ed., 1974)

Book Selection is a standard British work on the subject. Spiller presents the problem of selection as the means of resolving the conflict between two goals—education and demand. Although his work reflects a slight public library bias, the concepts can be applied in any library.

Spiller feels that as far as the educational goal is concerned, two important factors must be present. First, there should be a minimum coverage of all subject fields, achieved with standard works. (A problem exists in determining what those standard works are as well as who will make the decision about superseded items.) The second factor is that all but the very smallest libraries initially should attempt to stock the standard works in both literature and subject fields for both adults and children. (In this area, Spiller's public library bias is most clear. He does not contend, nor suggest, that his book applies to special libraries or academic libraries; however, much of his material pertains to college libraries, including some of the references to children's literature.) As far as demand is concerned, he sees the situation as one in which:

1)   community needs and interests merit more than minimum coverage— including those of non-users if possible—so that special groups who would otherwise be without resources may be serviced [you do this only after the minimum is served, though] ;

2)   even small public libraries should:
    a)   change a large proportion of their stock frequently to give an indication of the total resources available;
    b)   attempt to serve along the wide range of tastes in the community rather than limiting choices entirely to popular material.

Certainly demand takes a secondary position to the combination of education and quality in Spiller's philosophy. This is further reflected in his identification of three main reading areas: factual, cultural, and recreational. Factual reading is defined as purposeful reading with emphasis on a need for practical information. Cultural reading expands an individual's world view, illuminates some aspect of life. Recreational reading, for amusement, is the least specific area; since alternate sources of recreational reading materials are usually available, a smaller range of such material can be made available. Spiller sees persons reading primarily for one of these three reasons, although he does indicate that at times the purposes may be mixed; of more importance to the book selector, a single title may serve all these purposes for one or more readers.

The library's approach to solving the goal conflict inherent in education versus demand is modified by its relationship to formal or informal educational programs in the community. The library may choose to complement or support these educational programs. In either case, the identified level of service will also modify the selection process. Finally, there is a factor not often discussed by other writers: the level and effectiveness of interlibrary loan systems. An extensive and effective interlibrary loan system can have a major impact on how you develop your collection. No matter what modifications took place, Spiller sees the final aim of any educational library service program to be to increase involvement—to widen the reading interests of present users from occasional, practical use to wider interest in cultural and purposeful reading, and to increase the number and type of clientele' using the library.

ROBERT BROADUS
Selecting Materials for Libraries (1973)

A relatively recent book on selection is Robert Broadus's *Selecting Materials for Libraries*. His principles are not as explicit as those in other works; instead, he produces an inventory of factors or attitudes present in the selection process. The inventory is a mixture of the desirable ideal and practical necessity. As to a personal philosophy of collection development, Broadus places first importance on the type of library and then is concerned about quality and demand. He thinks that the responsiveness of the library to its "parent institution" is the critical factor in shaping the collection. Intellectually a distinction can be made between responsiveness and demand; but on a practical day-to-day basis, the two are almost inseparable. If the library is established by a parent institution to support this or that function of that parent institution, it is difficult to contend that the purpose of the library is not to satisfy that demand.

Quality and demand are seen as factors that primarily affect public libraries. Regarding public libraries, Broadus takes the position that either factor may be stressed as desired, since the issue is usually never fully resolved in the library's policy. An attempt is made to present the case for both sides, but his position is that the library should meet both the "currently expressed" and "ultimate" needs of the community. To do this the library must make available the best in quality because: a) a small number of persons appreciate quality [this is a demand], and b) this can help meet future demands for high quality items after the community's conceptions of quality have been raised.

Broadus suggests a number of factors to consider in assessing demand:

1) be aware of the impact of publicity that may stimulate demand (an author interviewed on radio or television, a highly favorable review in a local newspaper, etc.);

2) be certain to consider the duration as well as the intensity of the demand (consider renting multiple copies of highly popular titles; the demand for certain titles may decrease after a short period of time);

3) be certain to weigh the amount of possible opposition to a title (controversy tends to stimulate demand);

4) be certain to have a reasonably high percentage of "standards" and classics [even if not extensively used, they can be employed as public relations devices with groups that may be concerned with the "quality" of the collection] ;

5) be certain to consider past loans of specific titles and subjects (past use is one of the most reliable predictors of future use);

6) be certain to make some provision for serving the needs of potential users in the community (having made such provision advertises the fact);

7) be certain to weigh the differences between "true" demand (reflecting individual needs) and "artificial" demand (organized propaganda efforts). This is especially important when assessing differences in reading abilities, ages, living conditions, ethnic backgrounds, economic conditions, etc.

Broadus also had some general advice about collection development that is somewhat different from that given by other writers:

1) the maxim "the right book for the right reader at the right time" means accounting for *individual* readership in selection policy, as there are various individual needs, interests, and capacities for reading, learning, and enjoyment;

2) a decision against a particular book should be based on justifiable selection standards concerned with merit and honesty, and it should not infringe on the freedom to read of either a majority or minority;

3) the present status of the collection influences the selection process:
   a) a gap revealed by an unsatisfied demand should be of concern—fill it for future users;
   b) a "balanced collection" should really be an *optimum collection* for a given community of users or ought-to-be users;
   c) insure the presentation of truth by providing materials on all sides of controversial issues and representing all responsible opinions—although quantitative equality in this matter is not always necessary;
   d) on occasion, a small part of any special collection can be strengthened—thereby gaining the library a distinction and serving a few people that other libraries cannot serve as well. Belief in "balance" should not interfere with this aim;

4) selection should be influenced by other collections in the community and by particular allegiances that the library may owe (membership in cooperatives or networks of various kinds);

5) written policy statements are desirable, especially for public libraries. They are of use in:
    a) clarifying the dimensions and limits of the collection being built (through reference to forms, subjects, and usership of materials collected);
    b) emphasizing patrons' rights, thus legitimately buffering unjust complaints. A written policy can effectively shift the focus of discussion from a certain title to a question of principle.

THOUGHTS ON THE SELECTION PROCESS

All of the foregoing material contains a wealth of information for anyone interested in collection development and/or book selection. Because the process of book selection is subjective, you will need to formulate a personal philosophy. In addition to this personal perspective, your selection work will be influenced by the type of your library, its policies, and the community it serves. The following are suggestions as to what a person should do if serious about becoming a first-rate book selector:

1) do not forget that collection development is a dynamic series of interrelated activities, and actual selection is but one of six of them;

2) take time to learn the basics of the book trade and audio visual production;

3) get to know book editors and producers of audio visual materials;

4) study the publishers who produce the best materials for your library—examine their catalogs in detail, look for advertisements, learn the names of their editors;

5) spend time reading reviews in a wide variety of sources, not just your favorites—determine what the review editors and reviewers both like and dislike, and compare these findings with what your library requires;

6) examine the trade and national bibliographies with great care—determine how accurately they report the materials that your library needs;

7) knowledge of the library's community is the foundation upon which to build its collection. *Do not* stay in the library and expect to have a useful (and used) collection. Only by getting out into the community, meeting people, and becoming involved in community organizations can you develop the necessary "feel" for what is needed;

8) read as much as possible about the philosophies and processes of book selection, reviewing, and acquisition activities;

9) make independent personal judgments about specific titles, and compare those judgments with those found in national reviews;

10) be interested in what is going on in the world around you, and READ, READ, READ!

WHAT HAPPENS IN SELECTION

No matter what type of library you work in two steps will always occur in the selection process. Assuming that areas of need have been identified, a list of books that will meet those needs must be secured. The procedures in this first step vary from library to library. In most situations, the identification of possible titles for acquisition draws heavily from published lists, catalogs, flyers, announcements, and bibliographies. (We will discuss categories of published aids later in this chapter.) After the list is secured (and this may be no more difficult than locating a copy of a current bibliography), a person or group of persons assesses the worth of various titles on the same topic. In some cases only one book will be available. When that occurs the only questions to resolve are: is the price reasonable for the level of use that the book will receive? and is the book physically suitable for the projected use? If both questions are answered in the affirmative or the negative, there is no problem. When they are answered differently, more information about the level of need for that item must be secured.

More often than not, though, the assessment is made using published information rather than a physical examination of the book. An item-by-item physical examination and reading would be ideal; however, for most libraries there simply is not enough time to secure examination copies and review each item, at least for everything they buy. School and public libraries generally devote more time to looking over "approval" copies than do academic libraries although large university and research libraries do use approval plans. Large public libraries frequently use the Greenaway Plan, discussed in chapter 3, for securing examination material. To reiterate, this Plan in essence is a contract between a library and a publisher for buying at a large discount one copy of all or most of that publisher's trade books. The purpose is to provide examination copies immediately after publication so that the library can decide which titles should be acquired in multiple copies. If the library exhibits no intent to buy multiple copies, however, publishers will not be willing to sign a Greenaway agreement.

Almost all wholesalers and jobbers will provide libraries with examination copies if there is a reasonable expectation of purchase of each title sent or of multiple-copy orders being placed. For example, if you requested 100 titles on approval and kept 90, the jobber would probably send other titles on approval. However, if you kept only 65 titles, you would have to convince the firm that there was good reason for this high rejection rate (unless you order additional copies of most of the retained titles) before you would receive another approval shipment. The reason is simple: it costs as much to select, pack, and ship an approval order as it does an actual firm order. (This is true for both the library and vendor.) Thus, the more a library can depend upon published selection aids to reduce the number of examination copies it would otherwise receive, the better off everyone will be. Most academic libraries use a jobber approval program, but the principle remains the same for all types of libraries: the return rate must be low. Vendors usually get upset if the rate gets above 10 percent.

SELECTION AIDS

No one involved in collection development ever forgets how dependent they are on bibliographies and review sources for information essential to building a library collection. It is possible to imagine a situation without published aids, but either the size of the library staff would go up dramatically or the number of items acquired would go down in the same fashion. What the aids provide is some degree of control over the output of publishers and media producers. Imagine, if you will, the problems that a library staff would have if no bibliographies or review sources existed. Each publisher and audio visual producer would flood the library with catalogs and announcements of their products, and developing a filing and retrieval system for that material would be a significant problem for the library. How many books exist on vegetable gardening? Going through thousands of catalogs and announcements to cull all relevant items would be very time-consuming. This merely underscores the fact that despite their shortcomings and the complaints that libraries have about various individual aids, these tools are timesavers; and for today's output, they are essential if libraries are to function with any degree of efficiency.

A number of aids will be described along with a few representative titles. It is emphasized that the listing is selective, as there are literally hundreds of titles in most of the categories when you consider the world-wide nature of publishing and audio visual production. In many libraries it is a matter of world-wide (or at least multi-national) selection. All of the aids that follow will save you time and frustration *if* you take the time to study the titles in each one. As with any reference tool, the first step is to read the introductory material that the publisher or producer provides. A good introduction will answer the following questions:

1) why does this work exist?

2) what does it do that other works fail to do?

3) what does it contain?

4) if it is selective in coverage, how was the selection made and who made it?

5) how is the material arranged?

6) how do you go about using the work most effectively?

7) how current is the information?

If the introductory material does not answer all or most of these questions, then the item is probably either brand new (and may not last) or else an old established tool. Should it be an established tool, information about it may be found in the basic guides to reference books (such as Sheehy, *American Reference Books Annual*; Walford; etc.).

We will examine six general categories of selection aids for books and one each for serials and microforms:

1)   current sources for in-print books;

2)   catalogs, flyers, announcements;

3)   current reviews;

4)   national bibliographies;

5)   recommended, best, core collection lists;

6)   subject lists;

7)   serial selection aids;

8)   microform selection aids.

Remember, the examples within each category are selective; to give complete, world-wide coverage to all the titles in each would require one or two books at least as long as this one.

Current Sources for In-Print Books

New books (those acquired during the year they were published) represent the majority of the materials acquired by most libraries. In some of the large research and/or archival libraries, this may not be quite the case; but even in such libraries, new books would still be a major share of the total. Every country in the world with any significant amount of publishing has some publication that attempts to list that nation's books in print. Naturally, the degree of success varies, and access to such a list may be easy or difficult. For countries with a high volume of publishing (such as the United States, Great Britain, and other industrialized countries), there may be weekly listings of new books (examples are the *Weekly Record* of the R. R. Bowker Company, or the *Bookseller* of Whitakers). Lists of this type (in-print) normally provide information on author, title, publisher, place of publication, date of publication, and price. Beyond this minimum, there may be information about length, special features, series information, International Standard Book Number (ISBN), and sometimes cataloging information, including subject headings. The last item can be very helpful in selection, as too often the title of a book does not provide enough information to allow anyone to make an informed judgment about its content. More often that not, though, weekly lists allow only an author search, so they are time-consuming if you are doing a subject search.

Monthly lists are also common, either as the first listing or as cumulations of weekly lists. If it is a monthly accumulation of weekly lists such as *American Book Publishing Record* (Bowker) or *Books of the Month* (Whitaker), it will contain the same information as the weekly listing but also provide several means of access—usually subject, author, and title. In a few countries, pre-publication announcements are compiled in one source, such as *Forthcoming Books* (Bowker) and *Books of the Month and Books to Come* (Whitaker). [The latter combines current and future listings for a three-month period.] While such aids can be of some value in planning purchases of new books, two major factors limit their use: 1) many announced books do not appear as scheduled, and 2) a few announced titles are never released.

For many countries, an annual list is the only one, or at least the only one that you will be able to secure in the case of countries with low new book outputs. Annual lists may range from only a few hundred pages to multivolume sets. All contain the basic bibliographic information required to order a specific book (author, title, publisher, date, price); and most include many of the other features listed above and provide author, title, and subject access. Examples of annual lists are *Books in Print* (Bowker); *Cumulative Book Index* (H. W. Wilson); *British Books in Print, Paperbacks in Print,* and *Whitaker's Cumulative Book List* (Whitaker); *Les livres de l'année—Biblio* (Hachette) [often *Biblio*]. Almost every major language in which there is active publishing has an in-print book list.

Anyone concerned with collection development must remember that most "comprehensive" in-print lists issued by a commercial publisher are *not* complete. In almost all cases, the listing is based upon titles or information sent in by the original publishers. Thus, if a publisher forgets or does not wish to send in the data on a title or group of titles, nothing can be listed. Naturally, since in-print lists are so widely used as a buying tool, most publishers send in the information, as it almost provides free advertising. Nevertheless, many smaller publishers do not appear in such works, so never assume that because you did not find a specific title in the national in-print list that it is out of print or does not exist. Even if other titles by the same publisher are listed, it is wise to write to the publisher inquiring about the availability of the book you need. Some suspicious persons have suggested that a few publishers may be excluded from commercial in-print lists because of inter-company jealousies. To date no evidence suggests that this has or does happen.

Thus, the national in-print list becomes a primary tool in selection by virtue of its identifying new materials as they become available. Individuals involved in selection and acquisition work must be very familiar with these tools if they are to be effective in their work.

Catalogs, Flyers, and Announcements

Publishers also use catalogs and other forms of promotional material to inform buyers of what is available. Some publishers use a direct mail approach almost exclusively, feeling that national in-print lists bury their books among too many others. Also, they feel that such in-print lists do not provide enough information to sell their books. Such publishers will distribute catalogs that list all their available books and, in addition, send out flyers and announcements of new titles. Even publishers who participate in combined in-print lists employ these sales methods.

Generally, such announcements contain more information about a book and its author(s) than do national in-print lists. When it is not possible to secure a review copy or find a published review, the catalog and flyers listing the book can provide useful selection data. It probably should go without saying that such information must be used with caution. Very few publishers would lie about a book, but the purpose of the catalog and flyer is to sell the items; therefore, everything will be presented in the most favorable light. As you get to know publishers, you will learn which ones are reasonably objective and which tend to "puff" their books more than the content would warrant.

All this means that libraries must maintain files of publishers' catalogs and flyers. When you buy extensively in just one language, the number of publishers is large; when you buy on a world-wide basis, the problem is immense. But no matter on what level you buy, you must maintain the catalogs and flyers. Occasionally, there will be an attempt to publish a collection of publishers' catalogs (e.g., Bowker's *Publishers Trade List Annual*). Perhaps at some point this concept is valid, generally speaking; however, as the number of publishers and titles increase, the system fails. One major reason is that the information in the catalogs has to be updated by a library system. If you can get a catalog for free from the publisher and have to maintain an update system for any new materials, why pay someone else for giving you the catalog? A few years ago Bowker's *Books in Print* was based solely upon the information from the catalogs in *Publishers Trade List Annual*. Today this is not the case. Too many publishers could not afford to be in PTLA. Thus, fewer and fewer libraries buy it, depending instead upon their own filing system. (Also see the section on bookseller catalogs, pages 82-87).

Current Review Sources

Wherever there is a flourishing book trade, there is usually an equally strong book reviewing system. You can divide book reviewing into three general types: 1) reviews for persons making their living buying books (trade-professional booksellers and librarians), 2) reviews for subject specialists, and 3) reviews for the general public. Book selectors will use all three types, but the greatest use will be in the area of trade-professional reviews.

Trade-professional reviews can be divided into two subcategories: a) those designed to promote the book, and b) those designed to evaluate the book. With trade journals such as *Publishers Weekly* (Bowker) and *Bookseller* (Whitaker), although the primary market is the bookseller (both wholesale and retail), librarians can and do make effective use of their reviews. In essence, the reviews serve to alert booksellers to new titles that the publisher plans to push. Publishers have a reasonably good grasp of which titles will sell well and which will not, so not every title they publish will receive the same amount of advertising and promotion. A potential good seller frequently gets extra promotion in the hope that it will become a top seller. Bookstore owners would like to know about such titles ahead of time in order to have enough copies to meet the demand, since best sellers have relatively short life spans—high interest usually lasts for a month or two. (Library patrons want to read the best sellers when they are best sellers, not when the demand is down.) If selection staffs read the trade reviews, they too can have the best seller in their collection by the time interest in it peaks, rather than months later. When a trade review ends with something like "book club selection for April; national newspaper and television ads; nation-wide author tour," there is reason to expect more than average interest in the book. Although these reviews do not solve the problem of anticipating which new books will be in high public demand, they do help. Regularly reading these reviews will help you to identify the clues that could lead you to discern top demand items in your library.

Evaluative reviews prepared by librarians and by specialists for librarians are also extremely important in selection, especially in public and school libraries. You will find these reviews in almost all library publications (*Library Journal, Wilson Library Bulletin, LA Record*, etc.). Normally, such reviews are both descriptive and evaluative; occasionally, they will also be comparative. Reviews of this type are particularly useful because they are prepared with library needs in mind.

Despite the fact that many library publications contain book reviews, only a small percentage of the total publishing output for any year are reviewed. Some titles are heavily reviewed; others, never.

An analysis of ten major American book review journals (both professional and general public) for the year 1976 showed the following total of books reviewed: *Choice*–6,402; *Library Journal*–5,819; *Booklist*–4,719; *Publishers Weekly*–4,184; *Kirkus Services*–4,050; *School Library Journal*–2,430; West Coast *Review of Books*–1,352; *New York Times*–1,186; *Bulletin of the Center for Children's Books*–798; *Horn Book*–429; and *New York Review of Books*–314 [not all NYRB reviews concern new books]. The magnitude of the problem of coverage is clear when you realize that at least 24,951 titles were published in 1976. The total number of reviews published in the ten journals was 31,683. If there was no overlap—and it is known that some overlap does exist—the average number of reviews per title was 1.27. *Choice* probably covers the largest percentage of new books of primary interest to academic libraries. However, just in the fields of sociology and economics, 4,303 hardcover new titles were issued in 1976. If you include history (1,531 new hardcover titles), there would be only 568 reviews left for all other fields of academic interest, assuming that all economics, sociology, and history books were reviewed. The messages that these data convey are clear: 1) no one book review source will cover more than a fraction of the total output; 2) even if every book were to be reviewed, you would only find 1¼ reviews per title; and 3) it is very likely that a number of new titles will never be reviewed.

Another limitation on the use of the reviews is that they tend to be delayed in publication. Most trade reviews appear before the publication date; most professional (library) reviews usually do not appear until several months after the publication date. One reason for this latter situation is that books are sent to librarians and subject specialists, a strength in this method of reviewing. But first, the book is sent to the journal's book review editor, who then must identify a reviewer and send the book to that person. The reviewer may or may not be able to read and review the book immediately. Eventually, the review is sent to the editor, who will edit the text and schedule the review for publication. This is a complex process but necessary if one wants a number of librarians to be involved in the review process.

In addition to the general professional reviews, some journals focus on a type of library; for example, *School Library Journal, Choice* (academic), and *Booklist* (public). Naturally there is some overlap in materials, and journal editors try to make their publications somewhat useful to all types of libraries. Nevertheless, they do have a primary field of emphasis. They focus on certain classes of books, and their reviewers are qualified to present an opinion on the value of a book for one type of library.

Occasionally, a journal will have a policy of only publishing reviews of books that are recommended. The major limitation here is that you are never certain as to which books were sent for review but got a negative evaluation and which books never were sent for review. Just as the general professional review sources cannot cover every new book, neither can the specialty sources. If you are dependent on, or required to use, published reviews in selecting books, this drawback can be important. You will wait a long time before you are certain that a book will not be reviewed and still not know whether it was negatively reviewed and not listed for that reason.

One important area of concern in book reviewing is how competent the reviewer is in the field of review. Nonfiction titles require subject expertise if the content of the book is to be evaluated. For general trade books, it is not so essential that the reviewer has an in-depth subject knowledge for every book reviewed. When you get beyond the "introduction to . . . " and average readers' guides, the need for depth in background increases until you can reach the level where the expert is reviewing another expert's book for just a few other experts in the field. Most academic fields have one or two journals that publish scholarly reviews of books in the field. Expert reviews of this type could be of great assistance in developing a research collection in a subject. Unfortunately, despite the scholarship and length of such reviews, they seldom play a significant role in developing a collection. The major reason for this is that the reviews are not published soon enough; commonly, books reviewed in scholarly journals are one or two years old when the review appears, which is much too slow for libraries with patrons who need up-to-date material. The best thing you can do in the United States is to use *Choice*. Most of the reviewers are subject experts, and the reviews normally do appear within a year of publication (often only three or four months after publication). In order to gain wide coverage the reviews are relatively short—one or two paragraphs; thus, you lose depth to gain coverage and speed.

A final category of review sources are the general public sources such as the *New York Times Book Review, Times Literary Supplement*, etc. Anyone concerned with building a collection geared to current popular reading must examine these as a normal part of the selection process. Editors of such book review sources must keep in touch with current interests and tastes in order to hold their readership. Therefore, although they are only able to review a very small percentage of the new titles, they select the ones they do review with great care. The value of these reviews lies in two areas: 1) the books are selected with an eye toward current popular taste; and 2) the titles reviewed will be seen by thousands of readers, thereby creating a demand for them. Because these sources are geared to current interests, and because most of their reviewers are paid for preparing reviews, most of the books that do get reviewed are covered within a month or two after their publication date.

The data on the number of book reviews published each year in only ten journals made it clear that you will be facing a search problem if you use only reviews for selection purposes (where *has* that book been reviewed?). To some extent, indexing services that cover book reviews will help, but indexes of book reviews are of little assistance for the very current new titles (from publication date to about eight months old). Not only is there the delay (described earlier) in publishing the review, but there is another delay in indexing the review journal and in publishing the index. However, for older titles, the indexes can be a major timesaver. *Book Review Digest* and *Book Review Index* are two major American tools of this type. Another clue to the problem in review coverage of new titles is found in *Book Review Digest* (BRD). Each year BRD publishes citations to and summaries of 5,000 to 6,000 new books. Titles are included only if a nonfiction title receives two reviews or a fiction title receives four reviews. BRD editors examine seventy leading journals and newspapers that have large book review sections. Even in this large number of potential sources for reviews, though, only 5,000-6,000 new books out of 24,000-plus are reviewed at least twice. In addition to the index publications that only cover book reviews, many of the general periodical indexes include book review citations, and these should be noted for future use.

Book reviews are useful for most libraries because there is insufficient time available to have the staff read and review all of the new books that might be suitable additions to the collection. Reviews *must not* be used as a substitute for local judgments; just because review X claimed that the book is great does not mean that the book will be great for your library. As the title of this section indicates, reviews are aids in selection, not the means of selection. When you gain more and more familiarity with book review editors and the reviewers' biases, these tools will become more valuable as a source of useful information.

National Bibliographies

Up to this point the discussion has focused on new (in print) books. At some point in time, however, almost every library will need to add some books that are not in print. Retrospective collection development (adding books that are out of print) is a normal part of most academic and research library programs. School and public libraries will have to buy replacement copies for some of the books that wear out but are still used. Special libraries, as a class, do the least retrospective buying, but they do, on occasion, have to acquire out-of-print materials. (The sources for acquiring out-of-print books were covered in chapter 3.) However, before you buy the material you must identify it. Your sources for identifying authors, titles, publishers, and dates of publication of out-of-print items are varied, but one major source is the national bibliography network.

Most countries with a strong book trade have a national bibliography of some type. (There are many specific types of bibliographies—trade, national, general, etc., which are covered in reference books. For purposes of this book, a national bibliography is a listing of books published in a country or about a country.) One common feature of most of these bibliographies is that they are produced by nonprofit organizations—in many cases the national library or a very large research library. Some examples are the *British National Bibliography* (Council of the British National Bibliography), *Catalogue général des livres de la Bibliothèque Nationale* (Bibliothèque Nationale), and *National Union Catalog* (Library of Congress).

Frequency of publication varies from weekly to yearly, and in some cases, simply whenever there is enough material to warrant issuing a volume. A few of these bibliographies are based in part upon books received by the country's copyright office (*British National Bibliography*—BNB). In those cases, if it also includes out-of-print titles added to the library's collection, the bibliography serves as both an in-print and retrospective aid. A number of the national and large research libraries have or are publishing their public catalogs in multivolume sets (British Museum, Library of Congress, Bibliothèque Nationale). If you have access to a full set plus the updated material, then you have an almost complete record of official holdings of the library.

Because these libraries are so large, and in most cases, collect almost everything produced in and about their country, the published catalogs are valuable bibliographic checking sources. Use them to verify the existence of a particular work, and locate at least one source for the work if you cannot acquire the book from any other source. (For a fuller discussion of the process of bibliographic verification see chapter 8 on acquisition work.) When you use the *National Union Catalog* (NUC) volumes, you will find entries for libraries other than the Library of Congress. These volumes contain information about other libraries holding a particular book, and in some cases, the book is not even in the Library of Congress collection.

You should be able to establish all of the following information in any of the existing national bibliographies: author, full title, publisher, place and date of publication, pagination, and form of main entry for the book in the library. Beyond this, in most cases, you can usually get information about special features of the book—bibliographies, illustrations, charts, maps, whether part of a series, scope notes, and subject information (the classification number and subject heading tracings). In a few national bibliographies you will find the original price of the book.

Large academic and research libraries may use the current issues of NUC, BNB, and other national bibliographies as a selection aid. For most other types of libraries, these tools are used more to verify the existence of a title, rather than as a selection tool. But no matter what the purpose is, these items must be used with care. For example, both the United States and Great Britain have a reasonably comprehensive bibliographic network for new books. Several years ago, for use in another book, *Introduction to Technical Services for Library Technicians*, 3rd edition (Libraries Unlimited, 1976), three books were searched through the basic American and British bibliographies (fourteen items—PW through NUC and *Bookseller* through *British Museum General Catalog*).* The results are of some interest here.

Books searched:
1) all had personal author entries;

2) all were monographs;

3) two of them were available in both hardbound and paper covers;

4) two of the books were American and one was British.

Bibliographies searched:
1) although each title was searched through all available approaches to each bibliography (author, title, and sometimes subject), only two of the fourteen bibliographies searched listed all three books;

---

*(1) *Publishers Weekly* (PW), (2) *American Book Publishing Record* (BPR), (3) *Publishers Trade List Annual* (PTLA), (4) *Books in Print* (BIP), (5) *Subject Guide to Books in Print*, (6) *Paperbound Books in Print*, (7) *Cumulative Book Index* (CBI), (8) *National Union Catalog* (NUC), (9) *Bookseller*, (10) *British Books in Print* (BBIP), (11) *Whitaker's Cumulative Book List* (CBL), (12) *British National Bibliography* (BNB), and (14) *British Museum General Catalog.*

2)   American titles are slow to appear in British sources and vice versa;

3)   when a title is released in England and the United States at the same time, it appears in the trade bibliographies of both countries;

4)   subject entries varied even within the same bibliography;

5)   there is little consistency in the listing of series;

6)   when searching a library catalog, you must know that particular library's rules for establishing the main entry.

Best Books, Recommended Lists, and Core Collections

Earlier in this chapter we touched on the problem of generating lists of the "best of ... " or items recommended for purchase. They are useful aids when employed carefully. If there is any doubt that book selection is a subjective process, it should be dispelled upon looking over the number of titles that exist in this category. Titles such as *Public Library Catalog* (H. W. Wilson), *Books for Public Libraries* (R. R. Bowker), *Books for College Libraries* (ALA), or *Opening Day Collection* (Choice) have some overlap, but also some differences. The differences arise from the purposes of the list makers and individuals who make the selection. Personal opinions vary, and these lists are either one person's opinion or a composite of many opinions about the value of a particular book.

Few specialists in collection development would claim that a library ought to hold any title just because it was on two or more recommended lists. If the list is something like basic books for undergraduate programs in mathematics, and is produced by a national association of mathematics teachers, and the library is at an institution with an undergraduate program in mathematics, there is reason to expect that a high percentage of the titles in the list would be in the collection, *but not every title*. Why not? A major reason would be differences in emphasis in the school's program; there may be no need for a particular title. Another factor is that often several equally good alternatives are available. A good list for collection development purposes will indicate alternatives (for example, *A Basic Library List: For Four-Year Colleges*, 2nd ed., Mathematical Association of America, 1976). A final factor is that the list is out of date the day it is published; new titles may have appeared that supersede the titles listed. Also, trying to get a copy of every title on a list can be very time-consuming. Unless there is agreement that it is important to secure every title, do not spend the time; retrospective buying requires considerably more time than buying in-print titles.

Subject Bibliographies

Subject bibliographies suffer from many of the same limitations as the "best" or "recommended" lists: currency and selectivity. If the bibliography is prepared by one or more subject experts and contains critical evaluations of the items listed, it can be of great value in both selection and collection evaluation. The range of possible titles in subject areas is limited only by the imagination of the compilers. First, however, learn the contents of some of the bibliographies covering broad subject fields, such as: *Fine Arts* (D. H. Ehresmann; Libraries Unlimited, 1975); *The Humanities* (A. R. Rogers; Libraries Unlimited, 1974); *Use of Social Science Literature* (N. Roberts; Butterworths, 1977); or *Use of Physics Literature* (H. Coblans; Butterworths, 1975). In most broad fields more than one bibliography has been published. Compare earlier titles to current titles. Where these have been multiple editions, check on the amount of change between editions. Do new editions merely add more titles or is there a real revision with older, superseded titles dropped and new assessments made of all the items? Do not depend upon published reviews; do your own checking before using such a bibliography as a selection aid.

Serials

Serials present another entirely different bibliographic network. Few of the book selection aids described above include newspapers, periodicals, or serials. Although all of the same categories of book selection aids do not exist for serials (used throughout the text to mean newspapers, periodicals, and serial publications), several similarities can be seen.

Several in-print lists do exist for serials. Most of these provide such information as title (perhaps even former title), place of publication, price, frequency, sometimes circulation figures, publisher's and/or editor's address, and where the title is indexed and/or abstracted. Earlier it was noted that a library normally uses a serials jobber for handling the placement of subscriptions; a useful guide to subscription jobbers is *International Subscription Agents*, 4th edition (ALA). However, as with books, some serials must be ordered directly from the publisher. Also, a number of publications have similar or even identical titles. Place of publication information and any data on institutional affiliation can be invaluable in entering a subscription to the right serial. Examples of in-print lists, somewhat analogous to *Books in Print*, are: *Ulrich's International Periodical Directory* (R. R. Bowker), *Ayer Directory of Publications* (Ayer Press), *Standard Periodical Directory* (Oxbridge), *Guide to Current British Journals* (Library Association), and *Willing's Press Guide* (Thomas Skinner Directories). *New Serial Titles* (Library of Congress) is somewhat akin to a national serials bibliography, especially if it is used in conjunction with *Union List of Serials* (H. W. Wilson).

Reviews of new periodicals and serials are not too easy to find if you are looking for reasonably comprehensive coverage. Some professional journals such as *Library Journal* and *Wilson Library Bulletin* include a few reviews of periodicals, but a journal such as *Serials Librarian* does not. In most cases if you want to see what you will be getting, ask for sample copies from the publisher. Another place to examine new titles is at the combined book and serials exhibits at professional conventions. But do remember an earlier point—serials can change dramatically between issues; just because the sample issue looks excellent does *not* always mean the journal is worth acquiring. Naturally, if a library near you has a long current run of the serial, go there to examine the title. Examining issues and/or runs of a periodical title is important because the decision to subscribe is usually a long-term expensive commitment. Not only is there the annual subscription (which will go up in price), but the repetitive record-keeping (a library labor cost) for as long as you subscribe and, finally, a bindery cost (at least for most serials). Thus, taking a few extra hours or even days to make a decision based on an examination of the journal is a worthwhile investment.

Just as is true of books, lists of serials by subject area or type of library exist. The same limitations exist except current lists of periodicals are less likely to contain o.p. titles. While the quality of a periodical can change radically between issues, most do not after a few years of existence. In this way, time can be a useful factor in selecting periodicals for inclusion in a list of recommended titles. Some examples of such subject-type library lists are: *Periodicals for School Libraries* (ALA), *Classified List of Periodicals for the College Library* (R. R. Bowker), *Guides to Scientific Periodicals* (Library Association), *U.S. Government Scientific and Technical Periodicals* (Scarecrow), and *Encyclopedic Directory of Ethnic Newspapers and Periodicals in the United States* (Libraries Unlimited).

Microforms

Where do microformats belong—books or audio visual? Probably in both places. However, in this text they are at the end of the book section and in front of audio visual. Most of the guides to microform materials cover microfilms and microfiche that contain printed information.

At several points in the text we have discussed retrospective collection development. One of the problems in that activity is finding a "hard" copy of all of the items that you might wish to add to the collection. Usually, if you wait long enough (perhaps years) you will find the book or periodical volume in an out-of-print shop. Sometimes the need for the item is so great that you cannot wait. If reprint dealers do not have the item, then a microform copy may be your answer.

Another reason for using microformats is to save space, especially with low-use back files of serials. (A back file or back run is a set of older volumes of a current serial subscription—for example, your current issues of *Newsweek* are from volume 92; volumes 1-91 would represent the back file for *Newsweek*.) When you have long runs and the use of the material is low, you may be wasting space by keeping the physical volumes in the library. A serial that occupies several hundred feet of shelf space may be reduced to less than a foot of space when each volume is put into a microformat. Naturally, there is a trade-off in space; the more material you have in microformat, the more equipment you will need in order for patrons to use the material. In addition to saving space, some serial librarians use a microformat for back files of popular titles that have a high incidence of mutilation or a habit of disappearing. Not many persons have microform readers in their homes, at least not yet; and if the library has reader-printers (a device that allows a person to read the microform and when he or she wishes, to push a buttom and receive a hard copy of the material being read), such loss and mutilation drops.

One major drawback to using microforms to any major degree in collection development is patron resistance. Many persons claim that they cannot read anything on microformats, that it gives them a headache, causes eyestrain, etc. Occasionally, someone will say it causes nausea. None of these has been established (headache or eyestrain) as a significant physiological problem for the majority of users. In most cases where the only source for the information is microform, an individual is able to use the material without a problem. Admittedly, it takes time to get used to using microforms—it is harder in some forms to locate a specific point in the text than when you have a book in hand. If the equipment is not properly maintained the image quality will be poor and will cause eyestrain; and equipment does break down and malfunction at times.

Despite these problems you will need to use more and more microformats as time goes on. The major factor in this increased use will be economic—new library buildings will be harder to secure; the prices of hard copies of older materials keep going up; and library book and materials budgets remain about the same or increase at a rate less than the inflation rate. Thus it is important to know the guides to microformats. Two guides to "in print" microformats are: *Guide to Microforms in Print* (Microform Review) and *National Register of Microform Masters* (Library of Congress). Both titles try to be international in scope, cover both commercial and non-commercial (libraries, historical associations, etc.) sources of supply, and cover over sixteen types of microformats. In the case of the latter title, only United States suppliers are covered, but the actual material available is international in scope. *Microform Market Place* (Microfilm Review) is an international directory of micro publishing, including microform jobbers. A major source for reviews of microform series, both current and retrospective, is *Microform Review* (Microfilm Review). Major producers have extensive catalogs of what they have available, and it is necessary to keep a file of their catalogs because even fewer micropublishers contribute information to the "in print" guides than do book publishers.

SUMMARY

In spite of the length of this chapter we have only reviewed the high points and basic issues of book selection. Even the following bibliography is highly selective. Learning to be a book selector is a lifelong process, and the items listed in the bibliography will provide you with further leads to material on all aspects about this challenging, exciting, and enjoyable aspect of collection development.

BIBLIOGRAPHY

General Works on Selection and Book Reviewing

Altick, R. D. *The English Common Reader: A Social History of the Mass Reading Public, 1800-1900.* Chicago: University of Chicago Press, 1957.

Arora, S. R., and R. N. Paul. "Acquisition of Library Materials: A Quantitative Approach." In American Society for Information Science. Conference, 1969, San Francisco. Proceedings, v.6: *Cooperating Information Societies.* Westport, CT: Greenwood, 1969. pp. 495-99.

Avant, J. A. "A Librarian Review of Reviews . . . Slouching Toward Criticism." *Library Journal* 96 (Dec. 15, 1971): 4055-59.

Bonny, H. V. *A Manual of Practical Book Selection for Public Libraries.* London: Grafton, 1939.

Bostwick, A. O. *The American Public Library.* New York: Appleton, 1929.

Broadus, R. N. *Selecting Materials for Libraries.* New York: H. W. Wilson, 1973.

Broderick, D. M. "Librarians and Literature." *Library Journal* 85 (Aug. 1960): 2709-2718.

Broderick, D. M. "Aftermath of an Article." *Library Journal* 85 (Oct. 15, 1960): 3261-65, 3234.

Carter, M., W. J. Bonk, and R. M. Magrill. *Building Library Collections.* 4th ed. Metuchen, NJ: Scarecrow, 1974.

"Case Studies of Six Public and School Library Systems." In Hensel, E., and P. D. Veillete. *Purchasing Library Materials in Public and School Libraries.* Chicago: American Library Association, 1969. pp. 25-80.

Clarke, J. A. "Search for Principles of Book Selection 1550-1700." *Library Quarterly* 41 (July 1971): 216-22.

The Climate of Book Selection: The Art of the Possible. Proceedings of a Workshop sponsored by Oregon State Library. N. R. Riggs, ed. Salem: Oregon State Library, 1971.

Crozet, L. *Manuel pratique du bibliothécaire.* Paris: Nourry, 1952.

Drury, F. K. W. *Book Selection.* Chicago: American Library Association, 1930.

Goldhor, H., ed. *Selection and Acquisition Procedures in Medium-Sized and Large Libraries. Papers Presented at an Institute Conducted by University of Illinois Graduate School of Library Science, November 11-14, 1962.* Champaign, IL: Illini Bookstore, 1963. (Allerton Park Institute Publications, no. 9).

Haines, H. E. *Living with Books.* 2nd ed. New York: Columbia University Press, 1950.

Hollander, J. "Some Animadversions on Current Reviewing." In Smith, R. H. *The American Reading Public.* New York: R. R. Bowker, 1963.

"Looking Inside NYRB." *Publishers Weekly* 205 (March 11, 1974): 36-40.

McColvin, L. R. *The Theory of Book Selection for Public Libraries.* London: Grafton, 1925.

Malcles, L. N. *Cours de bibliographie à l'intention des etudiants de l'université et des candidats aux examens de bibliothécaire.* Geneva: Droz, 1954.

Merritt, L. C., et al. *Reviews in Library Book Selection.* Detroit: Wayne State University Press, 1958. (Wayne State University Studies. Humanities, no. 3).

Monroe, M. E. "Meeting Demands: A Library Imperative." *Library Journal* 88 (Feb. 1, 1963): 516-18.

Naude, G. *Advis pour dresser une bibliothèque.* Paris: Renduel, 1836-39.

Peyre, H. "What's Wrong with American Book Reviewing." *Daedalus* 92 (Winter 1963): 128-44.

Ranganathan, S. R. *Library Book Selection.* Delhi: India Library Association, 1952.

Regnery, H. "Bias in Book Reviewing and Book Selection." *American Library Association Bulletin* 60 (Jan. 1966): 57-62.

Rowell, J. "A Total Book Selection Process." *Wilson Library Bulletin* 41 (Oct. 1966): 190-96.

Samore, T. "TLS or NYTBR: Does It Matter?" *Choice* 6 (June 1969): 473-77.

Shockley, A. A. "Black Book Reviewing: A Case for Library Action." *College and Research Libraries* 35 (Jan. 1974): 16-20.

Simmons, P. A. *Collection Development and the Computer: A Case Study in the Analysis of Machine Readable Loan Records and Their Application to Book Selection.* Vancouver: University of British Columbia, 1971.

Spiller, D. *Book Selection: An Introduction to Principles and Practice.* 2nd ed. Hamden, CT: Shoe String Press, 1974.

Stuttaford, G. "A Short Review of the Magazine Reviewers." *Publishers Weekly* 206 (Dec. 2, 1974): 38-41.

Totok, W., and R. Weitzel. *Handbuch der bibliographischen nachschlagewerke.* Frankfurt: Klostermann, c1972, 1977.

Weeks, K. R. *Determination of Pre-Acquisition Predictors of Book Use: Final Report.* Berkeley: Institute of Library Research, University of California, 1963.

Weyr, T. "The Making of the *New York Times Book Review.*" *Publishers Weekly* 202 (July 31, 1972): 36-49.

Selection in University and College Libraries

"Acquisition Policy: A Symposium." *College and Research Libraries* 14 (Oct. 1953): 363-72.

Association of Research Libraries. Systems and Procedures Exchange Center. *Acquisition Policies in ARL Libraries.* Washington: ARL, 1974.

Collection Development in ARL Libraries. Washington: Association of Research Libraries, 1974.

Bach, H. "Acquisition Policy in the American Academic Library." *College and Research Libraries* 18 (Nov. 1957): 441-51.

Bach, H. "The Junior College Library Collection." *California Libraries* 33 (April 1972): 88-99.

Brenni, V. J. "Book Selection and the University Library." *Catholic Library World* 38 (March 1967): 425-29.

Brubeck, K. M. "Emerging Problems in Acquisitions: The Junior College." *Library Resources and Technical Services* 12 (Spring 1968): 156-60.

Bryant, D. W. "The Changing Research Library." *Harvard Library Bulletin* 22 (Oct. 1974): 365.

Buckeye, N. "A Plan for Undergraduate Participation in Book Selection." *Library Resources and Technical Services* 19 (Sept. 1975): 121-32.

Buckland, M. K. *Book Availability and the Library User.* New York: Pergamon, 1975.

Byrd, C. K. "Subject Specialists in a University Library." *College and Research Libraries* 28 (May 1966): 191-93.

Christ, R. W. "Acquisition Work in College Libraries." *College and Research Libraries* 10 (Jan. 1949): 17-23.

Clapp, V. W. *The Future of the Research Library.* Urbana: University of Illinois Press, 1964.

Cohen, J. B. "Undergraduate Science Booklists." *Reference Quarterly* 13 (Fall 1973): 35-38.

Coppin, A. "The Subject Specialist in the Academic Library Staff." *Libri* 24 (1974): 124.

Danton, J. P. *Book Selection and Collections: A Comparison of German and American University Libraries.* New York: Columbia University Press, 1963. (Columbia University Studies in Library Service, no. 12).

Danton, J. P. "Selection of Books for College Libraries." *Library Quarterly* 5 (Oct. 1953): 419-56.

Danton, J. P. "The Subject Specialist in National and University Libraries, with Special Reference to Book Selection." *Libri* 17 (1967): 42-58.

Danton, J. P. "University Library Book Selection Policy Revisited." *International Library Review* 3 (1971): 61-65.

Evans, G. E. "Book Selection and Book Collection Usage in Academic Libraries." *Library Quarterly* 40 (July 1970): 297-308.

Gorchels, C. "Acquisitions Policy Statements in Colleges of Education." *Library Resources and Technical Services* 5 (Spring 1961): 157-59.

Grieder, E. M. "The Foundations of Acquisition Policy in the Small University Library." *College and Research Libraries* 10 (July 1949): 208-214.

Haro, R. P. "The Bibliographer in the Academic Library." *Library Resources and Technical Services* 13 (Spring 1969): 163-69.

Haro, R. P. "Book Selection in Academic Libraries." *College and Research Libraries* 28 (March 1967): 104-106.

Holbrook, A. "The Subject Specialist in Polytechnic Libraries." *New Library World* 73 (Sept. 1972): 393-96.

Humphreys, K. "The Subject Specialist in National and University Libraries." *Libri* 17 (1967): 29-41.

Jenks, G. M. "Book Selection: An Approach for Small and Medium-Size Libraries." *College and Research Libraries* 33 (Jan. 1972): 28-30.

Kosa, G. A. "Book Selection Tools for Subject Specialists in a Large Research Library: An Analysis." *Library Resources and Technical Services* 19 (Winter 1975): 13-18.

Kosa, G. A. "Book Selection Trends in American Academic Libraries." *Australian Library Journal* 21 (Nov. 1972): 416-24.

Kraft, M. "An Argument for Selectivity in the Acquisition of Materials for Research Libraries." *Library Quarterly* 37 (July 1967): 284-95.

Lane, D. O. "The Selection of Academic Library Materials: A Literature Survey." *College and Research Libraries* 29 (Sept. 1968): 364-72.

Lehman, J. O. "*Choice* as a Selection Tool." *Wilson Library Bulletin* 44 (May 1970): 957-61.

Lennenberg, H. "Another View of Selectivity." *Library Quarterly* 38 (1968): 286-90.

Lopez, M. D. "A Guide for Beginning Bibliographers." *Library Resources and Technical Services* 13 (Fall 1969): 462-70.

McGrath, W. E. "Correlating the Subjects of Books Taken Out of and Books Used Within an Open Stack Library." *College and Research Libraries* 32 (July 1971): 280-85.

Massman, V. F., and D. R. Olson. "Book Selection: A National Plan for Small Academic Libraries." *College and Research Libraries* 32 (July 1971): 271-79.

Metcalf, K. D. "Problems of Acquisitions Policy in a University Library." *Harvard Library Bulletin* 4 (Autumn 1950): 293-303.

Meyer, B. J., and J. T. Demos. "Acquisition Policy for University Libraries: Selection or Collection." *Library Resources and Technical Services* 14 (Summer 1970): 395-99.

Mitchell, B. J., J. White, and A. B. Griffith. "Junior College Materials." *Choice* 6 (March 1969): 28-33.

New, D. E. "Interlibrary Loan Analysis as a Collection Development Tool." *Library Resources and Technical Services* 18 (Summer 1974): 275-84.

Olson, K. D. "Communications of a Bibliographer." *Special Libraries* 66 (May/June 1975): 266-72.

Sable, A. P. "Death of Book Selection." *Wilson Library Bulletin* 43 (Dec. 1968): 345-48.

Schad, J. G., and R. L. Adams. "Book Selection in Academic Libraries: A New Approach." *College and Research Libraries* 30 (Sept. 1969): 437-42.

Schad, J. G., and N. E. Tanis. *Problems in Developing Academic Library Collections.* New York: R. R. Bowker, 1974.

Skelley, G. T. "Characteristics of Collections Added to American Research Libraries 1940-1970: A Preliminary Investigation." *College and Research Libraries* 36 (Jan. 1975): 52-60.

Stanford University Libraries. *Book Selection Policies of the Libraries of Stanford University.* P. A. Johnson, comp.; E. M. Grieder, ed. Stanford, CA: The Libraries, 1970.

Stevens, R. E., ed. "Problems of Acquisition for Research Libraries." *Library Trends* 18 (Jan. 1970): 275-421.

Stiffler, S. A. "A Philosophy of Book Selection for Smaller Academic Libraries." *College and Research Libraries* 24 (May 1963): 204-208.

Stueart, R. D. *The Area Specialist Bibliographer: An Inquiry into His Role.* Metuchen, NJ: Scarecrow, 1972.

Taggart, W. R. "Book Selection Librarian in Canadian Universities." *Canadian Library Journal* 31 (Oct. 1974): 411.

Tauber, M. F. "Faculty and the Development of Library Collections." *Journal of Higher Education* 32 (Nov. 1961): 454-58.

Tuttle, H. W. "An Acquisitionist Looks at Mr. Haro's Bibliographer." *Library Resources and Technical Services* 13 (Spring 1969): 170-74.

Voigt, M. J. "Acquisition Rates in University Libraries." *College and Research Libraries* 36 (July 1975): 263-71.

Vosper, R. G. "Acquisition Policy: Fact or Fancy?" *College and Research Libraries* 14 (Oct. 1953): 367-70.

Selection in Public Libraries

Bass, D. "Can This Marriage Be Saved?" *Library Journal* 94 (Sept. 1969): 3023-27.

Bendim, D. *Some Problems in Book Selection Policies and Practices in Medium Sized Public Libraries.* Urbana: University of Illinois Library School, 1959. (Illinois University Library School. Occasional Papers, no. 55).

Berry, J. N. "Demand for Dissent? Public Library Practice in the Selection of Dissident Periodicals." *Library Journal* 89 (Oct. 15, 1964): 3912-17.

Bone, L., and T. Raines. "The Nature of the Urban Main Library: Its Relation to Selection and Collection Building." *Library Trends* 20 (April 1972): 625-39.

Busha, C. H. "Evaluation of Four Book Review Media Commonly Used by Public Librarians for Acquisition Work." *South Carolina Librarian* 12 (March 1968): 29-34.

Enoch Pratt Free Library [Baltimore]. *Book Selection Procedures.* Rev. ed. M. E. Hawes and D. Sinclair, eds. Baltimore, The Library, 1961.

Enoch Pratt Free Library [Baltimore]. *How Baltimore Chooses: Selection Policies of the Enoch Pratt Free Library.* 4th ed. Baltimore: The Library, 1968.

Gant, M. D. "Vermillion Public Library Materials Selection Policy." *South Dakota Library Bulletin* 58 (April 1972): 90-97.

Garceau, O., et al. *The Public Library in the Political Process: A Report of the Public Library Inquiry.* New York: Columbia University Press, 1949; reprinted 1972.

Leon, S. J. "Book Selection in Philadelphia: The Survey of the Handling of Certain Controversial Adult Materials by Philadelphia Area Libraries." *Library Journal* 98 (April 1, 1973): 1081-89.

McClennan, A. W. *The Reader, the Library and the Book: Selected Papers 1949-1970.* London: Bingley, 1973.

McCrossan, J. A. *Library Science Education and Its Relationship to Competence in Adult Book Selection in Public Libraries.* Springfield: Illinois State Library, 1967. (Illinois State Library Research Series, no. 9).

McElroy, E. W. "Subject Variety in Adult Reading." *Library Quarterly* 38 (1968): 154-67, 261-69.

McNiff, P. J. "Book Selection and Provision in the Urban Library." *Library Quarterly* 28 (Jan. 1968): 58-69.

Tulsa City-County Library System, [Tulsa, Oklahoma]. *Book Selection Policies.* Tulsa: The Library, 1968.

Tulsa City-County Library System, [Tulsa, Oklahoma]. *Materials Selection Policy.* Tulsa: The Library, 1973.

Selection in Special Libraries and Subject Area Materials

American Library Association. Office for Research and Development. *Study of the Decision-Making Procedures for the Acquisition of Science Library Materials and the Relation of These Procedures to the Requirements of College and University Patrons.* Chicago: ALA, 1968.

American Library Association. Adult Services Division. "Guidelines for the Evaluation of Indian Materials for Adults." *American Libraries* 2 (June 1971): 610-11.

California. University. University Extension. Continuing Education in Librarianship. *Acquisition of Special Materials.* I. H. Jackson, ed. San Francisco: Special Libraries Association, San Francisco Bay Region Chapter, 1966.

Colaianni, L. A., and P. S. Mirsky. "Books: How to Select, Acquire, and Prepare Them for Use." In Bloomquist, H., ed. *Library Practice in Hospitals.* Cleveland: Press of Case Western Reserve University, 1972. pp. 76-93.

Fink, W. R., and N. S. Stearns. "Principles of Selection." In Bloomquist, H., ed. *Library Practice in Hospitals.* Cleveland: Press of Case Western Reserve University, 1972. pp. 63-75.

Grannis, F. "Philosophical Implications of Book Selection for the Blind." *Wilson Library Bulletin* 43 (Dec. 1968): 330-39.

Horn, A. H., ed. "Special Materials and Services." *Library Trends* 4 (Oct. 1955): 119-212.

Illinois, University of. Graduate School of Library Science. *Collecting Science Literature for General Reading: Papers Presented at an Institute Conducted by the University of Illinois Graduate School of Library Science, November 6-9, 1960.* F. B. Jenkins, ed. Champaign, IL: Illini Union Bookstore, 1961. (Allerton Park Institute Papers, no. 7).

Krummel, D. W. "Observations on Library Acquisitions of Music." *Notes* 23 (Sept. 1966): 5-16.

Lubetski, M., and E. Lubetski. "Sources of Current Acquisitions in the Jewish Field." *Library Resources and Technical Services* 18 (Fall 1974): 343-47.

Phelps, R. H. "Selecting Materials for Science-Technology Libraries." *Special Libraries* 44 (March 1953): 89-92.

Sadow, A. "Book Reviewing Media for Technical Libraries." *Special Libraries* 61 (April 1970): 194-98.

Smith, M. H. "Commentary on Book Reviewing Media." *Special Libraries* 61 (Nov. 1970): 515-16.

Swarthout, A. W. *Selecting Library Materials.* Bryn Mawr, PA: Church and Synagogue Libraries Association, 1974.

Taylor, B. W., and W. W. Gaunt. "Book Selection and Acquisitions: Comments and Annotated Bibliography." *Law Library Journal* 63 (Feb. 1970): 107-120.

Ward, K. L. "Collection Policy in College and University Libraries." *Music Library Association Notes* 29 (March 1973): 432-40.

Way, D. J. "Book Selection." *Law Librarian* 4 (Aug. 1973): 25-27.

Weinstein, F. D. "Book Selection in the Sciences." *American Library Association Bulletin* 52 (July 1958): 509-519.

Selection in School Libraries and Children's Materials

American Association of School Librarians. "Policies and Procedures for Selection of School Library Materials." *School Libraries* 11 (Oct. 1971): 37-38.

American Association of School Librarians. *Selecting Materials for School Libraries: Guidelines and Selection Sources to Insure Quality Collections.* Rev. ed. Chicago: American Library Association, 1967.

American Library and Educational Service Co. *Professional Guide for Use in the Elementary School Library.* Completely rev. Paramus, NJ: The Company, 1970.

American Library and Educational Service Co. *Professional Guide for Use in the Junior-Senior High School Library.* Completely rev. Paramus, NJ: The Company, 1970.

American Library Association. Children's Service Division. Library Service to the Disadvantaged Child Committee. *I Read . . . I See . . . I Hear . . . I Learn.* Chicago: ALA, 1971.

American Library Association. *Standards for School Library Programs.* Chicago: American Library Association, 1960.

Arbuthnot, M. H., and Z. Sutherland. *Children and Books.* 4th ed. Chicago: Scott, Foresman, 1972.

Baker, A. *The Black Experience in Children's Books.* New York: New York Public Library, 1971. [See also new edition by B. Rollock, 1974; listed below.]

Baur, E. "The Fader Plan: Detroit Style." *Library Journal* 92 (Sept. 15, 1967): 3119-21.

Broderick, D. M. *An Introduction to Children's Work in Public Libraries.* New York: H. W. Wilson, 1965.

California Association of School Librarians. *Instructional Materials: Selection Policies and Procedures.* Daly City, CA: The Association, 1965.

Canadian School Library Association. *Aids to Selection of Materials for Canadian School Libraries.* M. B. Scott, ed. Ottawa: Canadian Library Association, 1971.

Doebler, P. D. "Kids vs. Adults on Children's Book." *Publishers Weekly* 206 (Nov. 4, 1974): 22-27.

Egoff, S. "If That Don't Do No Good, That Don't Do No Harm: The Use and Dangers of Mediocrity in Children's Reading." *School Library Journal* 97 (Oct. 1972): 3435-39.

Gaver, M. V. *Patterns of Development in Elementary School Libraries Today.* 2nd ed. Chicago: Encyclopaedia Britannica, 1965.

Hanna, G. R., and M. K. McAllister. *Books, Young People, and Reading Guidance.* New York: Harper and Row, 1960.

Hodges, E. D. "Book Selection Practices in the Nation's Schools." *School Libraries* 6 (March 1957): 11-15.

Huck, C. S. *Children's Literature in the Elementary School.* 3rd ed. New York: Holt, 1976.

Issues in Children's Book Selection: A School Library Journal/Library Journal Anthology. New York: R. R. Bowker, 1973.

Ladley, W. C., comp. *Sources of Good Books and Magazines for Children: An Annotated Bibliography.* Newark, DE: International Reading Association, 1970.

Lowrie, J. E. *Elementary School Libraries.* 2nd ed. Metuchen, NJ: Scarecrow Press, 1970.

Rollock, B. *The Black Experience in Children's Books.* New ed. New York: New York Public Library, 1974 [omits Baker's original introduction].

Rufsvold, M. I., and C. Guss. "Software: Bibliographic Control and the NICEM Indexes." *School Libraries* 20 (Winter 1971): 11-20.

Schuman, P. "Concerned Criticism or Casual Cop-Outs? Fall Children's Book Sections and Supplements." *Library Journal* 97 (Jan. 16, 1972): 245-48.

"Selection Centers for Educational Materials." *Publishers Weekly* 198 (Sept. 1970): 35.

Smith, L. H. *The Unreluctant Years: A Critical Approach to Children's Literature.* Chicago: American Library Association, 1953.

Sutherland, Z. "Current Reviewing of Children's Books." *Library Quarterly* 37 (Jan. 1967): 110-18.

Wofford, A. *Book Selection for School Libraries.* New York: H. W. Wilson, 1962.

Chapter 7

SELECTION OF AUDIO VISUAL MATERIALS

Why a chapter on audio visuals? The basic philosophy of this text is that the library's most important products are information and service. If you accept this philosophy, then the library collection must consist of more than books. Books are and will be for some time, the least expensive method of conveying large amounts of detailed information to a large number of persons at one given time. Television may reach millions of persons at one time, but it does not convey *detailed* information except in the most exceptional circumstances. A major consideration in building a library collection is how to convey quantities of information to the patron at a comparatively low cost. However, books are only useful to persons who are literate. Depending upon what area of the world you are in, the percentage of persons who are "literate" ranges from 1 percent to 100 percent. For a great portion of the world the percentage of persons who can be considered literate is less than 50 percent of the total population. Even in countries where very high literacy rates are reported (such as the United States) there is a difference between what is reported and the true literacy rate. In the United States great concern is expressed in many areas about functional illiteracy; persons may have gone through the required educational system (12 years of schooling) but are not able to read beyond the level reached by the third or fourth year of schooling. Many colleges and universities are worried about the inability of entering students to read and write, but there seems to be a growing difference in the United States between young people's ability to use and understand the spoken, as opposed to the written, word.

WHY AUDIO VISUALS?

Given a certain percentage of persons who are incapable of using the printed word and yet another percentage unwilling to do so, can the library afford to ignore the needs of these persons? The answer certainly depends upon the goals and objectives of the library. If its purpose is to serve the total community then the answer must be no. When library operating funds come from all taxpayers, the librarian should expect a certain amount of pressure to serve all segments of the community to some degree. Should the library fail to do so, the unserved groups in the community will fail to support library funding. In fact, active opposition should be expected.

Audio and visual formats will help in reaching many groups in the community that would otherwise not be served. This is not only a problem for public and school libraries; academic and special libraries should also be concerned with the "other" formats. One major reason is that for some types of information these formats are really the only appropriate means of communication. Anyone concerned with the fine arts knows this and also knows that generally speaking, academic libraries are ill-equipped to meet their needs. Business and industrial libraries will find themselves more and more called upon to have video formats available, especially for training purposes. These factors only begin to indicate the need to build a collection incorporating all formats. Before exploring the basic issues of audio visual selection and evaluation procedures, a few words about costs are in order. Motion picture and many video formats are expensive in comparison to books and microforms. Assuming that a library is ready to embark on building a media collection, some factors need to be considered:

1) do other audio visual collections exist in the community?

2) if so, where and what are the primary purposes of those collections?

3) is there any chance the financial resources and the collection(s) might be shared?

4) can you develop a collection of formats
   a) that is useful to a large number of users and
   b) that does not already exist in the community?

5) to what degree do your users' needs correlate with those of other library users?

6) how much money can be devoted to audio visual hardware and software?

7) are there agencies other than libraries that might be interested in cooperating—museums, private institutions, etc.?

8) do you have or can you have staff members who can effectively develop an audio visual collection?

Because the unit cost is high (see chapters 1 and 2) mistakes in selection of certain types of audio visual materials are much more significant than with books. In addition, not only software but in most cases, equipment (hardware) of some type is needed: a projector, player, or display unit. Although the playback equipment may have a much longer lifespan than the software, it also requires the attention of highly qualified repair technicians—another significant cost factor. (In some large media operations there may be a staff technician; however, in most situations the library will have a repair and maintenance contract with an outside service agency.) Sharing the hardware, software, and maintenance expenses, then, makes good economic sense.

GENERAL EVALUATION FACTORS

To some degree the same factors that determine inclusion or exclusion of books apply to other formats. Obviously, factually incorrect items should not be acquired, and badly organized and presented materials are equally unacceptable. If the quality of a book is difficult to assess, with other media the problem is magnified. How many times have you gone to a film and enjoyed it only to hear some of your friends claim it is "absolutely *the* worst film" they had ever seen? Thus, subjectivity is a great problem. Basically the issues of authority, accuracy, effectiveness of presentation or style, and value and usefulness to the community are as valid for all other formats as they are for books.

Before embarking upon a program to develop the library media collection you should give careful consideration to evaluating each potential format in terms of its unique utility to the community. Each format has its strong and weak points, and similar information may be available in a variety of formats. The following are some general guidelines for assessing the strengths and weaknesses of various forms.

Formats that involve motion (such as 8mm, 16mm, and 35mm films and video tapes) are among the most expensive. Therefore, an important question to ask is whether motion really adds that much information. There are films in which there is no motion at all, or if there is motion, it may not be relevant to the content. For example, many "educational" films and video tapes simply alternate shots of one or two persons talking to one another or to the viewers; there are no other graphics or at least graphics that require this expensive mode of presentation. On the other hand, hundreds of pages can be read and dozens of still photographs of cell division viewed, but the reader may still not really understand how cell division takes place. A short, clearly photographed film combined with a good audio track can produce a quicker, more accurate understanding of the process than all the reading.

Detailed study is sometimes most effectively carried out with the use of still pictures, charts, and/or graphs. Another advantage is that the cost to produce and acquire these formats is much lower than for those that involve motion.

With both motion and still graphic formats, color is an important consideration. Color reproduction is more costly than black and white; so what must be considered is whether the color is necessary or just nice. In some instances it is absolutely necessary. Certainly anything that attempts to represent the work of a great artist must have excellent color work as do a great many medical and biological materials.

Audio formats also can provide greater understanding and appreciation. Your reading of a poem is never the same as hearing the poet recite it to you. We all know that tone, emphasis, inflection, etc., can dramatically change the meaning of a printed text. On a different level there are literally millions of persons in the world who cannot read music scores and yet get great enjoyment out of music being performed. Audio recordings also should be considered for any collection if there are persons to be served who are visually impaired. "Talking Books" is an important service for such persons.

Other general factors are cost, flexibility and manipulation, and, of course, patrons. Cost is a consideration in almost all major decisions in collection development; however, audio visual formats often require expensive equipment in addition to the rather expensive software. Cost factors need to be considered in light of what type of equipment patrons own—film or slide projectors, video tape players, tape decks, record players, etc. If the patrons do not own the necessary equipment can the library supply it free of charge, or on a rental basis? Should the library buy the equipment and allow its use only in the library? You must also consider *what* patrons like and use. Libraries ought not to get into the position of attempting to change patron format preferences when the community is not *known* to be actively interested in a particular format. Obviously it costs too much to attempt to change patron preferences, and librarians are really not in the business of marketing a particular format anyway. Thus, both cost and patron preference become significant in deciding what to buy or not to buy.

Flexibility and manipulation are interrelated. How can you use the format and equipment, and where? Some equipment can be used to produce local programs as well as to play back commercial software. Others, such as video tape equipment, will allow both motion and stop-action use or, even more sophisticated, instant replay. These features may be necessary, nice, or just gimmicks, depending on the local situation. Ease of operation is also important; can anyone operate the equipment or does it take a person who is fairly well trained in its use?

Although the following table (Figure 13, page 182) is not exhaustive it does provide an overview of the basic factors in planning a comprehensive media collection. It is important to remember that the statements are general and there are exceptions to almost every one. (You should also refer to Figure 8, page 57, which compares media to books.)

SELECTION CRITERIA

Once a library has decided to embark upon the acetate/vinyl path, how are appropriate items selected? There are three general factors to consider (content, technical aspects, and format) and then there are criteria for each format. In a short chapter only the highlights of the selection criteria can be included. The problems of how to put together effective audio visual programs for the library must be ignored. Programming (that is, use of the material) is important in deciding what to acquire and a number of articles and books have been written on this topic, some of which are listed in the bibliography at the end of this chapter. Some of the programming questions include: will the medium be used in a formal instructional situation? will it be used only for recreational purposes? will it focus on an adult audience, children, everyone? will it be used in the library with someone from the staff or an "expert" in the field to guide group discussions before or after its use? will the library be joining a formal network (for example, 16mm film networks are popular)? sharing with other libraries the use of the material? The full impact of these considerations will only be apparent after more reading.

Content Factors

The content of any format is the first concern in any selection process. The following are a sample of the type of questions that should be asked. Remember that audio visual selection, even more than book selection, tends to be done by a

Figure 13

Comparison of Audio Visual Materials

Medium	Motion	Visual	Aural	Flexibility	Manipulation	Cost if Purchased	Cost if Produced in Library	Cost of Equip- ment
16 mm film	yes	yes	yes	Equipment heavy but portable Darkening required Re-sequencing not feasible	Larger, smaller, slower, faster	high	med.-high	high
Records	no	no	yes	Good portability Shipping & re-sequencing easy	Slower, faster on occasion	low	not feasible	low-mod.
Tape record- ing	no	no	yes	Excellent, particularly cassettes Re-sequencing, editing, & shipping easy	Slower, faster on occasion	low	low	low-mod.
Paintings & art prints	no	yes	no	Easily circulated	none	low-high	framing & mounting— low-mod.	n/a
Video- cassettes	yes	yes	yes	Depends on distribu- tion system Re-sequencing, editing, shipping not feasible Limited to no. of pro- grams available	Larger, smaller, slower, faster	high	medium	mod.-high
Television— commercial or closed circuit	yes	yes	yes	Portability limited Shipping easy Re-sequencing not feasible	Larger, smaller, slower, faster	high	mod.-high	mod.-high
Overhead trans- parencies	rarely	yes	no	Very portable Re-sequencing, editing, & shipping easy	Larger, smaller	low-mod.	low	mod.
Filmstrips with/with- out recording	no	yes	pos- sible	Very portable Darkening req. for group use Re-sequencing not feasible	Larger, smaller	low-mod.	low	low-mod.
Simulations & games	n/a	n/a	n/a	Usually very portable	n/a	low-high	low-mod.	n/a
Computer- assisted, managed instruc- tion	yes	yes	no	Limited to location of terminal	Larger, smaller, slower, faster	high	high	high
Graphics, charts, posters, maps	no	yes	no	Depends on size	Larger, smaller	low	low	n/a
3 dimen- sional objects, realia, models, globes	on occasion	on occasion	yes	Depends on size & shape	Larger, smaller	low-high	low-mod.	n/a

Adapted from a classroom handout, with permission of instructor, William Speed.

group rather than one individual, which usually means that some type of evaluation form will be employed in the process. No matter what specific questions are on the form—and not all items listed in this chapter will be on one form—all of the items listed below should be considered:

1) what is the primary purpose(s) of the item? If there is a user's guide included, does it provide a specific answer to this question?

2) given the purpose(s) of the item, is the length of the program appropriate? An item can be too short, but more often than not they are too long;

3) is the topic a current fad or is it something that is likely to have long-term interest? (Long-term interest and lasting value are not always one and the same);

4) is the material presented in a well-organized fashion?

5) is it easy to follow the story line?

6) if the item is of relatively short duration and is an attempt to popularize a subject, does it do this with sufficient accuracy—sufficient in the sense that the simplification process does not cause misunderstandings or, worse, create misrepresentations?

7) when was the material copyrighted? Copyright information can be difficult to find for some formats. Motion picture films usually provide this information somewhere in the credits, often in roman numerals. Generally speaking, there is no national bibliographic description standard for the various media. Sales catalogs may or may not provide the date of production. Unfortunately, a large number of very dated products are or have been sold as if they were currently produced;

8) will the visuals or audio date very quickly? How many times have you viewed an educational film where the subject matter was important but the dress of the actors made it seem old-fashioned? If such films are not presented as historical or history films, the true purpose may be lost to most viewers. Audience attention is drawn away from the real subject. Needless to say, this ties back to the need for copyright information;

9) how many uses could be made of the material, in addition to those identified by the producer? Naturally, if there are a number of ways to use the format (different types of programs or audiences), it is easier to justify spending money on the item.

Technical Factors

Technical issues will vary in importance from format to format, but some general considerations apply to a number of forms. In most instances, judging technical matters is less subjective than many other selection criteria. On the other hand, it will take time and guidance from experienced selectors to develop a critical sense of these factors. This process will take longer for media than for books because school systems traditionally have emphasized literature, and to some degree everyone who completes twelve years of schooling has been exposed to some of the great works of literature. Most individuals going into library and information service work are usually even more attuned to good literature, good physical books, and the various methods of literary review than the average person. We may be exposed to as much (or more) television, film, and recordings as we are to books, but very few of us are exposed to the methods for assessing the technical aspects of these formats. This fact is evident when film and television awards are made—the general public is only interested in the best film or program and performance categories; yet there are usually three times as many awards for technical aspects (direction, production, special effects, cinematography, etc.) as for the more obvious general categories.

The following questions should be asked:

1) are the visuals, assuming that there are visuals, really necessary?

2) are the visuals in proper focus, the composition effective, the shots appropriate? (These questions need to be asked because out-of-focus, strange angles, and jarring composition may be used to create different moods and feeling);

3) is the material edited with skill?

4) does the background audio material contribute to the overall impact?

5) is there good synchronization of visuals and audio?

6) how may format be used—small or large group viewing, or both? in darkened, semi- or fully-lighted room?

Format Factors

Many of the format factors are identified in Figure 13. Additional factors to consider are:

1) is the format the best one for the stated purposes of the producer?

2) is the format the least expensive of those that are appropriate for the content?

3) will the carrier medium stand up to the level and type of use that your library would give it?

4) if it is damaged can it be repaired (locally or by producer), or must it be replaced? Does it require maintenance, and if so, what kind?

5) what type of equipment is required to use the medium? How portable is it and how heavy?

It is possible to group all audio visual materials into six broad categories. Again, some general questions can be asked about each category.

Still pictures (slides, filmstrips, transparencies, microformats, flat pictures, and art reproductions):

1) does the lack of movement cause the viewer to misinterpret the original meaning?

2) how accurate is the color reproduction? Is the color necessary?

3) are the mountings/holders compatible with existing library equipment?

4) for filmstrips and microforms, is the sequence of frames logical and easy to follow?

5) if there is an audio track does it aid in understanding the materials?

6) are microformat images readable when enlarged? What is the reduction ratio that has been employed? Can it be used in equipment that will allow the user to make a copy of single frames as desired?

7) is the ratio of pictures to narration appropriate? (A frequent problem with slide or tape programs or narrated filmstrips is too few illustrations which often results in a product that seems to last too long.)

Motion pictures (35mm, 16mm, 8mm films, videoformats; most of these are available in reel-to-reel, cartridge, and cassette configurations):

1) does the motion add to the message?

2) are variable speed capabilities (fast, normal, slow, stop) used effectively?

3) is the running time appropriate to the content? Too long? Too short?

4) if it is a recreational film using either performers or animation, has that fact caused a problem in presenting an accurate picture of the true events?

5) has the sound been properly synchronized with the visual materials?

Audio recordings (discs or tapes):

1) how much use can the format withstand and not distort the quality of the sound?

2) how easily damaged is the format?

3) does the recording provide coverage of the full range of sound frequencies?

4) is there any distortion of the sound?

5) was the recording speed held constant? (This is seldom a problem with major producers but it can be significant with those who do not produce many recordings);

6) if the recording is multiple channel, were the microphones properly placed to ensure a balanced recording?

7)   was the recording site suitable for the purposes or was it a matter of convenience? (For example, if the goal is to produce an excellent recording of a musical composition, then a recording studio or a concert hall with excellent acoustics and no audience is the best location—not a concert. With "live" performances you should not expect the best sound quality.)

Graphic materials (maps, charts, posters, etc.):

1)   has there been an attempt to convey too much information? (Maps, charts, etc., can become so complex as to be almost unusable if too much data is included on any one item);

2)   are the symbols employed standard ones or unique to the particular item?

3)   is the printing of high quality? (When color is employed, especially with maps, the presswork must be of high quality or all the efforts of the cartographer are wasted);

4)   is the scale appropriate for your library's needs?

5)   how durable is the paper or cloth on which the information is printed?

6)   can a user determine the intended message with a single look?

7)   is the surface treatment appropriate—glossy, semi-glossy, etc.?

Three-dimensional objects (models, realia, dioramas, globes, etc.):

1)   are objects of less than life size reproduced in an appropriate scale?

2)   is the scale sufficient to illustrate the necessary details?

3)   when horizontal and vertical scales must be different, is the distortion so great as to create a false impression?

4)   are the colors used accurate in terms of the original object?

5)   are the objects constructed of materials that will stand up to the type of handling that it will receive in the library?

Other formats (simulations, games, self-guided instruction formats):

1)   can a patron understand the directions without assistance from the library staff and/or does it require training to set up and use?

2)   does the system allow for a variety of speeds in learning?

3)   if it is a computer system, does the system cover areas that cannot be handled as effectively in any other format?

4)   will the patron be able to take the item home or must it be used in the library?

5)   if it must be used in the library, will it be available anytime the library is open, or just during certain hours?

6) are the right answers predictable in a manner that does not ensure true learning?

7) if it is a printed system, are there additional answer sheets available or will the library have to produce extras?

These are but a few of the considerations that must go into the selection of audio visual formats. Just as there are few, if any, universal questions to raise about selecting books, so it is with audio visuals. Each library will develop its own selection criteria as it gains experience in the field.

PREVIEWING

As noted earlier the actual selection process of audio visual materials is usually a group rather than individual activity. This is particularly true of films and video formats. To some degree it is the cost of the decision rather than intellectual collection development factors that brings this about. In essence, making a mistake on a 20-minute sound, color, 16mm film has more serious economic consequences for the library budget than most single mistakes with a book, a transparency, a recording, etc. Such a film will cost anywhere from $300 to $500. As we have seen, the criteria for selection tend to be highly subjective. As a result, it is safer to get multiple opinions about a possible purchase. An audio visual selection committee is the typical mechanism employed for securing such multiple points of view.

How does the book selection committee—rather common in public and school libraries—differ from the audio visual selection committee? Audio visual selection committees usually function as a true group decision-making body. Materials being considered for purchase are normally previewed by the entire group; films (both motion pictures and filmstrips) and video formats are viewed in their entirety. A group discussion usually then takes place after each screening wherein each person expresses a reaction to and an evaluation of the item. Everyone sees the same material and group interaction ends in a decision to buy or not to buy. Sometimes the product is rerun several times when there are strong differences in opinion.

Book selection committee meetings normally operate on a more individual basis. That is, each person is assigned certain books to review and report on, including indications of what published reviews of the book have said. A brief synopsis is given and a purchase recommendation is made. There may or may not be an extended discussion of the recommendation. In any case, only one (or perhaps two) person(s) on the committee will have examined the book in detail—examined rather than read completely, because most libraries do not have enough professional staff time to allow for the complete reading of every book purchased. In some library systems the selection process is conducted solely on the basis of published reviews, bibliographic data, and the knowledge the selectors have of various authors, editors, and publishers. Very few libraries can afford to or should select films and video formats on the basis of published reviews.

Another important difference is the sequential nature of films and video formats. It is not really possible to skim a film as you do a book; you must run it at its normal speed in order to get the proper impression. A 20-minute film requires

20 minutes to preview. Simple arithmetic tells us that in an 8-hour work day a maximum of 24 20-minute films could be viewed. A book selection committee that only discussed 24 titles in 8 hours of meetings would be considered something of a disaster. Realistically, though, no group can preview 24 films in 8 hours as the figure does not provide for discussion time between films or for breaks. It is possible that with three playback units you could actually run 24 films, but it would require that someone do nothing but set up one playback unit after another—it does require a few minutes to thread and rewind. Finally, it is not feasible to have people sit and view materials for four straight hours; they need a break. All of this means that a more realistic figure would be somewhere between 10-12 audio visual items per day could be evaluated.

Standardization of the evaluation process is probably a long way away in the media field but several professional associations have attempted to bring some order to previewing by developing evaluation forms. Until such time as your library decides to commit a major segment of its materials budget to audio visual forms, you can save effort by using one of the association forms. Sources of the forms are the Unesco Film Appraisal Information Form, the Educational Film Library Association form, the Council on International Nontheatrical Events, Inc. (CINE) film rating sheet, and the Educational Product Report evaluation form (this latter form covers more than motion picture formats).

This means that not only do these formats cost more to buy, but they also cost a great deal more to select. The two cost factors are significant. Thus one cannot conclude that just because a library does not have a collection of films or video materials that there is necessarily a reluctance to accept new formats. A significant difference exists between reluctance and the lack of money and qualified staff to select the newer formats. Your only question should be whether the monetary factor is being used as an excuse to avoid trying out other mediums.

AUDIO VISUAL SELECTION AIDS

Despite the desirability of previewing audio visual materials, and even with previewing, published evaluations are important in this field. Each year there is a little more progress toward bibliographic control of the field, including reviews of most formats. Perhaps when multiple published reviews of most formats are available there will be less and less need for hundreds of audio visual librarians to spend hours and hours in preview screening rooms.

At this time, still no comprehensive source exists for audio visual materials similar to *Book Review Digest* or *Book Review Index*. In 1974, *Media Review Digest* was announced as an annual (a renaming of *Multi Media Review Index*—1970). Each month *Audiovisual Instruction* publishes a supplement that reviews instructional media. If it continues to develop it will become the most important selection aid for such media. In 1970, *Film Review Index* started; in 1974, the title was changed to *International Index to Multi-Media Information*. The publication now covers more than sixty periodical titles.

Some services are reasonably comprehensive and successfully focus on one format. The series of indexes from the NICEM group (National Information Center for Educational Media) focuses on educational materials; however, as they have a rather broad definition of education, the publications are useful to all types of libraries. Some of their basic publications are:

Index to 16mm Educational Films. 6th ed. (1976)

Index to 35mm Educational Filmstrips. 6th ed. (1976)

Index to 8mm Motion Cartridges. 5th ed. (1976)

Index to Overhead Transparencies. 5th ed. (1976)

Index to Educational Audio Tapes. 4th ed. (1976)

Index to Educational Records. 4th ed. (1976)

Index to Educational Slides. 4th ed. (1976)

Index to Educational Video Tapes. 4th ed. (1976)

Index to Producers and Distributors. 4th ed. (1976)

NICEM publishes other format indexes and has several subject indexes on current topics such as ecology and ethnic studies. You can locate basic descriptive information (producer, title, source) and a brief annotation about the content and grade level, and in this regard, this series is not unlike many other tools. That is, they describe rather than analyze or criticize the materials covered. Lacking such critical evaluations, then, a media librarian still must preview items. The NICEM series is the closest that the audio visual field comes to having an equivalent to *Books in Print.*

A major problem in the field is its vast size and diversity. As a result very few aids are published annually that cover more than one or two formats. You also must be alert to the fact that this field changes very quickly. Indeed, the field is so volatile that although the titles and dates of publication of the aids identified in this chapter were correct at the time the chapter was written, there is no assurance that they will reflect the state of the art by the time this book is published (and that time frame is only a few months). With that caution in mind the following is offered as a selective list of guides, aids, and review sources. Books include:

Audiovisual Market Place: A Multimedia Guide. New York: R. R. Bowker, 1970- [1970 (biannual) 1977- (annual)].

Brown, J. W. *Educational Media Yearbook.* New York: R. R. Bowker, 1973- (annual).

Chisholm, M. E. *Media Indexes and Review Sources.* College Park, MD: University of Maryland, School of Library and Information Services, 1972.

Coster, Y. *Aids in Media Selection for Students and Teachers.* Washington: U.S. Office of Education, 1971.

Perkins, F. *Books and Non-Book Media: Annotated Guide to Selection Aids for Educational Materials.* Urbana, IL: National Council of Teachers of English, 1972.

Rufsvold, M. I. *Guide to Educational Media: Films, Filmstrips, Kinescopes, Phonodiscs, Phonotapes, Programmed Instructional Materials, Slides, Transparencies, Videotapes.* Chicago: American Library Association, 1977.

Sive, M. R. *Selecting Instructional Media: A Guide to Audiovisual and Other Instructional Media Lists.* Littleton, CO: Libraries Unlimited, 1978.

Wynar, C. L. *Guide to Reference Books for School Media Centers.* Littleton, CO: Libraries Unlimited, 1973.

Wynar, C. L. *1974-75 Supplement: Guide to Reference Books for School Media Centers.* Littleton, CO: Libraries Unlimited, 1976.

Journals (review sources) include:

Audio Visual Instruction	*Landers Film Review*
Booklist	*Library Journal Previews*
Canadian Audio-Visual Review	*Media & Methods*
EFLA Evaluations	*Media Mix Newsletter*
Film Library Quarterly	*School Library Journal*
Filmmakers' Newsletter	*Stereo Review*
Film News	*Wilson Library Bulletin*
High Fidelity	

Although all of the preceding lists of sources are intended to provide a general overview, there is a slight emphasis on films. One reason for that is historical, since after microforms and phonograph records, motion picture films are the most commonly held audio visual forms in libraries. Also, 16mm films cost significantly more than either of the other two formats, making previewing very important. Because of its popularity, cost, and longer history of use, film review and evaluation have had more time to become established. Increased popularity of other formats in time will make it economically feasible to publish journals supporting just one form.

ORDERING AUDIO VISUALS

For all practical purposes ordering materials in the formats discussed in this chapter is the same as for books and serials, with only a few exceptions. The exceptions are related to those items acquired after previewing.

There is a major difference between review copies of books and preview copies of other media. With books, if you like what you see, you keep it, pay the invoice, and perhaps order multiple copies at the same time. For a number of reasons (risk of loss, damage, etc.), audio visual preview copies are requested from the supplier, viewed, and then *returned.* (A few film vendors now ship an approval copy with a 10 percent discount if the library buys the film.) Also, almost all filmstrips are sent on approval. Suppliers only have a few preview copies of each title available, so this means that in most cases, you must *schedule* the preview copy well in advance. Normally you will write to the producer or supplier asking for preview copies of titles X, Y, and Z, and list a number of alternative dates. Remember you will be previewing in a group, so the meeting must be set up in advance. You also must know when you will have what items available for previewing. A preview file thus becomes a very important aid in the selection process; it should contain a listing of each title requested, the dates requested, when it is scheduled for previewing, and the result of the preview.

Several other factors should be kept in mind. Your preview copy will probably have been used before; therefore, the quality will not be as high as for a new copy. If you can determine from the supplier how often the preview copy has been used you then can gain an insight into the durability of the product. In assessing this information (assuming that you can get it), remember that the copy was used by persons who are more skilled in using the medium than is the average library patron.

If you decide to buy the item, you return the preview copy and order a new print. When the new print is received you should screen it to be certain it is: a) a new print, b) the same content as what was ordered, and c) technically sound—no breaks, sound track coordinated with visuals, and properly processed. Generally, other media are not mass produced in the same manner as are books; sometimes it is just on an "on-demand" basis. That is, the producer has several preview copies and a master copy; when an order arrives the master copy is used to produce a new print. Thus there is no assurance that the preview copy is reflective of the quality of the print that you will receive.

EQUIPMENT FACTORS IN SELECTING AUDIO VISUALS

Part of the expense of developing an audio visual collection is in buying and maintaining the equipment required for use of the various formats acquired. Increasing standardization in equipment means that the problem of compatability is not as great as it once was, but newer formats always go through an early stage in which there are competing and incompatible lines of equipment. In those cases where you must buy such a format—that is, before standardization has occurred— you should decide on the basis of which equipment line has the greatest number of available titles. Do not believe more than one-quarter of what the sales representative tells you about plans for the future development of a strong line of titles. Look at what *is*, not what may be.

A good example of a format's going through the early development phase is the video disc. Currently (late 1978) many newspapers are carrying advertisements for video cassette tape recording units for the home. This may now seem to be an area where a library might begin to build a collection of video cassettes for public loan, as a considerable number of programs are now available in this format. The library could handle video cassettes in the same manner as they do phonorecords and tapes. However, for the past five years or so there have been attempts to develop a video disc, similar to the phonorecord. Four systems are about to be marketed; unfortunately they are neither compatible with one another nor with any other existing system. Should you ignore the development of the disc and go with the tape format? Should you wait to see what happens? Unless you are among the fortunate few who work in a library that has no fiscal problems, the wait-and-see approach seems safest. Also currently in developmental stages are hologram programs (a laser technology), and this may make *both* tape and disc video obsolete.

The above example illustrates two points: 1) standardization takes time to accomplish; and 2) the media field is always changing. These two factors combine to make equipment buying hazardous, and to some extent, they keep libraries from building collections outside the areas of sound recordings (records and tapes) and films (filmstrips, 8mm and 16mm).

When you do decide to buy equipment several annual guides are available:

Audiovisual Market Place: A Multimedia Guide (published by R. R. Bowker) is really a directory of manufacturers and distributors. You will find only the briefest description of the type of equipment and the names and addresses where you can get additional information.

The Audio-Visual Equipment Directory (published by National Audio-Visual Association) is much more detailed than *A-V Market Place*. Whenever possible each piece of equipment will have information on its technical details, operation, and price, and usually a photograph. The list is as comprehensive as possible but does depend upon manufacturers and distributors to supply the information, in much the same manner as PTLA. The content is descriptive, not evaluative.

Library Technology Reports (published by the American Library Association) provides, from time to time, valuable evaluations of equipment for the media library (record players, filmstrip projectors, and microform equipment, have all appeared). The *Reports* are published as a looseleaf service and include reports on new products, articles on the use of a type of equipment as well as testing and evaluation information. Unfortunately, the LTR program is not well supported, so no attempt is made to be comprehensive or to necessarily update information previously published. The *Reports* and program are very useful and it is too bad that more support cannot be found to develop it more fully.

You can also find information on 16mm film projectors, 35mm slide projectors, and phonorecord and tape player/recorders in popular magazines. The major drawback to these sources is that the evaluation is normally made in terms of home or personal use rather than institutional. Institutional use requires the same ease of operation as home use; however, the equipment must be much more durable and designed to withstand misuse. Most popular magazines do not examine durability in this light. Some sources may be of some help—one is the *Educational Product Report* (EPR), published several times a year by Educational Products Information Exchange Institute. Again the problem is there are few comparative tests. EPR provides information on the "how to" of selecting educational media equipment and on basic technical operating data, but is not the *Consumer Reports* or *Consumers' Research* for educational media equipment.

All of this means that you can do your homework in the above sources, perhaps visit a showroom or convention and examine the equipment and see it demonstrated. But the final decision is yours. Before you commit yourself by signing a purchase order for the equipment, spend some time and effort in locating a library or educational institution that already has the equipment. Talking with individuals who have used equipment on a day-to-day basis is the best insurance against getting equipment that is continuously breaking down. Find out how easy it is to get parts when the unit does go down. Can local technicians repair the unit or must it be returned to the manufacturer? If your informants say that their experience proves the equipment to be durable, reliable, and easy to maintain, then you may have what you need. If they say less than that, perhaps more searching will save you time and trouble in the long run.

SUMMARY

This chapter has tried to convey the fact that building a media collection for the library is a time-consuming activity and an expensive undertaking. It probably has done that, but it was *not* intended to convey the message: do not bother with audio visual materials. Previewing and seeking out published evaluations of hardware and software do take time. Additional to the cost in time is the cost of the equipment and software. Also, new formats seem to appear every day, threatening to make one or two existing formats obsolete. On the other hand, photography (still and motion), radio, television, etc., have not made the book nor one another obsolete, despite pronouncements of the forthcoming demise of this or that format. Each new format is capable of doing certain things that no other format can do, but each also has its limitations and as a result, supplements rather than replaces other formats. What is also clear is that different persons respond to different formats in different ways, as they have different preferences in seeking and enjoying information. If the library is to be responsive to the total community it must build a collection of materials that reflects that community's variety of interests and tastes.

BIBLIOGRAPHY

Alexander, E. "The School Libraries." *Library Resources and Technical Services* 12 (Spring 1968): 148-52.

American Library Association. Public Library Association. Audiovisual Committee. *Guidelines for Audiovisual Materials and Services for Large Public Libraries.* Chicago: ALA, 1975.

American Library Association. *Recommendations for Audiovisual Materials and Services for Small and Medium Sized Public Libraries.* Chicago: ALA, 1975.

Ball, H. G. "A Model for Program Planning in Media." *California Librarian* 36 (July 1975): 16-21.

Belland, J. C. "Educational Media: Why Bother?" *School Media Quarterly* 3 (Spring 1975): 219-36.

Billings, J. "Selecting for the Instructional Materials Center." *Wisconsin Library Bulletin* 64 (Jan. 1968): 9-12.

Blake, F., and E. Perlmutter. "Libraries in the Marketplace." *Library Journal* 99 (Jan. 15, 1974): 108-111.

Bouchner, B. G., et al. *Handbook and Catalog for Instructional Media Selection.* Englewood Cliffs, NJ: Educational Technology Publications, 1973.

Brown, J. W. *A-V Instruction: Technology, Media and Methods.* 4th ed. New York: McGraw-Hill, 1973.

Brown, J. W. *New Media in Public Libraries.* New York: McGraw-Hill, 1976.

Bukalski, P. J. "Collecting Classic Films." *American Libraries* 3 (May 1971): 475-79.

Burr, R. L. "Library Goals and Library Behavior." *College and Research Libraries* 36 (Jan. 1975): 27-32.

Currell, H. F. J. *Phonograph Record Libraries: Their Organization and Practice.* 2nd ed. Hamden, CT: Shoe String Press, 1970.

Dougherty, R. M. "The Unserved—Academic Library Style." *American Libraries* 2 (Nov. 1971): 1055-58.

Eash, M. J. "Evaluating Instructional Materials." *Audiovisual Instruction* 17 (Dec. 1972): 12-13.

Elstein, H. "Standards, Selection, and the Media Center: Where Are We Now?" *Audiovisual Instruction* 17 (Dec. 1970): 35-39.

Emery, R. "Philosophy, Purpose and Function in Librarianship." *Library Association Record* 73 (July 1971): 127-29.

"Evaluation and Selection of Media." *Audiovisual Instruction* 20 (April 1975): 4-45.

Fleischer, E. "Decks, Cassettes, Dials or Buffers: Systems for Individual Study." *Library Journal* 96 (Feb. 15, 1971): 695-98.

French, J. "The Evaluation Gap: The State of the Art in A/V Reviewing with Special Emphasis on Filmstrips." *School Library Journal* 16 (March 1970): 104-109.

Geller, E. "This Media Matter." *Library Journal* 96 (June 15, 1971): 2048-53.

Grove, P. *Nonprint Media in Academic Libraries.* Chicago: American Library Association, 1975.

Harrison, H. *Film Library Techniques.* New York: Hastings House, 1973.

Hicks, W. B., and A. M. Tillin. *Developing Multi-Media Libraries.* New York: R. R. Bowker, 1970.

Hicks, W. B., and A. M. Tillin. *Managing Multi-Media Libraries.* New York: R. R. Bowker, 1977.

Hug, W. E. *Instructional Design and the Media Program.* Chicago: American Library Association, 1975.

Improving Materials Selection Procedures: A Basic "How to" Handbook. EPIE Educational Product Report no. 54. New York: Educational Products Information Exchange Institute, 1973.

Jones, J., and R. Lawson. "Intellectual Freedom and Material Selection." *School Media Quarterly* 1 (Winter 1973): 113-16.

Kemp, J. E. "Which Medium?" *Audiovisual Instruction* 16 (Dec. 1971): 32-38.

Neville, S. H., and A. S. Clark. "How Can a University Library Support Educational Needs in a Period of Change?" *Educational Technology* 15 (Sept. 1975): 48-55.

Prostano, E. J., and J. S. Prostano. *School Library Media Center.* 2nd ed. Littleton, CO: Libraries Unlimited, 1977.

Romiszowski, A. J. *The Selection and Use of Instructional Media: A Systems Approach.* New York: Halsted Press, 1974.

Shoner, J. M. "Selecting Initial Media Equipment for New Facilities." *School Media Quarterly* 2 (Spring 1974): 227-33.

Standards for the Development of School Media Programs in California. Joint Committee of the California Association of School Librarians and the Audiovisual Education Association. Burlingame, CA: California Association of School Libraries, 1970.

Topper, L. "Back to Basics: Some Problems and Pointers for Those Introducing A-V Materials into the Library." *Wilson Library Bulletin* 47 (Sept. 1972): 42.

Topper, L. "Evaluating Audio-Visual Material." *Educational Technology* 13 (May 1973): 19-20.

Waldron, G. *The Information Film.* New York: Columbia University Press, 1949.

Woolls, B. "Who Previews What . . . " *AV Guide* 51 (July 1972): 4-7.

Chapter 8

ACQUISITION WORK

ACQUISITION—WHAT IT IS AND WHAT IT IS NOT

Many persons assume that selection and acquisition work are one and the same process. Nothing could be further from the truth. They are closely related but distinctly different activities. By now you should have a clear picture of what is involved in the selection process. In this chapter we will examine the acquisition work, the process by which the library physically secures (through buying, gifts, or exchange) the items that selection personnel have identified as desirable additions to the collection.

The acquisition department usually does not have the responsibility for selection. Individuals in the department may have selection responsibility, but that would be a result of their special knowledge or skill, not because they work in the acquisition department. Selection personnel and the acquisition department must have a close cooperative work relationship in order to be effective. Poor coordination will mean wasted effort, slow response time, and high unit costs. Library budgets are never adequate to meet all the information needs of the community, and wasted effort lowers the quality of service. Coordination can only be achieved when all parties involved in the work understand the other groups' processes, problems, and potential utility.

Beyond the obvious purpose of supporting overall library objectives, the acquisition department has both specific library-wide goals and departmental goals. Library-wide goals can be grouped into five very broad categories: 1) develop a knowledge of the book and media trade (discussed in earlier chapters), 2) aid in the selection and collection development process, 3) process requests for items to be added to the collection, 4) control the expenditure of collection development funds, 5) maintain all of the required records regarding the expenditure of funds.

By collecting and disseminating information about book publishers and media producers and vendors, the acquisition department aids in the selection process. Collections of publishers' catalogs, pre-publication announcements, and book dealer catalogs are maintained in most acquisition departments. Information regarding changes in publishing schedules, publishing houses, and new services is also collected. Many acquisition departments serve as central clearinghouses for this type of information for their entire library. Indeed, in larger libraries, the department sometimes operates a small-scale selective dissemination system by routing information to selectors, based on each individual's subject or area responsibility.

Processing requests for materials involves a number of activities to ensure that the library secures the needed items as quickly and inexpensively as possible. Time and money would be wasted if requests were simply forwarded to a publisher or vendor. Inaccurate information, duplicate requests, unavailable material, etc., cause increased costs for both the library and the supplier (and considerable ill-will on the part of the latter). Each acquisition department develops its own set of procedures to reduce problems of this type, and while there are hundreds of variations, the basic process is the same (we will discuss that basic process later in this chapter).

Everyone working in the acquisition department must know something about bookkeeping and accounting. Selectors need to know enough about financial reporting to be able to interpret the reports that the acquisition department prepares for them. The acquisition department controls the expenditure of collection development funds for two reasons. First, the department must meet legal requirements regarding the reporting of expenditures of public funds. Meeting these requirements does not, however, provide the day-to-day financial information that selection and acquisition personnel require. Second, special internal accounting records are used and maintained by the department to meet the staff's needs.

In addition to financial records, the acquisition department keeps files of information on all aspects of its business transactions. Files may be in the form of correspondence, catalogs, monthly fiscal reports, statistics, etc., used by the department selectors and the library administration. File maintenance requires a considerable amount of staff time, thereby making recordkeeping and file control an important activity in the department.

In addition to its library-wide goals, the acquisition department has four primary internal goals: 1) acquire material as quickly as possible, 2) maintain a high level of accuracy in all work procedures, 3) keep work processes simple so as to achieve the lowest possible unit cost, 4) develop close, friendly working relationships both with other library units and with vendors. These internal goals are important in the achievement of the broader, library-wide goals discussed earlier, since all of the department's decisions regarding internal goals will have some impact on other operating units in the library. With this fact in mind, it should be clear why selection and acquisition personnel must understand each other's needs and procedures.

Speed is a significant factor in meeting patron demands and determining patron satisfaction. Many patrons want their material "yesterday," and an acquisition system that requires three or four months to secure items will create problems in public relations. A system that is very fast but has a high error rate will increase operating costs and waste time and energy for both departmental staff and suppliers. In many medium- and large-sized libraries, studies have shown that the costs of securing and processing an item are equal to or greater than the price of that item. By keeping procedures simple, and by periodically reviewing work flow, the department can aid the library in providing better service. Speed, accuracy, and least cost should be the watchwords in acquisition departments.

STAFFING

Its staffing pattern will naturally affect the way that the department accomplishes its various goals, and thoughtful staff planning will go a long way toward providing efficient service. Efficient staffing is usually accomplished by utilizing four classes of employees: 1) professionals, 2) library/media technical assistants, 3) clerks, and 4) part-time help. Persons in each category supply certain skills and knowledge required for the optimum operation of the department.

Librarians provide in-depth knowledge of library operations and the book and media trade. They should decide the objectives and goals of the department, prepare operating plans, develop policies, and supervise the operation of the department. In addition, they carry out tasks that require special skill or knowledge, such as verifying out-of-print requests or checking rare or special collection items. If the acquisition department does not have any selection responsibility (and very few do), there is little need to have a large number of professionals on its staff except in the very largest departments. A high percentage of the department's activities can be handled by technicians and clerks—if the work has been properly planned.

Library/media technical assistants (LMTAs) are staff who have had some training in librarianship. Many LMTAs are graduates of community college library technician training programs and also hold a bachelor's degree. If staff members with the B.A. degree have completed a one-year assistant program, they have a background very similar to that of a library school graduate. One ought to make considerable use of this category of employee in planning work in an acquisition department. Acquisition work does require considerable knowledge of librarianship, yet it is rather structured and routine. LMTAs have enough background to operate effectively while not being so highly trained as to waste otherwise valuable skills and training in such tasks. The most routine of tasks (e.g., typing and filing) are usually left to clerical and part-time staff.

The following sections describe the major activities carried out in an acquisitions department. These are general descriptions and you should not expect to find any acquisitions unit conducting its work exactly as outlined below. Each jurisdiction has different regulations regarding accounting methods, different staffing patterns will cause certain modifications, and the method of selecting materials may also affect the system. However, the categories of work and the reasons that they are performed should remain consistent throughout the library world.

REQUESTS

Searching begins with the receipt of a request for an item. The form of this request will vary from an oral request from a patron at a public service desk to a scrawled note on a paper napkin from the local coffee shop to a completed request card. However, all requests eventually will be put on a formal request card, after the individual(s) responsible for selection approve the request. Each library will have its own special request format or order in which information is given.

Despite individual variations, the following categories of information are normally requested: 1) author, 2) title, 3) publisher, 4) date of publication, 5) edition, 6) price, 7) number of copies, 8) requestor's name. Other information requested may be: a) series, b) vendor, c) fund to be charged, and d) approval signature. For any person not familiar with library book trade practice, the most confusing item on such a request card is the space entitled "date/year." The most frequent assumption by patrons is that the library is interested in the date on which the request card was filled out, rather than the date on which the item was produced. Anyone with acquisition department experience knows how often this item is confused. If the form specifically calls for "date of publication," there will be no problem.

Because, in most libraries, anyone can request any book, some preliminary work must be done before starting the formal search/verification procedure. First, duplicates must be removed. Remember also that patrons often request items already in the collection because they do not know how to use the public catalog. Frequently patrons are somewhat confused in that they combine information about more than one popular title: the author of one book with the title of a book by someone else. As a person gains experience with various requestors and stays up to date with new titles being published, the preliminary sorting can go very quickly.

BIBLIOGRAPHIC SEARCHING

Bibliographic searching/verification consists of two elements. One element is the establishment of the existence of a particular item—search. The other element is the establishment of the need for the item by the library—verify. In searching, the concern is with the author, the correct title, the publisher of the work, etc. Verification is concerned with whether the library already owns the item, whether it needs a second copy or multiple copies, and whether the item already has been ordered but not received. *Note*: The search may be done using either printed sources or one of the on-line systems such as OCLC; whichever one is employed, the basic issues in searching remain the same.

Which step should you start with? The answer will depend upon the collection development system employed by each library. It is true that all requests will have to be verified. It is also true, however, that not all request cards have sufficient information to do this accurately. If the majority of request cards are filled out from bibliographies, dealer catalogs, etc., by book selection personnel, then the procedure could start with verification. When a large percentage of the selections are from non-librarians, it is advisable to start with the search procedure.

One of the major problems for a searcher is the question of author entry. Some selectors, usually non-librarians, know very little about cataloging rules of entry. Even bibliographers may not keep up to date on rule changes. Yet, because often in published tools only the main entry citation provides complete information, this question is important in saving time and effort in searching. Needless to say, the main problem areas are corporate authors and conference papers, proceedings, or transactions. If the files in the acquisition department are maintained by title rather than main entry, you may be able to reduce bibliographic training of clerical help to a minimum. Titles seldom change after the item is published; main entries, on the other hand, may change several times between the time the item is selected and is on the shelf. Main entry searching requires a greater knowledge of cataloging rules, which in turn requires more time for training searchers and more time spent in searching.

If the author main entry search procedure does not verify between 60 percent and 90 percent of the items, the procedure should be examined very closely, as it is probable that either requests have been made improperly (i.e., they lack adequate information) or the search is being conducted with the wrong tools. For the remaining items, the title approach should be the next step in the procedure. Most bibliographies provide both author and title access to their contents, and a title search should verify most of the remaining items. Occasionally, an item cannot be located in any source; when this happens, the original requestor might be contacted in the hope that she or he can provide some additional information.

If the requestor cannot give any further information, the searcher may try a subject approach, provided enough information is available to determine what the subject might be. The success ratio of subject searches is generally low for a number of reasons. One is that not many bibliographies provide a subject approach, therefore making it impossible to use this method consistently in some of the more commonly used bibliographies. Another, and more critical, one is the assignment of subject; it is quite arbitrary, and even with a work in hand, two individuals may very well provide two different subject categories for the same book. As one can imagine, the searcher must then look under as many subjects as possible and still can never be certain that all the appropriate headings were used. Because of its low success ratio, the subject method of verification should only be used as a last resort measure for items that are urgently needed.

Occasionally, it will be necessary to examine three or four sources in order to establish all of the required order information. One may quickly find the author, title, publisher, date of publication, and price, but it may be difficult to find information regarding whether the item is in a series. Two new publications—*Books in Series in the United States 1966-1975* (R. R. Bowker, 1977) and its *Supplement* (1978), which extends coverage into but not comprehensive of 1977—may be the answer to the problem of searching multiple sources for information on series. Both verification and searching procedures, though, involve the use of a number of bibliographic tools, the major categories of which were described in chapter 6. Book dealer catalogs are another helpful source (see chapter 3).

There are several files to check to establish the library's need for the selected item. The most obvious place to start is with the public catalog. A checker would look first under the assumed main entry; if the results were negative and there was some doubt as to the validity of the main entry, then a title search should be made. Some librarians suggest that checkers begin with the item's title rather than with its author because there is less variation in titles. In some libraries, a number of other public catalogs list phonograph records, government documents, series, collections in special libraries, or subject areas (such as fine arts). These specialized catalogs must be checked if the item falls into one of these categories and if the public catalog does not list all such collections. Other public service files to be examined are those for lost and missing books or damaged books (replacement file). The checker would not examine all of these files for all items, but merely for those popular items not marked "added copy" or "replacement."

In the technical service area, several files can be checked to determine whether the item is being processed. Technical service units tend to maintain a number of files that somewhat duplicate one another, so at least three basic files should be examined: the *in-process file*, the *verified requests file* noting items waiting to be typed on order forms, and the *standing order file*. The in-process file represents books on order, books received but not yet sent to cataloging, and books in the cataloging department. The standing order file represents items to be received automatically from a supplier. Usually these items are in publishers' series, and it is important that the checker examine the standing order file after establishing that an item is in a series.

ORDER FORMS

There are three basic types of order forms. One is the single card, which is essentially a request card. (Not often used, it cannot serve as many functions as the multiple copy order form, although some small libraries use it and then photo-reproduce several copies for their file needs.) The second and most common type of order form is the multiple copy order form. A third type is the punched card (not yet very common, except in larger libraries or in cooperative library systems with a high volume of business). Regardless of the form employed, it must provide the supplier with enough information to assure shipment of the correct materials: author, title, publisher, date of publication, price, edition (if there are various editions), number of copies, order number, and any special instructions regarding invoicing or methods of payment. Also, more and more suppliers are asking for the International Standard Book Number (ISBN).

The multiple copy (fan-fold) order form is most common, as noted. These forms are available in a number of formats, containing anywhere from four to twelve copies. The normal size is 3x5-inches (standard library file drawer size). Normally, each copy is a different color for easy identification, but no standard dictates a particular color for a certain purpose. A minimum of four copies is typical in all libraries: 1) an outstanding order copy, 2) a dealer's copy, 3) a claiming copy, and 4) an accounting copy. The number of potential uses seems to be limited only by the imagination of the librarians. In some libraries, two copies are sent to the dealer, while three or four may be kept in the in-process file. In the past, most libraries used one slip to order a catalog card either from the Library of Congress or a commercial cataloging service. Today such use is diminishing, as more and more libraries use only on-line cataloging systems such as OCLC. In the not-too-distant future, libraries may not have to type up order slips. One large American book jobber already has an on-line order system available for library installation. Other uses for the slips are for bookkeeping purposes: one for the bookkeeper in the acquisitions department, one for the agency that supervises the library's expenditures. In some larger systems, where selectors lack close contact with the acquisitions department (as in an academic library, where faculty members do much of the selecting), a copy is sent to the selector, who then knows that the order was placed.

The outstanding order slip is one of the most important because of its many uses. It is essential that this be a clear, readable copy (usually either the ribbon copy or the second or third copy in the multiple order form). The most common places in which this might be filed are the outstanding order or in-process file. Often the in-process file contains several copies of the order. For example, when the order is sent, the in-process file might receive five slips. The first represents on-order status, the next three slips will be used in cataloging, and the final one remains in the file, indicating that the book is being processed but is not yet ready for public use. When the book is received, all slips except the in-process slip are removed. When the book is ready for circulation, one slip from cataloging is returned to the acquisition department to signal the removal of the in-process slip. Presumably at this point, a set of cards will be filed in the public catalog indicating that the book is now available for the public.

Since dealers find individual slips easier to use than a long list of books, this means reserving at least one, but usually two, slips from the multiple copy form. A single long list is less likely to get lost; but if only part of the required items are available, then individual slips make shipment of partial orders much easier. If the library sends only a listing on an order blank, the dealer will usually make up individual slips for easier access to the stock. Obviously, then, the copy sent to the dealer must be a clear copy. If only one slip is sent, some space must be provided in which to report the status of an item that cannot be supplied. It is usual to supply the dealer with two slips, one to retain if the book is out of stock, and one that can be returned to indicate that the item is temporarily unavailable but will be supplied as soon as it is restocked.

A claiming copy is a slip retained by the library for inquiry when an item has been ordered but not received. While this copy must be readable, it does not have to be one of the most legible, as very few of them usually are used and most will be thrown away when the order is received. The claiming slip asks the dealer the status of the order and what he will do about filling it. On the verso of the slip are printed four or five different status categories (out of stock, out of print, etc.), so the dealer merely checks the appropriate category and returns the slip to the library. Claiming slips should also record the date on which the claim was sent, because many libraries automatically cancel any order outstanding and unreported for more than 90 or 120 days.

An accounting copy is often used by the bookkeeper to encumber funds (that is, to set aside the full list price of each item, as the percentage of discount will not be known in advance usually; the difference, once determined, returns to the unexpended funds category). Some libraries find it more convenient to maintain more than one copy for accounting. Since many libraries do not pay invoices until an order is complete, the first system works very well. Where it is possible to make payments on partially filled orders, then individual slips make it easier to forward this information to the accounting office.

After the verification process is finished, a number of steps still must be taken to complete the order procedure. The assignment of the dealer is first. To do this effectively requires some knowledge of the entire operating routine of the individual library, which is not something that can be taught in school but can only be learned on the job.

VENDOR (PUBLISHER, JOBBER, OR WHOLESALER) ASSIGNMENT

When one has a choice between two or more vendors, some consideration should be given to the discounts offered. Usually these will be quite similar, with not more than one or two percent difference. Even if there is a great difference in the discount, the vendor with the lower discount might be selected because of the type of service offered. If, for instance, the firm is prompt in filling orders, quickly reports the status of items not in stock, quickly follows up on items that are temporarily out of stock, and does not hold an order for an inordinate length of time while buying items not in stock—the service would be worth the higher cost. Other considerations are the speed with which the vendor handles both returns and the many problems that arise with frequent shipments of large quantities of material. Mistakes do happen, and the ease with which one may correct them is important. Also, the vendor who has had a number of transactions with a given library is more likely to understand and abide by its accounting system and special bookkeeping procedures, while a new dealer may not fully understand some of the variations. Sometimes it is faster to send rush orders directly to the publisher than to a jobber or wholesaler, another reason for knowing what these firms can do for you.

ASSIGNMENT OF ORDER NUMBER

After the vendor has been assigned, the assignment of the order number is very simple and straightforward. It is simply a matter of checking with the bookkeeper as to the last order number used and assigning the next number in the sequence. Fund assignments, however, are made on the basis of department (in academic libraries: English, history, etc.; in public libraries: children, reference, etc.), and the items selected by members of a department will be assigned to that department's fund.

PREPARING ORDERS

When the assignment of the vendor, order number, and fund are completed, the order is ready to be typed. This entails at least two operations. A standard form cover letter is typed giving the dealer information and details regarding billing, credit memos, invoicing procedures and so forth. The other step in this procedure is typing the multiple copy order forms. Normally, a list is also sent to the dealer (typically, an alphabetical author listing).

In many libraries, all orders must be signed by the person authorized to spend library funds (e.g., the director of the library or the head of the acquisition department). This requirement is something of a nuisance when one sends out several hundred orders, each one requiring a signature. It is helpful to arrange the signing time so that orders may be sorted and prepared for mailing by the time the library's mail is picked up.

ORDER RECEIPT

Receiving orders, although not difficult, must be carefully planned. As strange as it may seem, the careful unpacking of shipments can save everyone in the department a great deal of time, energy, and frustration. One of the first steps in the unpacking process is to find the packing slip and/or invoice. A packing slip is simply a list of items sent in a particular shipment; an invoice is an itemized bill, which is required before a business office will issue a voucher or check. Either or both items will or should accompany any shipment. Without either item, it is impossible to determine whether or not the shipment is complete, because there is no itemized listing of what was sent. Because of the importance of the invoice—no invoice, no money—many vendors mail the invoice to the acquisitions department rather than send it packed with the merchandise.

No matter which format is used (packing slip/invoice), the person unpacking a shipment may find himself at times playing "who has the packing slip?" Happily, most vendors attach an envelope containing the slip to the outside of one of the boxes, and it is clearly marked as such. Unfortunately, a few vendors delight in hiding the slip in the strangest places: one technique is to enclose the slip inside one of the items, while another favorite hiding place is in the bottom of a box under a cardboard bottom liner. If unpacking a shipment for which no slip has been found, it is *essential* to keep the items separated from other materials in the receiving area. Mixing shipments can create trouble.

Normally, as each item is unpacked, it is checked against the packing slip. This serves to check what the shippers think they sent against what the library received. Boxes go astray in shipment, items are overlooked in packing rooms, and sometimes items disappear from the library before they are processed.

The next step in the receiving process is to check the physical condition of the items received and then check each item against the original order. Some of the more common problems are:

1) the wrong edition is received. [Note: The checker must be aware of the difference between an edition and a printing. A new edition indicates that the item has been changed—material added and/or deleted; a new printing merely indicates the item was reprinted with *no* change] ;

2) items ordered are not received;

3) items not ordered are received;

4) too many copies of an item are received;

5) imperfect copies received.

Imperfections can be of many kinds. With books, some of the typical problems are missing or blank pages, or improperly collated texts. Audio tapes should be checked for gaps, blank tapes, and proper speed of recording. Film items should be examined for proper developing. Many times a film is "fogged," "streaked," or spotted with hypo residue. Any imperfect item *can* be returned for replacement.

The next step in the process is to "property mark" the items. As noted above, sometimes items disappear, so the sooner items are marked, the more difficult it will be for them to disappear. Property marking takes many forms. Books are usually stamped on the fore-edge and on the title page. When a library is required to "accession number" items, the number is recorded in the book and in the accessions book. (Accessioning is a system of assigning a unique number to each item purchased for inventory control.)

Films often have a special leader attached, which has the name of the library imprinted in it. If an accession number is used, the leader is perforated with that number. Phonograph records may have the label on the record stamped as well as a stamp on the record jacket. Cassette items may have a special label attached, or may have the library name and accession number engraved into them.

The last step in processing a received order is approval of the invoice for payment. Normally this may only be approved by the head of the department or that person's representative. The approval of payment is only made when the order has been fully received or items not supplied have been cancelled so that the order is "complete" (that is, all items have been accounted for). When the invoice is approved, the bookkeeper passes this information to the agency that actually writes the check. Rarely does a library itself write such checks; it is done by the governing agency.

GIFTS AND EXCHANGE

Very often, the acquisitions department has a unit to handle gifts and exchange. This unit checks items received against the library's holdings and also against the want list. A wanted item is sent to the catalog department for processing, along with any relevant bibliographic information. Occasionally, gifts and exchange will receive items that are not in the want file but still are considered worthwhile additions. (It also is common to receive a great many duplicates or items that simply are not appropriate for the collection. They must be disposed of in some way, frequently through an exchange program.) The gift section has a number of responsibilities. In a large library with a special collections department, active efforts may be made to secure gifts from various donors. Frequently, there is an interest in acquiring an individual's private collection. Even the smallest library will receive a few gift items during a year, and the section's primary function is to evaluate donated materials and decide what to do with them.

An important tool is a written policy regarding gifts, one that provides a framework within which the unit makes its decisions. Normally, the same criteria should be used for purchasing as well as receiving. Even a gift item is not cost free; neither is it always a worthwhile addition. For instance, if a library would not buy the material, it probably should not be retained. The policy should include information regarding disposal rights, deposit items, memorial gifts, special labeling for gift items, and the acceptance of funds to purchase materials. Without such a policy, it is almost impossible to establish an effective gifts unit (see chapter 5).

The checking process is important, because the library cannot afford to add unnecessary items and processing and storage costs *must* be considered. But it cannot afford to discard valuable or needed items. Older books must be carefully checked, as variations in printings and editions determine whether an item is valuable or worthless. (Second or third printings lessen the value of a work.) This must be done by persons with extensive training and experience in bibliographic checking.

Only a small percentage of gifts will be added to the collection. In larger libraries, gifts are rejected if they are already in the collection, but this means a rather high cost per item added. Careful training and efficient work procedures will help keep the unit cost as low as possible, but it will still be higher for gifts in comparison with purchased items. This also means that the library is confronted with the problem of disposing of a great many unwanted items, which is usually the responsibility of the exchange unit.

There are two basic types of exchange activity: the exchange of unwanted and duplicate materials, and the exchange of new materials between libraries. Exchange of new materials is usually confined to large university or research libraries; in essence, cooperating institutions trade publications. For example, the University of California libraries might exchange UC publications with State University of New York libraries for SUNY publications. Occasionally, this system is employed to acquire materials from countries in which commercial trade operations are limited or restricted in some manner. Exchanges like this are established through formal agreements between the cooperating organizations; the technician's role is confined to maintaining records of what has been sent and received.

One method libraries use for disposing of unwanted items is to prepare a list of them. This list is then sent to exchange units in other libraries, and the first library to request an item gets it for the shipping cost (usually book rate postage). Another method is to sell the material to a o.p. dealer. These are usually block purchases rather than by a price per item. Cash is generally not involved; instead, credit is extended by the dealer to the library in the amount agreed upon. The credit memo then is given to the bookkeeping department for recording as a credit that the library will use when buying materials from that dealer. Holding a book sale is yet another method of disposing of unwanted material. It is time-consuming. Staff must choose the materials to be sold, find a suitable location, and work during the sale. Most libraries do not find this profitable in terms of the amount of staff time involved and the return realized, although it does clear out a number of items that might not be disposed of by any other method.

ACCOUNTING

Every librarian must know something about accounting, especially those individuals in acquisitions. Accounting has a specialized language system to measure the consequences of organizational activities and to communicate that information to interested parties in a uniform manner. Although public service agencies—including libraries—use a fund accounting number system, accountants still use many private sector accounting terms when discussing their work. Therefore, some knowledge of their terminology is useful.

The modern method of double entry bookkeeping, developed in the fourteenth century, is premised on equating business transactions. That is, every transaction represents a duality of elements, a flow in which something of tangible or intangible value is received but at the same time an equivalent value is given up. Each transaction results in increases or decreases in assets, liabilities, and net worth (these expressed in monetary units).

Accounting provides a record of business transactions in financial terms, and such records are needed by non-profit organizations as well as by business enterprises operated for profit. Book selectors and order unit personnel must know how much money is available to be spent at any given time. Accounting also makes available the financial information required by supervising agencies (governmental or not) and by present and prospective creditors, investors, and the general public. In academic libraries where book funds are allocated by department or subject areas, monthly fiscal statements are prepared.

Anyone who deals with accounting is frequently confused by the way in which the terms debit and credit are employed. Accounting practices have given conventional meanings to these words, which are not the same as the general public's definition. Debit (DR.) refers to the left side of an account sheet, and credit (CR.) refers to the right side. When used as a *noun*, a debit is an entry on the left side, and a credit is an entry on the right side of the account. As an *adjective*, the debit side is the left, and the credit side is the right. As a *verb*, to debit is to make an entry on the left side, while to credit is to make an entry on the right. (Sometimes the word charge is used instead of the word debit.)

Remembering the debit and credit side of the account sheet, the increases and decreases shown on it can be summarized as follows: *debit* indicates asset increase, liability decrease, proprietorship decrease, income decrease, expense increase; *credit* indicates asset decrease, liability increase, proprietorship increase, income increase, expense decrease. Since there is a two-fold aspect to each transaction, the complete record of transaction requires that the *total* amount for the debits and credits must be equal. This gives rise to a fundamental rule of accounting: *for every debit there must be a credit.* It is *not* necessary that there be the same number of debit and credit *items*, but the debit and credit *amounts must be equal.*

A group of accounts is normally entered into a book called the ledger. It is a derived (secondary) record, presenting in analytical form the accumulated effects of transactions on the assets, liabilities, and proprietorship. Its sources of information are the account books of entry, called journals. Usually only one account is placed on each page of the ledger.

Accounts may be classified objectively, that is, according to object or nature, so there can be an account for each general class or type of object on which the entreprise desires separate information. A more detailed classification may be desired by department or according to functional activities of the enterprise. Such a classification by function requires that those accounts relating to departmental activities be subdivided in order to keep the results of the operations of each department separate.

The journal is a chronological record of the transactions of an organization. It is the book of original entry in which transactions are recorded in their chronological order, showing debits and credits for each, amounts and accounts to be debited and credited, and an explanation of transactions. The journal may also be files of documents, punched cards, reels of punched magnetic tape, or other media. The journal is considered to be the book of first entry, despite the fact that its entries may be based on memoranda prepared previously in auxiliary records that give the details of each transaction.

The journal and the ledger are the basic books of the double entry accounting system. Both books are essential to an efficient and complete accounting system. The journal is the chronological record; the ledger is the analytical record. The journal is the book of original entry, the ledger is the book of second entry, a derived record. Therefore, the journal, as a book of first entry, ordinarily has greater weight as legal evidence than the ledger.

BOOKKEEPING

The primary function of the bookkeeping section is to oversee the financial transactions of the library. This is done in three basic steps: 1) encumbering of funds at the time the order is placed (to repeat, this is crediting an account with the full list price of the item ordered, since the discount is usually not known until the order is filled); 2) maintaining a list of accounts indicating the amounts encumbered but not yet expended (that is, money being held to pay for items on order but not yet received); 3) approving payment for those items received (that is, actually expending funds).

One of the major problems confronting a bookkeeper in the acquisitions department is the sheer number of funds against which items may be charged. In some systems, this may run as high as 50, 80, or even 100 accounts. And only specific types of materials may be charged against specific accounts. While it may not be the bookkeeper's job to assign those charges, it is necessary that he or she be able to tell approximately how much money remains, how much has been committed (encumbered), and how much has actually been spent from each account. It is the librarian's job to make certain that items are charged against the proper accounts. Some libraries allocate funds by subject area (X number of dollars for humanities, etc.). Again, the allocation of the monies available to the various sub-accounts is the librarian's responsibility. Yet another method of allocation is on the basis of services (children's, reference, etc.). Very often, there are separate funds for such things as phonograph records, serials, motion picture films, and art prints.

From the bookkeeper's point of view, perhaps the best method is no fund allocation at all. It reduces the number of running accounts to the minimum, and there is no question of improperly charged items. When many accounts exist, a great deal of time is spent preparing statements regarding the status of each. An almost equal amount of time then is devoted to explaining to those concerned with spending the money why an account is at a certain level.

RECONCILIATION OF ACCOUNTS

One difficulty facing the bookkeeper is knowing precisely where the library stands financially. The encumbered funds are always greater than the amount expended because some items have discounts. How many items are discounted and by how much are only known when the bill is received. The average discount will be around 10-15 percent, but some items will have no discount at all; others will have perhaps 33 percent or even 40 percent. For all of the items ordered during a year, the average is well under 20 percent.

The bookkeeper is also responsible for many routine, end-of-fiscal-year library duties. The library is normally on a one-year fiscal basis, and any money granted to it as part of its budget normally reverts to the granting agency if it is not expended within the fiscal year. Therefore, several months prior to the end of the fiscal year, acquisition staff must check with vendors on all outstanding orders to determine whether or not they will make delivery in time. If they cannot, the old order is cancelled, and a new one is placed for items to be delivered at the beginning of the following fiscal year. The bookkeeper's primary duty is to ensure that the library neither overspends nor underspends its budget. Since discounts and cancellations are unknown quantities until the moment they are received, it becomes quite a challenge to the bookkeeper to make an accurate estimate of just where the library stands financially.

SUMMARY

In such a short chapter on such a complex issue as managing an acquisition department, we have only touched upon the basic activities and problems. As more and more libraries are able to make use of on-line systems such as OCLC and BALLOTS, the amount of routine recordkeeping will be reduced. However, the importance of the acquisition department is never likely to diminish. It requires considerable professional skill and knowledge to operate such a department successfully.

The following bibliography will aid you in reading further and in greater depth on many of the topics touched upon, and thereby, you can gain much of the needed knowledge. Again, the remainder comes through actually working in an acquisition department.

BIBLIOGRAPHY

General Works

Adams, C. J. "Statistical Chaos: Technical Services in Public Libraries." *Library Journal* 91 (June 1, 1966): 2278-80.

American Library Association. "Lending to Reprinters." *Library Resources and Technical Services* 11 (Spring 1967): 229-31; 12 (Fall 1968): 455-56.

American Library Association. *Study of the Decision-Making Procedures for the Acquisition of Science Library Materials.* Chicago: ALA, 1969.

Applebaum, E. L. *Reader in Technical Services.* New York: NCR, 1973.

Arms, W. Y., and T. P. Walter. "A Simulation Model for Purchasing Duplicate Copies in a Library." *Journal of Library Automation* 7 (June 1974): 73-75.

Bach, H. "Junior College Library Collection." *California Librarian* 33 (Feb. 1972): 88-99.

Bagshaw, M. G. "Enter Computer: Book Ordering Practices and Procedures of the Toronto Public Library." *Top of the News* 23 (Nov. 1966): 39-42.

"Book Purchasing by University and College Libraries." *Publishers Weekly* 188 (July 10, 1965): 44-45.

Bowman, B. C. "Zerography, Possible Solution to the Bad-Paper Book Problem." *College and Research Libraries* 18 (May 1958): 185-89.

Boyer, C. J. "State-Wide Contracts for Library Materials: An Analysis of the Attendant Dysfunctional Consequences." *College and Research Libraries* 34 (March 1974): 86-94.

Butler, W. R. "Acquisitions." *Library Journal* 91 (May 15, 1966): 2271-74.

Christ, R. W. "Acquisition Work in College Libraries." *College and Research Libraries* 10 (Jan. 1949): 17-23.

Clapp, V. W. "Re-Evaluation of Microfilm as a Method of Book Storage." *College and Research Libraries* 23 (Jan. 1963): 5-15.

Dougherty, R. M., and L. L. Leonard. *Management and Costs of Technical Processes: A Bibliographical Review, 1876-1969.* Metuchen, NJ: Scarecrow, 1970.

Downs, R. B. "Libraries in Miniscule." *College and Research Libraries* 17 (Jan. 1957): 11-18.

Farley, E. "Combined Procedures for Technical Services." *Library Resources and Technical Services* 8 (Summer 1964): 257-65.

Ford, S. *Acquisition of Library Materials.* Chicago: American Library Association, 1978.

Franklin, R. D. "Book Acquisition Cost." *Library Journal* 90 (April 1, 1965): 1612-13.

Frarey, C. J. *The Processing Services of the Dallas Public Library.* Dallas, TX: Public Library, 1959.

Fristoe, A. J. "Bitter End: The Searching Process." *Library Resources and Technical Services* 10 (Winter 1966): 91-95.

Gold, S. D. "Allocating the Book Budget: An Economic Model." *College and Research Libraries* 36 (Sept. 1975): 397-402.

Goyal, S. K. "Allocation of Library Funds to Departments of a University—An Operation Research Approach." *College and Research Libraries* 34 (May 1973): 219-22.

Insel, E. *Purchasing Library Materials in Public and School Libraries.* Chicago: American Library Association, 1969.

Jackson, I. H. *Acquisition of Special Materials.* San Francisco: Special Libraries Association, San Francisco Bay Region Chapter, 1966.

Johnson, R. K. "Some Aspects of Acquisition Work in Selected Military Academy Libraries." *Library Resources and Technical Services* 2 (Winter 1958): 16-24.

Kaser, D. E. "Acquisitions Work in the Next Twenty Years." *Southeastern Librarian* 15 (Summer 1965): 90-94.

Koenig, M. E. D. "Expediting Book Acquisitions." *Special Libraries* 65 (Dec. 1974): 516.

Kountz, J. "Library Cost Analysis: A Recipe." *Library Journal* 97 (Feb. 1, 1972): 459-64.

Ladenson, A. "Budget Control of Book Purchase and Binding Expenditures in Large Public Libraries." *Library Resources and Technical Services* 4 (Winter 1960): 47-58.

Lazorick, G. J., and T. L. Minder. "A Least Cost Searching Sequence." *College and Research Libraries* 25 (March 1964): 126-28.

Los Angeles, Bureau of the Budget. *Organization, Administration and Management of the Los Angeles Public Library.* Vol. 2: *Technical Services.* Los Angeles: Bureau of the Budget, 1974.

Lowy, G. *A Searcher's Manual.* Metuchen, NJ: Scarecrow, 1965.

McGrath, W. E. "An Allocation Formula Derived from a Factor Analysis of Academic Departments." *College and Research Libraries* 30 (Jan. 1969): 51-62.

McGrath, W. E. "Determining and Allocating Book Funds for Current Domestic Buying." *College and Research Libraries* 28 (July 1967): 260-72.

McGrath, W. E. "A Pragmatic Book Allocation Formula for Academic and Public Libraries with a Test for Its Effectiveness." *Library Resources and Technical Services* 36 (Fall 1975): 356-69.

Malkin, S. "University Microfilms/Xerox/O.P." *AB Bookman's Weekly* 36 (Oct. 18, 1965): 1415-16.

Massman, V. F., and K. Patterson. "A Minimum Budget for Current Acquisition." *College and Research Libraries* 31 (March 1970): 83-88.

Melcher, D. *Melcher on Acquisitions.* Chicago: American Library Association, 1971.

"SDC (Systems Development Corporation) Develops New Book Purchasing System." *Special Libraries* 55 (Dec. 1964): 703-705.

Saul, M. "The Business of Book Buying—As Special Libraries See It." *Library Journal* 86 (July 1963): 2637-40.

Schachtman, B. E. "Technical Services: Policy, Organization and Coordination." *Journal of Cataloging and Classification* (April 1955): 61-114.

Schad, J. G. "Allocating Book Funds: Control or Planning." *College and Research Libraries* 31 (May 1970): 155-68.

Shaw, R. R. *The Use of Photography for Clerical Routines.* Washington: American Council of Learned Societies, 1953.

Sweet, A. P. "Forms in Acquisition Work." *College and Research Libraries* 14 (Oct. 1953): 398-401, 452.

Tauber, M. F. "Some Problems of Technical Services in Special Libraries." *Special Libraries* 49 (July 1958): 241-45.

Thompson, E. "The Automatic Ordering of Replacement Titles for Libraries in Metropolitan Toronto." *Library Resources and Technical Services* 11 (Spring 1967): 215-20.

Voigt, M. J. "Acquisition Rates in University Libraries." *College and Research Libraries* 36 (July 1975): 263-71.

Weeks, K. *Determination of Pre-Acquisition Predictors of Book Use.* Berkeley: Institute of Library Research, University of California, 1973.

Acquisition of Foreign Material

"Acquisition of Library Materials from Newly-Developing Areas of the World." *Library Resources and Technical Services* 7 (Winter 1963): 7-46.

Fall, J. "Problems of American Libraries in Acquiring Foreign Publications." *Library Quarterly* 24 (April 1954): 101-113.

Orne, J. *The Language of the Foreign Book Trade.* 3rd ed. Chicago: American Library Association, 1976.

Samore, T. *Acquisition of Foreign Materials for U.S. Libraries.* Metuchen, NJ: Scarecrow, 1970.

Schick, F. L. "Acquiring Books from Abroad." *Library Resources and Technical Services* 3 (Winter 1959): 46-50.

Shepard, H. D. "Cooperative Acquisitions of Latin American Materials." *Library Resources and Technical Services* 13 (Summer 1969): 347-60.

Wertheimer, L. *Books in Other Languages: How to Select and Where to Order Them.* Ottawa: Canadian Library Association, 1976.

Approval Plans, Blanket Orders, and Standing Orders

Axford, H. W. "The Economics of a Domestic Approval Plan." *College and Research Libraries* 32 (Sept. 1971): 368-75.

DeVilbiss, M. L. "Approval-Built Collection in the Medium-Sized Academic Library." *College and Research Libraries* 36 (Nov. 1975): 487-92.

DeVolder, A. L. "Approval Plans, Bounty or Bedlam." *Publishers Weekly* 202 (July 3, 1972): 18-20.

DeVolder, A. L. "Why Continue an Approval Plan?" *Mountain-Plains Library Quarterly* 17 (Summer 1972): 11-16.

Dobbyn, M. "Approval Plan Purchasing in Perspective." *College and Research Libraries* 33 (Nov. 1972): 480-84.

Dudley, N. "Blanket Order." *Library Trends* 18 (Jan. 1970): 318-27.

Evans, G. E., and C. W. Argyres. "Approval Plans and Collection Development in Academic Libraries." *Library Resources and Technical Services* 18 (Winter 1974): 35-50.

Gamble, L. "Blanket Ordering and the University of Texas at Austin Library." *Texas Library Journal* 48 (Nov. 1972): 230-32.

International Seminar on Approval and Gathering Plans in Large and Medium Size Academic Libraries, 1st; Western Michigan University, 1968. *Approval and Gathering Plans in Academic Libraries; Proceedings.* P. Spyers-Duran, ed. Littleton, CO: Libraries Unlimited, 1969.

International Seminar on Approval and Gathering Plans in Large and Medium Size Academic Libraries, 2d; Western Michigan University, 1969. *Advances in Understanding Approval and Gathering Plans in Academic Libraries.* P. Spyers-Duran and D. Gore, eds. Kalamazoo: Western Michigan University, 1970.

International Seminar on Approval and Gathering Plans in Large and Medium Size Academic Libraries, 3d; West Palm Beach, FL, 1971. *Economics of Approval Plans; Proceedings.* P. Spyers-Duran and D. Gore, eds. Westport, CT: Greenwood Press, 1972.

Jacob, E., and B. Salisbury. "Automatic Purchase of University Press Books." *Library Journal* 83 (March 1, 1958): 707-708.

McCullough, K. "Approval Plans: Vendor Responsibility and Library Research: A Literature Survey and Discussion." *College and Research Libraries* 33 (Summer 1972): 368-81.

McCullough, K., E. D. Posey, and D. C. Pickett. *Approval Plans and Academic Libraries: An Interpretive Survey.* Phoenix, AZ: Oryx Press, 1977.

Martin, M. S. "Series Standing Order and the Library." *Choice* 10 (Oct. 1973): 1152-55.

Merritt, L. C. "Are We Selecting or Collecting?" *Library Resources and Technical Services* 12 (Spring 1968): 140-42.

Morrison, P. D., et al. "A Symposium on Approval Order Plans and the Book Selection Responsibilities of Librarians." *Library Resources and Technical Services* 12 (Spring 1968): 133-45.

Ready, W. B. "Acquisition by Standing Order." *Library Resources and Technical Services* 1 (Spring 1957): 85-88.

Rebuldela, H. K. "Some Administrative Aspects of Blanket Ordering: A Response." *Library Resources and Technical Services* 13 (Summer 1969): 342-45.

Taggart, W. R. "Blanket Approval Ordering: A Positive Approach." *Canadian Library Journal* 27 (July 1970): 286-89.

Thom, I. W. "Some Administrative Aspects of Blanket Ordering." *Library Resources and Technical Services* 13 (Summer 1969): 338-42.

Wedgeworth, R. "Foreign Blanket Orders: Precedent and Practice." *Library Resources and Technical Services* 14 (Spring 1970): 258-68.

Wilden-Hart, M. "Long-Term Effects of Approval Plans." *Library Resources and Technical Services* 14 (Summer 1970): 400-406.

Gifts

American Library Association. Association of College and Research Libraries. Rare Book Section. "Statement of Recommended Library Policy Regarding Appraisals." *Antiquarian Bookman* 26 (Dec. 19, 1960): 2205.

American Library Association. Association of College and Research Libraries. Rare Books and Manuscripts Section. Committee on Manuscripts Collections. "Draft Supplement on Legal Title." *AB Bookman's Weekly* 50 (Oct. 9, 1972): 1116.

American Library Association. Association of College and Research Libraries. Rare Books and Manuscripts Section. Committee on Manuscripts Collections. "Statement on Appraisal of Gifts: Draft Statement—Gifts Appraisal." *AB Bookman's Weekly* 50 (Oct. 9, 1972): 1116.

Brewer, F. J. "Friends of the Library and Other Benefactors and Donors." *Library Trends* 9 (April 1961): 453-65.

Briggs, D. R. "Gift Appraisal Policy in Large Research Libraries." *College and Research Libraries* 29 (Nov. 1968): 505-507.

Kebabian, J. S. "Book Appraisals." *Library Trends* 9 (April 1961): 466-70.

Lane, A. H. "Gifts and Exchanges: Practicabilities and Problems." *Library Resources and Technical Services* 14 (Winter 1970): 92-97.

Society of American Archivists. "Draft Standards of Appraisal of Gifts." *American Archivist* 35 (Oct. 1972): 455-56.

Society of American Archivists. "Standards on Appraisals of Gifts." *American Archivist* 37 (Jan. 1974): 154-55.

Thompson, D. E. "Gifts." In *The State of the Library Art.* R. R. Shaw, ed. New Brunswick, NJ: Rutgers University Press, 1961. Vol. 1, p.4 [Bibliography].

Thompson, L. S. "Of Bibliographical Mendicancy." *College and Research Libraries* 14 (Oct. 1953): 373-78.

Exchanges

"Adoption of New Conventions on the Exchange of Publications." *Unesco Bulletin for Libraries* 13 (Feb. 1959): 29-35.

Avicenne, P. "The Mission of the National Exchange Services." *Unesco Bulletin for Libraries* 18 (Nov.-Dec. 1964): 253-58.

Blake, F. M. "Expanding Exchange Services." *College and Research Libraries* 24 (Jan. 1963): 53-56.

"Brief History of USBE." *Library Resources and Technical Services* 14 (Fall 1970): 608-609.

Diakonova, O. A. "International Book Exchange of Soviet Libraries." *Libri* 15 (1965): 180-85.

Draft Conventions Concerning the International Exchange of Publications. Paris: Unesco, 1958.

"Duplicate Exchange Union of ACRL." *College and Research Libraries* 17 (Nov. 1956): 511.

"Duplicates Exchange Union." *Library Resources and Technical Services* 8 (Summer 1964): 333.

Eggleton, R. "The American Library Association Duplicates Exchange Union—A Study and Evaluation." *Library Resources and Technical Services* 19 (Spring 1975): 148-63.

European Conference on the International Exchange of Publications, Vienna, 1972. *The International Exchange of Publications: Proceedings.* M. J. Schiltman, ed.; sponsored by IFLA. München-Pullach: Verlag Dokumentation der Technik, 1973 [English or French].

Galejs, J. E. "Economics of Serials Exchanges." *Library Resources and Technical Services* 16 (Fall 1972): 511-20.

Gambocz, I. "European Conference on the International Exchange of Publications." *Unesco Bulletin for Libraries* 27 (Jan. 1973): 54-56.

Hamann, E. G. "Out-of-Print Periodicals: The United States Book Exchange as a Source of Supply." *Library Resources and Technical Services* 16 (Winter 1972): 19-25.

Kanevskij, B. P. "International Exchange of Publications." *Unesco Bulletin for Libraries* 10 (Nov. 1965): 302-307.

Kanevskij, B. P. "International Exchange of Publications and the Free Flow of Books." *Unesco Bulletin for Libraries* 26 (May 1972): 141-49.

Kanevskij, B. P. "International Exchange of Publications at the Lenin State Library." *Unesco Bulletin for Libraries* 13 (Feb. 1959): 48-52.

Lane, A. H. "The Economics of Exchange." *Serial Slants* 3 (July 1952): 19-22.

Letheve, J. "Project for Standard Book-Exchange Request Forms." *Unesco Bulletin for Libraries* 25 (Sept.-Oct. 1971): 283.

MacIver, I. "The Exchange of Publications as a Medium for the Development of the Book Collection." *Library Quarterly* 8 (Oct. 1938): 491-502.

Novak, V. "Let's Exchange Profitably." *Library Resources and Technical Services* 9 (Summer 1965): 345-51.

Shinn, I. E. "Toward Uniformity in Exchange Communication." *Library Resources and Technical Services* 16 (Fall 1972): 502-510.

Slabczynski, W. "New Trends in International Exchange of Publications." *Unesco Bulletin for Libraries* 22 (Sept. 1968): 218-24.

Thom, I. W. "Duplicates Exchange: A Cost Analysis." *Library Resources and Technical Services* 1 (Spring 1957): 81-84.

Thompson, D. E. "Exchanges." In *The State of the Library Art.* R. R. Shaw, ed. New Brunswick, NJ: Rutgers University Press, 1961. Vol. 1, p. 5.

United Nations Educational, Scientific and Cultural Organization. *Handbook of International Exchanges.* Paris: Unesco, 1967.

United Nations Educational, Scientific and Cultural Organization. *Handbook on the International Exchange of Publications.* 3rd ed. Ed. and rev. G. von Busse. Paris: Unesco, 1964.

Williams, E. E. *A Serviceable Reservoir: Report of a Survey of the United States Book Exchange.* Washington: The United States Book Exchange, 1959.

Chapter 9

WEEDING THE COLLECTION*

Selection in reverse is one way that some persons like to think about weeding or collection control. Unfortunately, weeding is something most librarians think about but seldom do. Nevertheless, this process is as important as any other in the system of developing collections, for without an on-going weeding program, a collection can quickly become obsolete. The major function of a library is to acquire, store, and make available knowledge resources; and know that at this time and for the foreseeable future, no library can acquire and store the total world production of knowledge resources for any current year. Some of the world's largest libraries (the Library of Congress, the British Museum Library, Bibliothèque Nationale, et al.) do manage to secure a major portion and, perhaps in combination, succeed in getting most of the important items. Nevertheless, even these giants of the library world cannot do it alone. Eventually they are confronted, just as is the smallest library, with three alternatives as they reach their limits of growth: 1) secure new physical facilities; 2) divide the collection (which also requires space); or 3) weed the collection (which may or may not require new space). Only if a library acquires a completely new and adequate building can a librarian avoid selecting items for relocation.

WHAT IS WEEDING?

Weeding is defined as "the practice of discarding or transferring to storage excess copies, rarely used books, and materials no longer of use."[1] Purging is defined as "officially withdrawing a volume (all entries made for a particular book have been removed from library records) from a library collection because it is unfit for further use or is no longer needed."[2] The term purging applies more to the

---

*This chapter is based upon several workshops that the author has given. The results have been published in the *California Librarian* and are to be published in the Norwegian library journal, *Bibliotek og Forsknig.* The workshops were at the Norwegian Library Association meeting, May 1975; California Library Association, Collection Development Chapter meeting, October 1976; and a seminar on collection development and weeding at the Statens Bibliotekskole, Oslo, November 1976.

library's files than to items themselves. Also, it is rare that a purged item will be destroyed. Rather, it is disposed of in some fashion—gifts and exchange programs, friends of the library book sales, "sold" to an out-of-print dealer for credit against future purchases. The end result, however, is as though the library never owned the item (so a patron who needs it would have to use interlibrary loan).

Storing, however, maintains the item in the library system but in a "second level" of access—a system either in the library or in a warehouse arrangement. In either case, the patron usually is not allowed to go to the location to get the book; a library staff member does this. Such second-person retrieval may mean that the patron does not get the desired item for some time (anywhere from one-half hour to forty-eight hours). Nevertheless, this arrangement is usually faster than an interlibrary loan.

Before any selective weeding program (for discard or storage) is implemented, an evaluation of library policies and goals must take place. This evaluation should also include analysis of the present situation, consideration of possible alternatives, feasibility of a weeding program in terms of all library operations, faculty cooperation, types of libraries involved, types of materials collected, and, very important, cost. Actually, an active (i.e., on-going) weeding policy should be an integral part of that library's selection policy. Selection and weeding are the same function: first, because they both are part of the same process (collection development), and second, if each is considered in relationship to the other, they both can be more effectively implemented. Book selection policy will determine weeding policy.[3]

Unfortunately, very few libraries have active weeding policies. It is not difficult to repeat the reasons that weeding policies are almost non-existent; what is difficult to determine is how to combat these deep-seated obstacles to weeding. That is, the librarian must question whether the basic assumption that the collection and preservation of all printed materials are the primary functions of research libraries is no longer valid or realistic.

Selection policies, if properly prepared, will help reduce the weeding problem by controlling growth. Nevertheless, the time eventually will come when something will have to be done to control the growth of the collection. Either there will be no more space in the stacks or else access to the material will have become so cumbersome that most persons fail to find what they need. As has been noted, at that time, some hard, costly decisions will have to be made: build a new building, split the collection, or weed it. These three major alternatives are time-consuming and expensive processes. A policy of continuous weeding will be much more effective in the long run. Lazy librarians, like lazy gardeners, will find that the weeding problem only gets larger through neglect.

Unfortunately, there seem to be two natural laws about weeding that every experienced librarian knows, even if not everyone is able to put them into words:

1) no matter how strange an item may seem, at least one person in the world will find it valuable;

2) no matter how long a library keeps these strange items, ten minutes after one has been discarded, the one possible user in the world will walk in and ask for that item.

The basic rule seems to be: one person's garbage is someone else's greatest treasure. This is the fundamental problem confronted by collection development staffs every day, and when the collection is based upon current user needs, weeding can be a major activity as those needs change.

TYPE OF LIBRARY BACKGROUND

Because different types of libraries have significantly different clientele and goals, we will look at them from slightly different points of view. Although the basic problems, issues, and methods of weeding apply to all libraries, variations occur in what is done with the "weeds" after they have been pulled.

The Public Library

The purpose of the public library may be viewed as supplying those library materials that meet the current needs and interests of a very diverse community of users. In the public library, demand for materials should be an important factor influencing selection and weeding; and therefore, materials no longer of interest or of use to the public are the ones that should be considered for storage or discard. Storage is usually considered only for large municipal public libraries whose collections include research materials. As for discarding, it has been estimated that a complete turnover in public library collections should take place once every ten years, although actual practice probably falls far short of this. If storage is contemplated, this usually means separating the little-used books from a working collection that will receive a high degree of use, and then discarding duplicates, worn out volumes, and obsolete material. It is said that if a collection contains many items of little interest, those that are useful will not be so readily visible or accessible. Costs involved in maintaining a large collection are also a consideration.

The Special Library

Special libraries have had to exercise the most stringent weeding policies because severe limits to expansion of their collections usually result from a lack of space. As Paula M. Strain[4] indicates, the cost of industrial floor space is so high that libraries must make very efficient use of each square foot. The library in such a situation is examined with the businessperson's eye toward economy and efficiency. Also, the collections of such libraries are often comprised of technical materials, much of it in periodical format with a rapid and regular rate of obsolescence. The major concern of special libraries is meeting the *current* needs of their clientele. In such a situation, weeding materials is easier because of the comparatively straightforward and predictable use patterns, the homogeneous nature of the clientele and its small size, and the relatively narrow goals of the special library. Weeding is done with little hesitation because costs and space are such prime considerations.

The Academic Library

Traditionally, the purpose of the academic research library has been to select, acquire, organize, *preserve*, and make available the full record of human knowledge. Demand for a book has not been considered a valid measure of its worth in these institutions, since many books are or may be of research value even if little used. Why then are weeding programs being considered in the context of the academic library? The role of the college and university library is changing. Whenever change of role is discussed, the information explosion is cited as one cause. It is clear to most rational collection development staffs that it is futile to expect any one institution to locate and acquire all of the printed matter that is coming into existence. Nor can they organize it, house it, or make it readily accessible to their public. (No one person can manage to absorb all the relevant material that would supposedly be available to him if everything in fact were being collected and preserved.)

School Libraries and Media Centers

As noted in chapter 1, school libraries and media centers are more highly structured in their collection development practices than other types of libraries. In most schools and school districts, the library's funds are expended by a committee made up of teachers, administrators, and librarians. The need to coordinate collection growth with curriculum needs is imperative. Generally speaking, these libraries have a very limited amount of space; thus, when there is a major shift in the curriculum (new areas added and old ones dropped), the library must remove (weed) most of the old material. To some degree, the school's problems in weeding are lessened by the fact that usually other community libraries or a larger school district library exists to serve as a major back-up resource.

WHY WEED?

Three important reasons are always cited for weeding:

1) to save space;
2) to improve access;
3) to save money.

These are the theoretical reasons that one finds stated in the literature. And if the volume of literature is any indication of the degree to which weeding is practiced, there would be no need for conferences and workshops on the subject. Unfortunately, librarians tend to write more about weeding (and cooperative networks) than they work at implementing the concept(s). In part, this is due to the fact that theory and the real world do not exactly coincide. Often, from a realistic point of view, no other solution to space problems suggests itself except weeding. Existing space is filled, and there is no more space in the library, which means that something must go. If C. N. Parkinson had written about libraries, he probably would have proposed a collection development law—collections expand to fill the space available.

In 1944, Fremont Rider determined that between 1831 and 1938, American research libraries doubled the size of their collections every sixteen years, an annual growth rate of 4.25 percent.[5] Since then, studies have shown a gradual decrease in the annual growth rate (to about 2.85 percent), but even now, the actual number of holdings has continued to grow, a cause for serious concern to numerous libraries of all types. The implications of an annual growth rate are fairly obvious. In addition to the problem of limited shelf space, rapid growth of library collections leads to several other problems: 1) existing space is often not utilized efficiently; 2) obtaining additional space is expensive; and 3) servicing and use of collections becomes difficult due to undifferentiated access to materials of all ages, types, and subjects.

Do theory and practice concerning saving space coincide? Very definitely! Compact storage systems do, in fact, save space. Conventional shelving is geared to housing 15 volumes per square foot (500,000 volumes thus would require more than 33,000 square feet). A compact shelving system similar to "Conserve-a-File" (a sliding shelf arrangement) can handle 500,000 volumes in slightly more than 14,000 square feet—a savings of more than 50 percent (an average of about 35 vol./sq. ft.). Using a rail system such as "Compactus" or "Elecompact-B," savings of more than 80 percent can be achieved; you need less than 7,000 square feet to house one-half million volumes. "Randtriever," the automatic compact storage system, achieves even more dramatic results. In about 3,600 square feet you could store the 500,000 items—an increase in storage density of almost ten times over that of conventional shelving.

Obviously, a price must be paid for saving space: special shelving costs more than conventional systems. It is interesting to note, however, that according to Ralph Ellsworth, conventional systems are also very expensive: only one compact system (Library Bureau "ABC-801") costs more per volume stored than open shelving. His 1969 cost figures were: conventional shelving, $1.31 per volume; "Conserve-a-File," $1.24; "Elecompact-B," $0.91; and "Randtriever," $1.08.[6] Thus, one aspect of cost can be lowered by using a storage system; however, these figures are only for the building and shelving costs. A number of other important cost factors must be considered (more about these later).

One basic theme of this book is that libraries exist to provide service. An archival library provides service, so our discussion naturally includes this type, as they also eventually run out of space. However, service and size frequently do not go together. Anyone who has used a major research library knows that they are neither quick nor easy to tap. Often, such a library will be the only location for certain materials, which is a service; however, very few persons actually claim that such libraries are easy or convenient to use. Generally speaking, though, people still like (or at least are made to think that they like) convenient, easy-to-use things. Thus, it is possible that a smaller, well-weeded collection will be viewed as providing better service than a fuller collection—so long as it has what patrons want.

Is there improved access? Here theory and practice start to diverge. Some staff members and patrons would give enthusiastically positive answers. Others would be equally definite in their negative response. For those who value quick, easy access to current materials, the thoughtfully weeded collection becomes ideal.

Dated, seldom used materials are out of the way and, perhaps, the cards may even be out of the main public catalog. If the material you want falls into the right category, access will be fast and easy. Should it fall into the other category, you may find that it takes twice as long to determine whether or not the library owns the item in question. Furthermore, it may take several days to see the actual item if it must be retrieved from a storage area. Thus the answer to the question of whether weeding improves access is sometimes yes, sometimes no.

Finally, does weeding save money? Here the answer is probably no. Theory and practice are again far apart at this point. As indicated, the cost per volume stored is usually lower using a compact storage system. However, a number of important costs were not included in the quoted figure. For instance, it is possible to quickly reduce the size of a collection by some arbitrary figure or percentage. One method of weeding in a public library would be to withdraw all books published before 1920 (or some other date) that have not circulated in the past five years. Unfortunately, just withdrawing the items from the shelves does not complete the process. All of the public and internal records must be changed to reflect the new status of the withdrawn books. For each item removed from the active collection, all of the cards in the public catalog either must be removed or have that item's new status recorded on them. If the item is placed in a storage collection, another catalog must be created for that collection, although this is an inconvenience for the patron. And all of this activity costs the library money.

Cost has always been a major factor in implementing any library procedure, and weeding is no exception. In fact, even in libraries where the need to weed is recognized, lack of sufficient funds often means eliminating low priority programs—and weeding is usually the lowest. Cost must be measured in terms of whether the expense of not weeding would be greater than that of leaving unused materials on the shelves (i.e., cost of extra shelving and space versus inventory time; longer response time for the user; etc.).

In addition to the cost of changing the public record, and perhaps creating a new record, you must consider the cost of deciding which items to remove, the cost of collecting and transporting them to their new location, and, if they are stored, the cost of paging them when required. Even if the system of storage is a dollar or more cheaper per volume than conventional stacks, these hidden costs can quickly mount well beyond the apparent savings. Despite the cost factors, however, every library will be eventually confronted with a space and access problem, which can only be solved by some type of weeding program.

Almost every large library has some form of weeding program. They may not call it a weeding program, but the effect is the same. Yale University, for example, boxes certain classes of material after they are acquired and processed—they call it book retirement. The University of California, Los Angeles, library system has something called the TOE (temporary one entry) system. Here the order slip with an accession number is filed in the public catalog, and the book is shelved by accession number. Books in this system are not classified and are, therefore, separately housed. Other libraries use "brief listing" or some other labels and processes that, in effect, create storage collections of limited access. Most of these systems are not viewed as methods of controlling collection growth. If they were, perhaps librarians would be more receptive to the idea of weeding, and the items going into these collections would be reviewed more carefully.

BARRIERS TO WEEDING

Weeding is a process to which everyone gives lip service, but few librarians are able or willing to practice the art. A story of questionable veracity, but one to the point, is that concerning a library school teacher of book selection who insisted that there was only one possible test to determine a person's suitability to be a librarian. The test would be conducted in a doctor's office and the candidate librarian's blood pressure would be taken on arrival at the office. The person is given a new book and told to rip out one page and throw the book in a waste basket. If the candidate's blood pressure rises above the first reading, the individual cannot be a librarian. True or not, the story does emphasize one of the most significant barriers to weeding—the psychological one.

Some of the most frequently given excuses for not weeding are:

1) lack of time,
2) putting it off,
3) fear of making a mistake,
4) reluctance to throw a book away.

These reasons are, to a greater or lesser extent, psychological in nature. No matter how long the book about to be weeded has remained unused, a librarian's reaction may be that someone will need it tomorrow. Also, an unused book or audio visual raises two important questions: why wasn't it being used? and why did the library buy it in the first place? Very few librarians, anymore than anyone else, like to admit that a selection was a mistake.

The possibility of discarding some books erroneously will always exist. But to use this fear of making a mistake as the reason for not weeding a collection is inexcusable. A library does not discontinue acquiring all books because a few of those selected have never been used, or ought not to have been acquired.

Another barrier to weeding, political as well as psychological, derives from the users and governing boards of the library. An academic library may feel that it needs to institute a weeding and storage program but fails to do so because of faculty opposition. If past experience is any indication, you can count on everyone being in favor of weeding the collection *except* in their special areas of interest. Sometimes librarians assume that there will be opposition and, therefore, never suggest such a program. There will, naturally, be opposition; however, if the issue is never raised, there is no chance of winning over support. The possibility also exists that assumed strong opponents will not materialize and that persons you least expect will turn out to be strong advocates. Certainly any weeding and storage problem will cause some inconvenience to some users. Fear of political consequences has kept many library programs from even being proposed—and thus the problem extends far beyond trying to set up a weeding program.

Related to the political barrier is the problem of size and prestige. Many librarians, library boards, and users rate a library's quality according to its size. This brings us back to the epigraph of this book: "No library of a million volumes can be all BAD!" Quantity does not insure quality. *Nevertheless, we continue to take the quantity road rather than the quality road, and we all arrive at chaos the sooner.*

Collecting everything and throwing nothing away is much easier than selecting and weeding a collection with care. We risk no political opposition, our prestige remains high, and only the taxpayer is hurt.

Prestige and size can create a barrier for governing boards as well. In spite of rising costs and lack of space, many persons associated with libraries (staff, patrons, and governing boards) rather frequently equate an increase in the size of the collection with an increase in the library's prestige. When this is the case, it is rather hard to demonstrate to such persons that a weeding program that causes a reduction in collection size is in the best interests of the library. Perhaps the equation of size with prestige is an American phenomenon, but it appears that the contagion is world-wide.

Practical barriers to weeding also exist. Time can be a practical as well as psychological barrier to weeding. Just the processes of identifying the most suitable criteria to employ and then developing and selling a useful weeding program can be time-consuming. Beyond this is the time required to train the staff to pull the "weeds," to change the public records, and finally, to dispose of the "weeds." With a small library staff, it will be very hard to find the time to undertake a major weeding project. This is one excellent reason for having a continuous program—there will be no need for a major program. For any library to start a weeding program is, inevitably, a major project. After the major project is finished, then an on-going procedure can be implemented as part of the normal workload. The best way to approach this major project, perhaps, is by seeking special funds and extra, temporary staff to support the work. In the section on criteria for weeding, we will discuss further the practical aspects of selecting criteria, selling the project, and training staff.

There are, occasionally, legal barriers to weeding. Although this is not a frequent problem, when it does arise, it is very difficult to handle. This is particularly true in public-supported libraries where regulations govern the disposal of anything purchased with public funds. In some cases, no disposal is allowed, whereas in other instances, you may have to attempt to sell the material (often by means of bids or auctions). Any means of disposal that gives even the impression of "government book burning" will cause public relations problems and should be avoided, even if legal.

IMPLICATIONS OF WEEDING

Weeding has both positive and negative implications for the library. In the long run, an effective weeding program is essential for a viable library system. Thus, the positive aspects far outweigh the negative. No matter how carefully one selects materials for the collection and no matter how slowly the collection grows, a space problem will arise eventually. If you know your community, develop a collection development policy based on the knowledge of the community, and have exercised good judgment, the space problem will be delayed. However, when it does arise, you may have an extremely difficult problem to resolve: all of the material seems too useful to be disposed of and new space seems to be the only solution. More often than not, you think you have abided by the above criteria and that asking for more space is an easy solution. But careful checking probably will reveal more deadwood than expected, and little will be lost by storing the material in a low cost storage unit.

Certainly, the patrons will be affected by a weeding program, but a good program will have for the majority of users, more positive than negative effects. If this is *not* the case, the program is clearly a bad one. Access should be improved so that it is easier to locate a desired item and easier to secure current relevant information. For a few patrons a weeding program will be all "bad"—at least they will think so at first, and perhaps it will be. Individuals interested in historical studies—no matter what the field—and those who like to browse through the *complete* collections will not like a weeding program. Items in storage can be made accessible to that class of user if you provide a few work stations in the storage area.

Cost is another important consideration. Weeding programs are not cheap, but neither is constructing a new building every twenty or thirty years. It is a matter of trading off costs and setting priorities: *which set of expenditures will provide the greatest service to the greatest number of people?* More often than not, a weeding program comes out ahead upon careful analysis—even if new physical facilities monies are capital expenses and the weeding program draws off operating expense monies.

CRITERIA FOR WEEDING

Weeding is not an overnight process, and it is not a function that can be performed in isolation. You must consider the library's goals; the funds for buying more satisfactory titles, if any are available; the relationship of a particular book to others on that subject; the degree to which the library is to function as an archive; and the possible future usefulness of a book. Only when you have these in mind can you develop a successful weeding program.

Once the need for a weeding policy is recognized, several lists of criteria can help to determine which items to weed. One fairly comprehensive list was compiled by H. F. McGraw:

1) duplicates;
2) unsolicited and unwanted gifts;
3) obsolete books, especially science;
4) superseded editions;
5) books that are infected, dirty, shabby, worn out, juvenile, etc.;
6) books with small print, brittle paper, and missing pages;
7) unused, unneeded volumes of sets;
8) periodicals with no indexes.[7]

Of course, the mere fact that a book is duplicated or worn out does not necessarily mean that it should be discarded. The usage factor is an extremely important one—but nonetheless crucial. If the item is out of print, microforms can be used for replacement.

The most recent and comprehensive work on weeding is by Stanley J. Slote, *Weeding Library Collections*.[8] This book will tell you everything about the problems of weeding a collection. Slote covers all the published lists of weeding criteria and how they are employed.

In examining the literature, three broad types of criteria can be discerned regarding the weeding of books: physical condition, qualitative worth, and quantitative worth. Physical condition, for most researchers, is not an effective criterion. In most cases, poor physical condition results from over-use rather than non-use. Thus, books in poor condition are either replaced or repaired. In any event, unless the library has a major environmental control problem (e.g., too much heat or light, insects), only a small percentage of books will be in poor physical condition. Consequently, if you use condition as a criterion, only a few items will probably be withdrawn, and it may be years before you can use it again.

Qualitative worth as a criterion for weeding collections has been employed, but because of the highly subjective nature of value judgments, this generally has not been too effective. In essence, the same factors governing the selection of a title are in effect when weeding. Is it possible for the person who selected an item some years ago to now say "remove it"? The answer is yes, but all of the psychological barriers to weeding come into play. Probably the best way to employ this method is to use a group decision process, and in this case, patrons ought to be consulted, even if it is just a storage decision.

Any group assessment will be slow, however, and it has been demonstrated that past usage as a criterion has been as effective as a subject specialist in predicting future use (need). Also, it is faster and cheaper when you have the past use data at hand. We will explore this in depth later in the chapter when we review some of the major studies that have been conducted on weeding.

C. A. Seymour summed up weeding problems as follows: "When the usefulness and/or popularity of a book has been questioned, the librarian, if the policy of the library permits discarding, must decide the following:

a.   if the financial and physical resources are present or available to provide continuing as well as immediate housing and maintenance of the book;

b.   if the book can be procured, within an acceptably short time, from another library at a cost similar to, or lower than, the cost of housing and maintenance within the library;

c.   if allowing the book to remain in the collection would produce a 'negative value.' "[9]

The problems that plague weeding of monographs also apply to serials. Similar criteria seem to be applicable, although the amount of space required to house serial publications is often greater than that required to house monographs. Thus the cost is often the determining factor in weeding (i.e., although there may be some requests for a particular serial, the amount of space that a publication uses may not economically warrant retaining the full set in the collection).

Of course, the poor library patron must not be forgotten (although it seems sometimes he is the last to be considered). Limited space is not the only reason that a library collection should be weeded. The pros and cons of patron benefit from an active weeding program are also vital considerations. Based upon personal research projects, this author can say that the percentage of librarians who feel that a patron should be able to make personal decisions concerning which materials to use from *all* possible materials available (i.e., no weeding) is much less than the percentage who strongly feel that a no-weeding policy is, in fact, detrimental to the patron.

Academic faculty members often lack total familiarity even with materials in their own subject fields; faced with two to seven million volumes in a collection, how can a student be expected to choose the materials most helpful to his or her research? Although he is referring to a public library collection, F. Wezeman has an applicable point: "how can we expect the public to get excited about books and library service when we (librarians) demonstrate by the condition of the book stock our lack of professional pride and standards?"[10]

A second element of weeding, and definitely of major concern to research libraries, is book *storage*. This subject requires a separate explanation because weeding to discard and weeding to store are two different processes. Criteria useful in making discarding decisions often do not apply to storage decisions. It is important to recognize that the primary objective of differential treatment is not necessarily to reduce the total amount of money spent for library purposes. Instead, the primary objective is to maximize the amount of research material made available to the patron. Two fundamental considerations are involved then in a weeding for storage program: 1) how will books be selected for storage? and 2) how will they be physically stored? (Books on storage will be found listed in the bibliography.) At this point, though, concrete programs will be discussed in order to provide a more solid basis for discussion.

In 1960, Yale University embarked upon its Selective Book Retirement Program funded by the Council on Library Resources, to determine how best to cope with the problem of limited shelf space with as little detriment to library resources and the program as possible. The Council outlined the objectives to be carried out by Yale:

a. to expedite the Yale University Library's Selective Book Retirement Program (from 20,000 to 60,000 volumes per year) and to extend it to other libraries on the campus;

b. to study (in collaboration with the faculty) the bases of selection for retirement for various subjects and forms of material;

c. to study the effects of the Program on library use and research by faculty, graduate and undergraduate students;

d. to ascertain what arrangements may compensate for the loss of immediate access caused by the program;

e. to explore the possible effectiveness of the Program toward stabilizing the size of the immediate-access collection;

f. to publish for the use by other libraries of the policies, procedures, and results thus discovered.[11]

According to the report, all but objective "d" were fulfilled.

The decision as to which books would actually be removed from the first level of access to storage was based on:

1) a study of books on the shelves;

2) value of a title as subject matter;

3) its importance historically in the field;

4) availability of other editions;

5) availability of other materials on the subject;

6) use of volume;

7) physical condition.

In other words, selection was based on the *subjective judgment* of individual librarians, some of whom were subject bibliography specialists—and not on objective criteria. The librarians determined that general policies regarding weeding were easier to formulate than those that applied to specific fields, that it was easier to recommend weeding of specific titles than groups or kinds of books in specific fields, and that unanticipated mechanical problems greatly affected weeding procedures. These last problems included:

1) lack of regularity in weeding (i.e., finding an adequate number of faculty and staff members and the time to keep the process going satisfactorily);

2) diminishing returns over a long period (i.e., the longer the program existed, the more difficult the weeding process became);

3) the "Ever-Normal-Granary" theory (one of the purposes of the selective retirement program was to discover whether a library can control the growth of its collection by annually removing from the stacks the same number of volumes as it adds); it was discovered that in order for the theory to be practical, fragmentation into department libraries must occur, or the library administration must be willing to manage its collection and facilities solely on the principle of stabilization—neither of which Yale was willing to do;

4) disagreement among weeders (i.e., the narrower viewpoint of faculty due to subject specialty versus the broader viewpoint of librarian).

Another unforeseen problem was a general feeling of discontent among faculty members and students. Neither group really understood the storage problem, and both objected to any type of change. Students particularly disliked the fact that they could not browse through the storage area.

It is evident that Yale's Selective Book Retirement Program did not make any significant contributions to the solution of problems associated with collection growth and selective weeding for storage. In the concluding statement, R. P. Morris said: "We found very little that can be reduced to a formula or routine . . . the execution of selective book retirement becomes increasingly a matter of knowledge, judgment, and wisdom."[12]

Fussler and Simon (University of Chicago), on the other hand, in their *Patterns in the Use of Books in Large Research Libraries*, reported some very interesting ideas and statistical findings concerning the *usage factor* in selective weeding of books for storage. Although they recognized that frequency of circulation or use of books is not always an accurate measure of the *importance* of books in large research libraries, Fussler and Simon hoped to determine whether "any kind of statistical procedure (could) predict, with reasonable accuracy, the frequencies with which groups of books with defined characteristics, are likely to be used in a research library."[13] They based their investigation on the assumption that use of it as a criterion for selectively weeding books for storage can be applied, but only to those books used very infrequently or not at all (i.e., for frequently used books, the concern is to provide good access at the first level).

The conclusion reached in the investigation was that "by far the best predictor of *future* use of a title is its *past* use. Because of the low probability of use in any one year for titles in the marginal value range in a library the size of that at the University of Chicago, a 15- to 20-year observation period produces considerably better results than an observation period of five years."[14] For libraries that do not have records of past use, Fussler and Simon's findings can still be used to help select the best functions for their own collections (although the authors suggested that a study of records for the past five years of use be conducted before a storage program is implemented).

Fussler and Simon's study is considered valuable because of their outlining of factors that affect the validity of comparing (i.e., between two research collections) criteria for removing books for storage, and because of their findings concerning the advantages of libraries devising "similar rules." These factors will be helpful reminders to any library considering a selective weeding program:

1) differences between libraries in composition of the collection in specific subject areas;

2) differences in size of collections;

3) differences in size of university populations;

4) differences in nature of university populations;

5) differences in kind of record-of-past use.[15]

In addition to these factors that affect comparisons, Fussler and Simon's findings indicated that "if libraries of different sizes and populations put into effect similar rules, the results will be quite similar in terms of *percentages* of total use that would be accounted for by the title sent to storage."[16] From this, they concluded that scholars at different institutions have very similar reading interests.

In their concluding remarks, Fussler and Simon summarized what they found to be the present realistic alternatives for selecting books for storage:

1) judgment of one or a few expert selectors in a field;

2) an examination of past use of a book and/or its objective characteristics;

3) a combination of these two approaches.

Of these alternatives, they concluded that an *objective system (i.e., statistical measure) ranks books more accurately by probable value than does the subjective judgment of a single scholar in the field.* They did recommend, however, that subject specialist faculty review the books determined by objective means for storage before they actually were stored.[17]

Richard Trueswell (Northwestern University, 1965) quantitatively measured the relationship between the last circulation date of a book and user circulation requirements, and their effect on weeding. He hoped to determine a quantitative method of maintaining a library's holdings at a reasonable level, while at the same time providing satisfactory service to the user (i.e., his method could also be used to determine multiple copy needs, thus increasing the probability of a user's finding the needed books).[18]

Trueswell's basic assumption was that the last circulation date of a book is an indication of that book's "value." In his analysis, he determined the cumulative distribution of the previous circulation data (which he assumed to represent the typical circulation of a given library), and then determined the 99 percentile, which was used as the time cut-off point for stack thinning. By multiplying the previous monthly circulation figures and the distribution for each month after the 99 percentile point was established, he was able to calculate the expected size of the main collection.

In applying this method to a sample from the Deering Library at Northwestern University, he predicted that 99 percent of circulation requirements could be satisfied by 40 percent of the library's present holdings (i.e., 60 percent of the holdings could be removed to storage without significantly affecting the core collection). Trueswell does admit that many of his basic assumptions are questionable, but only through future research can more reliable information be obtained.

Another study of note is Aridamen Jain's 1968 investigation, another quantitative study of book use, but one based on very different assumptions than the two previously described studies.[19] Although his statistical manipulations may completely baffle a non-statistician, the theory behind his method of measuring book use is easily understood. The purpose of his study was to examine mathematical models and statistical techniques for determining the dependence of circulation rate on a book's age and certain other characteristics. He hoped to indicate that the *age* of a book is the most significant variable both in predicting rates of monograph usage and in deciding which books should be taken from the first level of access and transferred to storage. He reviewed other studies in terms of whether the frequency with which groups of books with defined characteristics are likely to be used in a research library can be predicted by statistical methods. He hoped to point out by comparison that the probability of a book's *not* being used is an efficient method of predicting use by age of book.

Jain's model seems to be particularly valuable in selective weeding for two reasons. One is that, contrary to the "total library collection" sampling method utilized by Fussler and Simon in their studies, Jain (like Trueswell) derived his data from all of the books checked out for a *specific time period* (i.e., with no regard for the total library collection). Jain felt that this method was superior to that used by Fussler and Simon because, although their method ensures the gathering of information on the *same* books over a longer period of time, his method is much more conducive to a statistical design and data collection, and missing data and lack of control are no longer problems. A second reason for this model's importance is that by using the specific time period sampling method, *relative use* of books within the library can be determined. Using the method of Fussler and Simon, this is not possible. Jain felt that the relative use concept was more efficient in studying the usage of books than the collection method.

Other studies of weeding library collections were conducted by Cooper at Columbia,[20] Lister at Purdue,[21] and Raffel and Shisko at MIT.[22] Generally, they all agreed that weeding based on past use data provided the most satisfactory results. Although these studies were geared to academic libraries, Slote found that the method *also worked in public libraries*. It should be noted that a more recent British study by J. A. and N. C. Urquhart has taken exception to these findings, especially for serials.[23] As so many reports conclude, further research is needed; however, in this case, past usage is a reasonable criterion if you are weeding for storage. Regarding purging materials, on the other hand, the questions raised by the Urquharts would seem to indicate that librarians should go slow when applying the past usage criterion.

Almost every conceivable combination of "objective" criteria has been investigated at one time or another to find the best ones for weeding. Language, date of publication, subject matter, frequency of citation, and listing in bibliographies, indexes, and abstracting services have all been tried. Citation analysis and presence or absence of indexing or abstracting have usually been used with serials and periodicals. About the only factors not considered are book size and color of binding.

The preponderance of evidence points to the past use criterion as the one most reliable for weeding for storage. If the library has a circulation system that leaves a physical record of use in each book or if it has a memory store (automated system) that can be easily used, there will be little difficulty. Unfortunately, over the past twenty years, many libraries have switched to circulation systems that do not allow easy or economical access to usage data. To date, no one has thought of a rapid, inexpensive method of gathering it in such situations. Consequently, the best method then would be a staff/patron committee using a qualitative approach.

SUMMARY

One way to overcome some of the psychological barriers to weeding is to develop cooperative programs such as the Center for Research Libraries (see chapter 11, on cooperation). As long as there is a continuing emphasis on independence and size, our patrons will be badly served. Too much material to buy, too little money to spend, too little space to service and store adequately what we do buy, too few staff members to truly help bewildered patrons find what they need, and too little time and money to weed collections to a human scale—these are but a few of the problems that librarians face. It is to be hoped that the need to plan NOW for solutions to these problems has been made clear. Clearly, any solution will directly involve the concept of cooperation—whether that occurs in centralized processing, cooperative selective weeding policies, or cooperative storage programs. Preferably, it would occur in all of these.

NOTES

[1] H. F. McGraw, "Policies and Practices in Discarding," *Library Trends* 4 (Jan. 1956): 270.

[2] Ibid.

[3] Ibid., p. 275.

[4] P. M. Strain, "A Study of the Usage and Retention of Technical Periodicals," *Library Resources and Technical Services* 10 (Summer 1966): 295.

[5] F. Rider. *The Scholar and the Future of the Research Library* (New York: Handen Press, 1944), p. 17.

[6] R. Ellsworth. *The Economics of Book Storage in College and Research Libraries* (Washington: Association of Research Libraries, 1969).

[7] McGraw, pp. 278-79.

[8] S. J. Slote, *Weeding Library Collections* (Littleton, CO: Libraries Unlimited, 1975).

[9] C. A. Seymour, "Weeding the Collection," *Libri* 22 (1972): 189.

[10] F. Wezeman, "Psychological Barriers to Weeding," *ALA Bulletin* 52 (Sept. 1958): 639.

[11] L. Ash. *Yale's Selective Book Retirement Program* (Hamden, CT: Archon, 1963), p. ix.

[12] Ibid., p. 66.

[13] H. H. Fussler and J. L. Simon. *Patterns in the Use of Books in Large Research Libraries* (Chicago: University of Chicago Library, 1961; revised ed., 1969), p. 4 [1961 ed.].

[14] Ibid., p. 31.

[15] Ibid., p. 122.

[16] Ibid., p. 125.

[17] Ibid., p. 208.

[18] R. D. Trueswell, "Quantitative Measure of User Circulation Requirements and Its Effect on Possible Stock Thinning and Multiple Copy Determination," *American Documentation* 16 (Jan. 1965): 20.

[19] A. K. Jain, *Report on a Statistical Study of Book Use* (Lafayette, IN: Purdue University, 1968).

[20] M. Cooper, "Criteria for Weeding Collections," *Library Resources and Technical Services* 12 (Summer 1968): 340.

[21] W. C. Lister. *Least Cost Decision Rules for the Selection of Library Materials for Compact Storage* (Washington: U.S. Department of Commerce, 1967).

[22] J. A. Raffel and R. Shishko. *Systematic Analysis of University Libraries* (Cambridge, MA: MIT Press, 1969).

[23] J. A. Urquhart, and N. C. Urquhart. *Relegation and Stock Control in Libraries* (London: Oriel Press, 1976).

BIBLIOGRAPHY

Allen, W. H. "Call the Junkman Last." *Catholic Librarian* 36 (April 1965): 497-99.

Ash, L. *Yale's Selective Book Retirement Program.* Hamden, CT: Archon Books, 1963.

Bedsole, D. T. "Formulating a Weeding Policy for Books in a Special Library." *Special Libraries* 49 (May 1958): 205-209.

Brooks, B. C. "Growth, Utility and Obsolescence of Scientific Periodical Literature." *Journal of Documentation* 26 (Dec. 1970): 283-94.

Buckland, M. K., and S. Woodburn. *Some Implications for Library Management of Scattering and Obsolescence.* Lancaster, PA: University of Lancaster, 1968. (Occasional Papers, no. 1).

Carter, M. D., and W. J. Bonk. "How-and-Where-to-Weed." *Library Journal* 85 (Jan. 15, 1960): 198-200.

Cooper, M. "Criteria for Weeding of Collections." *Library Resources and Technical Services* 12 (Summer 1968): 339-51.

"Costs of Weeding a Library Collection." *Library Journal* 91 (Jan. 15, 1966): 194.

Davis, D. A. "Maintenance of Circulating Books in an Academic Library." *California Librarian* 38 (April 1977): 22-31.

Ellsworth, R. E. *The Economics of Book Storage in College and University Libraries.* Washington: Association of Research Libraries, 1969.

Evans, G. E. "Limits to Growth or the Need to Weed." *California Librarian* 38 (April 1977): 8-16.

Fussler, H. H., and J. L. Simon. *Patterns in the Use of Books in Large Research Libraries.* Chicago: University of Chicago Library, 1961; revised 1969.

Gawrecki, D. *Compact Library Shelving.* Chicago: ALA Library Technology Program, 1968.

Gosnell, C. F. "Obsolescence of Books in College Libraries." *College and Research Libraries* 5 (March 1944): 115-25.

Gribbin, L. S. "Keep or Discard?" *Library Journal* 89 (March 15, 1964): 1193.

Harris, T. C. "Library Storage or Collections Access: A Point of View." *California Librarian* 38 (April 1977): 38-43.

Jain, A. K. *Report on a Statistical Study of Book Use.* Lafayette, IN: Purdue University, 1968.

Line, M. B. "Half-Life of Periodical Literature: Apparent and Real Obsolescence." *Journal of Documentation* 26 (March 1970): 46-54.

Lister, W. C. *Least Cost Decision Rules for the Selection of Library Materials for Compact Storage.* Washington: U.S. Department of Commerce, 1967.

Lopez, M. D. "Compact Book Storage: Solutions Utilizing Conventional Methods." *Library Trends* 19 (Jan. 1971): 352-61.

McGraw, H. F. "Policies and Practices in Discarding." *Library Trends* 4 (Jan. 1956): 269-82.

McIntosh, C. W. "College President Examines a Weeding List." *Library Journal* 85 (Jan. 15, 1970): 201.

Mumford, L. Q. "Weeding Practices Vary." *Library Journal* 71 (June 15, 1946): 895-98.

Neufeld, J. "S-O-B. Save Our Books." *Reference Quarterly* 6 (Fall 1966): 25-28.

Perkins, D. "Periodical Weeding, or Weed It and Reap." *California Librarian* 38 (April 1977): 32-37.

Raffel, J. A., and R. Shishko. *Systematic Analysis of University Libraries.* Cambridge: Massachusetts Institute Press, 1969.

Reagan, E. D. "An Interior Solution to an Overcrowded Academic Library." *California Librarian* 38 (April 1977): 44-49.

Rider, F. *The Scholar and the Future of the Research Library.* New York: Hamden Press, 1944.

Schrieffer, K., and I. Mostecky. "Compact Book Storage: Mechanized Systems." *Library Trends* 19 (Jan. 1971): 362-78.

Seymour, C. A. "Weeding the Collection." *Libri* 22 (1972): 137-48, 183-89.

Slote, S. J. "Approach to Weeding Criteria for Newspaper Libraries." *American Documentation* 19 (April 1968): 168-72.

Slote, S. J. *Weeding Library Collections.* Littleton, CO: Libraries Unlimited, 1975.

Stone, E. O. "A University Library Reappraises Its Holdings." *Wilson Library Bulletin* 29 (May 1955): 712-14.

Strain, P. M. "A Study of the Usage and Retention of Technical Periodicals." *Library Resources and Technical Services* 10 (Summer 1966): 291-304.

Trueswell, R. D. "Quantitative Measure of User Circulation Requirements and Its Effect on Possible Stack Thinning and Multiple Copy Determination." *American Documentation* 16 (Jan. 1965): 20-25.

Wezeman, F. "Psychological Barriers to Weeding." *ALA Bulletin* 52 (Sept. 1958): 637-39.

Chapter 10

COLLECTION EVALUATION

At some point, every library is confronted with the need to assess its collection. The reasons for the assessment can vary from curiosity to the need to defend the manner in which funds were used to build the collection. Since different purposes require different methods of evaluation, in this chapter, we will explore the methods that are most frequently employed. To some extent, this chapter completes the cycle of collection development discussed in chapter 1.

WHAT IS COLLECTION EVALUATION?

One might expect that in the many years since library surveys were first seriously undertaken, librarians would have made considerable progress in defining the values, methods, scope, and the purposes of collection evaluation. But such is not the case. Elizabeth Stone revealed the problems in collection evaluation in 1941 when she wrote:

> the book collection may be measured in terms of any one or a combination of two or more of the following qualifications; number of volumes; number of volumes per capita; number of volumes per borrower; relationship between college student enrollment and the number of books as reported in inventory; proportional representation; comparison of circulation, purchases and book stock; average number of volumes added annually over a five-year period, or percentage of increases in book collection during ten years; number of accessions per student year; amount spent annually for additions; average cost of accession; comparison of book collections of teacher colleges and art colleges for non-professional courses; examination; duplication of books; recency of publication; questionnaire; and checklist.[1]

From this statement it would appear that the library pays its money and takes its choice of the particular method or combination of methods that would win the highest rating for its book collection. Unfortunately, things have not changed that much in 35-plus years. Today, collection evaluation appears to be in the same state of confusion despite the outstanding article by Verner Clapp and Robert Jordan written in 1965. They concluded their article on collection evaluation with these words:

> ... the attempt to identify and weigh the factors which affect the need for books in academic situations reveals gaps in our knowledge, to the filling of which research might profitably be directed. Among these questions requiring answers are:
>
> What are the tests of adequacy of an academic library?
>
> What is learned from experience regarding the contents of an undergraduate collection of minimum adequacy?
>
> How are these contents affected by variable factors, such as geography, curriculum, teaching methods, intellectual climate, etc.?
>
> What constitutes adequacy for particular kinds of materials at various levels of use—e.g., periodicals, government documents?
>
> What correlation, if any, exists between size of student body and that of collection?
>
> Is there a renewal or replacement cycle? What are its characteristics? Does it affect acquisition, weeding, or the estimates of cost of collection building?
>
> What constitutes adequate resources for graduate work and research on various subjects and at various levels?
>
> Questions similar to the foregoing may be asked with respect to the collections of junior and community colleges.[2]

The authors state further: "the adequacy of an academic library collection may be difficult to determine, but there is no mystery about it. The difficulty arises simply from the quantity of detail and the number of variables involved, far beyond the capacity of any visiting committee to assess merely on the basis of easy observation or sampling."[3] With only a few minor changes, all of the above statements could be applied as well to public, school, or special libraries.

Before proceeding further, it will help to reiterate what evaluation is: a judgment as to the value of X, based on a comparison, implicit or explicit, with some known value, Y. Problems can be seen here immediately when the unknown and the (presumably) known values involve abstracts, or things that do not lend themselves directly to quantitative measurement. If we consider a book's value, or even that of an entire collection, we must keep in mind the various kinds of values that may be involved—economic, moral, religious, aesthetic, intellectual, educational, political, social, etc. A single item may be valuable in any one of these respects, or in any combination of them. In any case, value judgments of this type are entirely subjective, just as each one was when items were originally purchased.

Therefore, it becomes important to consider to whom a book or a collection has what kind(s) of value, for how long, and in whose judgment. There are no right and wrong answers to these basic questions, yet this has not discouraged attempts at evaluation, nor should it destroy the usefulness of such evaluations. It is, however, important that such questions be taken into account in choosing evaluative methods and in interpretation of the results of the method(s) chosen. Otherwise, perspective may be lost and any number of slavish attempts to meet unrealistic goals may result.

Libraries often have been interested to see how they compare with other libraries in regard to the size and presumed quality of their respective collections. However, the individual library must beware of falling into an evaluation trap. Like all other aspects of evaluation, the use of comparative data presents a number of significant problems of definition and interpretation. What, for example, does library A stand to gain by comparing itself with library B—except perhaps an inferiority complex or a delusion as to its own status. No doubt some libraries are better than others, and comparisons may well be important in discovering why this is so. Yet, comparison presupposes a close approximation of needs and that norms developed for several organizations or municipalities "approximate optimum conditions," and neither assumption is well founded. The point is, of course, that while comparisons of libraries may be interesting and even helpful in some respects, each is unique, and at least part of its real value lies in that uniqueness.

If a library undertaking evaluation of its collection must be aware both of its own identity and of the tenuous nature of the evaluation process, it must even more surely have in mind clear reasons for making the evaluation. These may range from the more or less idealistic to the purely practical, and from the generally stated (but not vague) to the very specifically formulated. Robert B. Downs, who has had many years of experience in surveying library resources, suggests that:

> from the internal point of view, the survey, if properly done, gives one an opportunity to stand off and get an objective look at the library, to see its strengths, its weaknesses, the directions in which it has been developing, how it compares with other similar libraries, how well the collection is adapted to its clientele, and provides a basis for future planning.[4]

In addition, Downs believes that such surveys are preliminary steps to library cooperation in acquisitions and in availability of resources. Unfortunately, most libraries appear to have done little to implement this cooperative aspect of evaluation.

A library may have all of these reasons for evaluating its collection, or only want a broad view of the adequacy and availability of the library's book resources; the development of an intelligent, realistic acquisitions program based on a thorough knowledge of the existing collection; a justification for increased fund demands or for particular subject allocations; or merely want to increase the staff's familiarity with the collection. The major purposes of evaluation in education have also been applied to library collection evaluation, resulting in suggestions that such an evaluation would provide:

a check of the effectiveness of the library; . . . a kind of psychological security for the library staff and for the college faculty; . . . a valuable instrument in public relations for the library; . . . (and it would) force the library staff to formulate clearly the objectives of the library itself.[5]

This formulation of library objectives is often mentioned as a "must-do-first" for any library attempting an evaluation of any kind. An evaluator, whether librarian or scholar, should be aware not only of the objectives of the library in relation to the community that it serves, but also of the objectives of any larger institution of which it may be a part (e.g., a college, business, school district). These objectives provide a background for interpretation, which lends significance to the results of evaluation.

Given a set of objectives, evaluators still must answer such questions as:

1) can a satisfactory formula be derived for evaluating the library?

2) can a library reporting a small number of volumes be termed adequate when compared with another library reporting a much larger collection?

3) what has been the experience of others in attempting the evaluation of a collection?

4) what should be the approach in evaluating and what factors should be considered?

5) what standards are applicable?[6]

In evaluating a collection, questions associated with the value or effectiveness of use are as follows:

1) is the collection broad, varied, authorative, up-to-date; supplemented by source, monographic and periodical material for specialized study and research?

2) is the collection sufficient for specialized and technical fields of interest to the agency, institution or group with which associated?

3) is the collection being expanded so as to fill in the gaps; weeded efficiently to keep it solid and current?

4) is the collection supplemented but not replaced by interlibrary loans?

5) is the collection being added to enough in terms of new titles to keep abreast of advances in the fields of interest?[7]

Once library objectives are clear, decisions must be made on the most effective method(s) of evaluation given the reasons for carrying out the evaluation. As indicated earlier, a number of techniques are available, and choice depends in part upon the purpose and depth of the evaluation process. George Bonn, in a 1974 state-of-the-art review, listed five general approaches to the problem of evaluation:

1) compiling statistics on holdings;

2) checking standard lists—catalogs and bibliographies;

3)   obtaining opinions from regular users;

4)   examining the collections directly;

5)   applying standards [which involves use of various methods mentioned above], and listing the library's document delivery capability, and noting the relative use of a particular group.[8]

Most of the new methods developed in the past ten to fifteen years have employed statistical procedures. Even the revised standards and guidelines of professional associations and accrediting agencies have employed statistical approaches and formulas in order to give evaluators some quantitative indicators of what is considered adequate. Standards, checklists, catalogs, and bibliographies are also tools of the evaluator. In general, there are four types (if one combines two of Bonn's types): 1) impressionistic, 2) checklist, 3) statistical, and 4) usage.

IMPRESSIONISTIC METHOD OF
COLLECTION EVALUATION

What kinds of impressions does this method of collection evaluation comprise? Some evaluators suggest examining a collection in terms of the library's policies and purposes, and thus preparing a distinctly subjective impression of the collection's worth and/or of its problems. The impression might represent an overview of the collection as a whole, it might be confined to a single subject area, or, as is frequently the case, it may be drawn by gathering impressions of various subject areas within the collection. Concern is directed toward estimating such qualities as the depth of the collection, its usefulness in relation to the curriculum and for research, specifically known deficiencies, and strengths in special collections. Only very rarely is the impressionistic technique used alone in its most basic form, that is, an evaluator walks into the collection stacks, looks around, and comes out with a feeling for the value of the material. None of the surveyors who use this technique limit it to a glance around the shelves. Rather, they prefer to collect the impressions of others (though these may be based on similar vague feelings) and thus draw more reliable, but still impressionistic, conclusions. It is essential, however, to note that every patron makes such a judgment about the collection—often after only one brief visit. Therefore this approach is important at least in terms of a measure of patron opinion.

Frequently this approach is used by an outside consultant, an experienced librarian, or an accrediting committee. The evaluation is based upon information drawn from various sources—personal examination of the shelves, quantitative measures, and the impressions of others more directly connected with the library in question. Subject specialists (often teachers in the field under consideration) may be asked to give their impressions of the strengths and weaknesses of a collection in certain areas. This can be done by questionnaire and interview. Less frequently, specialists' impressions may constitute the evaluation. Members of the library staff are also often asked to give their impressions of the depth and usefulness of the collection in certain areas, with that information sometimes being compared to that given by the outside subject specialist.

Library self-surveys have also made effective use of the impressions of subject specialists and librarians, again often in combination with list checking and other evaluative methods. A recent example of a collection evaluation project carried out by librarians is that at the State University of New York at Buffalo (SUNYAB).[9] The library's subject bibliographers were chosen to make the evaluation, and an impressive set of guidelines were developed. The bibliographers were to make a preliminary statement based on their own impressions of the state of the collection in their fields, and then to check the holdings against various appropriate bibliographies. They were to use their ingenuity in approaching the research collection, and they were to evaluate the book selection procedures and faculty interest and aid. Once the actual data had been gathered, the original statement of impressions was to be re-evaluated. Note that many large public libraries employ subject specialists, most special libraries have an in-depth subject specialty, and school libraries can draw on teachers for subject expertise. Thus, the method can be used in every type of library.

The major weakness of the impressionistic technique, in whatever form it may be found, lies in the fact that it is so overwhelmingly subjective. This is not to say, however, that it has no place in meaningful collection evaluation, although this place may be difficult to determine. The opinions of those who are supposed to know obviously have some importance, even if only in a library's public relations efforts. Impressions may be most useful as part of an evaluation—i.e., in connection with other methods of examining a collection—but their importance depends on the objectives of the individual survey, and their significance depends on their interpretation.

CHECKLIST METHOD OF COLLECTION EVALUATION

The checklist method of evaluation has been used by many different evaluators with many different purposes in mind. It may be used alone, or in some combination with other techniques—usually to come up with some numerically-based statement such as "we (or they) have X percentage of the books on this list (or these lists)." Outside consultants frequently check holdings against standard bibliographies or suggest that the library do it and report the results. Checklists are a means of approaching the holdings for purposes of comparison.

Accreditation committees frequently use checklists in evaluation, particularly for reference and periodical collections. The attitude of such committees is, of course, closely connected with the idea of "standards" for various kinds of libraries. For example, the Committee on Standards for College Libraries makes the following recommendation:

> Library holdings should be checked frequently against standard bibliographies, both general and subject, as a reliable measure of their quality. A high percentage of listed titles which are relevant to the program of the individual institution should be included in the library collections.[10]

Self-surveys by the library staff also frequently make use of checklist methods. The "grand-daddy" of all checklist self-surveys was the evaluation of the University of Chicago libraries conducted by M. Llewellyn Raney in 1933. This survey used several hundred bibliographies to make an essentially complete check of the entire collection for the purpose of determining future needs. There is little question that this was a pioneer effort in using checklists and in thoroughly examining the book collection in each subject area.

Obviously, a wide variety of checklists may be used in any situation. Libraries have most often used standard lists of "basic" collections, but recently there seems to be a tendency to expand these lists to include more specific subject area lists. Some surveyors (notably R. B. Downs) have advocated increasing use of periodical and other indexes as additional checklists. Large research libraries (academic, public, or special) might consider using the basic lists to check basic collections, but they are far more inclined to use standard subject bibliographies and specially compiled lists.

Actually, the specially prepared bibliography is probably the best way to go if the checklist method is to be really effective. A library may feel that compilation of a special list is impractical and therefore, choose to make use of various standard lists. This is an acceptable procedure only if the lists are carefully chosen and used with the individual library's particular characteristics and needs in mind, and if the evaluator gives much attention to interpreting the results. Very often, for any number of particular purposes, the lists will represent only a sample of the total whether they are specially compiled or merely abbreviated versions of standard lists. Further, it should be remembered that unless an examination of a collection is as thorough as, say, the University of Chicago survey, any checklist system is really only a sample.

The shortcomings of the checklist technique as an effective means of evaluation are many, and they are repeated again and again in literature. Leon Carnovsky has enumerated seven major criticisms of checklists and has made helpful comments on each. A summary of these criticisms, together with Carnovsky's observations, follows:

1) checklists are highly arbitrary selections of titles, and many more worthwhile items are omitted.

    —Standard lists are based on the judgment of librarians and reviewers, and the titles included may be assumed to be "qualitatively superior." They are not, however, of equal value; yet their value for particular persons and purposes must be considered;

2) the titles often have little relevance for a specific library's community.
    —Only those checklists should be used whose titles do have some relation to the objectives of the specific library;

3) the lists may well be badly out of date.
    —It should be remembered that "an old book is not always a dead one";

4) many titles that a library has on the same topic may be ignored by the checklist.

—It may well be true that other books are equally good in many cases, yet since books are unique, often one is not a satisfactory substitute for another;

5) interlibrary loan is not taken into account.

—Even small libraries should remember that book circulation often depends on what is available on the shelves. A group of libraries that borrow from each other may find benefits in list checking with a view toward cooperative acquisitions;

6) checklists are always "approved" titles; there is no penalty for having poor titles also.

—Checklists do not criticize obsolete and worthless books, and so they fail to do a complete job of evaluating. "The method is designed to reveal riches and to identify areas of poverty, not to set up a scorecard for libraries in which good books are balanced off against poor ones."

7) checklists fail to take into account special materials which may be very important to a particular library.

—The checklist method is not definitive, and other devices must be used to measure special materials.[11]

A number of these criticisms would have the checklist be all things to all libraries, and, as Carnovsky points out, this just is not the case. Unfortunately, there is a tendency to stop one's judgment of a list at the assumption that the titles may be assumed to be qualitatively superior. All too often there seems to be little realization that works are not of equal value and may not necessarily be valuable at all for a specific library. It might also be noted that while old books may well continue to be useful for many years, an out-of-date checklist is a significant problem. It is not feasible to keep standard lists up to date, and the checklist method is thus essentially obviated as a means of keeping an evaluative eye on current acquisitions.

Obviously the time element involved in checking lists effectively is a problem with this method. Spotty or limited checking does little good, but most libraries are unable, or unwilling, to involve themselves with checking extensively enough to give a reasonably complete picture of the collection. It has been suggested that sampling techniques, in which lists might serve as "polls" or "strainers," might be an effective solution to the time problem. It has been mentioned that checklists are often used to show that the collection has a certain percentage of a certain number of titles. This may sound fine, but no one can say exactly what proportion of a list a library *should* have. Likewise, it is not possible to find true significance in the comparison of one library's holdings with another's on the basis of percentages of listed titles. It should be noted that use of a checklist assumes some correlation between the percentage of listed books held by a library and the percentage of desirable books in the library's collection. This may be an unwarranted assumption.

Just as unwarranted is the assumption that listed books not held necessarily constitute desiderata, and that the proportion of items held to items needed (as represented on the list) constitutes an effective measure of a library's adequacy.

This lengthy discussion of the shortcomings of the checklist method should be considered more as a warning rather than a prohibition. There *are* benefits from using this method in evaluation. Many librarians feel that checking lists helps to reveal gaps and weaknesses in a collection, that the lists then provide handy selection guides if the library wishes to use them for this purpose, and that the revelation of gaps and weaknesses may lead to reconsideration of selection methods and policies.

STATISTICAL METHOD OF COLLECTION EVALUATION

The quantitative method of evaluating a book collection is based on the assumption that a sufficient quantity of books is one valid indicator of the quality of the collection. Thus, this method compiles statistics concerning the number of volumes in the total collection and in its various parts, the expenditures for acquisitions, the relation of this amount to the size of the collection or to the total institutional budget, and other, similar data.

The standard checklists for opening-day collections operated on this premise. Thus Pirie, in his *Books for Junior Colleges,*[12] assumed that to support a liberal arts curriculum, a junior college library must have 20,000 volumes. *Books for College Libraries*[13] assumes that a four-year college must have a minimum of 150,000 volumes, 20 percent of which should be bound periodical volumes and the other 80 percent monographic titles. Similar assumptions are made in ALA's Public Library Association "shorter list," *Books for Public Libraries: Nonfiction for Small Collections,* 2nd ed. (R. R. Bowker, 1975).

The quantitative method has obvious limitations when it is applied to collections beyond those meeting basic minimal standards. While there cannot be quality without a certain quantity, quantity alone does not guarantee quality. Thus, Guy Lyle states unequivocally, "The adequacy of the college library's book collection cannot be measured in quantitative terms. To judge a collection as superior or inferior on the basis of the volume holdings is as absurd as rating a college on the basis of its enrollment."[14] The basic weakness in the quantitative method of evaluation lies in the use to which statistics are put in making value judgments. Almost invariably, these statistics are used to compare one particular library with other libraries or with fixed, external standards. In either case, the pitfalls are obvious.

Comparison with Other Institutions

Comparison with other institutions can offer no objective criterion for evaluation, because institutions differ in their objectives, programs, and curricula. For instance, a junior college with only a liberal arts program will require one type of library, whereas a community college that offers both a liberal arts curriculum and a wide variety of vocational courses will require a much broader collection.

Trying to compare the library of the first institution with the library of the other would be like comparing apples with oranges. There is simply no basis for comparison, and thus, no point in it.

Comparison among various libraries, moreover, is rendered difficult, if not almost impossible, by the different ways in which libraries generate statistics about their own collections. On paper, two libraries may present very similar statistics; yet in reality, their book collections may differ widely. Eli Oboler documents this increasingly acute problem when he writes:

> One library, without any footnote explanation, suddenly increased from less than twenty-five thousand volumes added during 1961-62 to more than three times that number while the amount shown for books and other library materials only increased approximately 50 per cent. Upon inquiry the librarian of this institution stated that, "from storage in one attic we removed forty thousand items, some of which have been catalogued, but in the main we are as yet unsure of the number which will be added. The addition of a large number of volumes also included about one-fourth public documents, state and federal, and almost fifty thousand volumes in microtext."[15]

One is reminded here of the aphorism, "figures don't lie, but liars can figure."

In summary, compiling statistics is a means of evaluating a library in purely quantitative terms, but library collections have always been difficult to evaluate validly in such terms. It is generally agreed that the adequacy of a library's collection cannot be determined or measured solely in quantitative terms. Number of volumes is a poor measure of the growth of the library's collection in relation to the programs and services it provides. However, when standards are not developed in quantitative terms, then budgeting and fiscal personnel, who cannot avoid quantitative bases for their decisions, are compelled to adopt measures that seem to have the virtues of simplicity but may be essentially irrelevant to the library's function. It is, therefore, necessary to develop quantitative approaches for evaluating collections, methods that can be used by officials in decision-making, but that still retain the virtue of simplicity while remaining relevant to the library's program and services.

In recent years, the development of formulas as statistical approaches to evaluating library collections has increased in all types of libraries. Formulas that have been given considerable attention in the literature of librarianship are Clapp-Jordan, Washington State, California State, the recent ACRL formula for college librarians, and Beasley's work with public libraries. Some advantages associated with these statistical approaches are that they generally allow for more reasonable, in-depth comparisons between libraries, and they are usually more easily available, easily understood, and easily compared. The disadvantage associated with some of these approaches is an inability to assess qualitative factors important in the relationship between the library collection and patron needs. Furthermore, there is a lack of standard definitions of what is to be measured (e.g., no uniformity in use of the terms titles and volumes).

Clapp-Jordan Formula

Because there has been general disagreement with standards that have been devised, some librarians have developed additional criteria for determining the adequacy of a collection. One example of this type of formula is the Clapp-Jordan Formula, developed in order to have a firm argument for the planning, budgeting, and appropriating bodies with whom the authors had to deal. Although formula approaches such as Clapp-Jordan have been accepted, there are always arguments as to whether these approaches best fit the library environment. An empirical study by R. M. McInnis (using linear regression analysis) is one example of an evaluation of a validity test of one of these approaches. After considerable analysis and manipulation of data, McInnis concluded that: 1) minimal level(s) of adequacy cannot be conclusively determined; 2) over-prediction or too high results are not produced; and 3) the Clapp-Jordan Formula can serve as a computed guide to minimum levels of library size.[16]

Washington State Formula

This formula is based on the approach developed by Clapp-Jordan. Through this approach, it is possible to develop a single formula applicable to both colleges and universities, since it takes into account both enrollment and program factors. Two elements used by Clapp and Jordan are not included in the formula: an allowance of 335 volumes per undergraduate major and 12 volumes per honor student. Both elements are subject to such wide variation of interpretation as to make their inter-institutional use extremely questionable. The formula used for determining quantitative adequacy of holdings in unit* of library resources is presented in Figure 14.

California State Formula

This formula is based on the U.S. Office of Education Standards that take into consideration opportunities for resource sharing by libraries in close proximity to one another. These goals are determined by specific, approved fields of graduate study and by the number of FTE (full-time equivalent) students projected as follows:

---

*A "Unit of Library Resources" is defined as follows: 1) one volume as defined by and reported to the U.S. Office of Education in the annual Higher Education General Information Survey, i.e., "a volume is a physical unit of any printed, typewritten, handwritten, mimeographed, or processed work contained in one binding or portfolio, hardbound or paperbound, which has been classified, cataloged or otherwise prepared for use. Includes government documents that have been classified and cataloged, contains as a volume such material as is contained in one binding or portfolio." 2) One reel of microfilm or eight micro-cards or microfiche as reported on the same survey.

1)   to a basic allowance of 75,000 volumes, for the opening day allowance of new college libraries and the first 600 FTE students;

2)   *add* 10,000 volumes for each additional 2,000 FTE students;

3)   *add* 3,000 volumes for each subject field of graduate study listed by the Office of Education in application for Title II funds;

4)   *add* 5,000 volumes for each approved joint doctoral program;

5)   *subtract* from the total computed 5 percent of such allowance when the college is closer than 25 miles from the nearest public institution of higher education, as determined by the Chancellor.[18]

Figure 14

Washington State Formula:
Determining Quantitative Adequacy of Holdings
in Unit of Library Resources for Colleges and Universities

	(1)	Units of Library Resources (2)
1.	Basic or Opening Day Collection	85,000
2.	Allowance per FTE Faculty	100
3.	Allowance per FTE Student	15
4.	Allowance per Masters Field When No Doctorate Offered in Field	6,100
5.	Allowance per Masters Field When Doctorate Is Offered in Field	3,050
6.	Allowance per Doctoral Field	24,500

Formula A—ACRL Standards for College Libraries

In a recent revision of the 1949 Standards for College Libraries, an ad hoc ACRL committee on revision proposed, in "Standard 2—Collections," the amount of materials that a college library should have in its basic collection. The Standards indicate that:

The library's collection shall comprise all corpuses of recorded information owned by the college for educational, inspirational, and recreational purposes, including multi-dimensional, aural, pictorial, and print materials.

The library shall provide quickly a high percentage of such materials needed by its patrons.

The amount of print materials to be thus provided shall be determined by a formula (Formula A) which takes into account the nature and extent of the academic program of the institution, its enrollment, and the size of its teaching faculty. [A volume is defined as a physical unit of any printed, typewritten, handwritten, mimeographed, or processed work contained in one binding or portfolio, hardbound or paperbound, which has been cataloged, classified, or otherwise prepared for use. For purpose of this calculation microform holdings should be included converting them to volume-equivalents. The number of volume-equivalents held in microform should be determined either by actual count or by averaging formula which considers each reel or microform as one and five pieces of any other format as one volume-equivalent.]

Formula A is based on the approach developed by Clapp-Jordan and is similar to the Washington State Formula. One of the elements used by Clapp and Jordan is not included in the proposed formula, the allowance of twelve volumes per honor student. It added one element that was not in either the Clapp-Jordan formula or the Washington State formula, 6,000 volumes per "6th year specialist degree field."

The Standards state that "libraries which can provide promptly 100 percent as many volumes or volume-equivalents as are called for in this formula shall, in the matter of quality, be graded 'A'. From 80-99 percent shall be graded 'B'; from 65-79 percent shall be graded 'C'; and from 50-64 percent shall be graded 'D.' "

As can be seen from examples presented above, academic libraries have made significant use of statistical tools for the purposes of evaluating collections. There have been very few examples specifically concerning the public library field; however, one outstanding example is Beasley's *Theoretical Framework for Public Library Measurement* (a statistical reporting system for public libraries). Beasley indicated that a statistical reporting system for libraries must have the following features:

1) the expressions should be stated in such a way that they themselves do not set values;

2) there should be a statistical or mathematical formula for each discrete element of a library program;

3) enough variables must be used to delineate clearly the total pattern;

4) the statistics should state clearly the characteristics of the present— where we are now—and in such a manner as to facilitate forecasts of the future.[19]

The major elements of the Beasley formula as stated below are familiar to most librarians. The formula is stated as follows:

$$\text{Potential Service} = \frac{B}{P} \cdot \frac{C}{P} \cdot S$$

The elements or variables defined by Beasley are as follows:

B = all resource materials (perhaps) weighted

P = population served

C = circulation

S = study or research factor

This formula makes no attempt to measure quality, on the assumption that it is primarily a function of a type of personnel.

USAGE METHOD OF COLLECTION EVALUATION

The study of the usage of a book collection as a method of evaluating it comes last in this chapter, because it is the method that has been practiced least. Consequently, there is the least data about it, yet it is the method with perhaps the greatest potential as a valid measure of a collection. This is even more the case today with the increasing use of computer-based library processes that facilitate data gathering.

There are two basic assumptions underlying this method, both enunciated by Lewis Steig, who was one of the first to have used it. Writing about his studies at Hamilton College, a small liberal arts college in New York State, he states these two assumptions as: "1) the adequacy of the book collection is directly related to its use by students and faculty. 2) the circulation records of books withdrawn for home use give a reasonably representative picture of the use made of the library."[20]

This basically pragmatic method of collection evaluation has proven generally distasteful to academicians. Thus Carnovsky writes:

> In general surveys of college and university libraries, where surveyors have devoted attention to use, they have focused on rules and regulations, physical convenience of facilities, and stimulation of reading through publicity, browsing rooms, open stacks and similar matters. They have not been concerned with circulation statistics, and in fact, the statistics for college and university libraries issued by the Library Services Branch do not include them at all. This is tacit recognition of the fact that circulation is largely a function of curriculum and teaching methods, and perhaps also of the realization that the sheer number of books a library circulates is no measure at all of its true contribution to the educational process. In spite of the fact that Wilson and Tauber advocated the maintenance of circulation records, Wilson and Swank, in their survey of Stanford University reported: "Because statistics of use are kept for only a few of the University libraries and those that are kept are not consolidated and consistently reported, it is impossible for the surveyors to present any meaningful discussion or evaluation of this significant aspect of the Library Program."[21]

It might also be added that public libraries, on the whole, have kept much more accurate and detailed circulation records and statistics, although they have not generally used these statistics to evaluate the book collection as such.

Wilson and Tauber, as already indicated by Carnovsky's article, advocate a similar pragmatic test to evaluate a library. They write:

> The true evaluation of a library should be arrived at by a study of the extent to which its clientele accomplishes its purposes. Company and other special libraries are compelled constantly to justify their existence—they are either integral parts of the organization supporting them or they are short lived. There is no reason why other types of libraries should not justify their expenditures in terms of the achievements of their patrons.[22]

This method does provide hard, objective data with which to make an evaluation. Moreover, the data are not affected by legitimate peculiarities in the objectives of the college that the library serves. Like Clapp and Jordan's method or quantitative criteria, this method can be tailor-made to suit each particular library rather than force the library into a Procrustean bed.

While certainly not the one and only method of collection evaluation, this method would serve as a most useful check on one of the other methods. This method is also most helpful in weeding the collection to keep it useful and living. Steig indicated that the greatest disadvantage of this method is the "considerable amount of work ... necessary to collect the data."[23] However, as a computer-based library operation becomes more common, this kind of usage data should become relatively easy and inexpensive to gather.

As yet, the usage method has not been used sufficiently to draw firm conclusions from the data gathered. For instance, what should be considered as adequate or acceptable levels of usage has not yet been determined. Also, sometimes there may be little relationship between the intellectual value of a book and its circulation. This would be especially true for large research collections. Moreover, one cannot always assume that because a book is checked out, that it is actually used. And yet, determining the level of usage of a particular borrower would be as difficult as trying to discover the deepest thoughts of a person's mind.

While this method of collection evaluation has not yet been tested sufficiently to make any final conclusions about it, nevertheless it seems to have outstanding promise. For in a day of increasing competition for money in tight budgets, every agency is required to justify its existence on pragmatic grounds or give way to clearer priorities.

SUMMARY

It is clear that much research must be done before collection evaluation can assume its most useful role in collection development. There is no disagreement that collection evaluation is a difficult task, and its results probably will always be somewhat relative, for measuring, testing, and evaluating a collection is as difficult as measuring, testing, and evaluating a human personality. Thus, the evaluator must be willing to live with what are, at best, always provisional results.

Although no one evaluation method is adequate by itself, each becomes quite effective when supplemented by one or more alternative methods. The alternative methods used today generally tend to be quantitative in approach. While quantitative approaches may be accurate, concise, and compelling, what librarians, administrators, legislators, and governing boards do with the results is another matter. However, as in every other human endeavor, evaluation is necessary for testing whether aims, objectives, or goals have been achieved. Therefore, evaluation is expected to continue to be an important part of librarianship as well.

Because of the time and money required for comprehensive collection surveys, such surveys have been few in number. However, the advent of the computer in library processes makes comprehensive collection surveys less burdensome in time if not in money. We may, therefore, expect more activity in this area of librarianship in the future. As values become more unanimously accepted and methods become better refined in collection evaluation, less reliance will be placed upon the outside expert; more evaluation will be performed by the local library staff, which is more adequately prepared to do the job because of its more intimate knowledge of the collection in relation to the library's objectives and goals. If you are going to do a complete evaluation, the following steps are recommended:

1) develop your own set of criteria for quality and value;

2) draw a random sample from the collection and examine the use of the items (shelf list sample);

3) collect data about titles wanted but not available (ILL requests);

4) keep a record of titles picked up from tables and in stack areas (in-house use);

5) keep a detailed record of interlibrary loan activities;

6) find out how much obsolete material is in the collection (for example, science works over fifteen years old and not considered classics);

7) if there are some checklists that have some relevance for your library, check them; *but* also check the use of these;

8) relate your findings to the library's local goals and objectives.

Collection evaluation is time-consuming as an activity, but only after you finish the task will you *know* what strengths and weaknesses exist in the library's collection. Once you know that, you can formulate a plan to build on the strengths and correct the weaknesses. This assumes that the assessment of strengths and weaknesses is done in terms of the library's goals, objectives, and community needs. After the first effort, if you make the process an on-going one, the work will be less time-consuming, and you can create a cycle of the type mentioned at the beginning of this chapter.

NOTES

[1] E. O. Stone, "Measuring the Book Collection," *Library Journal* 66 (June 1941): 941.

[2] V. W. Clapp and T. Jordan, "Quantitative Criteria for Adequacy of Academic Library Collections," *College and Research Libraries* 26 (Sept. 1965): 380.

[3] Ibid., pp. 379-80.

[4] R. B. Downs, "Techniques of the Library Resources Survey," *Special Libraries* 32 (April 1941): 113.

[5] J. H. Russell, "The Library Self-Survey," *College and Research Libraries* 17 (March 1956): 128.

[6] M. Benton and S. Otterson. *A Critique on Standards for Evaluating Library Collections.* (Washington: George Washington University, 1970), pp. 4-5.

[7] Ibid.

[8] C. S. Bonn, "Evaluation of the Collection," *Library Trends* 22 (Jan. 1974): 267.

[9] M. B. Cassata and G. L. Dewey, "The Evaluation of the University Library Collection," *Library Resources and Technical Services* 13 (Winter 1969): 450-57.

[10] American Library Association, "Standards for College Libraries," *College and Research Libraries* 20 (July 1959): 277.

[11] L. Carnovsky, "Measurement of Public Library Book Collections," *Library Trends* 1 (April 1953): 466-68.

[12] J. W. Pirie, *Books for Junior College Libraries* (Chicago: American Library Association, 1969).

[13] M. Voigt and J. Treyz, *Books for College Libraries* (Chicago: American Library Association, 1967).

[14] G. R. Lyle, *The Administration of the College Library*, 4th ed. (New York: H. W. Wilson, 1974), p. 399.

[15] E. M. Oboler, "The Accuracy of Federal Academic Library Statistics," *College and Research Libraries* 25 (Sept. 1964): 494.

[16] R. M. McInnis, "The Formula Approach to Size: An Empirical Study of Its Efficacy in Evaluating Research Libraries," *College and Research Libraries* 28 (May 1972): 191.

[17] Washington State Universities and Colleges, The Interinstitutional Committee of Business Officers, *A Model Budget Analysis System for Program 05 Libraries* (Olympia: Evergreen State College, Office of Interinstitutional Business Studies, March 1970).

[18] California State Colleges, Office of the Chancellor, Division of Academic Planning, *Report on the Development of the California State Libraries: A Study of Book, Staffing and Budgeting Problems* (Los Angeles, Nov. 1970).

[19] K. E. Beasley, "A Theoretical Framework for Public Library Measurement." In *Research Methods in Librarianship: Measurement and Evaluation*, H. Goldhor, ed. (Urbana: University of Illinois, Graduate School of Library Science, 1968).

[20] L. Steig, "A Technique for Evaluating the College Library Book Collection," *Library Quarterly* 13 (Jan. 1943): 43-44.

²¹ L. Carnovsky, "Survey of the Use of Library Resources and Facilities," in. *Library Surveys*, Maurice F. Tauber and Irene R. Stephens, eds. (New York: Columbia University Press, 1967), p. 68.

²² L. Wilson and M. F. Tauber, *The University Library*, 2nd ed. (New York: Columbia University Press, 1956).

²³ Steig, p. 44.

BIBLIOGRAPHY

American Library Association. Insurance for Libraries Committee. "Evaluation of Library Materials for Insurance Purposes." *American Library Association Bulletin* 53 (June 1959): 540-41.

Asheim, L. *The Humanities and the Library: Problems in the Interpretation, Evaluation, and Use of Library Materials.* Chicago: American Library Association, 1957.

Bach, H. "Evaluation of the University Library Collection." *Library Resources and Technical Services* 2 (Winter 1958): 24-29.

Beasley, K. E. "A Theoretical Framework for Public Library Measurement." In *Research Methods in Librarianship: Measurement and Evaluation.* H. Goldhor, ed. Urbana: University of Illinois, Graduate School of Library Science, 1968.

Benton, M., and S. Otterson. *A Critique on Standards for Evaluating Library Collections.* Washington: George Washington University, 1970.

Bibliographic Planning Committee of Philadelphia. *A Faculty Survey of the University of Pennsylvania Libraries.* Philadelphia: University of Pennsylvania, 1940.

Bonn, G. S. "Evaluation of the Collection." *Library Trends* 22 (Jan. 1974): 265-304.

Boone, J. "When Are Two Better Than One: The Duplication of Research Collections." *Nebraska Library Association Quarterly* 3 (Summer 1972): 12-15.

Buckland, M. K., and I. Woodburn. *An Analytical Approach to Duplication and Availability.* Lancaster, PA: Lancaster University, 1968. (Occasional Papers, no. 2).

Buckland, M. K., and I. Woodburn. *Some Implications for Library Management of Scattering and Obsolescence.* Lancaster, PA: University of Lancaster Library, 1968. (Occasional Papers, no. 1).

Carnovsky, L. "The Measurement of Public Library Book Collections." *Library Trends* 1 (April 1953): 462-70.

Carnovsky, L. "Survey of the Use of Library Resources and Facilities." In *Library Surveys.* M. F. Tauber and I. R. Stophers, eds. New York: Columbia University Press, 1967.

Cassata, M. B., and G. L. Dewey. "The Evaluation of a University Library Collection: Some Guidelines." *Library Resources and Technical Services* 13 (Fall 1969): 450-57.

Clapp, V. W., and R. T. Jordan. "Quantitative Criteria for Adequacy of Academic Library Collections." *College and Research Libraries* 27 (Sept. 1965): 371-80.

Cooper, W. S., D. T. Thompson, and K. R. Weeks. "The Duplication of Monograph Holdings in the U.C. Library System." *Library Quarterly* 45 (July 1975): 253-74.

Dougherty, R. M. "Collection Evaluation and the Bibliographer." *Library Resources and Technical Services* 13 (Fall 1969): 449-70.

Downs, R. B. "Technique of the Library Resources Survey." *Special Libraries* 23 (April 1941):113-15.

Downs, R. B. *Cooperative Library Program.* Little Rock: Arkansas Foundation of Associated Colleges, 1963.

Downs, R. B. *A Survey of the Library of Brigham Young University.* Provo, UT: Brigham Young University, 1969.

Downs, R. B. *Resources of North Carolina Libraries.* Raleigh: University of North Carolina, 1965.

Downs, R. B. *Resources of Missouri Libraries.* Jefferson City: Missouri State Library, 1966.

Evans, G. E. "Review of Criteria Used to Measure Library Effectiveness." In *Reader in Library Management.* R. Shimmer, ed. London: Bingley, 1976.

Galvin, T. J. "Assessing the Problem: The Collection." *LACUNY Journal* 4 (Spring 1976): 12-19.

Golden, B. "A Method for Quantitatively Evaluating a University Library Collection." *Library Resources and Technical Services* 18 (Summer 1974): 268-74.

Goldhor, H. "Analysis of an Inductive Method of Evaluating the Book Collection of a Public Library." *Libri* 23 (1973): 6-17.

Gore, D. "Let Them Eat Cake While Reading Catalog Cards: An Essay on the Availability Problem." *Library Journal* 100 (Jan. 15, 1975): 93-98.

Gore, D. "The View from the Tower of Babel." *Library Journal* 100 (Sept. 15, 1975): 1599-1605.

Grant, R. S. "Predicting the Need for Multiple Copies of Books." *Journal of Library Automation* 4 (June 1971): 64-71.

Heinritz, F. J. "Rate of Growth for Library Collections." *College and Research Libraries* 35 (March 1974): 95-96.

Hirsch, R. "Evaluation of Book Collections." In *Library Evaluation.* W. S. Yenawine, ed. Syracuse, NY: Syracuse University, 1959, pp. 8-9.

Knightly, J. J. "Library Collection and Academic Curricula: Quantitative Relationships." *College and Research Libraries* 36 (July 1975): 295-301.

Leigh, R. D. "The Public Library Inquiry's Sampling of Library Holdings of Books and Periodicals." *Library Quarterly* 21 (July 1951): 157-72.

Lushington, N. "Overdue: Mini-title/Maxi-dup." *Wilson Library Bulletin* 49 (Nov. 1974): 254-55.

McInnis, R. M. "The Formula Approach to Size: An Empirical Study of Its Efficacy in Evaluating Research Libraries." *College and Research Libraries* 28 (May 1972): 190-98.

Neufield, J. "S-O-B: Save Our Books." *Reference Quarterly* 6 (Fall 1966): 25-28.

Ottersen, S. "A Bibliography on Standards for Evaluating Libraries." *College and Research Libraries* 32 (March 1971): 127-44.

Rosenberg, B. "Evaluation: Problems of Criteria and Methodology." *California Librarian* 38 (April 1977): 17-21.

Russel, J. H. "The Library Self-Survey." *College and Research Libraries* 17 (March 1956): 127-31.

Steig, L. F. "A Technique for Evaluating the College Library Collection." *Library Quarterly* 13 (Jan. 1943): 34-44.

Stone, E. O. "Measuring the College Book Collection." *Library Journal* 66 (June 1941): 941-43.

Tauber, M. F. "The Columbia University Self-Study." *College and Research Libraries* 19 (July 1958): 277-82.

Vagianos, L. "Scaling the Library Collection: A Simplified Method for Weighing the Variables." *Library Journal* 98 (March 1, 1973): 712-15.

Webb, W. "Project CoEd: A University Library Collection Evaluation and Development Program." *Library Resources and Technical Services* 13 (Fall 1969): 457-62.

PART C

COLLECTION DEVELOPMENT
AND RELATED ISSUES

Chapter 11

COOPERATION AND COLLECTION DEVELOPMENT

A few years ago, Richard Dougherty wrote an article entitled "Library Cooperation: A Case of Hanging Together or Hanging Separately."[1] Generally speaking, despite hundreds of articles on library cooperation, libraries are still hanging separately in terms of cooperative collection development. We have cooperated reasonably effectively in many other areas of librarianship, but for some ill-defined reason, most librarians seem to prefer splendid isolation and a somewhat ineffective interlibrary loan system over creating true cooperative collection development programs. As of 1978, no truly effective cooperative collection development program operates in the United States on a national scale.

THE NATURE OF COOPERATIVE SYSTEMS

In many ways, library cooperation is like the weather—we all talk about it, but none of us seems able to do much about it—yet. As with weather modification, many individuals work on the problem, but the degree of success has been less than amazing. A primary reason is that we do not really understand what we are trying to accomplish. Figure 15 (page 258) presents a very general overview of the possible combinations of cooperative collection development. This figure represents the hope we all have of reaching the librarians' millennium of total cooperation between libraries and access to all of the world's information resources.

This ideal is a long way off, even at the local level. Many classes of patrons still get different levels of service in different libraries in the same community. Even personality differences between chief librarians can create minor but real barriers to effective cooperation at any level. As one moves farther out in the circles of the figure, it is harder to work out major cooperative programs. No longer is it just library and patron needs that decide the issue of whether to cooperate or not. Legal, political, and economic issues tend to dominate the decision-making process.

Figure 15

Ideal of Inter-Library Cooperation ("Networking")

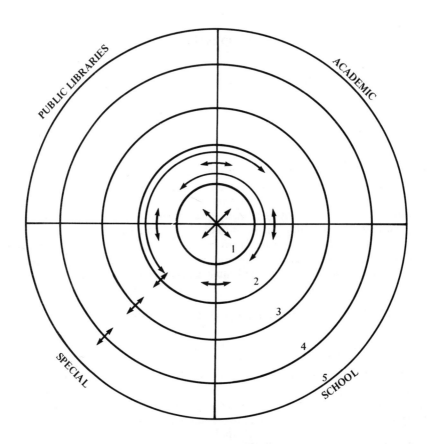

1   Community
2   Local Area
3   Region
4   National
5   International

Adapted from Mary Dugan, "Library Network Analysis and Planning," *Journal of Library Automation* 2/3 (Sept. 1969): 157-75.

MODELS OF COOPERATIVE ACTIVITY

Michael Sinclair, in his article of a few years ago entitled "A Typology of Library Cooperatives," proposed four theoretical models of cooperative activity (Figure 16).[2] Although the concepts are Sinclair's, the following interpretation is this author's. (Sinclair's article should be read in its entirety to gain a full understanding of his model.)

Figure 16
Models of Library Cooperative Activities

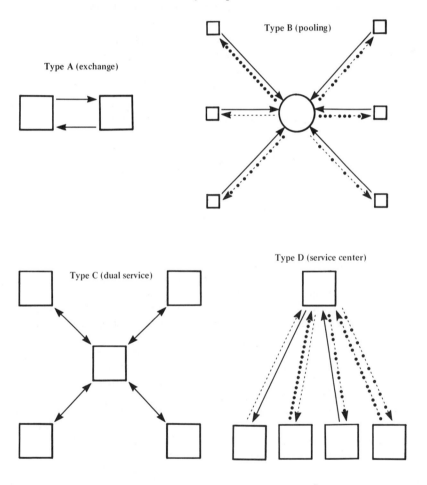

(Descriptions of model types begin on page 260)

A graphic interpretation of M. P. Sinclair, "A Typology of Library Cooperatives," *Special Libraries* 64 (April 1973): 181-86.

Type A. This is a bilateral *exchange model*, in which materials are exchanged between *two* participating libraries. In practice, where such an exchange is found, the exchange rate is usually calculated upon a proportional basis, according to some agreed-upon value (e.g., one for one, two for one).

Type B. This is a multilateral development of Type A and can be called, for convenience, the *pooling model*. In this model, more than two libraries contribute to and draw from a common pool of materials.

Type C. This *dual-service model* is one in which two or more participating libraries take advantage of the facilities of one of the participants to produce a common output—for instance, a union list. The term "dual-service" is proposed both to distinguish this model from the next and to emphasize the fact that *all* participants, including the facilitator, contribute to the common output.

Type D. The model is one in which a number of libraries employ the services of a facilitating participant to input and process materials for individual purposes rather than toward the end of a common output. Hence, it is called the *service-center model.*

These four types seem adequate to cover all existing systems; however, new systems now under consideration may not fit into his categorization.

SOMETHING-FOR-NOTHING SYNDROME

Any model of an existing library cooperation system is built on a series of important assumptions that need to be examined with considerable care. Perhaps the most important, although the one least often stated, is that all of the participants in the system are or will be equally efficient in their operations involving the cooperative system. No one assumes that every member will achieve the same benefits or contribute materials that are equally valuable; each is assumed to be somewhat unusual, if not unique. Why then do we assume that each is equally efficient? Given the slightest thought, it is clear that one cannot legitimately make such an assumption. We make the assumption because if we do not, it is very hard to convince ourselves that everyone will gain more, or at least get back the same value as was contributed. In a sense, librarians try to fool themselves that each will get something for nothing by joining a cooperative system. Each library hopes that it will be the one to get back more than it put into the system.

If a library enters into a cooperative program with the "something for nothing" goal in mind, there is little hope of success. There are always many real costs, which any good accountant could determine. In addition, there are many costs of cooperation that no cost accounting system can identify, much less help control. Two of the most important from a collection development point of view are ease of access and speed of delivery. Any cooperative system will place a higher cost on these two factors, if they are compared to local ownership; that is, it will always take as long, if not considerably longer, to gain access to a desired item, and it will entail more work for both the patron and the library. These costs are not often considered, as it is difficult if not impossible to translate them into monetary units. Often, then, this difficulty means ignoring costs and *assuming* that benefits will be high.

The patrons' costs are seldom considered in any manner; the assumption is that cooperation will only result in increased benefits for the users. Sometimes the extra work filling out one more form or answering one extra question is considered from the library point of view, but almost never from the standpoint of the patron. Small increases are usually thought to be insignificant, and while a single increase may be very small, in time or in aggregate, such increase(s) may be very significant. Nevertheless, a true cooperative collection development program can provide patrons with a much broader range of materials than would be possible for one library working in isolation.

Two examples of these problems will illustrate this point. In the United States, the interlibrary loan (ILL) system is slowly ceasing to function effectively. The early assumption was that *everyone* would gain as a result of the free exchange of resources. Yes, an increase in work load was seen for some of the better endowed libraries, but they would be doing some borrowing and the added volume of work was not expected to be great in any event. Today, we know the work load in the larger institutions is tremendous—so great that a solution must be found. (Something always costs something.) One proposed solution is to charge the borrowing library a fee that will recover most, if not all, of the direct costs of the lending library. The British National Lending Division arose as a direct result of the same problem; unfortunately, such a system is much harder to establish in the United States.

The second example is from Denmark. Copenhagen's public library has established systems for reciprocal patron borrowing rights with suburban public libraries. A high percentage of the persons living in the suburbs work in the central city. Danes are avid readers and are as inclined to use the convenient rather than the inconvenient as the rest of us. So it is not surprising to find them using the most convenient public library for their general library needs, and it seems that for a great many suburbanites, the most convenient is the Copenhagen system, not their local library. The cost for providing this free service has risen so much that several politicians have suggested either dropping the arrangement or charging the non-resident a fee. Certainly, the librarians do not like the idea of charging a fee. The debate goes on. The point again is that the original concept projection was based on the idea that it would be possible to expand service without increasing costs (something for nothing).

WHAT CAN BE GAINED THROUGH COOPERATION?

One can identify six general benefits that can be expected from any library cooperative effort. Improved access is certainly one of the major advantages (improved in the sense that there may be a greater range of material and/or better depth in a subject area). Generally, this does not mean more copies of a particular title, or at least not a significant increase. It certainly does not mean faster service—normally, it will mean an increase in the average time it takes to secure an item. This is offset by the increase in the number of titles available in a system.

A second benefit is that it may be possible to stretch limited resources. One danger in suggesting that cooperation may benefit the public or even the professional staff is that the idea of getting something for nothing will be implanted. Too often, people view cooperation as a money-saving device.

Cooperation does *not* save money for a library. If two or more libraries combine their efforts, they are not going to spend any less money—an effective cooperative program will divide up work and share results.

Sharing work results leads to two other benefits. If work is divided up, it can allow for greater staff specialization. One person can concentrate on one or two activities rather than on a great number, and the specialization should result in better overall performance. Naturally, better performance should provide the patron with better service, and thus perhaps greater satisfaction. Reducing unnecessary duplication is the second result of sharing work. The reduction may be in work performed or materials purchased, but just how much unnecessary duplication will be eliminated must be carefully studied *before* the cooperative agreement is signed. Vague discussions about reducing duplication, without an in-depth study of the situation, usually lead to high expectations and, all too often, to dashed hopes. Nevertheless, reduced duplication is a real potential benefit.

By actively advertising its presence and services, a cooperative program may reduce the number of places a patron will need to go for service. However, this benefit is more theoretical than real in most systems. A lack of union lists has generally negated this potential benefit.

A final benefit, and one not too frequently discussed, is an improvement in the working relationships between cooperating libraries. Several cooperatives have reported that this was an unexpected and pleasant benefit.[3] This is particularly true when there are different types of libraries involved in one system. Persons can gain a better perspective on others' problems as a result of working together on mutual problems. Also, learning about the special problems that another type of library encounters is useful in knowing what they can or cannot do. At least some systems have found this to be so important that they have set up exchange internships for staff members—both professional and non-professional.

More specific examples of what might result from a cooperative arrangement include such things as better or additional public services. For example, it may be possible as a result of shifting work loads to extend the hours of reference service or to increase the number of children's programs. Another possibility is to expand the service area. Perhaps the combined resources of the system will allow for providing service to persons or areas that no one system could reach using solely its own resources.

In terms of collection development, cooperative programs should force the library to have better knowledge of its collection. You have to know both what you have and what the other members have. It will also usually mean sharing problems of selection and collection development. If there is to be a division of collection responsibility by subject area, each library will have to have an in-depth knowledge of its own collection before reaching a meaningful cooperative agreement. Even if there is no final agreement, the process of examining the collection will be of great value in future work. Also, the opportunity to share with others the problems and solutions should improve each participant's capabilities as a selector.

Cooperative systems may also free time for such things as more in-service training, more and better public relations, or just more time for planning. All of these activities require a lot of time to be effective, but depending upon the nature of the cooperative, a considerable amount of time may be made available for such activities. Again, a little of the something-for-nothing syndrome comes out in thinking this way. It does *not* mean that someone else is doing your work for free, since if that is the case, the system will eventually fail, as is the United States interlibrary loan (ILL) system. What this does mean is that you will be doing something for other member libraries and they will be doing things for you.

Basically, a cooperative program properly organized will allow for more specialization, more service, and more time to do things effectively. Remember, there are trade-offs. You get *nothing* for nothing! Good service costs time and money, and there are no magic formulas for gaining extra time or services. What is required is hard work on identifying areas where each potential member has something to gain and something to contribute. In the long run, these two elements must be equal for all members of a system or it will fail.

BARRIERS TO COOPERATION

If so many positive benefits can be derived from cooperation and if the dangers in failing to cooperate are so great, why are there so few effective library cooperatives? A number of working cooperatives exist, but certainly not as many as the literature would lead you to expect. More time is spent talking about the benefits of cooperation than is spent building a cooperative system. Unfortunately, the list of barriers to cooperative activities among libraries is much longer than the list of benefits. This is not to say that all the items on the two lists are of equal importance—they are not. Many of the barriers are of a minor nature, from a theoretical point of view; however, there are still real, practical problems. You can divide the barriers into eight broad categories: 1) self-sufficiency versus sharing, 2) size and status, 3) technological aids, 4) psychological barriers, 5) experience barriers, 6) traditional/historical barriers, 7) physical/geographical barriers, and 8) legal, political, and administrative barriers.

Local Self-Sufficiency Factors

Local self-sufficiency traditionally has been the goal of the majority of libraries. Yet, almost all libraries now realize that the goal is unattainable, even for the great national libraries of the world. There are always some items that are not in their collections and never will be. Why be concerned with self-sufficiency? As you recall, one of the main factors in collection development is meeting patron demand. Being able to deliver a needed item from the local collection provides satisfaction for both the patron and the library staff. Furthermore, the speed of delivery is faster on the average than if the material must be secured through interlibrary loans.

Pressure for local self-sufficiency is probably greatest from patrons. Human nature seems to be such that when we want something, we want it now. Socialization slowly modifies an individual's desire for immediate need satisfaction but never completely eliminates this drive. (When we have our wants satisfied immediately, we are much happier than when we have to wait.) Admittedly, 99 percent of our information needs are not in a life-threatening category and thus we can afford to wait, but we still do not like it. How many times have you grumbled when an item you needed or wanted was charged out to another person? And, if you are like most persons, it has probably happened more than once.

Because librarianship is service oriented, it is not surprising to find the library staff trying to satisfy as many patron needs now as they possibly can.

Patron pressure is particularly strong when there is a proposal to share collection development responsibilities among libraries. Any knowledgeable library user knows something about the speed of interlibrary loans. (Some countries, usually relatively small ones, have very efficient interlibrary loan systems and thus have been able to do more with cooperative collection development.) A natural reaction from such a patron upon hearing the proposal might be, "what will happen to my area of interest? I do not want the library to stop buying my materials. I cannot afford to wait days or months for ILL!" If the library has carefully developed the collection in terms of patron needs, what can be given up? How do you respond to patron inquiries about the impact of the proposed cooperative? How can you be an effective member if you do not give up some areas? Almost always, the library's level of funding will not be enough to buy everything purchased before and still take on new cooperative obligations. Therefore, some areas will have to be given up or sharply reduced.

How nice it would be if easy, quick answers existed to those and a number of related questions. If easy answers existed, there would be many more collection cooperatives. In the absence of a speedy delivery system from other member libraries, librarians seeking cooperative arrangements will face strong patron opposition in many cases. An effective and truthful public relations program, one pointing out all the advantages to be gained by membership, will be the most important method to gaining support. Most of the answers to questions about cooperation will depend upon the local collection and those of the cooperating libraries.

Status and Size Factors

Related to self-sufficiency is an unfortunate situation in which a library's size and status are tied together. Size and status do not have as much impact on cooperative efforts as they do on weeding, but they are a factor, since giving up some areas of collecting responsibility may have an impact on growth. Not all areas have the same number of items produced per year, and thus they do not increase in size as fast. If your library must give up a fast growth area and has only low growth areas, your library's overall growth rate (annual increase in size) may drop. In addition to the growth rate within a subject area, there is the cost of materials. Many science and technology items cost 25 percent to 50 percent more than social science and humanities items, which can mean that you will acquire fewer titles for the same amount of money. If size and status are important for your library and parent institution, you may find it difficult if not impossible to find an agreeable breakdown of collecting responsibilities that does not have an adverse impact on the library's growth rate.

New Technologies Factors

New technologies also represent a barrier. Surprisingly enough, the hope that these new developments represent for storage of materials is also a problem. In some instances, pressure for cooperative collection development comes from a lack of physical space in which to store the collection. Eliminating unnecessary duplication of low use items can result in more space for heavily used materials. However, if new technology will allow you to store the equivalent of the Library of Congress or British Museum Library collections in space no longer than an office desk or less, why worry about running out of space? In addition, the potential for local self-sufficiency may be raised again. If you can buy a microfiche for one-quarter of the price of a hard copy, the book budget can be used to acquire a great many more items. Increased acquisition rate naturally will increase the title count and thus raise the status of the library. Increased depth and scope in the collection plus almost immediate satisfaction of patron needs are what libraries are all about, right?

Clearly, the new technologies will solve our problems and almost do away with the need to do any selection work. Or at least the persons selling the new devices claim that their systems will solve all our problems. Sometimes it seems as if the charlatans who once sold cure-all elixirs simply stopped peddling bottles of magic liquids because selling mysterious electronic black boxes to librarians is more profitable and easier. Many technological devices do work and work effectively for libraries, but to gain this result means a significant cost. In a sense, we still hope to get something for nothing. We hope that new developments will solve library problems at no increase in expenses. To date, there has been no such development. You trade one cost for another, and in some cases, what initially seems to be a reduction in cost later becomes a significant increase in long-term costs. Remember that many systems are not compatible with any other system, and if you select such a system, you may well find yourself trapped. Also, the longer you stay with an existing, limited system, the higher will be the cost of converting to a newer or more useful one.

Finally, new developments are continually being announced, as yesterday's latest cures all become obsolete overnight. Perhaps the hardest factor to handle is the announcement about what is under development and is being tested in a prototype system. Prototypes all too often fail to live up to expectations, but they do hold out a hope that will cause some libraries not to investigate joining cooperative efforts.

Psychological Factors

Psychological barriers are very important in the success or failure of a cooperative project. These barriers may exist for the staff members or patrons of the libraries attempting to establish a cooperative. Some of the factors arise from an individual's preferring the known to the unknown. Change can be threatening, and a move to cooperative programs from a program where self-sufficiency was the rule can be viewed as a threat. Job security may appear to be threatened, or at least personal status. Feelings of this type usually arise because the planners have not provided adequate information about the proposed system. Bits and pieces of information gleaned through the grapevine seldom provide more than enough fact and rumor to raise fears of things to come. Accurate information about the new system communicated directly to all concerned, even if there is a potential threat to employment, is better than allowing the rumor mill to operate. Unfortunately, even if the information is accurate, staff members sometimes will believe that communiques are deliberately false. In the first case, a slight extra effort will eliminate the barrier. As for the second case, the actual problem has nothing to do with the concept of library cooperation, and there will be little hope for a successful program until the credibility issue is resolved.

Loss of autonomy may be a real or imagined barrier to cooperation, and both patrons and the library staff may express this fear ("who will decide X?" "what voice will we have?" "won't Y library dominate the system?" etc.). There should be concern about the issue raised in such questions, and any good cooperative agreement will directly address these issues. However, the worry will be expressed, or at least be present, long before any written agreement exists. Dealing with this problem early in the planning process should help to ensure the successful conclusion of the project.

Inertia, indifference, or unwillingness to change are psychological factors often encountered ("things are going okay." "why make more work?"). Sometimes passive resistance is more difficult to overcome than active opposition. Persons actively opposing cooperation present arguments, which may be addressed and perhaps effectively countered. It is much harder to counter the spoken or silent attitude that "it is an outstanding idea but we need to work on the following local problems first. . . ." Even when the plan is implemented, too many indifferent persons in the system can cause the chances of success to go way down. Again, an active public relations program and good in-service orientation about the new system are the best insurance against inertia and indifference undermining the project.

In cooperative collection development, the problems of who makes decisions and specific local needs are frequently voiced. Also because selection is a very subjective matter, it is hard to get agreement on policies and priorities. The more persons who become involved in the process, the more difficult it becomes to achieve agreement. For a cooperative collection development program, agreement must be reached among the representatives of libraries in the proposed system regarding the system's priorities, a process that in itself may take a very long time. Even though representatives will have been checking back with their own libraries, when system priorities are fully set forth, each library will have to carefully examine the statement in terms of its own priorities. When conflicts arise between two sets of priorities, and there are often a great many, these will have to be resolved at the local level. If the library staff helped establish the local priorities, they then will need to be involved in resolving the conflict.

Dislike of "standardization" and unwillingness to accept "outsider errors" are two related barriers, attitudes normally based on deep personal feelings developed over a long period of time. Yet, almost every cooperative project will result in more standardization of activities or at least filling out more forms. Also, inevitably there will be mistakes by "outsiders." The full impact of either factor cannot be fully known until after the system is operative. Information on these factors from similar systems will help reduce such fears but will never completely overcome them.

Occasionally, personality differences can present significant problems in achieving a cooperative agreement. Strong or dominant personalities or a strong authority drive on the part of individual librarians are usually the source of these problems. If two or more such personalities become involved in the process of establishing or operating a cooperative system, there is little hope that the system will be able to operate effectively. Personal needs will almost inevitably take priority over system needs.

Past Experience Factors

Experience barriers are very real, practical problems that make it difficult to establish an effective cooperative system. Two interrelated factors involve the library's patrons. The first is whether we really have an adequate knowledge of what they need and want? Furthermore, even if we know the current situation, the needs and wants can change very quickly. To some degree, then, librarians must deal with these two issues every day in developing the collection. Why is it any greater problem for a cooperative? Lacking adequate knowledge of our local patron needs and future changes makes it very difficult to determine what we can both give up or effectively contribute to the cooperative. Each potential member is confronted with the same problem, but the major difficulty lies in the speed with which adjustments may be made in a network of more than two members. It is much easier to make adjustments in one local system in response to new needs when you do not need to worry about the impact that the adjustments will have on other libraries. Of course, any proposed change may have a major impact on the original agreement. Certainly most changes should have limited impact, but each one needs to be discussed on an individual case basis with other member libraries.

Perhaps the best known nationwide effort at cooperative collection development was the Farmington Plan. It no longer exists, though, for a number of reasons. One important reason was the changing interests of the member institutions. An area once considered important by a member would become less and less important *to its local patrons*, but pressures to buy materials in a new area while still maintaining the Farmington responsibilities became great. Some institutions were able to trade responsibilities with one another, while others devoted less and less attention to their assigned areas; occasionally, an area was simply ignored. With this type of experience recorded in the literature and in the background of the persons who attempted to make the Farmington program work, it will be difficult to convince libraries to try again.

A number of successful small-scale collection development cooperatives may exist; however, information about them is difficult to find. When a cooperative is formed, some formal announcement is made to the library press, but these announcements seldom get full coverage in the journals. Articles about a new small-scale system—unless there is an unusual feature about the program—are seldom published. Even when there has been good coverage of the establishment of a system, it is very difficult to get operational information. With the exception of major national programs (e.g., the Farmington and Latin American Cooperative Acquisition Plan—LACAP), very few announcements appear about the demise of a cooperative program. Once a program is functioning, no one seems to have time to write up what has been accomplished, beyond the necessary reporting to members. In-person assessment is therefore really the only way to find out what has happened.

Almost every program is modified in its first few years of operation, but again, these modifications are seldom described in the literature. Attempts to find out what has been accomplished by sending out a questionnaire are seldom very satisfactory, since response rates are low and a standard closed response form seldom produces enough useful information when surveying a wide range of activities. If such a form does cover enough topics, the length is usually so great that many persons refuse to answer it. On the other hand, open response forms are often viewed as too time-consuming to bother with.

The end result of all of the above is a general lack of knowledge about what has and has not succeeded in cooperative efforts. Another issue directly related to this lack of knowledge of accomplishments is a lack of adequate (depth and breadth) data on what the system will cost. So many factors go into figuring the cost of a system that very often the monetary figures from an existing system are of little value (not that many systems have made available detailed cost figures). Taking into account regional differences in salary, living conditions, and costs; computing direct and indirect cost factors; fixing methods of depreciating capital expense items; and deciding just what will or will not be included in overhead costs are just a few of the elements that make comparisons between cooperative system costs unsatisfactory.

Although time rates for activities in a cooperative could be of much greater value than the unit cost for persons planning a cooperative, such figures are even less often made available. "Standard times" for an activity can be useful for comparative and planning purposes. A major concern, however, is that any systems and activities being compared be identical, or the comparison tells nothing. For instance, typing a book order form might seem to be the same procedure from library to library, and a standard time for that activity would seem to be easy to determine. Naturally, though, the length of time to type a form is dependent upon both the complexity of the form itself and the format in which the typist gets the data that is to be included. How many order form variations exist? The safest answer would be somewhat fewer than the number of libraries that exist in the world. Thus, the concern must be with activities of an even smaller magnitude than typing an order form. Since each library in the proposed system may have a different order form (assuming the new system is an acquisition/collection development program), some agreement must be reached on a system-wide format. If the agreed-upon form is unique to member libraries, there will be no real basis for determining the time and cost to prepare it. Experiments, trial runs, etc., are never the same as operational times and costs. A good "guestimate" is all that such efforts can produce, unless data on the use of the format is available from another system. (What systems use *that* format? Who knows?)

Experience barriers take on great significance when it is a matter of planning the "nitty-gritty" for a cooperative. The order form typing example is just one small example of the problems related to experience that face planners. Great depth in planning is required, and while the body of useful published data is increasing, it still is very much a matter of local data collecting.

Traditional-Historical Factors

Variations in order forms are also an example of traditional and historical barriers. Incompatibility of procedures is a fact that must be faced at some point by all cooperatives. "We have *always* used *this* procedure, and *it* works" is a statement heard over and over again in cooperative planning meetings. Some of these problems—as in the order form example—are reasonably easy to overcome if everyone is really interested in forming a system. Other historical and traditional operational problems are not so easy to resolve, for example, differences in classification systems being used.

Examples of other types of historical and traditional barriers that must be overcome are institutional competition, special rules, funding problems, and inability to satisfy local needs. The last problem is and always will be with us. No matter how much money would be available to develop local service, some imaginative patron or staff member would think of a new need or service that would use up all available money. A variation on both Maslow's "wants hierarchy" and one of Parkinson's laws is that organizations, like people, always have wants slightly in excess of their ability to satisfy those wants. If this local need combines with the desire for local self-sufficiency, librarians will never be able to agree to any cooperative effort—unless we think we are going to get something for nothing, an impossibility in the real world.

Related to the inability to ever completely satisfy local needs with local resources are the institutional competition and funding problems. At the local level, often public, school, and community college libraries all compete for the same local tax money. Each type of library may have a certain legal minimum due it, but beyond the minimum, the situation is very competitive. In some manner, though, the community will establish a maximum total amount that it is willing to devote to library services. If allocations are not made by means of formulas, weighting systems, etc., the total will be determined through the politics of the budgetary process. Furthermore, each type of library will be counting as patrons a large number of persons who also use other types of libraries—a duplication of patron count. Collections, in fact, reflect the dual role of patrons. Educational libraries have "recreational" materials and recreational (public) libraries have "educational" materials. The "competition" for the same patron, resulting in a fairly high duplication of materials in some cases, results in significant funding problems. Attempts to extract additional monies for cooperative activities from local funding authorities are not likely to be successful unless those authorities see the request as a means to reduce or stabilize the level of local funding.

Finally, there are problems of rules and regulations to be overcome—usually a matter of who may use a certain type of library. As long as the cooperative membership is composed of one type of library, there are few problems of this kind. When several different types of libraries join a system, there may be significant problems. Archival and special collection libraries may have a number of restrictions on who may use the material, just as some professional libraries (e.g., law and medicine) do. Normally, this is not a major barrier, just time-consuming to make certain that all the rules and regulations are taken into account and adjusted.

Physical and Geographical Factors

Physical and geographical barriers are often such that they keep a cooperative from being formed or some libraries from being able to join a system. One example is lack of physical space in a library. Local patrons use the collection and reader stations to the maximum, so additional patrons would mean long waits or no service. Small archival libraries (special libraries where the materials must be used in the library) are often faced with this problem, without ever considering joining a cooperative. Even large physical facilities are often confronted with this problem— especially academic libraries; however, the opportunity to borrow materials provides a viable alternative if the library wants to solve the problem of lack of reader stations. Insufficient storage space for materials unfortunately is not as easy to resolve. Cooperative collection development proposals *may* reduce the need for storage space in some subject areas in the future, but they will add demands in other areas. Normally, such proposals *do not* address the issue of older materials already in a collection. If there is to be a new central storage unit for low use items from and for member libraries (for example, the Center for Research Libraries), then some space may be gained, but it usually does not solve the long-term space problem.

Physical distance between member libraries may mean that the delay in service will be too great for patron acceptance. Use of telecommunications continually make this less and less of a problem. Yet, as is so often the case, solving one problem creates a different one, and here the new problem is copyright. One of the major roadblocks to passage of the new U.S. copyright law was the new technology and efforts to establish resource sharing networks. What impact would such networks have on the property rights of the copyright holder? This is uncertain. Until the new law is tested in the courts, no one can determine precisely what influence it will have on efforts toward cooperative collection development.

One way to get around the use of telecommunications is to give patrons reciprocal borrowing rights. That is, a person holding a valid borrower's card from any member library is allowed to use it in any other library in the system. As long as the distances between the member libraries are not too great, this is a viable solution, up to a point. The major flaw is the general lack of union catalogs. How do you know if library X has the item you want without a visit? Union catalogs are one answer but they are very expensive to develop and maintain; the majority of libraries do not have a comprehensive, up to date union catalog—not even the public catalog and shelf list. (Most libraries do not include information on the latest issue of a periodical received in the catalog, and they seldom attempt to show broken runs of serial holdings in the public catalogs. Furthermore, many do not include government documents in the catalog unless they are part of the general classified collection. Many libraries maintain separate catalogs of audio visual materials. The list of exceptions is very long. The point is that in many libraries, a patron may have to consult several different catalogs in order to determine the total local resources on a single topic. Thus the problem of creating a systemwide, comprehensive union list is monumental.)

An alternative to a systemwide list is, of course, the telephone. As ITT is fond of saying, "don't be in doubt—phone ahead." Indeed this is a possibility; however, if there is a high use of reciprocal borrowing privilege, the level of telephone "reference" service may reach rather alarming proportions. Will member libraries be able to afford a separate "do you have?" telephone line and the personnel to handle the calls? At first, this may seem like a small matter—a cost that the local library can absorb. Perhaps and perhaps not; it appears to be more of the something-for-nothing concept. Copenhagen Public Library is not the first, only, or last library to find that reciprocal borrowing may carry a high price tag over the long run.

Two other barriers are differences in collection size and patron population. Libraries with large collections legitimately become worried about too great a pressure on their collection—becoming a net lender rather than having a balance between lending and borrowing. Research libraries in the United States are experiencing this problem with their interlibrary loan work. When this danger exists for a proposed system, planners must include a mechanism to balance off the contributions for the members. Balance is always a problem, but for resource sharing cooperatives, it is particularly hard to overcome. Size alone is not an adequate measure of a library's resources. Naturally, the size of user population enters into consideration. Of greater importance, though, is the composition of the entire group and their needs. For example, a medium-sized public library *may* not place as much pressure on a large academic library as might a small academic library. Thus, collection size, patron needs, and patron population combine to create a complex situation for developing a system that will balance each library's contribution and use.

Legal and Administrative Factors

Legal and administrative barriers can be both complex and unique to specific situations. One set of legal barriers can be illustrated by referring back to Figure 15 (page 258). Each circle represents a different level of government and political concern. To develop the least wasteful library system combining all four major types (wasteful in the sense of duplicating resources and services unnecessarily), we must cross a number of jurisdictional lines. We then are confronted with questions like: how are funds to be raised by multi-jurisdictional systems? how will the funds actually raised be controlled? will there be a lessening of local control? is it legal to raise money in one jurisdiction and spend it in another? what are the politics of securing enabling legislation for such a system? Attempts to start at the local level and work upward in the hierarchy of government sometimes succeed because the persons involved are more familiar with local needs as related to the political system. A major disadvantage of this approach is that it is very slow, and often a wide variety of systems are established that are not compatible with one another.

Starting at the national level usually reduces the number of jurisdictional questions and results in better funding. Although the national approach has some major advantages, it also has significant disadvantages. One of the most frequent responses to a national plan on the part of local authorities is, "what do the bureaucrats in the capital know about *our* problems? No one on the planning committee ever asks us what *we* need, much less comes to see our program." Suspicion is the keyword here, followed by possessiveness ("What is the real motive for this project, and why should we give up local control?"). These problems, of course, are not just library problems; they are part of the political process. Another problem is that the many national plans, in order to allow for local variation, are not developed in enough detail so as to make them functional. Unfortunately, reporting results to national authorities often consumes more administrative time than is saved by cooperative activities. Finally, regional jealousies and pure desire for political gain may dominate the entire process, thus negating most of the advantages that might have been achieved for library patrons across the country.

Other problems may be national and/or regional accreditation needs. Accreditation standards may present a few barriers for educational institutions, but by and large, these are minor and may pose no future problem as the economic necessity for cooperation is not only recognized but accepted.

Another problem is the need to maintain two systems for a period of time. Dual operations are always a part of the start-up procedure in any cooperative system, but generally, the two systems are simultaneously operative for only a short period of time. However, with tight operating budgets, even two or three months of dual operation may create a real economic burden for some members. All that can be done is to keep the transition period as short as possible. Finally, complex systems require extensive training of staff and thus some loss of normal productivity will occur while the staff is in training sessions. A complex system usually also means that more mistakes will be made, and longer transition periods will be observed.

Over the last few pages, we have looked at several kinds of barriers to establishing a cooperative system. By implication, the message has been that cooperatives are difficult to establish and cooperative collection development (resource sharing) systems are among the most difficult. Despite what may seem to be a litany of problems, *cooperatives can be established* and are becoming more and more a matter of economic necessity. The situation is summed up in the following quotations:

> The more a cooperative affects a library's local policies and procedures, the less the likelihood that the cooperative will be viewed with enthusiasm. —Richard Dougherty[4]

> ———

> The fact is, libraries can no longer afford to maintain the collections, staffs and service levels that libraries and users have come to expect in the last two decades.... We can rail against it and search for scapegoats, but it would be better if we come to terms with this painful reality and began to reduce our excessive commitments and expectations to match our declining resources.

> The importance of resource sharing mechanisms and particularly the most cost effective ones—the centralized libraries, libraries such as the Center for Research Libraries and the British Lending Division—is not so much that they will save us funds we can reallocate to other purposes, but that they will permit us to continue to have access to a large university or materials we can no longer afford, spending our diminishing funds on the materials we need and use most. —Richard DeGennaro[5]

WHAT TO AVOID

The following five points about what will cause a cooperative to fail are drawn from the literature on the topic. Avoid these pitfalls and the system will have a good chance of succeeding:

1) do not think of the cooperative as supplementary and something you can do without;

2) planners should spend time working out operational details;

3) the system *should* cause major operational changes in the member libraries;

4) do not think of the system as something-for-nothing for your library;

5) do have the cooperative's funding and operation handled by an independent agency.

An indication of the difficulties associated with developing resource sharing is found in an article by Maryann Dugan, "Library Network Analysis and Planning."[6] A group of 109 head librarians was asked to indicate what type of cooperative activities would be appropriate to develop. Ten major activities were identified; the librarians then ranked these in terms of their desirability and the need to develop cooperatives. Their ranking is indicative of the attitudes we have been discussing:

1)   union list;

2)   interlibrary loan;

3)   facsimile transmission;

4)   networking;

5)   reference service;

6)   regional centers;

7)   central facility;

8)   type of library centers;

9)   central processing;

10) collection management.

In one sense, resource sharing was both first and last; union lists, interlibrary loan, and facsimile transmission are forms of resource sharing. To be most useful, both in terms of cost-effectiveness and gaining access to the full universe of knowledge, collection management must also occur. Without cooperative collection management, the situation is the same as it has always been. Certainly, more union lists are needed, but if everyone is buying basically the same materials, what is really gained? We have used interlibrary loan for years as well as variations of facsimile transmission. The message would seem to be cooperate, so long as it does have an impact on local autonomy and self-sufficiency.

SUMMARY

Programs such as the Farmington Plan and the Latin American Cooperative Acquisition Plan (LACAP) are no longer operative. Both were highly complex, long-term efforts to share the problems of collection development and acquisitions (the bibliography at the end of this chapter lists works describing them in detail).

The Farmington Plan was an attempt by major American research libraries to have one copy of any currently published research work available somewhere within the United States. LACAP was a commercial effort to share the cost of acquiring materials from Latin America. Why did they cease to function? A number of persons have attempted to answer this question, but the answer is complex and to some extent impossible to determine. Certainly, both plans were affected by changes in user needs at member institutions. Another common factor was inflation. As the cost of materials climbed and book budgets remained almost stationary, it was harder for members to justify buying "marginal" items (marginal in terms of local user needs).

Acquisition responsibility in the Farmington Plan was originally assigned on the basis of institutional interests. In twenty years, those interests changed, but the goal of "one copy" remained. Who would take on the responsibility for acquisition after the shift in interest? Another problem was that some areas were not a major area of concern at any one institution. Sufficient *national* interest existed to warrant coverage, but deciding which institution should have the responsibility for buying such materials was a constant problem. The same type of problem will arise at the local level. A careful study of why the Farmington Plan and LACAP failed may provide invaluable data for future cooperative ventures. In the final analysis, both plans may have failed as a result of not avoiding the pitfalls listed earlier. The Scandia Plan in the Nordic countries has experienced similar problems. This plan has never achieved the same level of activity as the Farmington Plan, primarily due to problems of assigning responsibilities and changing needs.

Two of the most successful cooperative programs are the Center for Research Libraries (CRL), in the United States, and the British National Lending Division (BLD). One reason for their success is that they operate as independent agencies. Their purpose is to serve a diverse group of member libraries; in essence, they have *no local constituency* to serve. Another major difference for CRL is that there is no attempt to acquire high use items—in fact, just the reverse is true. With no local patron population to be served, the fiscal resources can be directed toward low-demand items of national interest. If more centers like CRL and BLD are established, the problems of collection development would be reduced—at the local level.

New on-line processing systems for technical services are coming into existence (e.g., OCLC, BALLOTS, etc.). Although not primarily intended as a means of resource sharing, a system that provides a union list function, as most of these do, offers the selector the information as to what library, if any, already owns a title. Some libraries use such systems for interlibrary loan work. In time, these or some variation will become an essential element in a cooperative system.

The day that every library is "on-line" with that great library computer in the sky is a few years away . . . if indeed it ever comes to pass. We must not let the promises of technological salvation lure us from working on less grand, but no less important, cooperative programs now. As DeGennaro said, "it would be better if we came to terms with this painful reality and began to reduce our excessive commitments and expectations to match our declining resources."[7]

NOTES

[1] R. M. Dougherty, "Library Cooperation: A Case of Hanging Together or Hanging Separately," *Catholic Library World* 46 (March 1975): 324-27.

[2] M. P. Sinclair, "A Typology of Library Cooperatives," *Special Libraries* 64 (April 1973): 181-86.

[3] B. Markoe, "The Cooperative Information Network," *California Librarian* 35 (July 1974): 16-21.

[4] Dougherty, p. 326.

[5] R. DeGennaro, "Copyright, Resource Sharing and Hard Times: A View from the Field," *American Libraries* 8 (Sept. 1977): 435.

[6] M. Dugan, "Library Network Analysis and Planning," *Journal of Library Automation* 2 (1969): 157-75.

[7] DeGennaro, p. 435.

BIBLIOGRAPHY

Cooperation and Generalization

California Department of Finance. Audits Division. Program Review Branch. *Library Cooperation: A Systems Approach to Interinstitutional Resource Utilization: Report and Recommendations.* Sacramento: The Department, 1973.

Center for Research Libraries. *Handbook.* Chicago: The Center, 1973.

Caudra, C. A., and R. J. Patrick. "Survey of Academic Library Consortia in the U.S." *College and Research Libraries* 33 (July 1972): 271-83.

DeGennaro, R. "Austerity, Technology and Resource Sharing: Research Libraries Face the Future." *Library Journal* 100 (May 15, 1975): 917-23.

DeGennaro, R. "Copyright, Resource Sharing and Hard Times: A View from the Field." *American Libraries* 8 (Sept. 1977): 430-35.

Dougherty, R. M. "Library Cooperation: A Case of Hanging Together or Hanging Separately." *Catholic Library World* 46 (March 1975): 324-27.

Dugan, M. "Library Network Analysis and Planning." *Journal of Library Automation* 2 (1969): 157-75.

Epstein, A. H., et al. "On Network. Cooperative Planning with Several Libraries." In American Society for Information Science. Conference, 1971, Denver: *Proceedings: Communication for Decision-Makers.* Vol. 8. Westport, CT: Greenwood Press, 1971.

Esterquest, R. T. "Aspects of Library Cooperation." *College and Research Libraries* 19 (May 1958): 203-208.

Evans, G. E. "The California State Department of Finance Report—Analysis of Library Cooperation: A Systems Approach to Intersegmental Resource Utilization." *California Librarian* 34 (April 1973): 5-15.

Hendricks, D. D. *A Report on Library Networks.* Urbana: University of Illinois, Graduate School of Library Science, 1973. (Occasional Papers, no. 108).

Kaplan, L. "Midwest Inter-Library Center, 1949-1964." *Journal of Library History* 10 (Oct. 1975): 291-310.

Kent, A., ed. *Resource Sharing in Libraries: Why, How, When, Next Action Steps.* New York: Dekker, 1974. (Books in Library and Information Science, v. 8).

Markoe, B. "The Cooperative Information Network." *California Librarian* 35 (July 1977): 226-35.

Research Libraries Group. [Proposals for Cooperation among the Libraries of Columbia, Harvard, and Yale Universities, and the New York Public Library.] "The Rosenthal Report for the Research Libraries Group." *Harvard Library Bulletin* 22 (July 1974): 356.

Reynolds, M. M., ed. *Reader in Library Cooperation.* New York: NCR Microcard Editions, 1972.

Sinclair, M. P. "A Typology of Library Cooperation." *Special Libraries* 64 (April 1973): 181-86.

U.S. National Commission on Libraries and Information Science. *Toward a National Program for Library and Information Sciences: Goals for Action.* Washington: Science Associates International, 1975.

Williams, G. R. "Center for Research Libraries: Its New Organization and Programs." *Library Quarterly* 90 (July 1965): 2947-51.

Cooperative and Centralized Processing

Adcock, E. "Comparison of the Operations of Various Processing Centers." *Library Resources and Technical Services* 8 (Winter 1964): 63-70.

American Library Association. Resources and Technical Services Division. Regional Processing Committee. "Guidelines for Centralized Technical Services." *Library Resources and Technical Services* 10 (Spring 1966): 233-40.

American Library Association. Technical Services Coordinating Routines Survey Committee. *Policies and Programs Designed to Improve Cooperation and Coordination among Technical Service Operating Units.* By R. M. Dougherty, et al. Urbana: University of Illinois, Graduate School of Library Science, 1967. (Occasional Papers, no. 86).

Bendix, D. "Regional Processing for Public Libraries, a Survey." *Library Resources and Technical Services* 2 (Summer 1958): 155-70.

Bundy, M. L. "Behind Central Processing." *Library Journal* 88 (Oct. 1, 1963): 3539-43.

Colorado Academic Libraries Book Processing Center. *Centralized Processing for Academic Libraries: The Final Report (Phase III, Jan. 1-June 30, 1969) of* the Colorado Academic Libraries Book Processing Center; The First Six Months of Operation. By R. M. Dougherty and J. M. Maier. Metuchen, NJ: Scarecrow, 1971.

"Colorado Academic Libraries Book Processing Center." *Mountain-Plains Library Quarterly* 14 (Spring 1969): 32.

Dougherty, R. M. "The Colorado Academic Libraries Book Processing Center Study." *Library Resources and Technical Services* 13 (Winter 1969): 115-41.

Flannery, A. "Processing En Masse." *California School Libraries* 36 (March 1965): 29-32.

Follett, R. J. R. "A Publisher Looks at Pre-Processing." *California School Libraries* 36 (March 1965): 5-8.

Hanley, M. *Centralized Processing, Recent Trends and Current Status: A Review and Syntheses of the Literature.* Urbana: University of Illinois, Graduate School of Library Science, 1964. (Occasional Papers, no. 1).

Hendricks, D. D. "Centralized Processing: A Directory of Centers." *Library Resources and Technical Services* 14 (Summer 1970): 355-89.

Inforonics, Inc. *Systems Design and Pilot Operation of a Regional Center for Technical Processing for the Libraries of the New England State Universities, NELINET, New England Library Information Network: Progress Report, July 1, 1967-March 30, 1968.* Prepared by J. E. Agenbroad, et al. Cambridge, MA: Inforonics, 1968.

Kurtz, H. G. "Centralized Processing—Diversified without Sophisticated Machines. Rhode Island Sets Up a Processing Unit to Serve All Types of Libraries in the State." *Library Journal* 95 (May 15, 1970): 1807-1812.

Leonard, L. E. "Colorado Academic Libraries Book Processing Center: A Feasibility Study." *College and Research Libraries* 29 (Sept. 1968): 393-99.

Leonard, L. E. *Colorado Academic Libraries Book Processing Center. Final Report, Phase I and Phase II.* Boulder: University of Colorado Libraries, 1968.

Leonard, L. E. "The Colorado Academic Libraries Book Processing Center Project Time Study Methodology." *Library Resources and Technical Services* 13 (Winter 1969): 116-27.

Leonard, L. E. *Cooperative and Centralized Cataloging and Processing: A Bibliography 1850-1967.* Urbana: University of Illinois, Graduate School of Library Service, 1968. (Occasional Papers, no. 93).

Leonard, L. E., J. M. Maier, and R. M. Dougherty. *Centralized Book Processing: A Feasibility Study Based on Colorado Academic Libraries.* Metuchen, NJ: Scarecrow, 1969.

Lively, G. M. "The Creative Elementary School Library and Centralized Processing." *Wilson Library Bulletin* 36 (May 1962): 753-57.

Nelson Associates, Inc. *Centralized Processing for the Public Libraries of New York State: A Survey.* New York: Nelson Associates, 1966.

Renfro, K. R. "Nebraska Centralized Processing." *Mountain-Plains Library Quarterly* 13 (Winter 1969): 4-6.

Summers, F. W. "State Libraries and Centralized Processing." *Library Resources and Technical Services* 14 (Spring 1970): 269-78.

Vann, S. K. "Cooperation between Different Types of Libraries in Technical Services." In Allerton Park Institute, 15th, 1968. *Cooperation between Types of Libraries: The Beginnings of a State Plan for Library Services in Illinois.* G. E. Thomassen, ed. Urbana: University of Illinois, Graduate School of Library Science, 1969. pp. 12-35.

Vincent, D. E. "New England State University Libraries Regional Processing Center." *American Library Association Bulletin* 61 (June 1967): 672-73.

Cooperative Acquisitions

"Clearinghouse for Costly Materials." *American Libraries* 4 (Dec. 1973): 661.

Cronin, J. W. "Library of Congress National Program for Acquisitions and Cataloguing." *Libri* 16 (1966): 113-17.

Downs, R. B. "Cooperative Planning in Acquisitions." *Southeastern Librarian* 8 (Fall 1956): 110-15.

Edelman, H. "Death of the Farmington Plan." *Library Journal* 98 (April 15, 1973): 1251-53.

Edelman, H. *Shared Acquisitions and Retention System (SHARES) for the New York Metropolitan Area: A Proposal for Cooperation among Metro Libraries.* New York: Metro, 1969.

El-Erian, T. S. "Public Law 480 Program in American Libraries." D.L.S. dissertation, Columbia University, School of Library Science, 1972.

Esterquest, R. T., ed. "Building Library Resources through Cooperation." *Library Trends* 6 (Jan. 1958): 257-383.

Farmington Plan Newsletter. Washington: Association of Research Libraries, No. 1- . March 1949- . [Title change: *Foreign Acquisitions Newsletter.* Washington: ARL.]

Goderich, M. "Cooperative Acquisitions: The Experience of General Libraries and Prospects for Law Libraries." *Law Library Journal* 63 (Fall 1970): 57-61.

Hamer, E. E. "Conferences in Europe on Shared Cataloging and Acquisition Program." *Library of Congress Information Bulletin* 25 (Nov. 17, 1966): 721-22.

Heard, J. N. "Suggested Procedures for Sharing Acquisitions in Academic Libraries." *Louisiana Library Association Bulletin* 35 (Spring 1972): 17-21.

Hendricks, D. D. "Interuniversity Council Cooperative Acquisitions of Journals." *Texas Library Journal* 47 (Nov. 1971): 269-70.

The Impact of the Public Law 480 Program on Overseas Acquisitions by American Libraries [proceedings of a conference]. W. L. Williamson, ed. Madison: University of Wisconsin Library School, 1967.

Ishimoto, C. F. "The National Program for Acquisition and Cataloging: Its Impact on University Libraries." *College and Research Libraries* 34 (March 1973): 126-36.

Jones, C. L. "Cooperative Serial Acquisition Program: Thoughts on a Response to Mounting Fiscal Pressures." *Medical Library Association Bulletin* 62 (April 1974): 120-23.

McNiff, P. J. "Farmington Plan and the Foreign Acquisitions Programmes of American Research Libraries." In Ligue des Bibliothèques Européennes de Recherche [LIBER]. *Acquisitions from the Third World.* D. A. Clarke, ed. London: Mansell, 1975.

Metcalf, K. D. "The Farmington Plan." In Reynolds, M. M., ed. *Reader in Library Cooperation.* New York: NCR Microcard Editions, 1972.

Metcalf, K. D., and E. E. Williams. "Proposal for a Division of Responsibility among American Libraries in the Acquisition and Recording of Library Materials." *College and Research Libraries* 5 (March 1944): 105-109.

Phinazee, A. H., and C. L. Jordan. "Centralized Library Purchasing and Technical Processing for Six Colleges in Alabama and Mississippi: A Report." *College and Research Libraries* 30 (July 1969): 369-70.

"Public Law 480 Program." *Library of Congress Information Bulletin* 24 (Aug. 9, 1965): 425; 22 (Dec. 30, 1963): 685.

Savary, M. J. *The Latin American Cooperative Acquisitions Program: An Imaginative Venture.* New York: Hafner Publishing Co., 1968.

Schmidt, T. M. "Cooperative Acquisitions." *Idaho Librarian* 26 (Jan. 1974): 5-9.

Skipper, J. E. "National Planning for Resource Development." *Library Trends* 15 (Oct. 1966): 321-34.

Stevens, N. D., ed. "The National Program for Acquisitions and Cataloging: A Progress Report on Developments under the Title II-C of the Higher Education Act of 1965." *Library Resources and Technical Services* 12 (Winter 1968): 17-29.

Stevens, R. D. "Library of Congress Public Law 480 Programs." *Library Resources and Technical Services* 7 (Spring 1963): 176-88.

Vosper, R. G. "Cooperation a l'Échelon National Pour la Selection et l'Acquisition des Livres Courants Éntrangers; Une Experience Recente des Bibliothèques de Recherche aux États-Unis." *Bulletin des Bibliothéques de France* 7 (Sept. 1962): 461-74. [Title translated: Cooperation at the National Level for the Selection and Acquisition of Current Foreign Books: A Recent Experience in the United States Research Libraries.]

Vosper, R. G. *Farmington Plan Survey: Final Report Presented at the Midwinter Annual Meeting of ARL, Chicago, January 26, 1959.* Chicago: Association of Research Libraries, 1959.

Vosper, R. G. *Farmington Plan Survey: A Summary of the Separate Studies of 1957-1961.* Urbana: University of Illinois, Graduate School of Library Science, 1965. (Occasional Papers, no. 77).

Vosper, R. G. "International Book Procurement; or Farmington Extended." *College and Research Libraries* 21 (March 1960): 117-24.

Welsh, W. J. "National Program for Acquisitions and Cataloging." In *Proceedings of the Canadian Library Association, 24th Annual Conference, St. John's, Newfoundland (June 7-13, 1969).* Ottawa: Canadian Library Association, 1970.

Welsh, W. J. "The Processing Department of the Library of Congress in 1968." *Library Resources and Technical Services* 13 (Spring 1969): 175-97.

Welsh, W. J. "The Processing Department of the Library of Congress in 1969." *Library Resources and Technical Services* 14 (Spring 1970): 236-57.

Williams, E. E. *Farmington Plan Handbook.* Rev. to 1961; abridged. Ithaca, NY: Association of Research Libraries, 1961.

Chapter 12

COPYRIGHT

IS COPYRIGHT AN ISSUE IN
COLLECTION DEVELOPMENT?

There is only one answer to the question—yes! Cooperative collection development efforts are dependent upon sharing resources through interlibrary loan or some reciprocal borrowing agreement. How will the new copyright law affect these programs? Only time will give us the definitive answer to that question. What is clear is that libraries will have to modify their copying policies as well as interlibrary loan practices. For example, under the new law, a library may not "borrow" more than six articles per year from any given journal. Should it borrow more than six, it is assumed that the borrowing was in lieu of placing a subscription and thus violates P.L. 94-553. If libraries may not freely exchange books, periodicals, or photocopies of these items, it will be difficult to develop effective cooperative systems. Some of the historical background and current concerns about copyright are explored in this chapter.

Copyright is granted to the creator of a work to protect that person's (or those persons') interest in the work. Originally, copyright was intended to protect against unauthorized printing, publishing, importing, or selling of multiple copies of a work: in essence, protection from the unauthorized mass production and sale of a work. Libraries, on the other hand, are established to disseminate information on a mass, free-of-charge basis. With the development of fast and cheap photocopying machines, a new problem arose—single copies per library patron but a high volume of copying. Actually, the volume of copying became so great that copyright holders felt their rights were being violated.

In the past, copying printed matter for personal use was limited. Word-for-word hand copying of extensive sections of books or complete magazine articles was very uncommon—people took notes. The photographic copy methods in use were expensive and took time as well. Today, quick, relatively inexpensive copy services exist everywhere. All of us have made photocopies of complete journal articles rather than take notes, and many of the articles were from current issues of periodicals that we could have purchased for not much more than the cost of the copied item. We have all done it and, if we thought about it at all, felt that "just one copy isn't going to hurt the author and publisher." Unfortunately, as the number of such single copies mounts, so does the problem.

As far as audio visual materials are concerned, the problem is very acute (in video and audio tapes, for instance). Institutions and individuals who own the hardware to use these materials also have the hardware to copy it, so control of this situation is even more difficult to achieve than book or journal copying. Preview copies help control the situation, as they tend to show wear to the degree that many persons would not want to reproduce a copy. If the preview copy is too worn, however, the buyer may decide that the item lacks technical quality and would, therefore, not buy it.

Library patrons and society in general have certain rights to have access to and use of copyrighted material. Where to draw the line between creators' rights and users' rights is a very complicated problem. An editorial from *Library Journal* sums up the complex of issues involved in library copying:

> Here at *LJ* we are often asked why the magazine has not come out strongly on one side or the other of the copyright issue. We are after all a library magazine. . . . In the case of copyright, however, our library-mindedness is somewhat blunted by the facts of our existence as a publication which is in copyright and is published by an independent, commercial publisher. Not only is copyright protection fundamental to our continued fiscal health, [but] we believe that authors and publishers deserve compensation for their creative work and for the risks taken to package and deliver that creative effort to users of it.
>
> Like any magazine publisher we have winced when it was obvious our rights in our published material have been violated. . . . Yet there is the other side, the flattery in the notion that people want to read what we print, and the gratification that so many share our view of its importance.
>
> So the issue of copyright, particularly of library copying, is deeply complicated for us. . . . We don't believe that "fair use" should be eliminated, but we can't subscribe to the view that wholesale copying should be allowed for "educational purpose."
>
> The answer has to be compromise.[1]

Several points need to be emphasized about copyright. First, the problem of how to handle the rights of creators and users is worldwide—worldwide in several senses. First, each country has to deal with its local copyright problem, and it must also be concerned about international copyright. Second, much of the controversy centers on educational and library copying. Third, copyright has divided authors, publishers, and producers from libraries and schools, with the result that a once very friendly working relationship now has become reserved. It has not yet reached the point of hostility, but unless true compromises are developed, that hostility may develop. Finally, there is concern over what new technological developments may bring—on-line systems are viewed both as threat and promise by all of the parties in the copyright controversy.

Most librarians agree that creator rights should be protected, and even that some creator rights have been violated in and by libraries. Recognition of those facts is tempered by direct daily contact with users and their needs. Often it is a matter of an item not easily available, or it involves articles reporting the results of work carried out using government funds. Since government documents are not copyrighted, many persons feel that reports of work carried out using government funds should be public property.

HISTORICAL BACKGROUND

Producers must be encouraged to risk creating something new and making it available to society, if society is to advance. This is true whether we are concerned with a capitalist or socialist economic system; without adequate incentives, the producer will not produce. For publishers and media producers, copyright is one of the main incentives. In essence, copyright says "Person(s) X owns this creation; if you are not person(s) X, before you make copies of this creation for more than your own personal use, you must get written permission from person(s) X."

England was the first country to legalize creative ownership; in 1710, the English Parliament passed the Statute of Anne, the first copyright bill. This law did two things: 1) it gave Parliamentary recognition to a royal decree of 1556, and 2) it gave legal recognition to a work's author as the ultimate holder of copyright on it. While contemporary copyright laws exist to encourage the creation of new, original works and encourage their wide public distribution, the 1556 decree had a rather less noble purpose: repression of the freedom of religion, in this case, the Protestant Reformation. Censorship rather than free public dissemination of information and thought was the goal. By investing all publishing rights with the Stationers' Company, which represented all major English publishers, the Star Chamber (which controlled the Stationers' Company), hoped to control the flow of information to the English people.

Certainly the Statute of Anne was a notable piece of legislation and did more than merely give legal sanction to censorship. In the two centuries preceding the Statute, many changes had taken place in English society. Although authors and publishers were by 1710 allied in the fight to retain or gain more control over the use of their creations, it was an uneasy alliance—uneasy in the sense that authors were and are the true creators of the copyrighted works. As the creators, authors felt that they should have a greater share and say in the way in which their works were distributed and the profits divided. Prior to 1710, all rights resided with the publisher. With the enactment of the Statute, authors were granted a fourteen-year monopoly on the publication of their works. An additional fourteen years would be granted at the end of the first period, if the author was still living. Thus, for 28 years the creator of a work could benefit from the publication of that work.

The American colonies developed a copyright concept similar to the English model. Indeed, the concept was so ingrained in American legal thought that it was incorporated into the Constitution, wherein the U.S. Congress has been delegated the power "to promote the Progress of Science and Useful Arts, by securing for limited Times to Authors and Inventors the exclusive Right to their Respective Writings and Discoveries."[2] Starting in 1790 and ending in 1891, Congress passed legislation granting exclusive rights to American authors and their representatives, but it refused to grant copyright to non-resident foreign authors. Only books, maps, and charts were covered by the original act (even in 1790, the act covered nonbook formats).

In 1831, Congress passed an act extending the copyright term—the new first term was for 28 years, while the second remained at 14 years. Extension of the exclusive right has been of concern in all countries since the start of the nineteenth century. Today, it is still the heart of the matter (how far and for how long does the copyright owner control the use of the item?). By 1870, copyright had been extended to cover art prints, musical compositions, photographs, "works of fine arts," translation rights, and the right to dramatize nondramatic works; performance rights were included for plays and musical compositions by 1897. The Chace Act of 1891 finally granted copyright to non-resident foreign authors, *if* their work, published in English, was *printed* in the United States. In 1909, a totally new copyright act was passed by Congress.

The 1909 Act was in force until January 1, 1978. While the 1909 Act passed through Congress more quickly than the current law, it was a matter of extended debate from 1905 to 1909. As with the 1978 law, several important issues had to be resolved in 1909—the libraries' rights to import books printed in foreign countries and the use of copyrighted music on "mechanical instruments"—phonograph records and piano rolls. After considerable debate, both rights were granted in the 1909 Act. Libraries could import a limited number of copies of a foreign work, and copyright owners were to be compensated for the use of their music in mechanical devices. (The later development of jukeboxes, which was not covered in the 1909 law, has caused many problems. These and similar problems were a major factor in the fifteen year debate over the form of the new law.) Composers were concerned with technological developments in 1909; authors and publishers are still concerned with technological developments in 1978.

Other provisions of the 1909 law (as passed and amended over the years) include: coverage of motion pictures; the owner of a nondramatic literary work controlling public "renditions" of the work *for profit* and the making of transcriptions or sound recordings of the work; foreign authors being given full copyright protection so that the United States could join the Universal Copyright Convention (in 1954); coverage of all sound recordings; two copyright terms of 28 years each, with a renewal requirement for the second term; all works being required to carry a notice of copyright. Several of these provisions have created barriers for American and foreign producers, and they have made it difficult also for the United States to be an effective member of a worldwide copyright program. The three major stumbling blocks have been the term of protection, the renewal requirements, and the manufacturing clause.

At the international level, there have been two important copyright conventions, Berne (1886) and Universal (1952). Until the Berne Convention was signed in 1886, international copyright was in a chaotic state with reciprocity only on the basis of bilateral treaties. Some countries, like the United States, made no such agreements; and during the nineteenth century, a new form of piracy appeared—literary piracy. Some countries signed the Berne Convention, notable exceptions being the United States and the Soviet Union. Basically, the signatories agreed to give one another the same copyright protection that their own citizens received. A 1908 revision required that this coverage be given automatically—no forms had to be filed by the individual copyright owner. As the convention now stands, the *minimum* term of copyright is the lifetime of the creator plus fifty years; this term of copyright protection holds for translations as well as the original work. Today, more than sixty countries participate in the Convention.

There are several reasons why the United States is not a party to the Berne Convention. Automatic coverage of a work (with no need for forms) means that the U.S. requirement that copyright notice appear on or in the work could not apply. Surprisingly, one of the most vocal and effective groups requesting retention of the notice requirement was librarians, who claimed that it would create problems and a hardship if the notice was not there. (Somehow this has not been a significant problem for libraries or librarians in the sixty signatory countries.) Another problem was the term of coverage: the U.S. only granted a total of 56 years, while the Convention minimum is life plus 50 years. The manufacturing clause was also a problem, because English-language books and periodicals written by foreign authors had to be manufactured in the U.S. to gain American copyright. Two other issues also played a role in keeping the U.S. from signing the Convention: one was the need to give retroactive coverage to foreign works that the U.S. now considers to be in the public domain; the other was the "moral" protection right for the copyright owner. The "moral rights" are concerned with protecting the copyright owner from misuse of the work and prevent "any action in relation to said work which would be prejudicial to the author's honor or reputation."

The United States did sign the Universal Copyright Convention (UCC) in 1954. How is it that the United States is able to sign one convention and not the other? There are two important differences between them. First, UCC does not provide automatic copyright without formalities. The formalities, however, are that a work carrying with the letter "c" in a circle, the name of the owner, and the date of first publication. This satisfies the U.S. notice requirement and presumably makes life easier for American librarians. The second difference is that the term of copyright may be whatever term the country granted its citizens at the time of signing; the only minimum is 25 years for all works other than photographs and applied arts (these last two categories must have at least 10 years protection). There are penalty provisions for a Berne Convention signer's withdrawing from the Berne Convention in order to belong to UCC. To date, forty of the Berne members have also joined UCC.

In 1971, both the Berne Convention and UCC were modified to ensure that certain licensing rights would be granted to developing countries. The revisions provide a mechanism for forcing a copyright owner to grant the use rights to developing countries under certain conditions, in effect, compulsory licensing. Most of the signatories of the two conventions have approved the revisions at this time. Certainly the revisions have helped control what was becoming the second age of international piracy of literary and creative works.

PL 94-553

On January 1, 1978, Public Law 94-553 went into effect. The new American copyright law had been passed on October 19, 1976, after more than fifteen years of work. After years of waiting and arguing, producers and users have a new set of regulations. Unfortunately, the issues that had caused the most disagreement are not really resolved by the law. The three major issues, as far as libraries are concerned, were and still are:

1) what is "fair use"?

2) what types of service may a library offer and not infringe on copyright?

3) what, if any, compensation, should be granted the copyright owner for use of the material, and how can it be paid?

The following highlights of the new copyright law are an extensive adaptation from the American Library Association's *Washington Newsletter*, November 15, 1976, a non-copyright item.[3] They provide an accurate summary of the major points in the law as they *may* affect libraries. Many sections of the law are vague as to their meaning—producers read the law one way, and users (librarians included) read it another. Librarians are particularly concerned about the impact in terms of a) being in the middle between the producers and the ultimate users, b) interlibrary loan practices, and c) cooperative acquisition and collection development programs, especially as intrasystem loans may be affected. At this time, no one is certain how the issues will be resolved. Everyone seems to agree, however, that in the last analysis, the issues will have to be resolved in the courts.

HIGHLIGHTS OF NEW COPYRIGHT LAW

Copyright protection is for the life of the author plus fifty years. The Register of Copyrights is to maintain current records of the death dates of authors of copyrighted works. Effective January 1, 1978, existing copyrights under the old system were extended to span a total of 75 years, automatically in the case of copyrights already renewed for a second term, but only if renewed in the case of first-term copyrights [sec. 302].

The "fair use" doctrine is given statutory recognition for the first time. Traditionally, fair use has been a judicially created limitation on the exclusive rights of the copyright owner, developed by the courts because the 1909 copyright law made no provision for any kind of copying. In the new law, fair use allows copying of a limited amount of material without permission from, or payment to, the copyright owner—where the use is reasonable and not harmful to the rights of the copyright owner [sec. 107].

The new law also extends copyright protection to unpublished works. Instead of the old dual system of protecting works under common law before they are published and under federal law after publication, the new law establishes a single system of statutory protection for all works, whether published or unpublished [sec. 301].

The manufacturing clause eventually is to be repealed. The clause, which grants U.S. copyright to English-language books and periodicals by American authors only if printed in the United States, is to be repealed on July 1, 1982. Canada is exempted from the manufacturing clause as of January 1, 1978 [sec. 601].

Copyright liability is extended to two previously exempted groups—cable television systems and the operators of jukeboxes. Both will be entitled to compulsory licenses [sec. 111, 116].

A five-member Copyright Royalty Tribunal has been established to review royalty rates and to settle disputes among parties entitled to several specified types of statutory royalties in areas not directly affecting libraries [sec. 801].

Suggested Approach to PL 94-553

To determine how the new law may affect current practices in your library, the following, at a minimum, should be considered (numbers refer to sections of the law):

works protected by copyright (sec. 102-105)

exclusive rights of copyright owner (sec. 106)

right of fair use (sec. 107)

library copying authorized (sec. 108)

library copying not authorized by new law (sec. 108[g])

importation of copies by libraries (sec. 602 [a] [3])

Works Protected by Copyright

Copyright protection extends to *literary* works; *musical* works; *dramatic* works; *pantomimes* and *choreographic* works; *pictorial, graphic,* and *sculptural* works; *motion pictures* and *other audio visual* works; and *sound recordings* [sec. 102].

Unpublished works by United States and foreign authors are protected by the new copyright statute, as are published works by United States authors. The *published* works of foreign authors are subject to copyright under certain conditions, including coverage under national treaties such as the Universal Copyright Convention [sec. 104].

U.S. government works are excluded. The new law does not change the basic premise of the prior law that works produced for the U.S. government by its officers and employees are not subject to copyright [sec. 105].

There is *no outright prohibition against copyright in works prepared under government contract or grant.* Both House and Senate Judiciary Committee reports on the copyright bill state:

> There may well be cases where it would be in the public interest to deny copyright in the writings generated by Government research contracts and the like; it can be assumed that, where a Government agency commissions a work for its own use merely as an alternative to having one of its own employees prepare the work, the right to secure a private copyright would be withheld. However, there are almost certainly many other cases where the denial of copyright protection would be unfair or would hamper the production and publication of important works. Where, under the particular circumstances, Congress

or the agency involved finds that the need to have a work freely available outweighs the need of the private author to secure copyright, the problem can be dealt with by specific legislation, agency regulations, or contractual restrictions.[4]

Exclusive Rights of Copyright Owner

Section 106 states the exclusive rights of copyright owners. The following are the five rights recognized: 1) to reproduce the work in copies or phono records, 2) to prepare derivative works (new versions), 3) to distribute copies or phono records publicly, 4) to perform the work publicly, and 5) to display the work publicly. It is important to understand the significant *limitations* to the exclusive rights stated in section 106, which are stated in sections 107 through 118.

The Right of Fair Use—Section 107

It was generally agreed that at least some kinds of copying were fair and should be permitted. The problem lies in defining what constitutes fair use. The law codifies the fair use doctrine in general terms. The statute refers to such purposes as criticism, comment, news reporting, teaching, scholarship, or research; and it specifies four criteria to be considered in determining whether a particular instance of copying or other reproduction is fair. The statutory criteria [sec. 107] are:

1) the purpose and character of the use, including whether such use is of a commercial nature or is for nonprofit educational purposes;

2) the nature of the copyrighted work;

3) the amount and substantiality of the portion used in relation to the copyrighted work as a whole; and

4) the effect of the use upon the potential market for or value of the copyrighted work.

Depending upon the circumstances, fair use might cover making a single copy or making multiple copies. For example, the statute specifically states that multiple copying for classroom use may fall within the category of fair use copying. In deciding whether any particular instance of copying is fair use, one must always consider the statutory fair use criteria.

Two sets of guidelines developed by educators, publishers, and authors provide some indication of what various parties thought at least minimally reasonable. These guidelines do not appear in the statute, but they are included in the House Judiciary Committee's report on the copyright bill. They are *Guidelines for Classroom Copying in Not-for-Profit Educational Institutions* and *Guidelines for Educational Uses of Music.*

Library Copying Authorized by Section 108

In addition to copying that would fall within the fair use section of the statute (discussed above), certain types of library copying that may not be fair use are authorized by sec. 108. In approaching sec. 108, understand that the specific types of library copying authorized in 108 in no way limit the library's fair use right (sec. 108 [f] [4]).

Section 108 (a) contains general conditions and limitations that apply to the various kinds of copying authorized in the rest of the section. These general conditions are as follows:

1) the copy is made without any purpose of direct or indirect commercial advantage;

2) the collections of the library are open to the public *or* available not only to researchers affiliated with the library but also to other persons doing research in a specialized field;

3) the copy includes a notice of copyright.

The status of special libraries in profit-making institutions with respect to the criterion "without direct or indirect commercial advantage" (sec. 108 [a] [1]) is clarified in the House Judiciary Committee's report and in the conference report: the library or archives within the institution must meet the criteria, and generally not the institution itself.

In addition to the general conditions of sec. 108 (a), it is possible that a library's own contractual obligations with a publisher or distributor might limit copying that otherwise would be authorized by sec. 108. By the same token, the limited types of copying authorized by sec. 108 could be augmented if the library and publisher agreed at the time of purchase that additional copying could be done [sec. 108 (f) (4)].

Possible Contractual Limitations on Section 108

Sec. 108 (f) (4) states that the rights of reproduction granted libraries do not override any contractual obligations assumed by the library at the time that it obtained a work for its collections. In view of this provision, librarians must be especially sensitive to the conditions under which they purchase materials; and before executing an agreement that would limit their rights under the copyright law, they should consult with legal counsel.

In general, sec. 108 authorizes, under certain circumstances, the making of a single copy of an entire work and, under other circumstances, the making of a single copy of an article or small excerpt for a library user. Each type of copying is summarized below.

Single Copy of Entire Work

Archival reproduction of an unpublished work: Sec. 108 (b) authorizes making a single copy of an entire unpublished work for purposes of preservation and security, or for deposit for research in another library if the copy is currently in the collections of the first library.

Replacement of damaged or stolen copy: Sec. 108 (c) authorizes making a single copy of an entire work for the purpose of replacing a copy that is damaged, deteriorating, lost, or stolen—if the library has, after a reasonable effort, determined that an unused replacement cannot be obtained at a fair price.

Replacement of out-of-print works: Sec. 108 (e) authorizes making a single copy of an entire work from the library's own collections or from another library if it has been established by a reasonable investigation that a copy cannot be obtained at a fair price. The scope and nature of a reasonable investigation will vary according to the circumstances of the particular situation.

Single Copy of Single Article or Small Excerpt

The library's own collections: Sec. 108 (d) authorizes making a single copy of a single article or a copy of a small part of a copyrighted work in the library's collections, provided that a) the copy becomes the property of the user; b) the library has no notice that the copy would be used for any purpose other than private study, scholarship, or research; and c) the library both displays prominently at the place where copying requests are accepted, and includes on its order form a warning of copyright in accordance with those requirements that the Register of Copyrights has prescribed by regulation.

On November 16, 1977, the *Federal Register* (pages 59264-65) published the new regulation and provided the form for the warning signs that need to be posted by library copy machines:

Figure 17

Official Copyright Warning Sign

NOTICE WARNING CONCERNING COPYRIGHT RESTRICTIONS

The Copyright law of the United States (Title 17, United States Code) governs the making of photocopies or other reproductions of copyrighted material.

Under certain conditions specified in the law, libraries and archives are authorized to furnish a photocopy or other reproduction. One of these specified conditions is that the photocopy or reproduction is not to be "used for any purpose other than private study, scholarship, or research." If a user makes a request for, or later uses, a photocopy or reproduction for purposes in excess of "fair use," that user may be liable for copyright infringement.

Figure 17 (cont'd)

This institution reserves the right to refuse to accept a copying order if, in its judgment, fulfillment of the order would involve violation of copyright law.

Interlibrary loan copying: Sec. 108 (d) authorizes making a single copy of a single article or a copy of a small part of a copyrighted work for purposes of interlibrary loan, provided that all the above conditions regarding a single copy of a single article from the library's own collections are met, and further provided (sec. 108 [g] [2]) that requests for interlibrary loan photocopies are not in such aggregate quantities as to substitute for purchases or subscriptions. The wording of the statute places responsibility for compliance on the library requesting the photocopy, not on the library fulfilling the request. The National Commission on New Technological Uses of Copyrighted Works (CONTU) in consultation with authors, publishers, and librarians has developed guidelines to assist libraries in complying with this provision. It is generally held that more than six articles per year from a journal is a violation of copyright.

Coin-Operated Copying Machines

Sec. 108 (f) (1) and (2) make clear that *neither libraries nor library employees* are liable for the unsupervised use of reproducing equipment located on library premises, provided that the machine displays the notice quoted above to the effect that the making of a copy may be subject to the copyright law. The library patron making the copy is not excused from liability for copyright infringement, however, if his or her copying exceeds fair use, as provided by sec. 107.

Library Copying Not Authorized by Section 108

With the exception of audio visual news programs, sec. 108 does not authorize a library to make multiple copies. Two general types of library copying that are not clearly defined in the statute are specifically not authorized by sec. 108. Stated only in the most general terms, these types of library copying are susceptible of many interpretations.

The first is called "related or concerted reproduction or distribution of multiple copies." This related or concerted copying by libraries is not authorized whether the copies are all made on one occasion or over a period of time, and whether intended for aggregate use by one individual or for separate use by individual members of a group (sec. 108 [g] [1]).

The second type of library copying not authorized by sec. 108 is called "systematic reproduction or distribution of single or multiple copies." Because many librarians feared that this term might be construed to preclude a wide range of interlibrary lending systems, this section of the bill was amended to make clear that whatever may be meant by the term "systematic," copying for purposes of interlibrary loan as specifically authorized by sec. 108 (d), discussed above, would not be prohibited by sec. 108 (g) (2) so long as it does not substitute for purchases or subscriptions. The wording of the statute places responsibility on the library requesting the photocopy from another library for the use of a patron, not on the library fulfilling the request (sec. 108 [g] [2]).

Agencies such as the National Commission on New Technological Uses of Copyrighted Works (CONTU) are now studying the types of library copying not authorized by sec. 108. The National Commission on Libraries and Information Science (NCLIS) funded a study to analyze library photocopying and to conduct a feasibility test of a possible royalty payment mechanism (see page 296). It is important to remember that the new copyright law does not set up any licensing or royalty payment schemes for library copying. It focuses primarily on the kinds of copying that libraries can do without such schemes. It merely states in sec. 108 (g) the two types of library copying that are not authorized by sec. 108.

Importation of Copies by Libraries

In general, the new law prohibits the importation of copies of works without the permission of the copyright holder. There are, however, certain exceptions to this general prohibition, one of which is directly related to libraries. Sec. 602 (a) (3) states that a nonprofit scholarly, educational, or religious organization may import no more than one copy of an audio visual work for archival purposes only, and no more than five copies of any other work "for its library lending or archival purposes, unless the importation of such copies or phonorecords is part of an activity consisting of systematic reproduction or distribution, engaged in by such organization in violation of the provisions of section 108 (g) (2)."

Guidelines in Relation to the Statute

Libraries should consult the statute in order to exercise fully what rights they have under the new copyright law. Look first in the statute *and* the accompanying congressional reports to determine whether a copy can be made by a library or archives in a given situation:

audiovisual news	108 (f) (3)
audiovisual work other than news	107, 108 (h)
book	107, 108
graphic work	107, 108 (h)
importing copies from abroad	602 (a) (3)
instructional transmission	107, 110
motion picture	107, 108 (h)
musical work	107, 108 (h)
periodical article	107, 108
pictorial work	107, 108 (h)
public broadcasting program	107, 118 (d) (3)
sound recording	107, 108, 114

Infringement

One who violates the rights of the copyright owner as defined by sec. 106-118 is a *copyright infringer*. Remedies available to the copyright holder for infringement include damages (actual or statutory, the latter set by statute at from $100 to $50,000), injunction, and recovery of court costs and attorney's fees. There is also criminal infringement (done willfully for commercial advantage or private financial gain), which is subject to $10,000 fine and/or one year imprisonment.

Statutory damages are to be waived entirely for a library or nonprofit educational institution when the institution or one of its employees acting within the scope of his or her employment "believed or had reasonable grounds for believing that his or her use of the copyrighted work was a fair use under sec. 107" (sec. 504 [c] [2]).

Librarians and media specialists have a professional responsibility to learn about the basic library-related provisions of the new copyright law, and to review current practices in the light of such provisions. If current practices seem likely to constitute infringement under the new law, plan now for needed change and be sure that the reason for such change is well understood by library users. Above all, take the time and trouble to master the basic provisions of the statute so that your library will be exercising fully the rights it has under the new copyright law. Anything short of this would be a disservice to library users everywhere.

RECOMMENDED PREPARATION FOR MANDATED FIVE-YEAR REVIEW IN 1982

Although the library community as a whole worked hard to get a flexible copyright law that would neither harm publishers and authors nor curtail the public's access to information, there is no assurance whatever that the new law as finally enacted will achieve such a balance. The law itself requires a review of its own library copying provisions every five years by the Register of Copyrights in consultation with librarians and representatives of authors and publishers. If a five-year review determines that the balance between the rights of copyright owners and the rights of the public is tilting too far in one direction, the Register is directed to make recommendations for legislative or other changes to correct the situation (sec. 108 [i]).

Librarians have a professional responsibility to pay close attention to the law's impact on library service. Is the public's access to information being curtailed by the library's attempted compliance with the new law? If so, to what extent? Is the record-keeping made necessary by the new law burdensome and time-consuming? Is staff time being diverted from service to copyright matters? Are copyright proprietors attempting to further restrict library copying by requiring libraries to sign contracts when materials are purchased? Keep track of the situation in your library.

Without documentation from libraries of all types in all parts of the country as to how the new copyright law is affecting library service, the library community as a whole will be ill-equipped in 1982 to press for changes in the law. We are assured by the statute of a review every five years, but to make such reviews beneficial to library users, librarians everywhere must begin *immediately* to prepare for the first one in 1982.

IMPLICATIONS FOR COLLECTION DEVELOPMENT

Although copyright law deals with unauthorized copying of a protected item, most efforts in cooperative collection development have been predicated on sharing resources—that is, one or two copies of an item being purchased, then being used by each member library as needed. The purpose of most cooperatives is to reduce the number of copies purchased of low use items. From a collection development point of view, if you can make one item do the work of four and use the savings to acquire other items, the patron is better served. The usual means of providing the patron with the low-use material in such arrangements has been photocopies, through either ILL or intrasystem loans. But from the publisher's and author's point of view, there is a loss of three sales in the above example. Thus photocopying, resource sharing, and copyright become intermixed, especially when one adds to this intrasystem (as opposed to intersystem) photocopying of copyrighted items.

As noted, two categories of legal copying are defined in PL 94-553: 1) fair use, and 2) interlibrary loan. Unfortunately, the other major area of library copying is not addressed in the law—intrasystem loan. A recent study by King Research, Inc. indicates that intrasystem copying for loan is somewhat higher than for interlibrary loan. The King study data indicated that in 1976, approximately 54 million copyrighted items were photocopied by library staff members—an aggregate number that is rather impressive, especially when you realize that these are items copied, not pages. When this number is reduced to consider only interlibrary loan copies of serials, 3.8 million copyrighted serial items were photocopied.

Because interlibrary loan copying is recognized in the law, however vague in terminology (sec. 108 [g] [2]), CONTU developed some guidelines that were incorporated into the House-Senate Conference Report of September 29, 1976. These "Guidelines for the Proviso of Subsection 108 (g) (2)" are the only thing we have to work with until the new law is tested in the courts; therefore, the full text is given below:

1.   As used in the proviso of subsection 108(g)(2), the words " . . . such aggregate quantities as to substitute for a subscription to or purchase of such work" shall mean:

    (a) with respect to any given periodical (as opposed to any given issue of a periodical), filled requests of a library or archives (a "requesting entity") within any calendar year for a total of six or more copies of an article or articles published in such periodical within five years prior to the date of the request. These guidelines specifically shall not apply, directly or indirectly, to any request of a requesting entity for a copy or copies of an article or articles published in any issue of a periodical, the publication date of which is more than five years prior to the date when the request is made. These guidelines do not define the meaning, with respect to such a request, of "... such aggregate quantities as to substitute for a subscription to [such periodical]."

(b)   with respect to any other material described in subsection 108(d) (including fiction and poetry), filled requests of a requesting entity within any calendar year for a total of six or more copies or phonorecords of or from any given work (including a collective work) during the entire period when such material shall be protected by copyright.

2.   In the event that a requesting entity—

(a)   shall have in force or shall have entered an order for a subscription to a periodical, or

(b)   has within its collection, or shall have entered an order for, a copy or phonorecord of any other copyrighted work,

material from either category of which it desires to obtain by copy from another library or archives (the "supplying entity"), because the material to be copied is not reasonably available for use by the requesting entity itself, then the fulfillment of such request shall be treated as though the requesting entity made such copy from its own collection. A library or archives may request a copy or phonorecord from a supplying entity only under those circumstances where the requesting entity would have been able, under the other provisions of section 108, to supply such copy from materials in its own collection.

3.   No request for a copy or phonorecord of any material to which these guidelines apply may be fulfilled by the supplying entity unless such request is accompanied by a representation by the requesting entity that the request was made in conformity with these guidelines.

4.   The requesting entity shall maintain records of all requests made by it for copies or phonorecords of any materials to which these guidelines apply and shall maintain records of the fulfillment of such requests, which records shall be retained until the end of the third complete calendar year after the end of the calendar year in which the respective request shall have been made.

5.   As part of the review provided for in subsection 108(i), these guidelines shall be reviewed not later than five years from the effective date of this bill.[5]

The crux of the matter is not libraries' losing the right to offer services of this type but how much royalty, if any, must be paid as a result.

Data from the King study would indicate that, under the CONTU guidelines, a minimum of 500,000 items that were copied for interlibrary loan purposes could be subject to royalty payments. Intrasystem data illustrates an even higher incidence of potential royalty payments (approximately 7 million items). One factor that could reduce the impact of the intralibrary loan data is that a high percentage of the copies were of only one page. Very probably, much of this copying was of tables of contents, which were used in a current awareness program for the library systems. Nevertheless, the volume of "illegal," or at least questionable, copying is high. A major issue to be resolved is how royalties might be collected. To date there is no generally accepted single method for such collections—suggestions for, and methods of, operation range from central clearinghouses to royalty stamps to individual publisher-library pre-purchase agreements.

As the King study concluded: "There are still uncertainties concerning the circumstances in which royalty payments would be legally required. Examples of these uncertainties are the following:

o   The lack of a concrete definition of the universe of publications to be covered by a royalty payment mechanism;

o   The lack of an unambiguous, quantitative definition of systematic photocopying;

o   The lack of an unambiguous definition of the term 'open to the public';

o   The lack of guidelines concerning serials older than five years;

o   The lack of guidelines governing the photocopying of library materials in response to local user and intrasystem loan requests;

o   The lack of a definition of 'library system.'

Until these uncertainties are resolved it will continue to be difficult to assess the impacts of alternative royalty payment mechanisms."[6]

SUMMARY

Without copyright, there would be little incentive for persons to produce creative and informative works. Without users of copyrighted material, the producers would realize little or nothing from their efforts. The two groups need to work together then, or everyone will lose. Perhaps now with a revised law, we can once again become partners rather than antagonists. Whatever does develop will not change the fact that you will not be able to develop a library collection without considering the impact of copyright laws. With that in mind, the following bibliography is offered to allow you to read further on this important topic. Also, the most important sections of the new law, as applied to libraries, are reproduced in the Appendix of this book (pages 321-30).

NOTES

[1] J. Berry, "Copyright: From Debate to Solution," *Library Journal* 100 (Sept. 1, 1975): 1459.

[2] *Constitution of the United States*, Article 1, sec. 88.

[3] American Library Association, "Librarian's Guide to the New Copyright Law," *Washington Newsletter* 28 (Nov. 15, 1976).

[4] U.S. House of Representatives, *Conference Report on General Revision of the Copyright Law 94-1733* (Sept. 29,1976), p. 55.

[5] Ibid., p. 71.

[6] King Research, Inc. *Library Photocopying in the United States* (Washington: National Commission on Libraries and Information Science and Government Printing Office, 1977), p. 199.

BIBLIOGRAPHY

Current American Copyright

Flacks, L. I. "Living in the Gap of Ambiguity: An Attorney's Advice to Librarians on the Copyright Law." *American Libraries* 8 (May 1977): 252-57.

Holley, E. "A Librarian Looks at the New Copyright Law." *American Libraries* 8 (May 1977): 247-51.

Holley, E. "A Look at Copyright: The Past and Likely Future." *Journal of Library and Information Science* 2 (April 1976): 1-15.

Johnston, D. *A Copyright Guide.* New York: R. R. Bowker, 1977.

Johnston, D. *A Copyright Handbook.* New York: R. R. Bowker, 1978.

King Research, Inc. *Library Photocopying in the United States: With Implications for the Development of a Copyright Royalty Payment Mechanism.* Washington: National Commission on Libraries and Information Science and Government Printing Office, 1977.

Martz, D. J. "Manuscripts as Literary Property: Everybody's Problem." *Manuscripts* 29 (Winter 1977): 23-27.

The New Copyright Law: Questions Teachers and Librarians Ask. Washington: National Education Association, 1977.

Ringer, B. "Finding Your Way Around in the New Copyright Law." *Publishers Weekly* 210 (Dec. 13, 1976): 38-41.

Stedman, J. C. "The New Copyright Law: Photocopying for Educational Use." *AAUP Bulletin* 63 (Feb. 1977): 5-15.

Wagner, S. "AAP Spells Out Clearinghouse Plan for Photocopying at CONTU Meeting." *Publishers Weekly* 211 (April 11, 1977): 15-18.

Wagner, S. "Copying and the Copyright Bill, Where the New Revision Stands on 'Fair Use.' " *Publishers Weekly* 210 (Oct. 18, 1976): 28-30.

Wagner, S. "Lawyers Warn Publishers: Copyright Countdown Has Begun." *Publishers Weekly* 211 (March 7, 1977): 38-41.

Wagner, S. "S. 22: Copyrighted 1976, Congress Approves 'Monumental Bill.' " *Publishers Weekly* 210 (Oct. 11, 1976): 22-24.

White, H. S., ed. *The Copyright Dilemma.* Chicago: American Library Association, 1978.

Whitestone, P. *Photocopying in Libraries: The Librarians Speak.* White Plains, NY: Knowledge Industry Publications, 1977.

Historical and International

American Library Association. *Williams & Wilkins Co. v. the U.S.* Chicago: ALA, 1974.

American Library Association [Washington Office]. *Libraries and Copyright: A Summary of the Arguments for Library Photocopying.* Chicago: ALA, 1974.

American Society of Composers, Authors and Publishers. *Copyright Law Symposium, No. 15.* New York: Columbia University Press, 1967.

Berne Convention for the Protection of Literary and Artistic Works, 1948. Berne: International Union for the Protection of Literary Works, 1948.

Brown, A. L. "Summary of Copyright Positions." *Special Libraries* 52 (Nov. 1961): 499-505.

Cambridge Research Institute. *Omnibus Copyright Revision: Comparative Analysis of the Issues.* Washington: American Society for Information Science, 1973.

Cecil, H. "Copyright in the Public Interest." *American Libraries* 5 (July-Aug. 1974): 343.

Clapp, V. W. "Library Photocopying and Copyright: Recent Developments." *Law Library Journal* 55 (1962): 10-15.

Clark, A. J. *The Movement for International Copyright in Nineteenth Century America.* Washington: Catholic University of America Press, 1960.

Clarke, R. F. "The Impact of Photocopying on Scholarly Publishing." *Library Journal* 88 (July 1963): 2625-29.

Gipe, G. A. *Copyright and the Machine Nearer to Dust.* Baltimore, MD: Williams and Wilkins, 1967.

Goldman, A. A. "Copyright and Archival Collections of Sound Recordings." *Library Trends* 21 (July 1972): 147-55.

Hattery, L. H., and G. P. Bush, eds. *Reprography and Copyright Law.* Washington: American Institute of Biological Sciences, 1964.

Intergovernmental Conference on Copyright, Geneva, 1952. *The Law of Copyright under the Universal Convention.* By A. Bogsch. New York: R. R. Bowker, 1964.

Intergovernmental Conference on Copyright, Geneva, 1952. *Universal Copyright Convention, an Analysis and Commentary.* By A. Bogsch. New York: R. R. Bowker, 1958.

Kaplan, B. *An Unhurried View of Copyright.* New York: Columbia University Press, 1967.

Keenan, S., ed. "The Copyright Controversy." *Drexel Library Quarterly* 8 (Oct. 1972): [entire issue].

Kent, A., and H. Lancour, eds. *Copyright: Current Viewpoints on History, Laws, Legislation.* New York: R. R. Bowker, 1972.

Kim, C. "Librarians and Copyright Legislation." *American Libraries* 2 (June 1971): 615-22.

Koepke, J. C. "Implications of the Copyright Law on the Dissemination of Scientific and Technical Information." *Special Libraries* 54 (Nov. 1963): 553-56.

Line, Maurice B., and D. N. Wood. "The Effect of a Large-Scale Photocopying Service on Journal Sales." *Journal of Documentation* 31 (Dec. 1975): 234-45.

Palmour, Vernon E., et al. *A Study of the Characteristics, Costs and Magnitude of Interlibrary Loan in Academic Libraries.* Westport, CT: Greenwood Publishing Company, 1972.

Patterson, L. R. *Copyright in Historical Perspective.* Nashville, TN: Vanderbilt University Press, 1968.

Pilpel, H. F., and M. D. Goldberg. *A Copyright Guide.* 3rd ed. New York: R. R. Bowker, 1966.

Roberts, M. T. "Copyright and Photocopying: An Experiment in Cooperation." *College and Research Libraries* 30 (May 1969): 222-29.

Roberts, M. T. *Copyright: A Selected Bibliography of Periodical Literature Relating to Literary Property in the United States.* Metuchen, NJ: Scarecrow, 1971.

Rogers, J. W. *U.S. National Bibliography and the Copyright Law: An Historical Study.* New York: R. R. Bowker, 1960.

Shaw, R. R. *"Williams and Wilkins v. the U.S.*: A Review of the Commissioner's Report." *American Libraries* 3 (Oct. 1972): 987-99.

U.S. Copyright Office. *Copyright Law Revision.* Washington: U.S. Government Printing Office, 1961-65. Pt. 1: Report of the Register of Copyrights on the General Revision of the U.S. Copyright Law; Pt. 2: Discussion and Comments; Pt. 3: Preliminary Draft for Revised U.S. Copyright Law; Pt. 4: Further Discussions and Comments on Preliminary Draft; Pt. 5: 1964 Revision Bill; Pt. 6: Supplementary Report of the Register of Copyrights and 1965 Revision Bill].

Williams & Wilkins Company, Baltimore [plaintiff]. *The Williams & Wilkins Case: The Williams & Wilkins Company v. the United States.* Comp. by M. G. McCormick. New York: Science Associates, International, 1974.

Chapter 13

CENSORSHIP AND COLLECTION DEVELOPMENT

All of the topics we have discussed so far are complex and some touch upon a wide variety of social issues and concerns. None, however, is more complex than the one we are about to explore. Intellectual freedom, free speech, freedom to read, and open access to information are possible alternative labels for this chapter. One of the standard questions in library school courses in collection development has been some variation of "collection development—book selection or book censorship? Please discuss."

We will *not* directly explore the issues of intellectual freedom and free speech in this chapter. Although these are interesting and important concepts for anyone involved in collection development, their complexity is so great that each one has been the subject of numerous books and articles. (The bibliography at the end of this chapter will provide a starting point for your reading on these topics.) It is important for librarians to gain an understanding of these areas; and certainly those persons directly responsible for collection development must know the laws relating to these issues. However, *anyone* working in a library may rather easily become involved in an intellectual freedom, or as it is more commonly labeled, a censorship controversy.

Many library associations have issued statements and taken public positions on questions of free speech and intellectual freedom. The American Library Association's "Freedom to Read" statement is a classic example. Most of such statements are filled with fine-sounding phrases, and the document(s) look useful when you are in the classroom or in a meeting discussing the theory or philosophy of intellectual freedom. On a day-to-day basis, these statements provide little assistance in collection development or in fighting off the censor.

Intellectual freedom and free speech controversies usually revolve around interpretations of points of law and possible violations of existing law. Therefore, the fight is usually resolved by attorneys and judges rather than in the library by the librarians and the community. We hear about the cases that reach the courts but seldom about day-to-day local problems. Naturally, each of the major cases started off as a local problem between the library and some of the community, but only a few escalate to the courtroom. Most often the problem starts because someone objects to an item already in the collection. Depending upon the nature of the material, the level of emotional involvement, and the prior administrative actions (policies), the issue may be quickly resolved; or it can escalate into the courtroom.

If a controversy is resolved without the aid of attorneys, it will be a result of a) a staff with an excellent background in interpersonal relations; b) a plan of action for handling complaints; c) a lack of strong feelings on the part of the person making the complaint; d) lack of concerted pressure from special interest groups; and e) backup material from library associations. If the individual(s) making a complaint feels very strongly about the matter, very likely the library's attorney will become involved. From that point on, depending on the emotional involvement and financial resources, the issue may go from the lowest court to the highest court in the country before it is resolved.

The local issue usually is, and should be, defined as censorship. Charles Busha has provided an adequate definition of censorship as it concerns the library: "the rejection by a library authority of a book (or other material) which the librarian, the library board or some person (or persons) bringing pressure on them holds to be obscene, dangerously radical, subversive, or too critical of the existing mores."[1] Actually, censorship has been a problem for libraries for just about as long as there have been libraries. Generally speaking, librarians attempt to resist censorship moves ("generally" because we don't know how many times complaints about an item are accepted and acted upon by removing the offensive item because the librarian personally agrees with the person making the complaint). As we will see later in this chapter, evidence suggests a difference between librarians' attitudes toward the concept and the actual act of censorship. Librarians' success in fending off the censors' efforts are varied—notable successes and spectacular failures. Unfortunately, no rules or guidelines will ensure success. You can do some things to forestall many complaints and quickly resolve those that are made; however, there is always a significant chance that the aids will fail and a legal battle will ensue.

CAUSES OF CENSORSHIP

What are the causes or motivations that underlie the actions of a censor? As with all human behavior, the answer is involved and never simple. In every case, psychological elements relate to the need that some persons have to restrain others from expressing ideas or creating works that the would-be censor will find offensive. Political motivations underlie the actions of governments when they attempt to maintain control over the communication systems that may threaten that government or its policies. Frequently, the censor (governments, groups, or an individual) claims to be operating on the basis of protective reasons. Clearly, though, censorship is a paternalistic art toward both adults and children in that it limits their experiences and environment to influences acceptable to the censor. Social factors, which are difficult to differentiate from paternal factors, result from a desire to preserve a wholesome social setting and/or to reduce crime, both of which the censor may see as related to the presence of objectionable material in the library.

Freedom and censorship create a contrast between the need to exercise some restraint so that social institutions intelligently protect citizens' rights and the need to ensure individuals' right to free choice. Some persons feel there should be no controls and would eradicate all laws, rules, and regulations. On the other hand, there are those who feel that everyone else must be tightly controlled. Somewhere between these extremes lies the necessary balance between freedom and restraint. Librarians, as is everyone else, are involved in an almost day-to-day attempt to achieve this balance.

The American Library Association (ALA) adopted a *Library Bill of Rights* (LBR) in 1948. ALA's Office for Intellectual Freedom vigorously promotes and publicizes the concepts contained in that statement. Unfortunately, the *Library Bill of Rights* is *not* a legal document and, therefore, provides no legal protection for libraries or librarians. What legal protection exists is contained in the freedom-of-speech provisions contained in the United States Constitution. With legal protection, every United States citizen has the right to express opinions freely in speaking, writing, or with graphics; to distribute them; and to seek information, from public sources, without unnecessary restraint. The *Library Bill of Rights* outlines the basic freedom-of-access concepts that ALA hopes will guide library public services. It states that persons should be able to read what they wish without intervention from groups or individuals—including librarians. Since its adoption in 1948, the provisions of the *Library Bill of Rights* have helped librarians recommit themselves to a philosophy of service based on the premise that users of libraries should have access to information on all sides of all issues. The text of the document, as amended February 2, 1961, and June 27, 1967, by the ALA Council, is presented below.

Library Bill of Rights

The Council of the American Library Association reaffirms its belief in the following basic policies which should govern the services of all libraries.

I.   As a responsibility of library service, books and other library materials should be chosen for values of interest, information and enlightenment of all people of the community. In no case should library materials be excluded because of the race or nationality or the social, political, or religious views of the authors.

II.   Libraries should provide books and other materials presenting all points of view concerning the problems and issues of our times; no library materials should be proscribed or removed from libraries because of partisan or doctrinal disapproval.

III.   Censorship should be challenged by libraries in the maintenance of their responsibility to provide public information and enlightenment.

IV.   Libraries should cooperate with all persons and groups concerned with resisting abridgment of free expression and free access to ideas.

V.   The rights of an individual to the use of a library should not be denied or abridged because of his age, race, religion, national origins or social or political views.

VI.   As an institution of education for democratic living, the library should welcome the use of its meeting rooms for socially useful and cultural activities and discussion of current public questions. Such meeting places should be available on equal terms to all groups in the community regardless of the beliefs and affiliations of their members, provided that the meeting be open to the public.

The *Library Bill of Rights* is an important guide to professional conduct in terms of intellectual freedom. It is a standard by which day-to-day practices can be gauged against desired professional behavior in the realms of freedom of access to information, of communication, and intellectual activity.

Despite LBR, there is and always will be pressure to limit the type of material put into the library's collection. Occasionally, someone tries to solve the problem by labeling material in the same manner as the U.S. Surgeon General's labels on cigarettes. To date, the efforts to label library materials have been about as effective in stopping persons from reading those materials as labeling cigarettes has been in stopping smoking. The practice usually takes the form of the placing of special marks or designations (stars, letters, bands, etc.) on certain classes of materials. Yet, the practice of labeling is prejudicial and can create a bias.

Labeling practices are generally a defensive method that indicates, in effect, that "these books, films, magazines, recordings, etc., may not meet with full community approval; therefore, if you wish to use them, be warned." Generally, labeling is considered to be contrary to principles of intellectual freedom, since librarians are not expected to establish and designate prohibited materials. Nor is it the librarian's duty to warn readers against such things as obscene language; descriptions of explicit sexual acts; or unorthodox political, religious, moral, and economic theories. If we are preservers and providers rather than censors, we need to bear in mind that most intellectual advances, in all fields, generally involve controversy. A librarian's primary responsibility is to provide access to information for the patron, not to restrict it. Thus, the formal position of ALA has been critical of labeling, and in 1951 the Association adopted an anti-labeling statement, which was last amended on June 25, 1971.

Statement on Labeling

An Interpretation of the Library Bill of Rights

Because labeling violates the spirit of the *Library Bill of Rights* the American Library Association opposes the technique of labeling as a means of predisposing readers against library materials for the following reasons:

1.   Labeling is an attempt to prejudice the reader, and as such it is a censor's tool.

2.   Although some find it easy and even proper, according to their ethics, to establish criteria for judging publications as objectionable, injustice and ignorance rather than justice and enlightenment result from such

practices, and the American Library Association must oppose the establishment of such criteria.

3. Libraries do not advocate the ideas found in their collections. The presence of a magazine or book in a library does not indicate an endorsement of its contents by the library.

4. No one person should take the responsibility of labeling publications. No sizable group of persons would be likely to agree either on the types of material which should be labeled or the sources of information which should be regarded with suspicion. As a practical consideration, a librarian who labels a book or magazine might be sued for libel.

5. If materials are labeled to pacify one group, there is no excuse for refusing to label any item in the library's collection. Because authoritarians tend to suppress ideas and attempt to coerce individuals to conform to a specific ideology, the American Library Association opposes such efforts which aim at closing any path to knowledge.

All of the ALA statements provide you with a philosophical base for resisting censorship. However, in the long run, success or failure will depend upon your personal feelings and attitudes.

You as a librarian will encounter three types of censorship: 1) legal or governmental, 2) individual or group pressure, and 3) self-censorship. As strange as it might at first appear, types 1 and 2 are easier to deal with than type 3. For type 1, you have two basic choices—comply or fight. Fighting to change a law or interpretation of a law is usually time-consuming and expensive, so because of the time and cost, this is seldom a matter of a single librarian or library's fighting to bring about a change. Even in a matter involving a local ordinance, if there is to be a modification, there must be community-wide support. The library staff working alone has little chance of success.

Literary censorship has existed for a long time. The United States has seen an interesting mixture of individual and governmental censorship. Anthony Comstock was one person of strong beliefs and personality whose efforts to control the reading materials of Americans were so vigorous and successful a word was added to the English language—Comstockery. Indeed, Comstock was so vigorous in his efforts that, in 1873, Congress passed a law that attempted to outline a structure of national morality. For almost 75 years, this law went unchallenged, with the U.S. Postal Service designated as the government agency primarily responsible for enforcement at the national level. At the local level, several elements were at work. State and local governments passed similar regulations, and thus local police departments became involved in the control of "vice." Law enforcement agencies also had a lot of help from two citizen groups—the Society for the Suppression of Vice, and the Watch and Ward Society. The Society for the Suppression of Vice was the vehicle that Comstock used to gain support, and show the depth of that support, for his views. A primary activity of the Society was to check on printed materials available to local citizens—whatever the source (bookstores, newsstands, libraries—both public and private). Occasionally, if the Society felt that local law enforcement officials were not moving fast enough, it would take matters into its own hands. Book burnings did take place, and great pressure was applied to anyone who was involved in buying or selling printed material to stock only items deemed moral by the censors. The phrase "banned in Boston" got its start as a result of the Society's activity.

From 1873 until well into the twentieth century, the United States experienced a mixture of all three types of censorship: official censorship because of the 1873 law; group pressure from organized societies concerned with moral standards of their communities; and self-censorship on the part of publishers, booksellers, and librarians. A public or even a private stance by librarians against such censorship was almost unheard of, and workshops and seminars were held to assist librarians to identify "improper" books. Most of the notable librarians of the past are on record somewhere (ALA proceedings, speeches, or writings), as being in favor of this type of collection "development." Arthur Bostwick suggested that it was reasonable that books such as *Man and Superman* should be purchased for the New York Public Library's reference collection (non-circulating), but not be purchased for branch library use.[2]

An interesting situation arose with foreign language titles. Many authors were available in their own language but not in English. Apparently, if you could read French, German, Spanish, Russian, etc., you were reading a moral book but if you read that same work in an English translation, it became immoral. To some extent, the censorship atmosphere caused a few American authors to live abroad and occasionally have a larger foreign readership than that in English-speaking countries (for example, Henry Miller). Librarians were no more vocal in protesting this situation than anyone else in the country at the time.

The period between 1873 and the mid-1950s represents all of the censorship problems you will encounter. From the 1930s to the mid-1950s, the 1873 law was slowly modified through various federal court decisions, including several by the U.S. Supreme Court. Today, we are still operating with that law as a part of the U.S. Code, but it is now so modified as to be a completely different law. Most court cases were between the government and publishers or booksellers, while librarians and their associations occasionally entered the suits as *amici curiae* ("friends" of the court) but very seldom as defendant or plaintiff.

Today, just as in the period of 1873-1950, you will have the most trouble with group- and self-censorship. While no active Society for the Suppression of Vice exists today, librarians are faced with occasional organized pressure groups. What may at first seem to be a simple matter of a person's objecting to one book can become a major confrontation between a library and an organized pressure group. Much depends upon the energy and time that the would-be censor is willing to devote to the issue. Influential persons may be able to organize a group to generate even greater pressure than one person could. You may encounter organized pressure groups based upon local interests and views (often religious or politically oriented), but seldom from a local group with broad national support. If such a group already exists, you will find it extremely difficult to avoid at least an occasional debate (if not all-out battle) over some materials in the collection. Policy statements about controversial materials, ALA "Freedom to Read" documents, etc., will help to slow the process; but they will not stop it. Local groups are particularly hard to resist, as they can have a fairly broad base of community support and their mere existence indicates some active interest in certain problems. Should these concerns be community welfare or moralistic issues, you can expect some problems.

When local pressure groups exist, you may find that you are asking how they will react if you buy an item. Thinking along these lines at least allows you to deal with your worries. The *real* danger in the situation is when that thought is not at the conscious level. At that point, the pressure group will have almost accomplished its purpose—control over the type of material being selected. And they will have accomplished it through self-censorship by the library.

Self-censorship is our greatest problem. We all feel that "I" would never let "that" happen to me, but it is very hard not to have it happen. A few librarians would agree with Walter Brahm's philosophy—retreat and fight another day.[3] He reasons that: censorship falls victim to time; public opinion can only dampen censorship; society's mores cannot be led or changed willfully, and certainly not by libraries and librarians; and libraries are not generally the main battleground of intellectual freedom. Most librarians would take a public stance against this position, *if* it is stated in a theoretical sense and does not directly affect them. When it becomes a real issue and they are personally involved, though, it becomes another matter.

EXAMPLES OF CENSORSHIP

Ramparts and *Evergreen Review*

A few examples of cases and surveys will illustrate the problem. In the late 1960s, two periodicals (*Ramparts* and *Evergreen Review*) caused libraries and librarians to confront the censorship issue head-on. In Los Angeles, the city librarian had to fight a city councilman's efforts to have ER removed from the library.[4] Eventually he was successful, but not until after the current ER issues had been removed from public areas while the problem was being debated. The journal went back on the open shelves after the final decision was reached—a short-term victory for censorship, but in the end, a final victory for freedom.

Not all librarians were so lucky. Richard Rosichan was dismissed as director of the Kingston Area (New York) Public Library because he fought to keep ER despite both library board and John Birch Society pressure to drop it.[5] At the same time, the American Legion was demanding that he remove *Ramparts* because of its "un-Americanism." Groton (Connecticut) Public Library managed to retain its staff, but lost its subscription to ER, after a four-month fight in the community when the library's board of trustees finally ordered that all issues be removed from the library and the subscription cancelled. This was done under the threat of fines and jail sentences for both the library board and staff. Head librarian John Carey issued a statement to the effect that this decision would affect the general acquisition policy.[6] One can only hope that he was wrong.

In between keeping an item on the shelves and its total disappearance is the "compromise" position to which librarians sometimes resort—restricted availability. The Philadelphia Free Library used this approach for ER when pressure began to be applied to have the title removed. The library renewed the subscription for the main building and one regional branch, but the issues were to be kept in closed stack areas and no one under eighteen could examine the title.[7] Emerson Greenaway, director of libraries, said this was done because ER was "important sociologically." Who was the winner here, the censor or the librarian?

The above is only a small sample of the problems that arose with *Evergreen Review* and *Ramparts*, and they are only two of hundreds of periodicals that have been attacked over the years. The list of books that have caused trouble is immense, and the short list at the end of this chapter illustrates the range of titles—indicating that you can never really tell what will cause an uproar.

Some topics are more sensitive than others, and you might expect trouble but not encounter any. However, sex, religion, and politics are always potential problems. Would you buy or recommend the use of Jerry Rubin's *Do It!*; *Portnoy's Complaint*; *Jesus Christ, Superstar*; *The Joy of Sex*; *The Last Temptation of Christ*; or the ALA film, "The Speaker"? If you would, in some communities, you would be safe; in others, you could be unemployed.

Do It!

Rubin's book got a non-tenured teacher fired, a tenured teacher reprimanded, and a department chairperson demoted—all in the same New Jersey county school system.[8] Although in this case it was the teachers who paid the price, the school libraries lost their copies of the book. On the other hand, Mary Cuarato of Philadelphia tried, unsuccessfully, to force the Free Library to remove *Do It!* from its collection.[9]

Portnoy's Complaint

Portnoy's Complaint (or librarians' lament) was and is almost as great a problem. Jamestown Public Library (New York) more or less succeeded in resisting the attempts of the New York State Committee for Responsible Patriotism to have all of the "smut" removed—particularly PC (it was placed on closed stack status buy stayed in the collection).[10] Librarians in Memphis, Tennessee, were less successful in their fight. After several months of attempting to counter charges of wasting tax money on "trash"—these charges were made by the mayor as well as other community spokespersons—the library placed restrictions on the use of *Portnoy's Complaint*.[11] No one under eighteen years of age could read the book. Not too much later the city passed an ordinance defining obscenity for minors and with clauses relating to library materials.

Jesus Christ, Superstar

Rockford High School, Michigan, was the location of a disagreement over music and texts. Materials relating to both the music and scripts for *Jesus Christ, Superstar* were removed entirely from the school system—both the library and the music department—because the musical was "sacrilegious."[12] Generally, you will have less difficulty with music than with other formats you add to the collection. However, at times there has been concern about the lyrics of rock music, especially when the song is about sex and/or drugs. Generally, though, these items come and go in popularity so fast that pressure groups seldom have an opportunity to develop before the song has fallen from favor.

Joy of Sex

Joy of Sex (JOS) is a type of book that you can always expect to cause some problems. The textual material in itself could and does cause some persons discomfort, although the vocal expression of concern will be about the "bad" influence that this book (or ones similar) will have on children. When you add to the text some rather explicit drawings, you have a title almost guaranteed to cause some librarians somewhere lots of trouble. Indeed, it did just that: Naomi Piccolo, the director of the Mount Laurel Public Library, New Jersey, lost her job as a result of a dispute with the library board over the circulation of JOS. Two board members had read the book and found it very objectionable. Although Ms. Piccolo was not fired, she was asked to submit her resignation.[13]

Spencer Public Library (Iowa) also had a problem with *Joy of Sex*. In this instance, the city attorney notified the library board of a number of citizen complaints that had been received about JOS, concerned with the fact that no restrictions were placed upon its circulation. Is restricted circulation a form of censorship? As far as Spencer, Iowa, was concerned, there was a new obscenity law aimed at regulating the availability of "obscene" materials to persons under eighteen, although the law did have a clause exempting educational materials in libraries.[14] A nice touch, but is *Joy of Sex* educational? As far as JOS was concerned the answer was no. What is obscene? Again, we are back to individual values and feelings. Each of us has developed these values over many years, and to some degree, each of us holds a unique world view that results in differences in opinion about such things as obscenity, quality, etc.

The Last Temptation of Christ

A different type of book, Nikos Kazantzakis's *The Last Temptation of Christ*, caused the same problem. Citizen groups were formed—"Citizens Committee for Clean Books"—in the hope that they could force the removal of all copies of the book. Generally libraries were able to resist the pressure.[15] In many respects, this book generated almost as many problems as the political problems of *Ramparts* and *Evergreen Review*. This perhaps reflects society's changing values, because to the best of this author's knowledge, no librarian lost a job because of LTOC, and most of the libraries received sufficient support from trustees and city councils to keep the book on the shelf.

The Last Temptation of Christ illustrates another phenomena with which you will have to deal—delayed but mass reaction. Kazantzakis's book was published in 1960, but many libraries had the title in circulation for three or four years before there was a problem. Once a title receives publicity—pro or con—interest will increase in the item. Thus, when you hear about a title causing problems in another library, you should not be surprised if it causes you similar trouble.

"The Speaker"

To this point, we have been concerned with pressure from outside the library. Unfortunately, we librarians also have some tendency to censor ourselves, and recently we put on what can only be termed an amazing performance. The situation surrounding the film "The Speaker" provides just about every element you are likely to encounter in any censorship case.[16] In order to fully understand all of the paradoxes that this event represents, you must read all of the references provided at the end of this chapter *and* view the film. A few years ago, ALA's Committee on Intellectual Freedom was given funds to have a film produced on the problems of censorship and intellectual freedom. At the June 1977 annual convention, the film was shown to the membership, which resulted in one of the bigger, longer debates in ALA history. Seldom has there been as long or as bitter debate within ALA over an issue that is presumably an article of faith in the profession. Most of the black members of the Association labeled the film racist. Many other members agreed the film was a problem for that or other reasons. An attempt to have ALA's name disassociated from the film failed, but not by much. Is that a move to censor? How does that differ from the definition given at the beginning of this chapter? Does that really differ from a publisher's deciding not to release a title because the work is found not to be in the best interest of the owner of the company?

As with every other problem of this type, we have no objective data on which to base a judgment. Not all blacks or minority persons who view the film see it as racist. Just because one (even large) group claims that an item is this or that, does the claim make it so? Is this really different from the Citizens' Committee for Clean Books' saying *The Last Temptation of Christ* is sacrilegious or the John Birch Society's claiming that *Ramparts* and the *Evergreen Review* are anti-American? One hopes that most librarians will agree with Dorothy Broderick regarding "The Speaker." There was a need to allow librarians across the country decide for themselves: "If they find the film boring, let them not buy it. If they find it racist, let them not buy it. If they feel that using it will stir up trouble in their community—as if they had invited 'the speaker'—let them ignore its existence. If the film is as bad as its opponents claim, it will die the natural death of an inadequate work in the marketplace."[17] If ALA's name had been removed, many persons would have felt that the first step in the suppression of the film would have occurred.

LIBRARIANS AND CENSORSHIP

Realistically, all the situations discussed so far are of the type that you can easily identify and choose to fight or not. Given the foregoing sample of the problems you may encounter, it should not be surprising to find librarians, including yourself, acting in a self-protective manner. How great a problem is this? Several studies have been done on this problem, but we will only explore the findings of two of the more widely known—Fiske's and Busha's.

Marjorie Fiske shook the library profession some years ago when she reported that a high percentage of librarians decided not to buy an item because it *might* cause a problem. Some titles are very likely to cause trouble—e.g., *Joy of Sex*—and are easy to identify. However, if you examine the sample list of titles that have caused trouble, you can see that some items are *not* easy to identify. Once you begin the process of not selecting a title that has the potential for controversy, you will have trouble breaking the habit. Unfortunately, like so many other habits, it is easy to slip into a behavior pattern and not even recognize that we have done so.

Reasons such as "lack of funds," "no demand," or "poor quality" may be true, or they may be just a rationalization for not selecting an item that might make life troublesome. Other excuses, such as "I will buy it when someone asks for it" or "I don't like that author or producer; he/she has never anything worthwhile to say," are even clearer danger signs. Just because you do not like an author or a subject does not mean that you have the right to keep others from having access. This may not be self-protective in the sense of job security, but it may be in terms of your own psyche. In any case, the result is the same—censorship.

One way to raise the level of self-awareness is to periodically check your holdings against various lists of "problem" items. How many do you have? Less than 50 percent might be cause to question what is happening in the selection process. There may be perfectly good reasons why you have so few items, but until you can give better reasons than the above, you cannot pat yourself on the back and say "I am not a censor."

Charles Busha's study examined librarians' attitudes toward censorship and intellectual freedom, which he compared to a standardized score on a test that is "an indirect measure of antidemocratic trends."[18] His concluding sentence is probably a reasonable picture of all librarianship in the United States: "It is evident, as a result of opinion research, that midwestern public librarians did not hesitate to express agreement with cliches of intellectual freedom but that many of them apparently did not feel strong enough as professionals to assert these principles in the face of real or anticipated censorship pressures."[19] Some persons may feel that the ALA debate about "The Speaker" is much the same.

A SAMPLING OF OTHER "PROBLEM" BOOKS

The following list comprises thirty books that have been attacked for a host of reasons. Some may surprise you, others may not:

1. Allen, ed.: *New American Story*
2. Baum: *Wizard of Oz*
3. Burroughs: *The Ticket That Exploded*
4. Catling: *The Experiment*
5. Cremer: *I, Jan Cremer*
6. De Berg: *The Image*
7. Dixon: *Hardy Boys*
8. Durrell: *Tunc*
9. Friedman: *Totempole*
10. Genet: *Miracle of the Rose*
11. Himes: *Pinktoes*
12. Jones: *Go to the Widowmaker*
13. Keene: *Nancy Drew*
14. Killens: *Sippi*

15. Kyle: *Venus Examined*
16. McMurtry: *The Last Picture Show*
17. Reage: *Story of O*
18. Rechy: *City of Night*
19. Richler: *Cocksure*
20. Rimmer: *The Harrad Experiment*
21. Robbins: *The Adventurers*
22. Selby: *Last Exit to Brooklyn*
23. Sterling: *The President's Plane Is Missing*
24. Susann: *Valley of the Dolls*
25. Sutton: *The Exhibitionist*
26. Twain: *Tom Sawyer*
27. Updike: *Couples*
28. Vidal: *Myra Breckinridge*
29. Williams: *Rabbit Wedding*
30. Yafa: *Paxton Quigley's Had the Course*

SUMMARY

You can see that the problem is complex, and you will need to do a lot of reading and thinking about this topic. A final example may help to illustrate just how complex the issue is. Assume that you are responsible for selecting materials for a small public library. Naturally, you depend upon your job to cover you and your family's living expenses. A small group of persons in the community wants you to buy a certain item for your library collection; but unfortunately, you also know of a large group of vocal and influential persons who would be very upset, and might even demand that you be fired, if you do buy it. Would you really buy the item and risk your family's welfare and your career over one item? If you do not buy the item, what would you tell the people who ask you to buy it? Does telling them they can get it somewhere else, or get it through interlibrary loan, really address *your* problem?

NOTES

[1] C. H. Busha, "Intellectual Freedom and Censorship: The Climate of Opinion in Midwestern Public Libraries," *Library Quarterly* 42 (July 1972): 283-84.

[2] E. Geller, "The Librarian as Censor," *Library Journal* (June 1, 1976): 1258.

[3] W. Brahm, "Knights and Windmills: Some Thoughts on the Holy Crusade for Intellectual Freedom," *Library Journal* 96 (Oct. 1, 1971): 3096-98.

[4] *Wilson Library Bulletin* 48 (Sept. 1969): 18; *Intellectual Freedom Newsletter* 18 (Nov. 1969): 92.

[5] *Wilson Library Bulletin* 48 (Sept. 1969): 18; *Library Journal* 93 (Nov. 1, 1969): 3947.

[6] *Wilson Library Bulletin* 45 (April 1971): 717; 45 (May 1971): 818-24.

[7] *Intellectual Freedom Newsletter* 18 (Jan. 1969): 5.

[8] *Intellectual Freedom Newsletter* 19 (Sept. 1970): 17; 19 (Nov. 1970): 12.

[9] *American Libraries* 1 (Dec. 1970): 1010-11; *Intellectual Freedom Newsletter* 20 (Jan. 1971): 2.

[10] *Library Journal* 94 (Aug. 1969): 2722.

[11] *Library Journal* 94 (Sept. 1, 1969): 2855; *Intellectual Freedom Newsletter* 18 (Nov. 1969): 98.

[12] *Intellectual Freedom Newsletter* 23 (May 1974): 54.

[13] *Intellectual Freedom Newsletter* 23 (Sept. 1974): 111.

[14] Ibid., p. 124.

[15] *Intellectual Freedom Newsletter* 12 (July 1963): 34, 48; *American Library Association Bulletin* 57 (April 1963): 305-306.

[16] *American Libraries* 8 (July/Aug. 1977): 371-75; *American Libraries* 8 (Oct. 1977): 502-505; *Interracial Books for Children Bulletin* 8 (Oct. 1977): 15-21.

[17] D. Broderick, "Son of Speaker," *American Libraries* 8 (Oct. 1977): 503.

[18] C. H. Busha, "Intellectual Freedom and Censorship: The Climate of Opinion in Midwestern Public Libraries," *Library Quarterly* 42 (July 1972): 285.

[19] Ibid., p. 300.

BIBLIOGRAPHY

Allain, H. P. "Public Library Governing Bodies and Intellectual Freedom." *Library Trends* 19 (July 1970): 47-63.

American Library Association. Office for Intellectual Freedom. *Intellectual Freedom Manual.* Chicago: ALA, 1974.

Anderson, A. J. *Problems in Intellectual Freedom and Censorship.* New York: R. R. Bowker, 1974.

Asheim, L. "The Librarian's Responsibility: Not Censorship But Selection." In Conference on Intellectual Freedom, Whittier, California, 1953. *Freedom of Book Selection: Proceedings.* F. J. Mosher, ed. Chicago: American Library Association, 1954.

Asheim, L. "Problems of Censorship in Book Selection." *Bay State Librarian* 52 (Winter 1962): 5-9.

Berninghausen, D. K. *The Flight from Reason: Essays on Intellectual Freedom in the Academy, the Press, and the Library.* Chicago: American Library Association, 1975.

Berninghausen, D. K. "Intellectual Freedom and the Press." *Library Journal* 97 (Dec. 15, 1972): 3960-67.

Berninghausen, D. K. "The Librarian's Commitment to *The Library Bill of Rights*." *Library Trends* 19 (July 1970): 19-38.

Berninghausen, D. K. "Social Responsibility vs. *The Library Bill of Rights.*" *Library Journal* 97 (Nov. 15, 1972): 3675-81; [Comment]. *Library Journal* 98 (Jan. 1, 1973): 25-41.

Boyer, P. S. *Purity in Print: The Vice-Society Movement and Book Censorship in America.* New York: Scribner's, 1968.

Brahm, W. "Knights and Windmills: Some Thoughts on the Holy Crusade for Intellectual Freedom." *Library Journal* 96 (Oct. 1, 1971): 3096-98.

Broderick, D. M. "Censorship-Reevaluated." *School Library Journal* 96 (Nov. 1971): 3816-18.

Broderick, D. M. "I May, I Might, I Must: Some Philosophical Observations on Book Selection Policies and Practices and the Freedom to Read." *Library Journal* 88 (Feb. 1, 1963): 507-510.

Broderick, D. M. "Son of Speaker." *American Libraries* 8 (Oct. 1977): 502-504.

Busha, C. H. *Freedom versus Suppression and Censorship: With a Study of the Attitudes of Midwestern Public Librarians and a Bibliography of Censorship.* Littleton, CO: Libraries Unlimited, 1972. (Research Studies in Library Science, no. 8).

Busha, C. H. "Intellectual Freedom and Censorship: The Climate of Opinion in Midwestern Public Libraries." *Library Quarterly* 42 (July 1972): 283-301.

Busha, C. H., ed. *An Intellectual Freedom Primer.* Littleton, CO: Libraries Unlimited, 1977.

Conference on Intellectual Freedom, Whittier, California, 1953. *Freedom of Book Selection: Proceedings.* F. J. Mosher, ed. Chicago: American Library Association, 1954.

Craig, A. *Suppressed Books: A History of the Conception of Literary Obscenity.* 1st American ed. Cleveland: World, 1963; British ed.: *The Banned Books of England and Other Countries: A Study of the Conception of Literary Obscenity.* London: Allen & Unwin, 1962.

Daily, J. E. *The Anatomy of Censorship.* New York: Dekker, 1973.

De Grazia, E. *Censorship Landmarks.* New York: R. R. Bowker, 1969.

Donelson, K. L. *The Students' Right to Read.* Urbana, IL: National Council of Teachers of English, 1972.

Ernst, M. L., and W. Seagle. *To the Pure: A Study of Obscenity and the Censor.* New York: Viking, 1928.

Fiske, M. *Book Selection and Censorship.* Berkeley: University of California, 1958.

Flanagan, L. N. "Defending the Indefensible: The Limits of Intellectual Freedom." *Library Journal* 100 (Oct. 15, 1975): 1887-91.

Gaines, E. J. "Moderation in Minneapolis." *Library Journal* 96 (May 15, 1971): 1681-86.

Geller, E. "The Librarian as Censor." *Library Journal* 101 (June 1, 1976): 1258.

Gillett, C. R. *Burned Books: Neglected Chapters in British History and Literature.* Port Washington, NY: Kennikat Press, 1964. 2v.

Good, P. "Politics of Pornography." *Evergreen Review* (Sept. 1971): 21-23, 54-63.

Haight, Anne Lyon. *Banned Books 387 B.C. to 1978 A.D.* 4th ed. Updated and enlarged by Chandler B. Grannis. New York: R. R. Bowker, 1978.

Haselden, C. "The Social Attitudes of Librarians and the Selection of Books on Social Issues." *Library Quarterly* 20 (April 1950): 127-35.

Jones, H., and R. Lawson. "Intellectual Freedom and Materials Selection; Phase I: Selection of the Book." *School Media Quarterly* 1 (Winter 1973): 113-16.

Kronhausen, E., and P. Kronhausen. *Pornography & the Law: The Psychology of Erotic Realism and Pornography.* 2nd ed., completely rev. and enl. New York: Ballantine, 1964.

McClellan, G. S., ed. *Censorship in the United States.* New York: H. W. Wilson, 1967.

McCormick, J., and M. MacInnes, eds. *Versions of Censorship: An Anthology.* New York: Anchor Books, 1962.

Merritt, L. C. *Book Selection and Intellectual Freedom.* New York: H. W. Wilson, 1970.

Molz, K. "The Public Custody of High Pornography." *Library Journal* 92 (Oct. 1, 1967): 3373-76.

Moon, E., ed. *Book Selection and Censorship in the Sixties.* New York: R. R. Bowker, 1969.

Moore, E. T. "The Intellectual Freedom Saga in California: The Experience of Four Decades." *California Librarian* 35 (Oct. 1974): 49-57.

Moore, E. T. "Threats to Intellectual Freedom." *Library Journal* 96 (Nov. 1, 1971): 3363-67.

Moore, E. T., ed. "Intellectual Freedom." *Library Trends* 19 (July 1970): 2-168.

Newsletter on Intellectual Freedom. Chicago: American Library Association, 1952- . [Bi-monthly].

Norwick, K. P. *Pornography: The Issues and the Law.* New York: Public Affairs Committee, 1972.

Pilpel, H. F. "Freedom of the Press—American Style." *Publishers Weekly* 203 (March 12, 1973): 26-29.

Pope, M. *Sex and the Undecided Librarian: A Study of Librarians' Opinions on Sexually Oriented Literature.* Metuchen, NJ: Scarecrow, 1974.

Rembar, C. *The End of Obscenity: The Trials of "Lady Chatterley," "Tropic of Cancer," and "Fanny Hill."* New York: Random House, 1968.

U.S. Commission on Obscenity and Pornography. *The Report.* Washington: Government Printing Office, 1970.

U.S. Commission on Obscenity and Pornography. *Technical Report.* Washington: Government Printing Office, 1971- .

Young, W. *Eros Denied: Sex in Western Society.* New York: Grove Press, 1964.

Chapter 14

CODA

COLLECTION DEVELOPMENT AND THE FUTURE

Looking toward the future is not as risky as predicting the future. None of these remarks, then, are intended to be predictions; rather, they are statements about possible developments.

Perhaps someday in the future, the book as we know it will be gone except as a museum piece or a collectors' curiosity. Certainly, video formats seem to be making tremendous strides and may in time be the sole format. We may, in our lifetime, see the end of the library as a physical facility to which patrons come to use materials. No matter what happens—changes in formats, services, and physical location—it seems likely that there will always be some system for disseminating information to the general population. It also seems very probable that the world's output of information and recreational materials will continue to increase. Should all of these factors come to pass, there will be just as much need for selectors who are capable of building appropriate collections as there is today.

Selection of information thus must become more important, not less important, in the future. As the volume of information and the forms in which it is available increase, libraries must be more selective. We now see that it is impossible on economic grounds alone for any library to be comprehensive in its collection. Yet, research and academic libraries for the past thirty years have been attempting this impossible task.

Early efforts at cooperative acquisitions failed for many reasons. One reason was that a period of large book budgets occurred, and vendors offered "pie in the sky" approval/blanket order plans that allowed rapid collection growth. Collection growth, though, is not the same thing as collection development. Selection personnel (subject bibliographers and specialists) were hired, but somehow real collection development seemed to be an exception rather than the rule. This author knows personally from research and consulting work that many of these persons spent the vast majority of their time writing reports, preparing statements of needs (mostly for more money to get more material), teaching courses, and working with the public. There is nothing wrong with these activities, but they are not selection activities. What developed were acquisition programs—acquire as much as possible—not collection development programs.

Today, economic realities have changed the picture. Approval/blanket order plans are too expensive, so libraries are more carefully defining their "profile" for such plans. This means a move back to real selection. A question that no one has answered is whether the users of the libraries where acquisition plans existed are or were happy with the collection? We can only speculate as to what the answer would be. Users of academic libraries that began to "develop" an engineering collection when no engineering program existed (nor would exist ten years later) felt that more selectivity was in order.

In the future, even if vast sums of money are available, the volume of information will have increased and will still be beyond the control of any library. Without question, there will be more need for in-depth subject knowledge in the library. Collection development personnel will have to have in-depth knowledge and work in only one or two very narrow fields in order to select the most useful items for patrons of that library. Gone will be the day of the social science bibliographer, if that day ever really existed. Perhaps it will not even be possible to be the anthropology bibliographer; it may be necessary to have even finer divisions. Cooperative acquisitions will be a normal part of library programs, as there will be no choice.

Whatever the future holds, one thing not likely to change is the intellectual challenge in creating the most appropriate resource collection for a community. Individuals with a great curiosity about what is happening in the world, an in-depth knowledge of information resources and their producers, and a knowledge of the problems and issues in building a library collection in their community will also find a rewarding and exciting career in librarianship.

APPENDIX

COPYRIGHT LAW

COPYRIGHT LAW

Public Law 94-553
94th Congress

An Act

Courtesy Of
S. I. Hayakawa

For the general revision of the Copyright Law, title 17 of the United States Code, and for other purposes.

Oct. 19, 1976
[S. 22]

Be it enacted by the Senate and House of Representatives of the United States of America in Congress assembled,

Title 17, USC,
Copyrights.

TITLE I—GENERAL REVISION OF COPYRIGHT LAW

SEC. 101. Title 17 of the United States Code, entitled "Copyrights", is hereby amended in its entirety to read as follows:

TITLE 17—COPYRIGHTS

Chapter 1.—SUBJECT MATTER AND SCOPE OF COPYRIGHT

§ 101. Definitions

17 USC 101.

As used in this title, the following terms and their variant forms mean the following:

An "anonymous work" is a work on the copies or phonorecords of which no natural person is identified as author.

"Audiovisual works" are works that consist of a series of related images which are intrinsically intended to be shown by the use of machines or devices such as projectors, viewers, or electronic equipment, together with accompanying sounds, if any, regardless

PUBLIC LAW 94-553—OCT. 19, 1976

of the nature of the material objects, such as films or tapes, in which the works are embodied.

The "best edition" of a work is the edition, published in the United States at any time before the date of deposit, that the Library of Congress determines to be most suitable for its purposes.

A person's "children" are that person's immediate offspring, whether legitimate or not, and any children legally adopted by that person.

A "collective work" is a work, such as a periodical issue, anthology, or encyclopedia, in which a number of contributions, constituting separate and independent works in themselves, are assembled into a collective whole.

A "compilation" is a work formed by the collection and assembling of preexisting materials or of data that are selected, coordinated, or arranged in such a way that the resulting work as a whole constitutes an original work of authorship. The term "compilation" includes collective works.

"Copies" are material objects, other than phonorecords, in which a work is fixed by any method now known or later developed, and from which the work can be perceived, reproduced, or otherwise communicated, either directly or with the aid of a machine or device. The term "copies" includes the material object, other than a phonorecord, in which the work is first fixed.

"Copyright owner", with respect to any one of the exclusive rights comprised in a copyright, refers to the owner of that particular right.

A work is "created" when it is fixed in a copy or phonorecord for the first time; where a work is prepared over a period of time, the portion of it that has been fixed at any particular time constitutes the work as of that time, and where the work has been prepared in different versions, each version constitutes a separate work.

A "derivative work" is a work based upon one or more preexisting works, such as a translation, musical arrangement, dramatization, fictionalization, motion picture version, sound recording, art reproduction, abridgment, condensation, or any other form in which a work may be recast, transformed, or adapted. A work consisting of editorial revisions, annotations, elaborations, or other modifications which, as a whole, represent an original work of authorship, is a "derivative work".

A "device", "machine", or "process" is one now known or later developed.

To "display" a work means to show a copy of it, either directly or by means of a film, slide, television image, or any other device or process or, in the case of a motion picture or other audiovisual work, to show individual images nonsequentially.

A work is "fixed" in a tangible medium of expression when its embodiment in a copy or phonorecord, by or under the authority of the author, is sufficiently permanent or stable to permit it to be perceived, reproduced, or otherwise communicated for a period of more than transitory duration. A work consisting of sounds, images, or both, that are being transmitted, is "fixed" for purposes of this title if a fixation of the work is being made simultaneously with its transmission.

The terms "including" and "such as" are illustrative and not limitative.

A "joint work" is a work prepared by two or more authors with the intention that their contributions be merged into inseparable or interdependent parts of a unitary whole.

"Literary works" are works, other than audiovisual works, expressed in words, numbers, or other verbal or numerical symbols or indicia, regardless of the nature of the material objects, such as books, periodicals, manuscripts, phonorecords, film, tapes, disks, or cards, in which they are embodied.

"Motion pictures" are audiovisual works consisting of a series of related images which, when shown in succession, impart an impression of motion, together with accompanying sounds, if any.

To "perform" a work means to recite, render, play, dance, or act it, either directly or by means of any device or process or, in the case of a motion picture or other audiovisual work, to show its images in any sequence or to make the sounds accompanying it audible.

"Phonorecords" are material objects in which sounds, other than those accompanying a motion picture or other audiovisual work, are fixed by any method now known or later developed, and from which the sounds can be perceived, reproduced, or otherwise communicated, either directly or with the aid of a machine or device. The term "phonorecords" includes the material object in which the sounds are first fixed.

"Pictorial, graphic, and sculptural works" include two-dimensional and three-dimensional works of fine, graphic, and applied art, photographs, prints and art reproductions, maps, globes, charts, technical drawings, diagrams, and models. Such works shall include works of artistic craftsmanship insofar as their form but not their mechanical or utilitarian aspects are concerned; the design of a useful article, as defined in this section, shall be considered a pictorial, graphic, or sculptural work only if, and only to the extent that, such design incorporates pictorial, graphic, or sculptural features that can be identified separately from, and are capable of existing independently of, the utilitarian aspects of the article.

A "pseudonymous work" is a work on the copies or phonorecords of which the author is identified under a fictitious name.

"Publication" is the distribution of copies or phonorecords of a work to the public by sale or other transfer of ownership, or by rental, lease, or lending. The offering to distribute copies or phonorecords to a group of persons for purposes of further distribution, public performance, or public display, constitutes publication. A public performance or display of a work does not of itself constitute publication.

To perform or display a work "publicly" means—

(1) to perform or display it at a place open to the public or at any place where a substantial number of persons outside of a normal circle of a family and its social acquaintances is gathered; or

(2) to transmit or otherwise communicate a performance or display of the work to a place specified by clause (1) or to the public, by means of any device or processs, whether the members of the public capable of receiving the performance or display receive it in the same place or in separate places and at the same time or at different times.

PUBLIC LAW 94–553—OCT. 19, 1976

"Sound recordings" are works that result from the fixation of a series of musical, spoken, or other sounds, but not including the sounds accompanying a motion picture or other audiovisual work, regardless of the nature of the material objects, such as disks, tapes, or other phonorecords, in which they are embodied.

"State" includes the District of Columbia and the Commonwealth of Puerto Rico, and any territories to which this title is made applicable by an Act of Congress.

A "transfer of copyright ownership" is an assignment, mortgage, exclusive license, or any other conveyance, alienation, or hypothecation of a copyright or of any of the exclusive rights comprised in a copyright, whether or not it is limited in time or place of effect, but not including a nonexclusive license.

A "transmission program" is a body of material that, as an aggregate, has been produced for the sole purpose of transmission to the public in sequence and as a unit.

To "transmit" a performance or display is to communicate it by any device or process whereby images or sounds are received beyond the place from which they are sent.

The "United States", when used in a geographical sense, comprises the several States, the District of Columbia and the Commonwealth of Puerto Rico, and the organized territories under the jurisdiction of the United States Government.

A "useful article" is an article having an intrinsic utilitarian function that is not merely to portray the appearance of the article or to convey information. An article that is normally a part of a useful article is considered a "useful article".

The author's "widow" or "widower" is the author's surviving spouse under the law of the author's domicile at the time of his or her death, whether or not the spouse has later remarried.

A "work of the United States Government" is a work prepared by an officer or employee of the United States Government as part of that person's official duties.

A "work made for hire" is—

(1) a work prepared by an employee within the scope of his or her employment; or

(2) a work specially ordered or commissioned for use as a contribution to a collective work, as a part of a motion picture or other audiovisual work, as a translation, as a supplementary work, as a compilation, as an instructional text, as a test, as answer material for a test, or as an atlas, if the parties expressly agree in a written instrument signed by them that the work shall be considered a work made for hire. For the purpose of the foregoing sentence, a "supplementary work" is a work prepared for publication as a secondary adjunct to a work by another author for the purpose of introducing, concluding, illustrating, explaining, revising, commenting upon, or assisting in the use of the other work, such as forewords, afterwords, pictorial illustrations, maps, charts, tables, editorial notes, musical arrangements, answer material for tests, bibliographies, appendixes, and indexes, and an "instructional text" is a literary, pictorial, or graphic work prepared for publication and with the purpose of use in systematic instructional activities.

17 USC 102.

§ 102. Subject matter of copyright: In general

(a) Copyright protection subsists, in accordance with this title, in original works of authorship fixed in any tangible medium of expression, now known or later developed, from which they can be perceived, reproduced, or otherwise communicated, either directly or with the aid of a machine or device. Works of authorship include the following categories:

Works of authorship.

    (1) literary works;
    (2) musical works, including any accompanying words;
    (3) dramatic works, including any accompanying music;
    (4) pantomimes and choreographic works;
    (5) pictorial, graphic, and sculptural works;
    (6) motion pictures and other audiovisual works; and
    (7) sound recordings.

(b) In no case does copyright protection for an original work of authorship extend to any idea, procedure, process, system, method of operation, concept, principle, or discovery, regardless of the form in which it is described, explained, illustrated, or embodied in such work.

§ 103. Subject matter of copyright: Compilations and derivative works

17 USC 103.

(a) The subject matter of copyright as specified by section 102 includes compilations and derivative works, but protection for a work employing preexisting material in which copyright subsists does not extend to any part of the work in which such material has been used unlawfully.

(b) The copyright in a compilation or derivative work extends only to the material contributed by the author of such work, as distinguished from the preexisting material employed in the work, and does not imply any exclusive right in the preexisting material. The copyright in such work is independent of, and does not affect or enlarge the scope, duration, ownership, or subsistence of, any copyright protection in the preexisting material.

§ 104. Subject matter of copyright: National origin

17 USC 104.

(a) UNPUBLISHED WORKS.—The works specified by sections 102 and 103, while unpublished, are subject to protection under this title without regard to the nationality or domicile of the author.

(b) PUBLISHED WORKS.—The works specified by sections 102 and 103, when published, are subject to protection under this title if—

    (1) on the date of first publication, one or more of the authors is a national or domiciliary of the United States, or is a national, domiciliary, or sovereign authority of a foreign nation that is a party to a copyright treaty to which the United States is also a party, or is a stateless person, wherever that person may be domiciled; or

    (2) the work is first published in the United States or in a foreign nation that, on the date of first publication, is a party to the Universal Copyright Convention; or

    (3) the work is first published by the United Nations or any of its specialized agencies, or by the Organization of American States; or

    (4) the work comes within the scope of a Presidential proclamation. Whenever the President finds that a particular foreign nation extends, to works by authors who are nationals or domiciliaries of the United States or to works that are first published in the United States, copyright protection on substantially the same basis as that on which the foreign nation extends protection to works of its own nationals and domiciliaries and works first published in that nation, the President may by proclamation extend protection under this title to works of which one or more

of the authors is, on the date of first publication, a national, domiciliary, or sovereign authority of that nation, or which was first published in that nation. The President may revise, suspend, or revoke any such proclamation or impose any conditions or limitations on protection under a proclamation.

17 USC 105.

§ 105. Subject matter of copyright: United States Government works

Copyright protection under this title is not available for any work of the United States Government, but the United States Government is not precluded from receiving and holding copyrights transferred to it by assignment, bequest, or otherwise.

17 USC 106.

§ 106. Exclusive rights in copyrighted works

Subject to sections 107 through 118, the owner of copyright under this title has the exclusive rights to do and to authorize any of the following:

(1) to reproduce the copyrighted work in copies or phonorecords;

(2) to prepare derivative works based upon the copyrighted work;

(3) to distribute copies or phonorecords of the copyrighted work to the public by sale or other transfer of ownership, or by rental, lease, or lending;

(4) in the case of literary, musical, dramatic, and choreographic works, pantomimes, and motion pictures and other audiovisual works, to perform the copyrighted work publicly; and

(5) in the case of literary, musical, dramatic, and choreographic works, pantomimes, and pictorial, graphic, or sculptural works, including the individual images of a motion picture or other audiovisual work, to display the copyrighted work publicly.

17 USC 107.

§ 107. Limitations on exclusive rights: Fair use

Notwithstanding the provisions of section 106, the fair use of a copyrighted work, including such use by reproduction in copies or phonorecords or by any other means specified by that section, for purposes such as criticism, comment, news reporting, teaching (including multiple copies for classroom use), scholarship, or research, is not an infringement of copyright. In determining whether the use made of a work in any particular case is a fair use the factors to be considered shall include—

(1) the purpose and character of the use, including whether such use is of a commercial nature or is for nonprofit educational purposes;

(2) the nature of the copyrighted work;

(3) the amount and substantiality of the portion used in relation to the copyrighted work as a whole; and

(4) the effect of the use upon the potential market for or value of the copyrighted work.

17 USC 108.

§ 108. Limitations on exclusive rights: Reproduction by libraries and archives

(a) Notwithstanding the provisions of section 106, it is not an infringement of copyright for a library or archives, or any of its employees acting within the scope of their employment, to reproduce no more than one copy or phonorecord of a work, or to distribute such copy or phonorecord, under the conditions specified by this section, if—

(1) the reproduction or distribution is made without any purpose of direct or indirect commercial advantage;

(2) the collections of the library or archives are (i) open to the public, or (ii) available not only to researchers affiliated with the library or archives or with the institution of which it is a part, but also to other persons doing research in a specialized field; and

(3) the reproduction or distribution of the work includes a notice of copyright.

(b) The rights of reproduction and distribution under this section apply to a copy or phonorecord of an unpublished work duplicated in facsimile form solely for purposes of preservation and security or for deposit for research use in another library or archives of the type described by clause (2) of subsection (a), if the copy or phonorecord reproduced is currently in the collections of the library or archives.

(c) The right of reproduction under this section applies to a copy or phonorecord of a published work duplicated in facsimile form solely for the purpose of replacement of a copy or phonorecord that is damaged, deteriorating, lost, or stolen, if the library or archives has, after a reasonable effort, determined that an unused replacement cannot be obtained at a fair price.

(d) The rights of reproduction and distribution under this section apply to a copy, made from the collection of a library or archives where the user makes his or her request or from that of another library or archives, of no more than one article or other contribution to a copyrighted collection or periodical issue, or to a copy or phonorecord of a small part of any other copyrighted work, if—

(1) the copy or phonorecord becomes the property of the user, and the library or archives has had no notice that the copy or phonorecord would be used for any purpose other than private study, scholarship, or research; and

(2) the library or archives displays prominently, at the place where orders are accepted, and includes on its order form, a warning of copyright in accordance with requirements that the Register of Copyrights shall prescribe by regulation.

(e) The rights of reproduction and distribution under this section apply to the entire work, or to a substantial part of it, made from the collection of a library or archives where the user makes his or her request or from that of another library or archives, if the library or archives has first determined, on the basis of a reasonable investigation, that a copy or phonorecord of the copyrighted work cannot be obtained at a pair price, if—

(1) the copy or phonorecord becomes the property of the user, and the library or archives has had no notice that the copy or phonorecord would be used for any purpose other than private study, scholarship, or research; and

(2) the library or archives displays prominently, at the place where orders are accepted, and includes on its order form, a warning of copyright in accordance with requirements that the Register of Copyrights shall prescribe by regulation.

(f) Nothing in this section—

(1) shall be construed to impose liability for copyright infringement upon a library or archives or its employees for the unsupervised use of reproducing equipment located on its premises: *Provided,* That such equipment displays a notice that the making of a copy may be subject to the copyright law;

(2) excuses a person who uses such reproducing equipment or who requests a copy or phonorecord under subsection (d) from liability for copyright infringement for any such act, or for any later use of such copy or phonorecord, if it exceeds fair use as provided by section 107;

(3) shall be construed to limit the reproduction and distribution by lending of a limited number of copies and excerpts by a library or archives of an audiovisual news program, subject to clauses (1), (2), and (3) of subsection (a) ; or

(4) in any way affects the right of fair use as provided by section 107, or any contractual obligations assumed at any time by the library or archives when it obtained a copy or phonorecord of a work in its collections.

(g) The rights of reproduction and distribution under this section extend to the isolated and unrelated reproduction or distribution of a single copy or phonorecord of the same material on separate occasions, but do not extend to cases where the library or archives, or its employee—

(1) is aware or has substantial reason to believe that it is engaging in the related or concerted reproduction or distribution of multiple copies or phonorecords of the same material, whether made on one occasion or over a period of time, and whether intended for aggregate use by one or more individuals or for separate use by the individual members of a group; or

(2) engages in the systematic reproduction or distribution of single or multiple copies or phonorecords of material described in subsection (d) : *Provided,* That nothing in this clause prevents a library or archives from participating in interlibrary arrangements that do not have, as their purpose or effect, that the library or archives receiving such copies or phonorecords for distribution does so in such aggregate quantities as to substitute for a subscription to or purchase of such work.

(h) The rights of reproduction and distribution under this section do not apply to a musical work, a pictorial, graphic or sculptural work, or a motion picture or other audiovisual work other than an audiovisual work dealing with news, except that no such limitation shall apply with respect to rights granted by subsections (b) and (c), or with respect to pictorial or graphic works published as illustrations, diagrams, or similar adjuncts to works of which copies are reproduced or distributed in accordance with subsections (d) and (e).

Report to Congress.

(i) Five years from the effective date of this Act, and at five-year intervals thereafter, the Register of Copyrights, after consulting with representatives of authors, book and periodical publishers, and other owners of copyrighted materials, and with representatives of library users and librarians, shall submit to the Congress a report setting forth the extent to which this section has achieved the intended statutory balancing of the rights of creators, and the needs of users. The report should also describe any problems that may have arisen, and present legislative or other recommendations, if warranted.

17 USC 109.

§ 109. Limitations on exclusive rights: Effect of transfer of particular copy or phonorecord

Disposal.

(a) Notwithstanding the provisions of section 106(3), the owner of a particular copy or phonorecord lawfully made under this title, or any person authorized by such owner, is entitled, without the authority of the copyright owner, to sell or otherwise dispose of the possession of that copy or phonorecord.

Public display.

(b) Notwithstanding the provisions of section 106(5), the owner of a particular copy lawfully made under this title, or any person authorized by such owner, is entitled, without the authority of the copyright owner, to display that copy publicly, either directly or by the projection of no more than one image at a time, to viewers present at the place where the copy is located.

(c) The privileges prescribed by subsections (a) and (b) do not, unless authorized by the coyright owner, extend to any person who has acquired possession of the copy or phonorecord from the copyright owner, by rental, lease, loan, or otherwise, without acquiring ownership of it.

§ 110. Limitations on exclusive rights: Exemption of certain performances and displays

17 USC 110.

Notwithstanding the provisions of section 106, the following are not infringements of copyright:

(1) performance or display of a work by instructors or pupils in the course of face-to-face teaching activities of a nonprofit educational institution, in a classroom or similar place devoted to instruction, unless, in the case of a motion picture or other audiovisual work, the performance, or the display of individual images, is given by means of a copy that was not lawfully made under this title, and that the person responsible for the performance knew or had reason to believe was not lawfully made;

(2) performance of a nondramatic literary or musical work or display of a work, by or in the course of a transmission, if—

(A) the performance or display is a regular part of the systematic instructional activities of a governmental body or a nonprofit educational institution; and

(B) the performance or display is directly related and of material assistance to the teaching content of the transmission; and

(C) the transmission is made primarily for—

(i) reception in classrooms or similar places normally devoted to instruction, or

(ii) reception by persons to whom the transmission is directed because their disabilities or other special circumstances prevent their attendance in classrooms or similar places normally devoted to instruction, or

(iii) reception by officers or employees of governmental bodies as a part of their official duties or employment;

(3) performance of a nondramatic literary or musical work or of a dramatico-musical work of a religious nature, or display of a work, in the course of services at a place of worship or other religious assembly;

(4) performance of a nondramatic literary or musical work otherwise than in a transmission to the public, without any purpose of direct or indirect commercial advantage and without payment of any fee or other compensation for the performance to any of its performers, promoters, or organizers, if—

(A) there is no direct or indirect admission charge; or

(B) the proceeds, after deducting the reasonable costs of producing the performance, are used exclusively for educational, religious, or charitable purposes and not for private financial gain, except where the copyright owner has served notice of objection to the performance under the following conditions:

Notice of objection to performance.

(i) the notice shall be in writing and signed by the copyright owner or such owner's duly authorized agent; and

(ii) the notice shall be served on the person responsible for the performance at least seven days before the date of the performance, and shall state the reasons for the objection; and

Regulation.

(iii) the notice shall comply, in form, content, and manner of service, with requirements that the Register of Copyrights shall prescribe by regulation;

(5) communication of a transmission embodying a performance or display of a work by the public reception of the transmission on a single receiving apparatus of a kind commonly used in private homes, unless—

(A) a direct charge is made to see or hear the transmission; or

(B) the transmission thus received is further transmitted to the public;

(6) performance of a nondramatic musical work by a governmental body or a nonprofit agricultural or horticultural organization, in the course of an annual agricultural or horticultural fair or exhibition conducted by such body or organization; the exemption provided by this clause shall extend to any liability for copyright infringement that would otherwise be imposed on such body or organization, under doctrines of vicarious liability or related infringement, for a performance by a concessionnaire, business establishment, or other person at such fair or exhibition, but shall not excuse any such person from liability for the performance;

(7) performance of a nondramatic musical work by a vending establishment open to the public at large without any direct or indirect admission charge, where the sole purpose of the performance is to promote the retail sale of copies or phonorecords of the work, and the performance is not transmitted beyond the place where the establishment is located and is within the immediate area where the sale is occurring;

(8) performance of a nondramatic literary work, by or in the course of a transmission specifically designed for and primarily directed to blind or other handicapped persons who are unable to read normal printed material as a result of their handicap, or deaf or other handicapped persons who are unable to hear the aural signals accompanying a transmission of visual signals, if the performance is made without any purpose of direct or indirect commercial advantage and its transmission is made through the facilities of: (i) a governmental body; or (ii) a noncommercial educational broadcast station (as defined in section 397 of title 47); or (iii) a radio subcarrier authorization (as defined in 47 CFR 73.293–73.295 and 73.593–73.595); or (iv) a cable system (as defined in section 111(f)).

(9) performance on a single occasion of a dramatic literary work published at least ten years before the date of the performance, by or in the course of a transmission specifically designed for and primarily directed to blind or other handicapped persons who are unable to read normal printed material as a result of their handicap, if the performance is made without any purpose of direct or indirect commercial advantage and its transmission is made through the facilities of a radio subcarrier authorization referred to in clause (8)(iii), *Provided*, That the provisions of this clause shall not be applicable to more than one performance of the same work by the same performers or under the auspices of the same organization.

17 USC 111.

§ 111. Limitations on exclusive rights: Secondary transmissions

(a) Certain Secondary Transmissions Exempted.—The secondary transmission of a primary transmission embodying a performance or display of a work is not an infringement of copyright if—

(Copyright Law continues through 90 STAT. 2602)

AUTHOR/TITLE/SUBJECT INDEX

"Short" discounts, 68
Simon, Julius—*Patterns in the Use of Books in Large Research Libraries*, 227
Simulations, 186
Sinclair, Michael—"A Typology of Library Cooperatives," 259
Single Copy Order Plan (SCOP), 77
Slides (35mm and 4x4"), 58, 61, 185
Slides (35mm and 4x4") outlets, 88
Slote, Stanley J.—*Weeding Library Collections*, 225
Social indicators, 107-108
Society for the Suppression of Vice, 304-305
"Speaker, The," 309
Special libraries
    collection development, 24-26, 127, 153
    evaluation, 240
    selection, 26-27, 131
    use of audio visuals, 179
    weeding in, 218
Specialty publishers, 39-40
    compared with media producers, 56
Specimen collections, 58, 61
Spiller, David—*Book Selection: An Introduction to Principles and Practices*, 153-54
Standard Periodical Directory, 167
Standard times, 268
Standing order file, 201
Standing orders and continuations, 71, 200
Statement on Labeling, 303-304
Statistical method
    assumptions behind, 242
    California State method, 244-45
    Clapp-Jordan formula, 244
    comparison with other institutions, 242-43
    Formula A—Standards for College Libraries, 245-47
    limitations of, 242
    Washington State formula, 244
    Statute of Anne, 283
Still pictures, 180, 185
Storage of books
    cost savings, 220-21
    improved access, 220-21
    past use criterion, 228-30
    second level access, 217
    selection for, 226-30
    space savings, 220
    studies of, 226-30
Subject bibliographies, 166-67
Subject specialists
    community analysis use, 101
    selectors, 26
Subsidiary rights
    See Book publishers—subsidiary rights

Surveys
    See Community analysis

Technical services, 24
Textbook publishers, 39-40
Three-dimensional objects, 186
Times Literary Supplement (London), 163
"Trade" discounts, 68
Trade list, 45
Trade publishers, 39
    contrasted with media producers, 56
Transparencies
    See Opaque materials and transparencies

U.S. Government Scientific and Technical Periodicals, 168
Ulrich's International Periodical Directory, 167
Union List of Serials, 167
Universal Copyright Convention, 284, 285
Unpublished works copyright, 286
Urquhart, John, and Nancy Urquhart—*Relegation and Stock Control in Libraries*, 230
Usage method
    as a check on other methods, 248
    assumptions behind, 247
    rejection by academicians, 247
    value of, 248
Use of and Attitudes toward Libraries in New Jersey, 34
Users
    See Patron community

Vanity presses, 40
Verified requests file, 201
Video disc, 190-91
Video formats, 58, 61, 88, 180, 185, 316
Vouchers, 70, 204

Warren, Roland—*Studying Your Community*, 98
Washington State formula, 243-44, 246
Watch and Ward Society, 304
Weeding
    barriers to, 222-23
    compared with selection, 145, 217
    criteria for storage decisions, 226
    definition of, 216
    existing programs, 221
    functions of, 21-22, 24, 217